Ruptured Histo

Ruptured Histories

WAR, MEMORY, AND THE POST—COLD WAR IN ASIA

Edited by

Sheila Miyoshi Jager

Rana Mitter

HARVARD UNIVERSITY PRESS

Cambridge, Massachusetts
London, England   2007

Library of Congress Cataloging-in-Publication Data

Ruptured histories : war, memory, and the post–Cold War in Asia /
    edited by Sheila Miyoshi Jager and Rana Mitter.
        p.   cm.
    Includes bibliographical references and index.
    ISBN-13: 978-0-674-02470-0 (cloth : alk. paper)
    ISBN-10: 0-674-02470-2 (cloth : alk. paper)
    ISBN-13: 978-0-674-02471-7 (paper : alk. paper)
    ISBN-10: 0-674-02471-0 (paper : alk. paper)
    1. East Asia—History—1945–   I. Jager, Sheila Miyoshi.
II. Mitter, Rana.   III. Title.
DS518.1.R87   2007
950.4'2—dc22   2006049772

Contents

List of Illustrations

Acknowledgments

THIS BOOK GREW OUT of a symposium entitled "War and Memory in Post–Cold War Asia," which I organized at Oberlin College on April 26–27, 2003. Funded by a grant from the Henry Luce Foundation's Luce Fund for Asian Studies, the symposium brought together fifteen scholars from various disciplines and regional specialties to discuss and debate the events and significance of the end of the Cold War and the impact that 1989 and 1991 have had on war memory in Asia. This book consists of revised versions of many of the original papers, as well as entirely new essays that complement our overall theme. I wish to thank all the authors, and also those who participated in the conference but whose work could not be included here. I am particularly grateful to Marilyn B. Young, Peter Zinoman, and Daniel Sherman for chairing the panels and for guiding us through rigorous discussions. Arthur Waldron, Leslie Pincus, and Chen Jian deserve special recognition for their participation in the symposium and for initiating some lively and heated debates. I also wish to thank Pam Snyder and Suzanne Gay for their unwavering and enthusiastic support of this project, as well as my two assistants, Lily Chang and Nana Uemura, who helped plan and coordinate the entire symposium and basically made it happen. Lily Chang, in particular, deserves special thanks for providing core technical support in putting the manuscript together at various stages of the project. It is a tribute to Oberlin College to have produced such fine and dedicated students.

I also wish to thank my coeditor, Rana Mitter, whose expert advice and collaborative spirit helped to transform the symposium into an edited book. Our ongoing discussions and our coauthorship of the introduction and epilogue, in particular, have been an experience that I will savor for many years to come. Rana also wishes to thank the Leverhulme Trust for the award of a Philip Leverhulme Prize, which enabled him to replace his teaching and free up time to work on this volume, and the British Academy–Chinese Academy of Social Sciences Exchange Scheme, which enabled him to carry out research in China. Both the Dean's Office at Oberlin College and the Sub-Faculty of East Asian Studies of the Faculty of Oriental Studies, University of Oxford, provided subvention support for this book.

Finally, I would like to thank Carol Gluck for guiding us through the arduous process of publishing this collection and for critically reading and editing the entire manuscript draft. Her generous input, meticulous care, and overall enthusiasm for this project has been a source of inspiration, and our debt to her is immeasurable. She epitomizes the best scholar/mentor that our field has to offer.

This book dovetails with Oberlin's goals for the initiative supported by the Luce Fund for Asian studies, which underwrote the symposium and offset costs associated with preparing the book manuscript, to promote the study of Japan, Korea, and China in a comparative, regional context. It is my hope that *Ruptured Histories: War, Memory, and the Post–Cold War in Asia* conforms to that spirit and promotes a way of thinking about history in a global, transnational perspective. The response to geopolitical demands means that international factors influence national memory even in its determinedly domestic precincts. *Ruptured Histories* seeks to explain how the influences of a changing global order in the decade following the end of the Cold War has fueled new interpretations of the past and how domestic politics and the politics of memory are intimately intertwined and shaped by global forces.

Sheila Miyoshi Jager
Oberlin, Ohio
October 2006

Ruptured Histories

Introduction

Re-envisioning Asia, Past and Present

SHEILA MIYOSHI JAGER AND RANA MITTER

IN MAY 2005, JAMES SOONG, leader of Taiwan's People First Party, paid homage to his ancestors at his family tomb in Hunan Province, China. He then made a rousing public speech asserting that China was one country and could never be divided. Such an encounter between a strong anticommunist and the leaders of the largest self-declaredly communist nation remaining on earth would have been unimaginable during the Cold War, when memories of the bitter civil war between Communists and Nationalists froze historical understandings into inflexible patterns. Yet such radical reworkings of past conflicts to shape the politics of the present are a characteristic of the post-1989 world, and East Asia in particular. The "ruptured memories" of the title are not always being healed, as may be the case between Taiwan and China, but the breaks, as well as continuities with the past, are now an inescapable part of what shapes the societies of East Asia.

The post–Cold War era has just begun to be treated as a coherent historical "moment" in its own right, rather than purely as part of the "history of the present." Studies of this moment have proliferated in the late 1990s, most of which focused on Eastern Europe.[1] The spectacle of an immensely varied and rapidly changing situation in this region has engendered numerous renegotiations of public and private memories of the communist past as contemporary historians try to make sense of the narratives of Soviet domination, the Cold War, and their local variations.

This volume explores the complex skeins of historical memory that have taken place in a region of the world that has been largely neglected in the contemporary literature of the post–Cold War period: East Asia. The events of 1989, which included the democratization movement in South Korea, the death of Hirohito in Japan, the Tian'anmen square uprising in China, and the economic reforms in Vietnam, all happened within national contexts. But the global changes that the end of the Cold War set in motion had far-reaching consequences, and not only in the domain of domestic politics and international relations. The end of the Cold War also became an important contextual marker in the realm of public memory as Japanese, Koreans, Chinese, Taiwanese, and Vietnamese began to grapple with a new layer of meaning added to the past by the changing present. A collaborative effort of an international group of scholars, this book presents diverse perspectives, and sometimes conflicting views, on post–Cold War Asia.

By the term "post–Cold War," we do not mean to refer to a period or series of events that occurred only after 1989. The failings of the Soviet regime and loss of confidence in communist ideology had been happening at least a decade before the collapse of the Berlin Wall. Indeed, a major step toward post–Cold War Asia occurred in 1972, when Japan established diplomatic relations with China. The subsequent forging of trade relations after 1972 signaled the beginning of the end of a bifurcated Asia. By "post–Cold War" we are instead referring to a particular historical process that occurred with the definitive end of a bifurcated Asia. The geopolitical changes of the late 1980s and early 1990s led to a significant restructuring of the political economy and strategic relationships in East Asia. The changes that accompanied the Soviet Union's decline and final collapse resulted in a series of new regional alignments in Asia that directly impacted Japanese, Chinese, Korean, Taiwanese, and Vietnamese peoples' understanding of their wartime past. These new understandings concern not only particular national events, such as the causes and impact of the 1989 Tian'anmen Square uprising in China, but also significant geopolitical events, such as the signing of the North-South Agreement in December 1991, which radically redefined the relationship between the two Koreas (and which later had far-reaching consequences on the United States' future relationship with South Korea). The notion of "post–Cold War Asia" also takes into account the rapid economic rise of China in the region as well as the rapid decline of North Korea, including the changing influence of the United States in the Pacific region. We suggest three arguments that underscore the significance of international and transnational developments that have had immense repercussions on the politics of wartime memory in Japan, South Korea, Taiwan, mainland China, and Vietnam.

First, the end of the Cold War represented a significant restructuring of relations between the United States and its Cold War allies in Asia, which in turn set in motion new interpretations of the wartime past. The bipolar rivalry that had existed between the two Cold War superpowers had created a linkage between domestic and international affairs in East Asia as these countries became inextricably intertwined with global Cold War interests and policies. For more than half a century, the United States provided stability in the Asia-Pacific region through its military presence there, its alliances with Japan and South Korea, and its commitment to fostering economic growth in the region. The end of the Cold War has, however, allowed a reassessment, first of the U.S. presence and role in East Asia, and second, of internal changes in the understanding of historical memory.

In South Korea, the end of the Cold War meant the contradictions of the continuing Korean War and the division of the peninsula became all the more apparent as a new generation of South Koreans began to seek reconciliation, rather than confrontation, with North Korea. This newer and more benign perception of North Korea among contemporary South Korean leaders has in turn precipitated marked tensions in the U.S.–South Korea security alliance, as both parties advocate radically different approaches to resolving the ongoing North Korean nuclear crisis. The changed post–Cold War global reality is reflected in a new remembering of the Korean War, as North Korean atrocities committed during the conflict, once the center of official South Korean historiography, are slowly being forgotten (or forgiven) in the name of achieving the peaceful unification of peninsula. Likewise, the threat from North Korea's nuclear and missile programs and new fears of a burgeoning capitalist China have led Japan on the path of rearmament, a development that is vehemently opposed by the nations Japan victimized during World War II, including China and South Korea. (Both countries forcefully opposed Japan's effort to obtain a seat on the United Nations [UN] Security

Council). Korean and Chinese memories of the Pacific War, and continuing tensions over Japan's "amnesia" about its wartime past, have led to a marked increase in anti-Japanese sentiments in these countries. Contemporary politics of memory and the history of Asia's wars must therefore be understood in light of the political and economic changes in the region after the end of the Cold War. The marked transformations in U.S.–South Korean and North–South Korean relations, including increasing tensions between both China and South Korea over Japanese remilitarization, have all found expression in new and competing memories of war.

Second, the post–Cold War period has placed more emphasis on Asian regional integration, which in turn has shaped the context in which the debate about war memory and postwar responsibility has become genuine public discourse. Unlike Europe, Asia lacks strong multilateral political institutions. Asian security is ensured not by multilateral treaties but by a series of bilateral treaties centering on Washington, in particular the U.S.-Japan Security Treaty and the U.S.–South Korean relationship. After 1945, both Japan and Germany had to convince their neighbors that they would no longer be a military threat, and while the new West Germany did so by ceding its sovereignty to a series of multilateral organizations, Japan did so by ceding sovereignty in security affairs to the United States. "Security ties thus took on a hub-and-spoke structure in Asia, with Washington playing a central mediating and balancing role."[2] But this Cold War system of security checks and balances centered on Washington is eroding. China has replaced the United States as South Korea's largest trading partner; China's leaders have also proposed a variety of new Asian multilateral economic arrangement with the Association of Southeast Asian Nations (ASEAN) (ASEAN plus one and ASEAN plus three, with Japan and North Korea) as well as China-ASEAN and East Asian free trade areas.[3] A new Asian multilateral framework is also emerging in the form of the ongoing six-party talks aimed at resolving the North Korean nuclear issue. And while the United States and Japan are saddled with huge and mounting debts, and in the case of Japan, stagnant growth rates and population decline, China is today the world's sixth largest economy with a population that is likely to stabilize at approximately 1.4 billion people.[4] According to some analysts, China is set to overtake the United States as the world's biggest economy as early as 2020.[5] China's economic and geopolitical rise in the region means that Asian nations are beginning to turn from the geopolitical West centered on the United States toward the geopolitical East centered on China.[6]

Partly in response to China's rapid rise and partly in reaction to China's recent and traditionally strong ties with the Korean peninsula, many Japanese citizens and grassroots organizations are taking steps to address their country's "history problem" in an effort to bring about Japan's peaceful reintegration within Asia. The result of these steps to confront the past has been what Carol Gluck has termed the "coming into memory" of various previously "forgotten" events—such as the comfort women issue and the Nanjing Massacre of 1937 during the 1990s—in Japan. The changing balance of power, as Japan is eclipsed by China, also means that South Koreans and Chinese are forcing the issue onto Japan, and demanding atonement, if not compensation. Fear of Japanese remilitarization and internal domestic politics in China and South Korea means that Japan's "history problem," largely buried by the Cold War, has resurfaced following the Cold War thaw. These new reevaluations of the past reveal how changes in the geopolitical landscape at the end of the Cold War have created the conditions for changes in the way in which the wartime past is being reevaluated.

Third, the post–Cold War period has given rise to new forms of nationalism that have moved to the center of official public discourse about the wartime past. Changing power relationships in the Asia-Pacific region have also unlocked nationalist passions and rivalries. Japan's program of incremental rearmament, sanctioned official visits to the Yasukuni Shrine, and ongoing textbook debates have led to rising anti-Japanese sentiments in both China and South Korea that have served to forge nationalist feeling at home. Several recent incidences come to mind. In 2005, observers of China, both within and outside of the country, were amazed at the frequency and virulence of anti-Japanese demonstrations in China's major cities. A series of events sparked the protests, including Beijing's fierce opposition to Japan's bid to gain a permanent seat on the UN Security Council. Many Chinese also felt outrage that a recent Japanese version of a school textbook did not provide a full account of Japanese World War II atrocities. South Korea also witnessed its share of vehement anti-Japanese demonstrations in recent years because of its ongoing dispute with Japan over the sovereignty of a chain of islands known as Tokdo in Korean and Takeshima in Japanese.[7] The

end of the Cold War initiated massive political and economic transformations that have already begun to rework the memory of war and revolution in Asia, and in ways that have shaped these countries' nationalist self-images, not only about their past but about their future as
well.

In the chapters that make up this volume, Japan occupies a prominent position. Just as the resolution of the "German question" shaped
much of European Cold War and post–Cold War politics, so the status
of Japan as a former enemy now finding a new identity stands central to
understanding East Asian politics since 1945. More than any other
Asian nation in the postwar era, the Japanese have debated their
wartime past as a central part of contemporary politics. This volume
reflects the prominence of these debates while also seeking to link
them to other national contexts.

From the end of World War II until the revolutions of 1989, the
American presence in Japan and South Korea helped to install a narrative of the wartime past that sought to promote the revitalization and
legitimacy of the Japanese and South Korean states and their
economies. In the case of South Korea, the division of the country that
was conceived at Potsdam and frozen in place after the Korean War
(1950–53) was shaped and perpetuated by the Cold War. South Korea's
relationship with other Asian countries, especially China and North
Korea, remained highly contentious because of the constraints of the
U.S.–South Korea security alliance. The positive uses to which the Korean wartime memories were put thus enabled the South Korean government to turn its engagement in a continuous war with communism
and North Korea into a powerful source of domestic mobilization in
support of its economic and national security policies. The South Koreans were thus *not* allowed to forget the brutality of their wartime experience in order to prevent the wounds of the war from healing,
which in turn promoted the legitimacy of the South Korean nation-
security state aligned with the United States. In contrast, the Japanese
were encouraged in a national amnesia about their wartime past.[8] The
American Occupation after 1945 reeducated the Japanese in a new narrative of their modern history in which Japan had been temporarily
"derailed" in the 1930s from its true democratic vocation. Such a view
also promoted nostalgia for the noble origins of Japan's modernity in
the Meiji period (1868–1912). By appealing to enduring cultural values
and forms through the celebration of an "endless present" that denied

the recent past, Japanese postwar politicians and intellectuals sought to continue "the very socio-economic endowment that had been fixed since the Meiji period and had figured the very fascism and imperialism that drove Japan into its conflict with the United States."[9]

This search for enduring cultural values and an "endless present" also complemented a narrative of self-victimization that blamed the military and the government for the war and focused on the atomic bombings of Hiroshima and Nagasaki. This victimization narrative silenced the memory of aggression by elevating the moment of defeat. The effect of this silencing was that Japan's prewar past, which might have explained the forces that propelled the Japanese into war, was eclipsed, while Japan, under American Occupation, was recast as a free and democratic society. In this way, Japan was portrayed as enacting a story of reform, reconstruction, and democratic renovation that derived from the idealization of the American experience.

The U.S.-Japan and the U.S.–South Korea security relationships thus represent one of the longest-standing restraints on war memory throughout the Cold War period. The question is whether the end of the Cold War, and the reevaluation of the U.S.-Japan and U.S.–South Korea security alliances in the changing international climate, will significantly alter Japan's and South Korea's view of their future as well as their reevaluations of their wartime past.

Scholars of Japan have arrived at different answers to these questions. For some, Japan's permanent postwar historiography did *not* disappear in 1989 with the collapse of the Berlin Wall.[10] Indeed, the kind of memory that surfaced at the time of Hirohito's death in 1989 and after made it permissible to talk about the war in increasingly positive terms. Linked to this narrative of the war was an aggressive and virulent call for revisions of history textbooks to deny the 1937 Nanjing Massacre and the forced prostitution of Asian women. Japan's right-wing nationalists thus perpetuate the narrative of self-victimization that encouraged Japan's forgetfulness about its war crimes. In appealing to this newer nationalism, the Yasukuni Shrine increasingly stands in contemporary Japan as a "symbol of Japan as future warrior, rather than a symbol of a defeated nation clinging desperately to its martial past."[11]

But these musings that largely deny a full accounting of Japan's World War II atrocities must be understood in the context of the end of the Cold War. Faced with a rising China allied with South Korea, a nuclear-armed North Korea and increasing tensions over Taiwan, Japan is considering easing constitutional limits on the development and deployment of its military forces. While both South Korea and China have made political use of the memory of Japan's wartime aggression, and their own experience of victimization, to oppose Japanese remilitarization, Japan's new right-wing forces downplay these memories in an effort to shore up its military independence from Washington.[12]

Hence, while it appears that the end of the Cold War has had little effect on war memory in Japan, at least among some segments of the Japanese population who continue to downplay Japan's war crimes, the reasons for this avoidance of history are in large part due to the new post–Cold War geopolitical arrangements. In response to a growing sense of insecurity over Japan's place in a regional order dominated by China, some sectors of contemporary Japan have witnessed the rise of nationalist sentiment and historical amnesia about the past. This historical amnesia, what Harootunian has called the "postwar repetition into the post-Cold War moment," legitimizes Japan's efforts toward rearmament while freeing the country from its dependency on the American "nuclear umbrella."

But this view of postwar repetition into the post–Cold War moment is complemented by that of other scholars, who argue that Japan's response to an increasingly global public culture that began in the late 1980s and continued into the twenty-first century marks a radical *shift* in Japanese war memory.[13] The impetus for this shift came not from within, but from the outside, as part of a response to a global order that began to change with the collapse of European communism in 1989 and the fall of the Soviet Union two years later. During the Cold War, the U.S.-Japan security alliance meant that Japan had faced the geopolitical West. However, in the post–Cold War era, Japan was suddenly confronted with doing the "memory work" necessary for its regional reintegration with Asia. As Carol Gluck has observed, "the accidental overlap of Hirohito's death in 1989, the end of the Cold War and the return of Asia to Japan's geopolitical agenda meant that 'Japanese official memory,' which had held its frozen ground practically until 1945, was now being forced by geopolitical pressures to deal with its 'history problem.'"[14] The surge of memory in the 1990s that brought World War II to the center of Japanese public debate generated a "transnational memory" of the war, that is, one that was not confined to a single national narrative, but included interactions across Asia. The post–Cold War world order created a new public space in which China–once declared out of political bounds by the U.S.–Japan alliance—had to be integrated into the new story of the war. Similarly, the comfort women who "came into memory" during the 1990s did so as part of "a transnational memory with social, legal and moral consequences that transcend national or cultural borders."[15] The "comfort women," the majority of whom were Korean, were women forced into service as prostitutes for the Japanese army during the 1930s and 1940s. A similar observation about the 1937 Nanjing Massacre can be made regarding the emergence of a new "community of memory" in Japan and China that has begun to recast this incident in international rather than purely domestic terms. The reaction of the international Chinese diaspora to Iris Chang's controversial 1997 bestseller, *The Rape of Nanking*, is an example of this phenomenon.

The challenge of reintegrating China into Asia following the end of the Cold War helps to explain why some Japanese—many civic groups and organizations—are now addressing past actions in China and Korea that had been neglected earlier. It is therefore significant that while China had largely disappeared in Japan's postwar narrative of war because of its "loss" to communism, South Korean suffering during the war was also silenced owing to the same Cold War geopolitics (the Taiwanese also refused to complain about their sufferings). For this reason, the increasing prominence of the comfort women issue during the 1990s represented not only the "coming into memory" in post–Cold War Japan, but also South Korea, where the comfort women issue was held hostage by the same geopolitical pressures binding South Korea to the United States and Japan. The result was the silencing of the issue within South Korean society as the state focused on economic development, which was heavily dependent on Japanese capital and investments. The need to appease Japanese sensibilities (and U.S. interests) meant that it was impolitic to recall the horrors of the war (or the colonial period) in official discourse. No doubt, then, that the demands of regional integration have exerted new pressures on war memory in both Japan and South Korea.

But if the nation-state was no longer in sole control of war memory in Japan and South Korea, memory struggles were everywhere dominated by considerations of national politics. In South Korea, the marked reevaluation of the U.S.–South Korea security alliance following the end of the Cold War, coupled with demands on the part of the South Korean public to revise the Status of Forces Agreement (SOFA) and South Korea's "client status" vis-à-vis the United States, has precipitated an active reremembering of the Korean War (1950–53), including the relationship of its closest Cold War enemy: North Korea.

Recent efforts throughout the late 1980s and 1990s in South Korea to revise the Cold War narrative of the Korean War, especially the demonization of North Korea, came on the heels of South Korea's global coming-out party during the 1988 Summer Olympics and new initiatives toward North Korea following the Soviet Union's demise in 1991. The new South Korean narrative of the war sees a shift from remembering the start of the war (June 25) to the end of the war (July 27), signaling the creation of a "post–Korean War" strategy to search for a peaceful resolution to the unfinished war.

In this rewriting, North Korea's divisive role in the conflict is being tacitly occluded, while America's actions have moved to the center of the story. The new war memory that has emerged in the post–Cold War context thus reflects a drastically changing view of the United States and the U.S.–South Korea security alliance (from savior from communism to perpetrator of war crimes). The active "remembering" of such alleged U.S. atrocities as the massacre of civilians at Nogŭn-ri in the new Korean War history, and the simultaneous "erasure" of North Korean culpability in the name of the peaceful reunification of the peninsula and ending the Korean War, reveal how war memory in South Korea is intimately caught up in the politics of reunification.

Post–Cold War unification politics may also help to explain South Koreans' brief remembering—and all-too-complete forgetting—of their country's role during the Vietnam War. The topic generated much discomfort and tension in 2000 when it was revealed that the South Korean military, the second largest force to deploy troops to Vietnam after the United States, had committed atrocities against thousands of unarmed Vietnamese civilians during the war. Revelations of the massacres were first reported by the Left-leaning newspaper *Hangyorae shinmun*, and the story created a brief stir during the summer of 2000 but it was quickly forgotten. While this "sordid history" came to light largely because of the forces of democratization in South Korea during the 1990s, its more recent "forgetting" has more to do with new post–Cold War regional alignments and unification politics. In contrast to the new remembering of the Korean War and the events of the 1930s and 1940s, as well as other moments of national "victimization" that can serve to bind North and South Korea in a *shared* memory of collective suffering, the memory of South Korea's role in Vietnam serves no nationalist purpose. Its complete erasure from new public discourse about the past (which has focused almost exclusively on Korea's victimization by other nations) is thus strategic. Memories of Vietnam do not help South and North Korea truly to end the Korean War and promote a pan-Korean nationalism that focuses on the shared experiences of victimization and suffering (colonialism and war).

The connection between the rise of a new post–Cold War regional order and new and emerging forms of nationalism in Asia is also evident in Vietnam and China. In Vietnam, war memory was invoked in an effort to shore up support for the Party-led state in the wake of the Doi Moi economic reforms of 1986. The ever-present orchestration of war references in contemporary Vietnam can thus be seen as the state's way of dealing with the move toward international economic integration and globalization. At a time when Vietnamese society is rapidly becoming more diverse, and less definable as a nation, the frequent invocations of war seek to hold on to the past and prescribe what is properly "Vietnamese" in the sense of "who is in" and "who is out." The post–Cold War response to the changing global order has been to effectively silence Southern viewpoints and regimes, all of them sustained by U.S. support, in order to define a particular version of Vietnamese-ness associated with the North. Precisely the opposite is happening in contemporary South Korea, where attempts to rewrite North Korea back into a shared history of the war is deemed necessary to finally end the Korean War and unify the two Koreas.

The post–Cold War regional realignment in China is heir to a much longer process. After the 1949 revolution, Confucian norms and assumptions of 2,000 years of statecraft were sidelined, at least ostensibly, by China's modernizing elites, whether Nationalist (Kuomintang) or Communist. Contesting interpretations of the past were more widespread before 1949, and in particular, before the Sino-Japanese War in

1937, than under the Communist government, because the Maoist state exercised tight control over public memory once it had attained power in 1949. At that point, much of China's recent past was written out of history because it did not fit a teleology of inevitable Communist victory.

One seemingly safe area for the Communist state was the memory of the imperialist past. The Opium Wars (1839–42) stood at the center of the narrative about imperialism, so much so that they became the starting point for China's modern history for Chinese and foreign historians alike. The Opium Wars exemplified imperialism, the highest form of capitalism, and they signified the threat that imperialism posed to China's sovereignty and to its proletarian population. Rhetoric about them was easy to justify.

It became a harder fit following normalization of relations with the United States in 1979, after which the rhetoric condemning Western imperialism was toned down. The collapse of the Soviet bloc at the end of the 1980s brought an even more serious crisis. The Chinese state was now left with two seemingly contradictory goals: on the one hand, to integrate China into global capitalist modernity, and on the other, to show China's continuing hostility to any forms of neo-imperialism that might bring back memories of past weakness and national fragmentation. War memory has been central to that realignment, which attempts to square the circle.

In the post–Cold War era, China's experience of World War II has played a significant role in reshaping public memory. During the Cold War, the People's Republic made little mention of the War of Resistance to Japan (*Kang-Ri zhanzheng*), as the war is known in China, although stylized versions of the conflict were found in sources such as Cultural Revolution–era model operas. The fact that Chiang Kai-shek's Nationalists had had a significant role in defeating the Japanese could not be easily discussed after the communist victory in 1949, and the many atrocities committed by the Japanese in wartime China were discussed only in muted terms, because Beijing wished to detach Japan from the United States's Cold War embrace. From the 1980s, however, this changed. Japan had recognized the People's Republic of China in 1972, and China's concerns became more and more fixed on structures that might rein in Chinese regional power, such as the U.S.-Japan Security Alliance. In addition, the desire for reunification with Taiwan encouraged a more positive attitude toward the former Nationalist government. New war museums accompanied changing popular textbooks, films, and other officially sanctioned outlets for the changing historiography of the war.[16] While the change in tone had started when the Cold War was still a reality, the fall of the Soviet bloc increased the speed and urgency of the changes. As the Chinese came to terms with a world dominated by a single power, its thaw toward the United States was in part replaced by a new wariness toward Japan, which in turn fed the incipient nationalism reflected in the new war memory. The revival of memory of Japanese war atrocities and Chinese collective suffering aimed to create an undivided loyalty and patriotism to the Chinese state in an uncertain world, which would serve as the basis for creating a "new" China. The contemporary Chinese focus on Japanese war crimes was also fed by growing anger at the rise of a nationalist right wing in Japan that claimed that Japan's wartime role in Asia had been noble and that atrocities in China had been exaggerated or invented. While this was by no means the mainstream viewpoint in Japan, it was shrill enough to fuel a counterreaction in China, and it is notable that the Chinese government chose to allow information about this discourse to filter in through China's controlled media. The reason it did so, no doubt, was to galvanize the people's allegiance to the "new" China by reviving memories of national victimization and imperialist aggression. China's response to the collapse of the communist world order was to offer up a new history of collective suffering that could serve to bind the nation together and thus thwart the rise of ethnic or regional divisions that had led to the downfall of the Soviet Union (which mirrored, in many ways, China's own downfall during the first half of the twentieth century). The end of communism would not be the end of communist China.

Taiwan's relationship with its memory of conflict, however, shows the complexity of the region's relationship with both China and Japan. Taiwan experienced a relatively benign period of Japanese imperialism, quite unlike the horrors of the Rape of Nanjing, which islanders contrasted with the brutal occupation by the Kuomintang after 1945 and the often unwelcome imposition of a new role as a Cold War ally for the United States after 1949. For the Taiwanese, the conflicts with which the current generations are coming to terms are not those that animate the mainland, the War of Resistance to Japan in particular, but rather the continuing aftermath of the still unfinished Chinese civil war.

The changing pattern of Asia's strategic and economic alignments means that the post–Cold War regional relations among South Korea, China, Japan, and Vietnam are creating new geopolitical pressures on war memory that are also opening up a new public space for remembering and forgetting the past. As long "forgotten" war crimes are being brought out into the open for public inspection, other crimes are being reburied in the name of reestablishing the bonds of community torn apart by the Cold War (a case in point being the two Koreas). These excavations and reburials of the past play an important part in the story of Asia's post–Cold War political transformations.

~ 1

Relocating War Memory at Century's End

Japan's Postwar Responsibility and Global Public Culture

FRANZISKA SERAPHIM

THE CHARACTERIZATION, IN THE public media, of contemporary political processes as "post–Cold War" is increasingly being refocused with reference to "9/11," a reminder that the events of 1989 and the changes they set in motion are now being refracted by a more recent incident collectively endowed with far-reaching consequences. The layers of meaning added onto the past by the changing present are obviously important contextual markers for students of public memory, who are interested in understanding the ways in which interpretations of a shared past function in public life. Both the fall of the Berlin Wall in 1989 and the attacks on the World Trade Center on September 11, 2001, had—in their different ways—immense repercussions on politics and culture everywhere and refocused the dynamics of global relations. The responses to 9/11 and to the Bush administration's global "war on terror" seem to have given sharper contours to what was new, and not so new, in the decade following the end of the Cold War. Japan, of course, did not experience these events as directly as Europe did the end of the Cold War and the United States (and specifically New York) the September 11 attacks. Indeed, it was the year 1995 that carried particular significance in the Japanese context, marked as it was by the Kobe earthquake in January, the sarin gas attack on the Tokyo subway in March, and the fiftieth anniversary of the end of World War II in August. The year 1995 revealed a society in flux, struggling with the demands of political reorganization, economic recession, and Asian regional integration, which had combined to engulf Japan in a genuinely public and highly contentious debate about its wartime and postwar past (in striking contrast to the seeming inability to produce viable visions for the future). Japan's response to the events of 1995 was symptomatic of significant shifts in international relations, domestic politics, and an increasingly global public culture that began in the late 1980s and continued into the twenty-first century, however differently nuanced by the demands of the United States' declared global war on terrorism. One important catalyst of this process was the gradual coming together of Asian and especially East Asian countries as a world region with both a past and a future of consequence for the forces of globalization. No longer conceived only in economic but also in political and cultural terms, relations between and among Asian countries became the critical space for building connections between national and global circuits of production and consumption.

While the dominant culture flows no longer bound Japan first and foremost to the United States, as had been the case in earlier postwar decades, the U.S.-Japan alliance remained central to Japan's international relations and even played into domestic conservative agendas in ways that both invoked and transcended Cold War structures. As Laura Hein argued in a thoughtful commentary on current affairs at the end of 2003, Prime Minister Koizumi's unqualified support for the Bush administration's unilateral foreign policy decisions in the aftermath of 9/11 suggested few new or independent goals, whereas his push for the Antiterrorism Measures Special Law of 2001 directly fed into newly fervent plans to amend the constitution and allow Japan's active participation in full-scale war.[1] The U.S.-Japan security relationship and constitutional revision certainly represent two of the longest standing issues with which war memory has been bound up since the end of the Occupation in 1952. The end of the Cold War transposed these issues from the domestic terrain of political contestation to the arena of international relations, which was being reshaped by the need of nation-states to respond collectively to violent ethnic conflicts in Asia, Europe, and Africa, and at the same time by the proliferation of transnational and nongovernmental organizations performing tasks formerly reserved for national governments. It was in this changed international context that the particularity of the U.S.-Japan relationship and Japan's constitutional disavowal of engaging in military action abroad assumed unprecedented urgency, not only in shaping the future but also in reevaluating the past.

Japan and the world as a whole faced new political challenges after the Cold War at precisely the time that the political, legal, and intellectual concern with restitution and the negotiation of historical injustices emerged as global phenomena with specific national inflections. While in Japan the political organization of memory was once intricately linked to the representation of powerful special interests, war memory and war responsibility emerged in the 1990s as a broad public issue no longer predictably aligned with established strategies to preserve or undermine the postwar status quo represented by the U.S.-Japan security system and the constitution. The Japan Socialist Party, for example, along with the biggest labor federation, simply ended its decades-long opposition to the U.S.-Japan security system in 1994 and considered constitutional revision while pressing for an official apology to China and Korea for Japan's war conduct. The nationalist Right emerged better organized than ever to protest such an apology, rewrite the constitution, and liberate Japan from its long subjugation to American hegemony. The government, experimenting with various coalition arrangements, had to address questions of war memory as a matter of foreign policy but without decentering its close relations with the United States. Meanwhile, a host of local and cross-national rights-based organizations inserted themselves as viable political players in restitution cases and other transnational issues, including war in Iraq.

My analysis of the changing locus of memory in the 1990s begins with a brief discussion of the ways in which diverse and incompatible memories of war and defeat secured legitimate niches in the political terrain in early postwar Japan, and how the political mechanisms of organized memory began to change in the 1960s and 1970s. The contextualization of "1989" writ large then sets the stage for a more detailed exploration of three larger themes central to the extraordinarily vivid debate about Japan's "postwar responsibility" *(sengo sekinin):* comparisons with other national experiences of this sort, a new wave of documenting war and postwar suffering in an explicitly international setting, and the search for practical solutions to as yet unresolved issues marked by the intersection of personal and political concerns, with national and global dimensions. The long-established interest groups that had articulated diverse political meanings of war and postwar for decades remained actively involved in memory politics, but now in an immensely broadened discursive and activist landscape.[2]

Finding Public Space for Diverse War Memories in Early Postwar Japan

The use of war memory to formulate political interests grew out of the experience of the immediate postwar period, when the realities of war, defeat, and foreign occupation mixed with visions of building a new and democratic society. While the government negotiated and implemented large-scale reforms under the direction of the Occupation powers, citizens formed various professional, social, religious, and other groups to bring "democracy" into the schools and communities. Civic organizations mushroomed in the first postwar years not only among people who had suffered repression before and during the war and emerged as popular heroes in the fall of 1945, in particular communists and participants in the early labor movement. Others organized for a variety of reasons, including the desire (or necessity under the Occupation) to redefine their public place from supporters of the war to builders of postwar democracy. Those who had been privileged during the war, such as military families and the Shintō establishment, organized in a literal effort to survive the Occupation as valid political and social actors. In this way, diverse political interests and ambitions came to be defined and represented on the basis of different prewar, wartime, and postwar experiences, combining memories of the past with visions for a democratic future. Public memory of World War II in Japan was rooted in the lived reality of the immediate postwar years, when multiple interpretations of war and postwar established legitimate niches in a (re)emerging public sphere, while the government formulated its policies with only minimal reference to its role during the war.

The Occupation period was a tumultuous time in politics as in everyday life, not only because the democratic process was in flux, but also because abrupt changes in Occupation policies soon compromised barely formed alliances in favor of politically more expedient ones in the context of the Cold War. Organizing special-interest groups thus had to position themselves within an extremely volatile political landscape, and it was not until the end of that period, when Japan regained its independence in 1952, that these groups were able to establish secure places for themselves on a stabilizing political map. The political landscape as it congealed in the years following the end of the Occupation came to be known as the "55-system" after the consolidation of the main political parties in 1955 into two opposing camps, the conservatives and the progressives. The institutionalization of diverse memories of the war in the form of contending special interests in the first half of the 1950s was a critical component of that process.

Five such associations serve as lenses through which the changing public landscape of contentious political memories in Japan can be traced from 1945 to the 1990s. On the Right, which constituted the governmental establishment for decades, the Association of Shintō Shrines *(Jinja honchō)* and the Japan Association of War-Bereaved Families *(Nihon izokukai)* formulated specific political agendas that focused on reversing some of the Occupation reforms and thereby establishing political continuities across 1945 that validated national unity based on wartime ideology, albeit reformulated within a democratic context. On the Left, which comprised a permanent opposition into the 1990s, the Japan Teachers' Union (JTU or *Nikkyōso*), the Japan-China Friendship Association *(Nitchū yūkō kyōkai)*, and the pacifist student-oriented *Wadatsumikai* (Japan Association for Commemorating Student-Soldiers Fallen in Battle) also turned against the Occupation by insisting on a cleaner institutional and philosophical break with the wartime past while resisting Japan's remilitarization and participation in international power politics.

Specifically, the Association of Shintō Shrines, the private umbrella organization comprising 75 percent of all Shintō shrines that had replaced the wartime governmental Shrine Board in early 1946, sought to rebuild the close ties that had existed during the war between Shrine Shintō, the Imperial House, and the public. But rather than condoning bureaucratic control, which it in fact criticized as having contributed to the "distortion" of Shintō during the war, the Association emphasized the historical centrality of the emperor for the Japanese polity, expressed through the use of official Shintō rituals in national politics. Although neither the Ise (imperial) nor Yasukuni (military) shrines counted among its members, both shrines enjoyed the Association's full support in efforts to recover their prewar public status. Two of the

Association of Shintō Shrines few, if politically significant, successes were the reestablishment of the Meiji holiday *Kigensetsu* (February 11), which celebrated Japan's allegedly unbroken imperial line since Emperor Jimmu (660 BC), as "National Foundation Day" *(kenkoku kinenbi)* in 1967, and the adoption of the Imperial Reign Law *(gengohō)* in 1979, which officially settled the continuation of the Japanese calendar according to imperial reigns.

The Japan Association of War-Bereaved Families, Japan's main association of the military war-bereaved, began in 1947 as a social welfare organization for military families who had lost their pensions under Occupation directives in the preceding year. By 1953, it had acquired the legal status of a foundation *(zaidan hōjin)* and was recognized as a political pressure group attached to the right wing of the conservative Liberal Democratic Party (LDP). From then on, the Association was represented in both houses of the Diet, and many powerful LDP politicians and bureaucrats came from its ranks. Its central leadership lobbied the Welfare Ministry for official recognition of the war-bereaved through pension payments (approved by the government in limited form in 1953) and state-sponsored ceremonies for the war dead. In particular, the Japan Association's leaders campaigned to revive the political clout that the surviving relatives of the military war dead had had during the war, when they represented the critical link between the state and the people through mutual obligations that perpetuated an organic national community. These mutual obligations consisted of military service by the people for the state, as well as proper state recognition of these services by way of official rites that celebrated the war dead as national deities and by pension payments to their bereaved relatives. The Japan Association of War-Bereaved Families was probably best known for its introduction in 1963 of the highly controversial "Yasukuni Bill," which proposed to make Yasukuni Shrine a state shrine for worshipping Japan's war dead. It was also in charge of Japan's first national war museum, the Hall of Shōwa *(Shōwakan)*, which opened in 1999 after more than a decade of heated public controversy about its design and management.

In their different ways, Shrine Shintoists and war-bereaved families remembered the war in terms of efforts to unite the national community in the face of an international crisis. The Association of Shintō Shrines was critical of the role of the wartime state even as it validated the underlying public value system expressed through Shintō ritual, whereas the Japan Association of War-Bereaved Families saw the state as the only viable agent that could foster national unity.

On the other end of the political spectrum, the Japan Teachers' Union (JTU) was formed in 1947 as the dominant labor union of school and university teachers affiliated with the left wing of the Japan Socialist Party (JSP) and radically critical of the Ministry of Education. It sought to empower teachers as agents of democratic change by enabling them to become the workers, professionals, and citizens that they had not been allowed to be under prewar and wartime state coercion, when they were controlled by a militaristic bureaucracy. Unionized teachers turned against the bureaucracy as a remnant of militarism incompatible with postwar democracy and established their labor union as a permanent critic of official educational policy. Especially in the 1950s and 1960s, the JTU engaged in fierce struggles with conservative offices over the reintroduction of compulsory ethics classes, the textbook screening process, the meaning of "peace education," and wage increases for teachers. Its opposition to the public use of Japan's national flag and anthem, the revival of prewar national holidays, and Yasukuni Shrine as a site of national mourning for Japan's war dead made it the arch-enemy of right-wing organizations such as The Association of Shintō Shrines and Japan Association of War-Bereaved Families. But by the mid-1980s, the JTU's political power had declined considerably, and in 1995, its leaders formally abandoned their longstanding opposition to the hoisting of the national flag at school ceremonies and adopted a generally conciliatory policy toward the Ministry of Education, which came under attack from newly founded nationalist groups of educators instead.

The Japan-China Friendship Association was established on the first anniversary of the Communist Revolution in China in October 1950 as an eclectic organization of businessmen, politicians, and intellectuals opposed to Japan's alliance with the United States and instead advocating a relationship with the People's Republic of China. Its leaders insisted on acknowledging Japanese war atrocities against Chinese people and supporting communist efforts to turn China into a peaceful, progressive country. The Friendship Association lobbied politicians of all parties interested in promoting trade and cultural exchange with China and was particularly successful in fostering informal contacts between the Japanese people (as opposed to the government) and the Chinese people (represented by the Communist Party) in what it called "people-to-people-diplomacy." It succeeded in 1953–56 in helping to administer the repatriation of thousands of Japanese left in China after the war's end, to expand trade relations with China on an informal basis, and to contribute to the eventual normalization of diplomatic relations in 1972. Throughout the postwar decades the Friendship Association spoke for the rights of Chinese residents in Japan, publicly commemorated anniversaries of Japanese wartime aggression against China, and especially since the 1990s, promoted research into Japan's biological warfare and the so-called military comfort women system.

Finally, the small pacifist organization *Wadatsumikai* (Japan Association for Memorializing Student-Soldiers Fallen in Battle) was a product of Japan's early peace movement, which quickly rose to public prominence at the outbreak of the Korean War in June 1950. It centered its activities on high school and university campuses and organized antigovernment protests around the notion of conscientious objection to war by invoking the tragic experiences of elite student-soldiers killed in the last years of the war. These it documented, among other publications, through a highly popular collection of testimonies entitled *Kike wadatsumi no koe* (Listen to the Voices from the Sea). Affiliates of elite universities and families of the student war dead who joined the organization shared a commitment to pacifism based on an overwhelming sentiment of grief and guilt toward their own dead relatives and colleagues. Whereas this sentiment was strongly present in Japanese society in the early postwar years, it gradually subsided as everyday life normalized. The Japan Association for Memorializing Student-Soldiers Fallen in Battle however, continued to keep this sentiment alive as a valuable tool to promote popular pacifism and conjure up emotional and intellectual strength to criticize and resist any government policies that could once again lead Japan into military conflict. In 1993, it stood at the forefront of strong public opposition to the newly passed PKO bill permitting Japanese troops to join international peace-keeping organizations in Cambodia and later elsewhere.

From their respective vantage points, the Japan Teachers' Union, the Japan-China Friendship Association, and the Japan Association for Memorializing Student-Soldiers Fallen in Battle remembered the war in terms of the state's victimizing the people—specifically but not exclusively teachers, Chinese imperial subjects, and elite university students moved by pacifist ideals—and sought to expose and fully replace what remained of the institutional and intellectual foundations of the war with democratic and internationally valid structures.

By actively promoting their respective agendas, civic organizations such as these identified the main issues through which war memories became political in the 1950s and remained contentious into the twenty-first century. First, the emperor system and the use of Shintō rituals for official political ceremonies, whose close connection had reached a peak under the wartime system, represented the most obvious continuity between the war and the postwar period and implied a hegemonic definition of national identity based on historical continuity. Second, questions over the appropriate commemoration of millions of war dead—military and civilian, Japanese and those of other nationalities, men and women—revealed different war memories and postwar identities among groups of war victims and war-bereaved. Third, school curricula and history textbooks provided material for ongoing battles over public information, interpretation, and representation of the national past in service of contemporary definitions of citizenship. Fourth, war victimization, both physical and spiritual, translated into a popular pacifism symbolized by the atomic bombs and the ethical conflict of students experiencing the horror of war and was used as a weapon of legitimate protest against the government. Fifth, Japan's relations with other Asian countries, especially China, remained highly contentious, for even though the U.S. alliance tended to eclipse "Asia" from public view at the height of the Cold War, unresolved legacies of the war periodically revealed contrasting memories of a shared past, within Japan as well as between Japan and its Asian neighbors. In fact, the degree to which the U.S.-Japan security relationship framed public memory was itself the subject of controversy, bound up with domestic political struggle over the validity and desirability of the alliance itself. The Japanese government was arguably the only political player that accepted and promoted the particular constraints set by the alliance, whereas interest groups on the political Right as on the Left understood their respective political goals in terms of transcending these constraints as a war legacy with which their own respective memory politics clashed. The emperor, Yasukuni Shrine, textbooks, Asia within

a Cold War framework, and the victims of war constituted the main issues around which political conflict over war memory swirled from the
1950s through the 1990s.

Changing Political Mechanisms of Organized War Memory

The issues may have remained the same, but the political workings of
public memory changed significantly over the postwar half-century.
Most obviously from a contemporary perspective, the temporality of
the past shifted as time passed and the prewar and wartime pasts were
joined by an increasingly longer postwar past, which was entangled
with the present and also the future. While war memory had served as
the means to articulate visions for a democratic future in the immediate
post-surrender period, a decade later it was joined by evaluations of the
early postwar years as part of an effort to explain how the realities of
the postwar present had deviated from those earlier visions. By the
1990s, the newly current concept of "memory" provided a broad
public with a lens through which to reexamine the entire postwar order
and discover missed chances or unresolved issues that might explain
the current social and political instability and point the way toward a
more equitable, unified, or less contentious society. This latest phase,
which is ongoing, resonated strongly with similar developments elsewhere, as heretofore unresolved historical injustices took center stage
in the renegotiation of international, regional, ethnic, gender, and
other social and political relations as part of an emerging global public
culture. The determination to overcome deep Cold War divisions in
the world after 1989 certainly provided an important impetus for political restructuring on a large scale, but so did other factors, from greatly
accelerated media flows to the rise of international terrorism. Gerrit
Gong made this point strongly when he argued that the most challenging revolution of the future was "the revolution of perception
management," by which he meant the increasing salience of "nonmate-
rial, psychological, and perceptual factors" reflecting "divergent histories, cultures, and national purposes."[3]

The focus here lies on one particularly salient aspect of this
changing public culture, namely the political organization of war
memory in post–Cold War Japan. The special-interest groups, which
had institutionalized diverse war memories as part of postwar demo-

cratic politics in the 1950s to the exclusion of a wider public, were joined in the 1960s, 1970s, and 1980s by different forms of political activism that gradually compromised the monopoly that the established institutions exercised over the contention of memory, until they became participants with many others in a vibrant and broadly public process. To document this development, specific historical moments or conjunctures must be brought into focus to explain how the political issues, to which memory continued to be connected, appeared differently in different contexts. At least three such conjunctures stand out at times when war memory became part of public debates characterized not only by established special interests but also by alternative forms of protest.

In the mid-1960s, Japan's place in the international community came into much sharper focus than it had since the end of World War II, from the Tokyo Olympics in 1964 and the phenomenal increase in Japanese exports worldwide (dubbed Japan's "economic miracle") to Japan's implicit role in the Vietnam War and its diplomatic negotiations in East and Southeast Asia. Within this context, issues of national identity, national interests in diplomatic relations with other Asian countries, and even national territory (i.e., of Okinawa's reversion to Japan) became anchors for negotiating conflicting lessons and legacies of the past on the terrain of postwar democracy as an institutionalized political system. Civic groups whose interests had always focused explicitly on national dimensions of public life, such as the Association of Shintō Shrines and its concern with Japan's national "essence," were important voices in the quest for a national identity. When diplomatic relations with Korea and communist China became politically viable, the Japan-China Friendship Organization gained public prominence with its insistence that Japan officially recognize its national responsibility for war atrocities. The Japan Teachers' Union among many others, found that its special interests resonated powerfully in the nationwide movement for Okinawa's reversion to Japan, which revealed the enormous complexity of a "Japanese" national memory if it were to include Okinawa's very different war and postwar experience, exemplifying precisely the *lack* of so-called postwar democratic accomplishments.

But this was also a time of significant shifts, splits, and realignments among such established organizations, especially on the opposition

Left, in the course of which the bureaucratized "system" itself—and the very *form* of organized war memory as special-interest politics—became a target of (popular) protest. New citizen movements proliferating after 1965 sought to create their own decentralized "participatory" democracy in opposition to both the government's "paternalistic" democracy and the old Left's "democratic centralism."[4] In rendering problematic not specific meanings of the war but the way these meanings competed within set bureaucratic structures, these popular movements posited a Foucauldian "counter-memory."[5] According to Oda Makoto, the colorful spokesman for the anti–Vietnam War movement Beheiren, such a counter-memory hinged on the recognition that memory as special-interest politics suffered from persistent "feelings of [wartime and postwar] victimization" against which a "personal sense of involvement and responsibility" needed to be fostered to "challenge the principle of ultimate state authority."[6] The considerable broadening of citizen political activism through movements such as these slowly altered the overly contained place of memory in public discourse. Yet it is also true that the ideal of the autonomous citizen did not itself produce a substantive examination of war memory and postwar responsibility and therefore did not supplant existing forms of memory as special interests.

Another conjuncture in the history of organized memory was the proliferation in the 1970s of conservative religious "grassroots" organizations whose central concern revolved around the (re)establishment of the state as the legitimate custodian of an "official memory" through the revival of state management of Yasukuni Shrine. This was a time when the ruling conservative elites struggled to adjust to new economic and political realities in the aftermath of the oil shocks, and foreign policy turned toward China while local governments sympathetic to the rise of environmental and other citizen movements on the Left were increasingly staffed with politicians of the opposition Socialist Party. Major political lobbying by the Association of Shintō Shrines and the Association of War-Bereaved Families in support of a bill legalizing the shrine's reconstitution as an official site of war memory had in fact encouraged some conservative LDP Diet members to distance themselves from these interest groups, and the bill never passed. In response, the Association of War-Bereaved Families promoted the establishment of new and complementary citizen groups committed to the Yasukuni Bill, of which the Society for Answering the Honorable War Dead *(Eirei ni kotaeru kai)* and the People's League for Protecting Japan *(Nihon o mamoru kokumin kaigi)* were the most prominent.

The significance of this development in the course of the 1970s was twofold. As political scientists have argued, nationalist grassroots organizations played an important role in once again firmly securing the LDP in power and ushering in a cabinet to the far right of center under Prime Minister Nakasone in the early 1980s.[7] Although state management of Yasukuni Shrine was never legalized, it became increasingly customary for cabinet members to overstep constitutional boundaries and participate in ceremonies honoring the Shrine's war dead, to which a number of executed Class A war criminals were secretly added in 1978. More important, for the subject of war memory, the organization of public support for the nationalization of Yasukuni Shrine in the form of citizens' or even residents' movements unwittingly helped to loosen the ties between memory and institutionalized special interests (although it hardly dissolved them) and to make war memory a public issue in its own right. When such localized memory was challenged by internationalized memory in the wake of Chinese and Korean protests against Japanese textbooks in 1982, the issue of war memory and responsibility began to emerge as a subject of general public interest in the context of reassessing the state of Japan's "postwar" in the late 1980s and 1990s.

1989 and Its Legacies

The year 1989 became a convenient marker for shifts in international relations, domestic politics, and an increasingly global public culture that had developed gradually over the preceding decade and formed the context in which war memory and postwar responsibility became issues of a general public debate rather than of particular special interest politics. Emperor Hirohito's death on January 7 ended the Shōwa era, which had begun when Hirohito ascended the throne in 1926 and encompassed Japan's greatest political transformations, all under the rule of the same imperial head. Not surprisingly, the end of Shōwa and beginning of the new era Heisei spurred a whole spectrum of public remembering, from the official Shintō rituals performed at Hirohito's funeral and Akihito's inauguration as the new emperor to an avalanche of personal war and postwar reminiscences and the heated debate about Japanese war crimes and Hirohito's responsibility for them. The unprecedented scale on which such public debates occurred in the late 1980s and early 1990s both reflected and contributed to the loosening of domestic political alliances and the gradually broadening recognition and purposeful rediscovery of the charged bonds between war victims and victimizers. Internationally, too, greater political and economic stability in China, South Korea, and elsewhere in East Asia as well as the end of the Cold War in some of its many facets (a divided Korea being the most notable exception) led to a gradual regional integration, which demonstrated to people in Asia that Japan's economic leadership was significantly constrained by a lack of political mandate rooted in different experiences and memories of Japan's conduct in the Asia-Pacific War.

When Emperor Hirohito died from cancer on January 7, 1989, at age 87, much of public life in Japan seemed enveloped by the rituals of mourning and remembering. Thanks to the success of an extensive conservative campaign in favor of the Imperial Reign Law (*gengohō*) in the late 1970s,[8] decisions about the funeral as well as inauguration rites and the new reign name were made quickly and largely at the highest levels of government without public participation. The law ensured that the official use of the Japanese calendar—organized by imperial reign span—would continue when Hirohito's son Akihito ascended the throne, thus reinforcing the centrality of the imperial institution in public life.[9] Celebratory events, both public and private, were called off, city lights dimmed, and voices hushed, creating the image of a whole nation in deep mourning. Supermarkets, bookstores, and vendors offered up-to-the-minute accounts of Hirohito's life seemingly overnight, portraying him as a dedicated botanist and pacifist, far removed from war. Not surprisingly, social and political organizations, large and small, all responded to the emperor's final days—more generally conceived as the end of the Shōwa period (1926–89)—from their respective positions, and equally predictably, their responses reflected familiar political divisions.

The emperor and the imperial household, after all, represented an institutionalized continuity across 1945, and all special interests organized around particular interpretations of the prewar and wartime past had to contend with this continuity. Like a "ghost at the historical feast," to borrow Carol Gluck's phrase, the emperor was an intricate part of war memory, however differently construed.[10] Embraced as the ultimate locus of Japanese tradition and national unity, rejected as the root of Japanese fascism, domesticated in popular discourse as *"Ten-chan,"* or ignored as an historical anachronism, the emperor served the purposes of many groups even while open public criticism remained unfashionable. Hirohito's demise provided the Association of Shintō Shrines with an unprecedented opportunity to declare authoritatively the unity of the Japanese people (in mourning their emperor) and the successful preservation of Japanese culture and tradition on the basis of official adherence to Shintō ritual.[11] The Association of War-Bereaved Families reaffirmed the close ties between the war-bereaved and the emperor, bounded by their common goal of securing their nation's integrity and their wishes for peace, and equally molded by the upheavals (*gekidō*) of Shōwa.[12] The Japan-China Friendship Association, on the other hand, all but ignored the emperor's death in its newspaper's mid-January issue and instead printed a scheduled report on various local meetings that had taken place a month before entitled "Pursuing the Emperor's War Responsibility."[13]

The Japan Association for Memorializing Student-Soldiers Fallen in Battle, in a more demonstrative move, issued a public statement on February 9 entitled "Hearkening to the Voices of Millions of War Victims" in protest of the late Shōwa Emperor's state funeral. The declaration, a rejoinder to an earlier one issued the preceding November, clearly stated that the emperor bore responsibility for Japan's war of invasion in Asia and the Pacific, and that there had been insufficient recognition of the emperor's, the government's, and the people's responsibility in the postwar period. But the urgency of the February statement derived specifically from the official rites of mourning adopted by the government that, for Wadatsumikai, indicated a gross continuation of the politics of irresponsibility.

> We inflicted much harm and damage, spiritually and physically, on peoples in Asia and the Pacific area, and have not as yet sufficiently atoned or compensated for that. We fear that for the Government to recompense the late Tennō, the person who himself bore the above-mentioned responsibility, with a national funeral would appear to exonerate not only him of his war responsibility

but also Japan itself. That would not only be contrary to the spirit of the Constitution but also debase the persons who died as victims of the war, and trample upon the feelings of tens of millions of people who still suffer heavily from the hurt.[14]

Meanwhile, in South Korea, a group of two hundred women gathered at the site of a wartime anti-Japan uprising to protest, for the first time, the sexual slavery of former Korean "comfort women" under the Japanese wartime military. In a courageous breaking of almost a half century of silence, these mostly old and poor ladies exclaimed, "What sort of thing is a condolence delegation to the funeral of Hirohito, murderer of the Korean people!"[15] Although obviously unable to compete with the international attention summoned by Hirohito's state funeral and Akihito's ascendance to the throne, their action signaled important shifts in the content and organizational practices of war memory on both sides of the Japan Sea. The economic boom and gradual democratization in South Korea in the 1980s, the increasing influence of international feminism, and Japan's greater regional involvement had aided these shifts, which came into full public view in the years that followed.

To the extent that the year 1989 symbolized important trends already well underway at the time of the emperor's death, it also came to be viewed as a harbinger of major political changes that were to characterize the new imperial era, Heisei. Seen by many as the crumbling of the postwar order, these changes related on the one hand to the electoral losses of the ruling LDP in the spring which—aided by the bursting of the so-called bubble economy a year later—led to the end of LDP hegemony in 1993 for the first time in thirty-eight years. In addition, the political challenges that emerged with the gradual dismantling of Cold War international structures after the fall of the Berlin Wall in 1989 placed more emphasis on Asian regional integration and an active political role for Japan in world politics. No other event brought this home to the Japanese as much as American demands for Japan's active participation in the Gulf War (1991) and the enormous disconnect between the international expectations for Japanese military and financial contributions and the domestic resistance to such contributions on the basis of the peace clause in Japan's constitution.[16]

The problem of constitutional revision itself dated back to the early 1950s and was inseparable from the particular political dynamic between the conservative LDP in power and the JSP in permanent opposition in which set positions, often tied to war memory, had been articulated for decades. The Gulf War brought this formerly domestic issue into the international arena, where it assumed an entirely new relevance as the only available tool with which to negotiate an unprecedented diplomatic situation. Prime Minister Kaifu's indecisive handling of the crisis, followed by furious debates in the Diet about a new bill allowing overseas deployment of the Self Defense Forces to participate in peace-keeping operations (passed in 1992) revealed two things: the inadequacy of the postwar (i.e., Cold War) political framework in the new decade, and the necessary realliance of political positions and forces. They clearly shaped the context in which the debate about war memory and postwar responsibility became a genuinely public discourse—broadly reflective of the postwar system's shortcomings and led by new forms of political activism.

Within this context, "postwar management" *(sengo shori)* and "postwar responsibility" *(sengo sekinin)* emerged as dual key terms in Japan's public life in the second half of the 1980s and preoccupied politics even beyond the fiftieth anniversary of defeat in World War II. International pressure, especially from China and South Korea, and rapidly increasing local and cross-national citizen networks pushed the issue forward until it became itself an important characteristic of the new "post-postwar" era. Propelled by, but no longer confined to, Left-liberal intellectual discourse, the interpretation of the war's legacies and its practical ramifications in government politics drew on older conflicts over war memory but significantly expanded their parameters. Educational policies, war dead ceremonies, financial compensation, and the like continued to define the contested territory of memory, but now this territory was recognized as a political issue in its own right that transcended national borders and included ordinary people as well as the highest wartime authority, the emperor.

Japanese War Responsibility and Global Public Culture

The changing spatial and sociopolitical topography of memory in the late 1980s and 1990s manifested itself particularly within three areas of debate and organized citizen activism. First, academics, critics, and the mass media readily compared and contrasted Japanese attitudes and policies toward the legacies of World War II with those of other countries, in particular (West) Germany and later, increasingly, Asia. Second, although most Japanese war atrocities had been documented decades earlier, a new wave of historical research for explicitly popular consumption swept Japan's public life, driven in part by the aging of victims and eyewitnesses. Third, a broad spectrum of organizations with varying degrees of governmental ties focused their activities on practical solutions to still outstanding humanitarian and cultural relations issues.

Comparing Postwar Responsibilities

As the politics of memory became increasingly more a phenomenon of global public culture, Japanese reassessments of the postwar in relation to the wartime past became increasingly guided by comparisons. Paradoxically, perhaps, the more other Asian nations made the war responsibility issue part of their relations with Japan, the more public discourse within Japan looked to (West) Germany in efforts to define and qualify what was politically and conceptually at stake. If earlier comparisons between Japan and West Germany had focused on the course of modernization or the characterization of wartime fascism, the public debate in the late 1980s and 1990s centered on the "management" of war legacies in the postwar period. At the time of the 1982 textbook scandal, Japanese audiences had already been exposed to sweeping comparisons in the media of the West German and Japanese education systems with respect to treatments of their wartime pasts. In 1986, Japanese and West German grassroots organizations formed the Japanese-German Peace Forum *(Nichi-doku heiwa fōramu)*, which was closely associated with Wadatsumikai and represented efforts in both countries to locate the initiative for articulating public memory of the war among citizens instead of the government.[17] Four years later, in 1990, Japanese and South Korean historians organized the Japan-South Korean Joint Study Group on History Textbooks, which was prompted by and modeled after German-Polish exchanges on history textbook development.[18] In August 1995, Japanese nongovernmental organizations invited former West German president Richard von Weizsäcker to

Japan for extensive television interviews on the issue of taking responsibility for the past, which were aired live on ETV on the eve of the fiftieth anniversary of the war's end.

Richard von Weizsäcker had held an extraordinarily high position among Left-liberal circles since his address to the German parliament on the occasion of the fortieth anniversary of defeat in 1985.[19] In it, von Weizsäcker linked the war with the Holocaust, commemorated various groups of victims of German aggression, and spelled out individual and collective (political) responsibilities. This speech took on a life of its own in Japan, where it was invoked over and over in the mass as well as "mini" media (organization-specific periodical publications) for at least a decade, complete with the appearance of the newly coined term *kako no kokufuku*, a translation of the German word *Vergangenheitsbewältigung* or "facing the past."[20] The comparison with Germany was designed to characterize and criticize postwar Japanese memory on the political, intellectual, and popular levels. It pointed to something lacking in postwar Japanese society, to missed opportunities, and to the incompleteness of the postwar project.[21] In almost all accounts Germany possessed the "better" postwar, even if Japan, for a good number of conservatives, had the better war.[22] For an example of the latter, Nishio Kanji, a crusader against what he and others termed *Nihon dameron* (Japan-bashing), devoted an entire book to the incomparability of the two countries, beginning with the different nature of their wars and ending with the evil intentions of a Germany newly unified, economically powerful, and ethically corrupted by the legacy of the East German *Stasi*.[23] On the center-Left, however, the appropriateness of the comparison itself was hardly questioned. Japan and Germany's parallel histories of wartime fascism, defeat, occupation, and war crime trials, followed by democratization and economic high growth, rendered the basis of the comparison self-evident. These basic commonalities then served to highlight the postwar divergences between the two countries, from geopolitical circumstances and occupation policies to the persistence of prewar social and cultural attitudes among the people and an unqualified though strong pacifism.[24]

The Japanese media's preoccupation with German modes of political memory in the early 1990s was nevertheless significant only as a catalyst for the heated debates on the subject that engulfed the public in unprecedented volume and variety at the end of the century. Indeed, the terminology that came to carry the new discourse on the one hand resurrected the old Japanese Left's terms "responsibility" *(sekinin)* and "reflection" *(hanshō)*, and on the other hand adopted the new American (and globally used) term "memory" *(kioku)*. The salience of "responsibility" attested to the persistence of an ideological Left-Right divide even if the power-political parameters had shifted to the extent that the nationalist Right now found itself in the opposition. At the same time, however, and similar to developments in Europe, the United States, and other parts of the world, the increasingly pervasive use of "memory" as an alternative to older and politically more charged vocabulary signaled the participation in post–Cold War cross-national and global conversations about historical injustices and their contemporary legacies. By the end of the 1990s, academic as well as popular publications explored various categories of "collective" memory, including ethnicity and gender, but the focus came to rest on "nationalism" versus "globalization," which captured, in a sense, the mutual imbrications of the Cold War *sekinin* and the post–Cold War *kioku* discourses.[25] Even the German-derived term *kako no kokufuku* enjoyed a comeback within the context of global memory cultures at an international symposium entitled " 'Facing the Past' and Truth Investigation: A survey of historical facts promoted in Japan, the United States, and Korea."[26]

Documenting War and Postwar Suffering

Nothing substantiated the conceptual talk about postwar responsibility as much as new, or newly public, information about real wartime events. Indeed, a long-overdue examination of Japanese war atrocities in Asia—as well as their vehement denial by a few right-wing politicians and their supporters—informed and characterized the politics of memory from the late 1980s on, complicating Japan's "victims' consciousness" *(higaisha ishiki)* with an emphasis on "victimizer consciousness" *(kagaisha ishiki)*. This brought into focus the public recognition of formerly neglected groups of victims as well as bearers of responsibility and linked the two in newly important ways. In terms of significance for the debate, strategies of disseminating knowledge and rousing public consciousness took precedence over finding new facts about particular wartime events, which, by and large, were well known to specialists. Yet, the discovery of new documents relating to Japanese war atrocities, paraded in front of both a domestic and an international audience, contributed critically to the emergence of the war responsibility issue as a political problem in its own right rather than an expression of special interests only.

The gruesome biological warfare experiments performed on Chinese, Russian, Korean, and other POWs under the direction of Japan's best scientists working for Unit 731 in Manchuria, as well as the American cover-up of these crimes in the immediate postwar years, captured public attention precisely because the doctors responsible had so entirely evaded responsibility.[27] Beginning with Morimura Seiichi's million-copy bestseller *Akuma no hōshoku* (The Devil's Gluttony) in the aftermath of the 1982 textbook controversy, the crimes of Unit 731 became an important focus of historical research, political activism, and cultural productions through a variety of public venues in which the Japan-China Friendship Association actively participated.[28] Another war atrocity, the Japanese army's rape and massacre of thousands of Chinese residents in the capital city of Nanjing in 1937, which ultra-conservatives in Japan tended to deny or minimize, for this very reason occupied historians and researchers with particular intensity. Iris Chang's discovery of the John Rabe diaries, manuscripts of a Nazi German eyewitness who helped many Chinese escape, lent a new immediacy to the sheer extent of the killing, and her polemical likening of Nanjing to Auschwitz not only made the book a bestseller but also sparked a heated international controversy about historical facts and contemporary politics.[29] Chang's use of historical sources was largely discredited in academic circles, but the public debate about it revealed much about the place of historical memory in post–Cold War transnational and citizen-led networks of political activism that came to characterize global public culture at century's end.

Politically even more explosive, however, was the discovery of archival materials that proved the wartime government's direct involvement in the recruitment of military "comfort women" (*jūgun ianfu*) from Korea and elsewhere, as well as in the establishment and supervision of so-called comfort stations at the war front.[30] In January 1992, historian Yoshimi Yoshiaki presented materials that forced the Japanese government to acknowledge its involvement, for which Prime Minister Miyazaki Kiichi offered an official apology on his visit to

Korea. Although some former "comfort women" began to organize earlier, many more came forth in the 1990s to testify and demand official acknowledgment of their mistreatment as well as government compensation.[31] An unprecedented number of academic and especially legal teams formed networks with citizen groups supporting individual victims, not only former "comfort women" but also forced laborers, convicted Class B/C war criminals, atomic-bomb survivors, and others in their quest for government compensation. At stake in all these cases was clearly the political, legal, and financial responsibility of the Japanese government, both past and present, as the official representative of a national memory. In other words, while public awareness of unresolved historical injustices had increased dramatically and protest was now organized by a host of grassroots organizations rather than established interest groups, the conceptual framework of public memory was slow to change.

In an ill-fated move, the cabinet of the socialist prime minister, Murayama Tomiichi, established the so-called Asian Women's Fund in 1995 from which the government was to offer each victim of the comfort women system an official letter of apology, medical and welfare funds, "atonement money," and the guarantee of government support for further historical research.[32] International law scholar and former board member Ōnuma Yasuaki has defended the Fund's intentions against the overwhelming public criticism that rendered it a failure, arguing that the joint governmental and private initiative represented a way for Japan as a whole to take responsibility.

> It was not only the Japanese government, but also the Japanese people, who gave birth to the abominable institution of "comfort women"; it was not only the Japanese government, but also the Japanese people who failed to confront the problem for almost half a century after the war; therefore, both the Japanese people and the government should take responsibility. Theoretically speaking, [the Asian Women's Fund] was an attempt for the Japanese nation as a whole, partly the government and partly the citizens, to take responsibility for the wrong that the Japanese nation as a whole had committed.[33]

It proved difficult, if not impossible, however, to break through the sharp divisions that decades of contentious interest politics had created on the terrain of war memory, where even basic meanings of a Japanese collectivity were elusive. Even if the old interest groups no longer dominated the public discourse, and even if the post–Cold War political landscape dictated major changes to postwar structures, established patterns of linking the wartime with the postwar past dissolved not abruptly but only gradually.

Another case in point was a concurrent project of documenting wartime (and postwar) suffering, namely that of families of Japan's war dead, at a new museum in Tokyo, the Hall of Shōwa *(Shōwakan)*. Both the content of the museum exhibitions and the public controversy that preceded the eventual building of the museum have received thoughtful attention;[34] here I focus on the place of the Shōwakan in the history of *Nihon izokukai*, the Association of War-Bereaved Families, who began lobbying the Welfare Ministry on behalf of such a commemorative project in 1979 and managed the museum since its opening in 1999. The Shōwakan offers displays of a variety of objects pertaining to the everyday life of Japanese within a trans-war framework between 1935 and 1955. In the absence of historical explanations of the political context that conditioned people's lives through this twenty-year time span, the displays focus on material culture, a media center invites visitors to explore documents on their own, and meeting rooms are available for group projects. Nothing in the Shōwakan suggests that this is in fact a national museum, or even that it is managed by Nihon Izokukai, except the long list of local Izokukai chapters as sponsors of displays. Yet it was built and is now managed with considerable financial support by the Health and Welfare Ministry, that is, with taxpayers' money.

The Shōwakan presents an instructively mixed record of contemporary nationalism in Japan with important parallels to similarly controversial museum exhibitions in the United States (i.e., the 1995 Enola Gay exhibit at the Smithsonian Institution) and Germany (e.g., the 1999 Wehrmacht exhibit). That it was built at all surely testifies to the continued strength of the Izokukai's close ties to the LDP and bureaucracy, an issue that itself became the explicit target of protests in 1993–95. Yet despite this structural continuity, a comparison of the Shōwakan as it stands today with earlier plans reveals that contemporary nationalism no longer easily relies on its most cherished symbols, for example, the emperor or the "manifestation of the heroic deeds of the war dead" *(eirei no kenshō)*. Instead, the Shōwakan was reduced to what was essentially a nationalistic interpretation of a common theme in the 1990s: victims of war, whether children or adults, men or women, Asians or Japanese. Moreover, in the final outcome the Shōwakan was situated on the commemorative landscape quite like the rest of Japan's museums had been throughout the postwar period, representing particular interests, ideologies, and memories. Rather than towering over all other war/peace museums as Japan's first national museum of World War II, the Shōwakan in effect ended up in its rightful place as a museum of the historical roots of the Izokukai, despite the troubling issue of state funding.

A closer look at the language used to describe the Shōwakan and its previously planned incarnations as part of the longer history of the Izokukai supports these claims. At the brief thirty-minute opening ceremony on March 27, 1999, four high-profile speakers gave addresses: Prime Minister Obuchi Keizō, Welfare Minister Miyashita Sohei, current Izokukai president Nakai Sumiko, and a delegate of former prime minister and former Izokukai president Hashimoto Ryūtarō, who did not appear in person. Prime Minister Obuchi steadfastly stuck to a narrative of suffering in his address:

> In the half-century that has passed since the end of the last world war, we have built, by the people's efforts, today's peaceful and affluent Japan. But when I think of the hardships defying both pen and tongue that you war-bereaved have endured, the loss of your loved ones in war and the painful struggle of life in the midst of the confusion and upheaval after the war, I am overcome by a flood of emotions . . . The need to collect, preserve, and pass on to the next generation historical documents and information of this experience and reality now looms large.

He went on to say that after the war, the country extended various support measures to the war-bereaved and war-injured in the form of state compensation. The opening of the Shōwakan, which "transmits to younger generations the hardships of the people's daily lives during and after the war, has an immensely deep meaning and achieves its stated goal completely by connecting broadly with the people of today. We expect that it will make great contributions to the twenty-first century."[35] Hashimoto Ryūtarō, in contrast, acknowledged that the project originated in the desire of the Izokukai to have the state build a Commemoration Hall for the War-Bereaved Children to *console* the war orphans and function as an added support measure for the war bereaved. Suehiro Sakae, spokesman for the Izokukai in 1996 when I interviewed him, asserted that the Japan Association of War-Bereaved Families considered this project (termed alternately "commemoration hall" and "prayer hall")[36] a way for the state to make up to the war-bereaved, who had been forced to rebuild their lives without the appropriate compensation and state-sponsored war dead ceremonies to which they were entitled. Neither this sense of entitlement nor the ritual aspect of "consolation" and "prayer" were present in the final version of the project. Instead, the outcome represented a long-resisted compromise to appease critics both on the Left, who protested the violation of the constitutional separation of state and religion, and on the Right, led by Yasukuni Shrine, who insisted that there could be no other legitimate place for ritual worship than Yasukuni itself. In the final outcome, the Shōwakan was defined simply as

> an institution that collects, preserves, and displays historical documents and information about the hardship of the people's everyday life that the war-bereaved families, beginning with the orphans, experienced during and after the war (1935–55), and that gives later generations the opportunity to learn about these hardships.[37]

This no doubt represented a significant failure for the Association of War-bereaved Families. The name "Shōwakan," of which members were unceremoniously informed only two months before opening, reflected none of its ideological concerns. The briefest of explanations asserted, "the emblem of the Shōwa era was the last great war, and the hardship of people who suffered in it became the cornerstone of the prosperity of postwar society."[38] Indeed, the clear linkage of wartime and early postwar material suffering with later postwar affluence placed at the center of the national community's (re)construction the memory of material and social conditions, which had served, under the Occupation, to justify the legitimacy of a war-bereaved organization, which at that time was still called the Japan League for the Welfare of the War-Bereaved (*Nihon izoku kōsei renmei*). Under Occupation censorship, all references to a *political* community of war-bereaved had to be avoided. Moreover, one of SCAP's (Supreme Command for the Allied Powers) conditions for allowing such an organization was that it not be limited to the military war-bereaved but also include war-bereaved with no connection to the military. It was as if the language of the Shōwakan reconnected with the earliest incarnation of the Izokukai as a social welfare group rather than the political pressure group into which it had evolved with the end of the Occupation.

A consideration of the Shōwakan's opening as a moment in the history of the Izokukai reveals a long-established special interest group at the crossroads. The opening ceremony actually had a twin event, smaller in scale but one that nonetheless made the front page of the Izokukai's newspaper while coverage of the museum opening appeared on page 2 of the same issue. On the eve of March 27, the day of the opening ceremony, the *sōnenbu* (Middle-Aged Section), a suborganization of the children of the war-bereaved, who stood at the center of the Shōwakan project, formally dissolved itself. It was a ceremony of closure, of reflection and remembering an almost forty-year history of activism. This section had formed in 1960 as the Youth Section (*seinenbu*), when the war orphans (*iji*) were becoming the new focal point of Izokukai activism. Generational change and the importance of transmitting a "correct" memory of the war and contemporary patriotism to those without concrete war experience had then become a critical objective of Izokukai activism. The Youth Section served as a tool to control this transfer of "correct" national sentiment rather than youth organizing on its own behalf. At the end of the century, these youths were of course past their prime, and it was as if the museum, which remembered their suffering and honored their strength in rebuilding the country, took their place in society—displayed memory replacing lived experiences, so to speak. From the coverage in the Association's newspaper it was clear that this dissolution marked a turning point in the Izokukai's history, one that had been pondered in general terms over the past years, namely the need to remake the organization and give it a new direction. It indicated not only the very reality of generational turnover, which war-bereaved associations inescapably face over time, but also of efforts to locate long-established special interests on a shifting and much widened terrain of civic political activism.

Seeking Practical Solutions to Unresolved Issues

No other postwar responsibility awaiting resolution after fifty years of postwar management caught the public imagination as much as "postwar compensation" *(sengo hoshō)*, the "super-keyword" of the 1990s as the *Postwar Compensation Handbook* boasted.[39] Individual lawsuits for compensation had worked themselves through Japanese courts since at least 1975, when former Korean forced laborers stranded in Sakhalin after the war's end and unable to return to their homeland sued the Japanese government for compensation.[40] But it was not until 1991 that lawsuits for compensation by non-Japanese, especially in the Tokyo District Court, increased rapidly and focused public opinion on this issue.[41] Shortly after Prime Minister Hosokawa Morihiro's apology in 1993—in which he explicitly included Asian war victims in an official invocation of the war dead—more than half of those questioned in a national opinion poll taken by the *Asahi shimbun* favored government compensation, with that trend on a steep rise in the following years. Among the 20- and 30-year-olds polled in 1993, 59 percent affirmed compensating former "comfort women," 78 percent felt those born in Japan's colonies were entitled to compensation for their suffering under Japanese colonial rule, and 78 percent wanted to see the government pay compensation to countries against which Japan had committed atrocities.[42]

Nonetheless, to the extent that postwar compensation, responsibility, and management had overlapping, sometimes interchangeable, and sometimes contrasting meanings as Japan commemorated "fifty years postwar" *(sengo gojūnen)*, the debate elicited a convoluted, crosscutting, and politically charged array of responses. The compensation debate gave public memory in the 1990s a particular inflection that drew its vitality from contemporary changes in public culture as well as from older patterns of organized memory. Most likely because the Asian women and men who sued the Japanese government for compensation formed a previously unrecognized group of victims and exposed heretofore little discussed war crimes, their plight became the terrain on which important political questions were fought out in the 1990s. Indeed, what began as an issue of financial compensation writ small turned before long into a politics of restitution writ large. The "imaginative power of the 'military comfort women'," to use Laura Hein's phrase,[43] became so compelling precisely because it engaged long-standing uses of war memory and responsibility in debates about democracy, citizenship, and social and national identity in a context now informed by the knowledges of an increasingly global public culture.

The politics of restitution in the 1990s stretched and challenged the older political framework of public memory in important ways. Formerly underrepresented issues of memory pertaining to non-Japanese victims of Japanese colonialism, and not just war, found vocal advocates in new citizen organizations outside established political circles. At a time when older political alliances began to break up, these new groups mobilized local, national, and cross-national networks and succeeded in pushing war responsibility issues into the international arena. The founding principles of the National League of War-Bereaved Families for Peace (*Heiwa izokukai zenkoku renkaku kai* or *Heiwa izokukai* for short), established on July 7, 1986 (the forty-ninth anniversary of Japan's invasion of China) in the aftermath of Prime Minister Nakasone's visit to Yasukuni Shrine, clearly linked the suffering of Japanese war victims to their role in a system that inflicted even greater pain on other Asians. The group called for an international alliance of war-bereaved to address the problem of war and postwar responsibility in a global context.[44] Absorbing dissenting members of the powerful Izokukai who had been meeting since 1982, especially in Hokkaido, in opposition to the central leadership's politics, the new Heiwa izokukai expanded rapidly and played a leading role in the promotion of the compensation issue in the 1990s.

The new agents of public memory in post–Cold War Japan engaged the older special-interest groups in what became a public debate incorporating various aspects of war memory that in earlier decades tended to be discussed separately. This was because the larger issues brought up in the 1990s had long been part of a highly politicized domestic discourse on memory, only now the challenger came from outside Japan (at least in a general perception) and thus warranted a "national" response that revealed the fragmented organization of Japanese memory as problematic. The focus on Asia and the legacy of Japanese colonialism, which could be argued reached back not fifty but one hundred years (to the Sino-Japanese War of 1894–95), lent a new specificity to a debate that became at once broader (international) and narrower in scope (Asian plaintiffs in Japanese courts). At the same time, the inherent multiplicity of issues associated with compensation as a political, legal, social, and ethical question elicited a variety of approaches and clashes of interests. Indeed, no sooner had former victims of Japanese aggression filed their lawsuits in Japanese courts than their individual claims were appropriated to long familiar problems of memory, from school textbooks to museums and back to the Tokyo War Crimes Trial and Cold War politics. A case in point is Tokyo University professor Fujioka Nobukatsu's Liberal View of History Study Group (*Jiyū-shugi shikan kenkyūkai*) and its notorious spinoff, the Society for the Making of New School Textbooks in History (*Atarashii rekishi kyōkasho o tsukuru kai*). Addressing themselves to students and teachers in Japan as well as abroad,[45] these groups—new in the mid-1990s—not only resisted the onslaught of the global memory critique but also took issue with it and thereby strengthened the viability of conservative nationalism within contemporary discourses. This self-styled "liberal" view of history claimed to offer a new paradigm to break out of the older, postwar Left-Right polarities, but it did so by openly denying some of Japan's newly documented war atrocities and actively campaigning to eliminate references to the "comfort women" system in textbooks.[46]

Meanwhile, the Supreme Court ruled in favor of including explicit references to Japanese war atrocities in textbooks in the final decision of Ienaga Saburo's third lawsuit, marking the conclusion of a thirty-year-long struggle led by Left-liberal organizations against the Ministry of Education.[47] No less significantly, the Japan Teachers' Union, which had lost much of its political salience along with the general decline of the labor movement in the 1980s, joined the Socialist Party in abandoning its radical opposition to the use of the national flag and anthem in schools, a position unthinkable in earlier decades. The political arena in which struggles over memory and history education took place had thus changed, albeit not beyond recognition. Many of the old interest organizations remained actively involved in memory politics, but now in an immensely broadened context in which they had to reposition themselves. The Association of Shintō Shrines won a significant victory in 1989, when it insisted on—and helped plan and execute—elaborate Shintō ceremonies at Emperor Hirohito's funeral and Akihito's ascendance to the throne. Shortly afterward, however, the association strongly opposed some of the new emperor's public actions, such as his trips to China and Korea. The Japan-China Friendship Association promoted a host of smaller cross-national groups and projects engaged in focusing public attention of Japanese war crimes against Asians. In 1995, the pacifist intellectual group Wadatsumikai published a new edition of its classic compilation of student-soldier testimonies, *Kike wadatsumi no koe* (Listen to the Voices from the Sea) and cooperated with the large commercial film company Tōei in releasing a new (and greatly changed) version of its 1950 antiwar movie *Kike wadatsumi no koe* (*Last Friends* in English). Both projects were explicitly guided by a critique of Japan's "victims consciousness" and reconsidered the student-soldiers not only as victims but also as perpetrators.

Finally, the compensation debate owed much of its significance to the recognition by all who participated in it that it took place "belatedly" in biological time (its would-be recipients neared the end of their lives or had already died) and in world time (comparatively to other countries facing similar issues). Public hearings and other testimonies as well as oral histories assumed a now-or-never urgency sustained by a new realization of the political consequences of half a century of silences and silencings. Of course Japan was not alone in this but was in fact in the good company of most of its Asian neighbors, who were also only now beginning to complicate and negotiate the politics of memory and restitution in their own countries and internationally. Moreover, the worldwide attention summoned by this intra-Asian memory debate suggested that war memory and responsibility were acute issues in other world regions as well. At the turn of the millennium, perhaps the most innovative attempts at conceptualizing and addressing issues of historical responsibility and relating them to contemporary war crimes were taking place in Asia, organized by international teams of women and men.

I refer here to the Women's International Tribunal on Japan's Military Sexual Slavery, which took place in Tokyo in December 2000 and presented its verdict a year later in The Hague, declaring all defendants, including Emperor Hirohito, guilty of crimes against humanity. This extraordinary "people's tribunal," in which judges, legal teams, and survivors from nine countries participated, was masterminded by three women, each head of a women's rights organization formed in the 1990s: the Korean Council for the Women Drafted for Military

Sexual Slavery by Japan, Violence Against Women in War Network (VAWW-NET Japan), and the Asian Center for Women's Human Rights (ASCENT). In the preamble of the Tribunal's charter, the organizers stressed the lack of international acknowledgment of Japanese war crimes against women in Asia as well as the continuation of violence against women in war today. They also recognized an ethical mandate in conducting this trial:

> Mindful that while the Tribunal, as a people's and women's initiative, has no real power to enforce its judgments, it nonetheless carries the moral authority demanding their wide acceptance and enforcement by the international community and national governments.

They urged once again that states and intergovernmental organizations take necessary measures to bring to justice the persons responsible for the crimes and to provide reparation including apology, compensation, and rehabilitation.[48]

As such, the Tribunal fits squarely within the global space of restitution that Elazar Barkan described, perhaps overly optimistically, to be a growing moral trend in the world today.[49] To the extent that changes in international relations and an increasingly global public culture influenced the politics of memory in Japan and Asia in the 1990s, it appears that developments in Asia were now in fact acting as catalysts in the cultures of memory elsewhere.

Conclusion

To be sure, the established special-interest groups that carried the political discourse about the meaning of World War II in Japan after 1945 were alive and well fifty years later, even if their future was far from clear. Although the LDP made a comeback after the loss of its long hegemony in 1993 and the JSP all but vanished from the political scene in the meantime, and although the battle over textbook reform was by the late 1990s led by conservative revisionists in place of progressive teachers, the Right did not in fact dominate public memory. The (overwhelmingly progressive) debate about (post)war responsibility, and official (conservative) attempts to represent a national memory through national symbols and ritual ceremonies no longer operate on separate planes. The multiple ways in which memories of a shared past (whether the war or the postwar) command public space—through diverse agents, different media, and contested concerns of the present—are more fully recognized today than they were when public memory was an object primarily of special interests. Although Asian regional integration is far from a foregone conclusion, it may well provide the context in which memory continues to be a staple of politics, not only in national but also increasingly in international terms. The organization and the politics of memory may change, but the contention over issues of the past, as well as its public representation and negotiation, is here to stay. The changing pattern of political conflict about multiple memories of the war and the postwar in Japan from 1945 to 1995 reveals not only how Japanese have publicly formulated, negotiated, and adjusted views of their past but also the mechanisms by which different and conflicting memories were deeply anchored, and in fact centered, in the political process in contemporary Japan.

~ 2

Operations of Memory

"Comfort Women" and the World

CAROL GLUCK

THE SURGE OF MEMORY in the 1990s brought World War II once again to the center of public attention. This was no parochial phenomenon but one that occurred in many countries, as the wartime past of fifty years before became pressingly present in politics and culture. One reason was generational—those who experienced the war would not let it pass from living memory without a collective autobiographical sigh, sob, or salute. Another was the seismic geopolitical shift after the end of the Cold War, which heralded change but also brought uncertainty and drove nations both old and new to nationalistic reviews of their recent history. Yet another reason was the late-twentieth-century obsession with memory itself—a seizure of interest in how societies, nations, and individuals told their stories, constructed their identities, and otherwise used the past to lay claim to the future. The diversity of these personal recollections and the welter of conflicting claims on collective memory characterized the international memoryscape of the 1990s. In 2005, sixty years after its end, World War II was not merely being commemorated but *re*-remembered in a struggle over the shape of public memory, frequently with high political and cultural stakes.

This process prompts two questions that while important are not at all easy to answer. First, how did public memory actually work in late twentieth-century mass society? What factors accounted for the contention and for the changes in the way war stories were told? *Where,* discursively, was public memory located and whose memory was it? Why did war memory follow different patterns in different countries, impelling the by now conventional comparison between postwar West Germany and Japan? Because the process of war re-remembering occurred in so many places at roughly the same time, I tried to frame these questions into something approaching an analytic of memory by focusing on the commonalities across societies rather than on the differences among them. In doing so, it seemed that what I call the "operations of memory" worked in similar ways in dissimilar contexts, leading to a stark statement I will make at the outset: cultural differences do not much affect the way public memory is created, maintained, and transformed in contemporary mass societies. The analytic corollary is that cultural explanations will not suffice to account for the differences in war memory in Japan, Germany, Indonesia, the United States, and elsewhere—or for the (erroneously) alleged preference for apology in Asian memory, or again for so-called cultural disparities in notions of guilt and responsibility. My argument thus addresses the common features of public memory, as found in Japan and other places, not the cultural (as distinct from historical) particularities that Japanese and other peoples use to insulate themselves from the rest of the world.

The second question relates to the world. World War II was made and fought by nation-states, a total war that demanded total mobilization and generated a kind of total memory, from which no one was meant to be exempt. The nation-state was the subject of war, and its subjects were twice mobilized, first for national sacrifice and then for national memory, in which all war stories were melded monolithically into a single national narrative. Not surprisingly, each country told the war from its own point of view, seeing victory, defeat, liberation, or division as an almost entirely national experience. The result was a memory of a *world* war with the *world* left out. Even when the viewpoint of enemies and victims on the other side was sometimes acknowledged, seldom did national horizons expand enough to include the geometry of global war. So it seemed that by imprisoning a world war within national borders, nations recapitulated in memory the nation-centered interests that had caused the war in the first place.

Yet counterforces did exist. In the postwar world international pressures made it difficult for people to wall themselves off in the inner courtyards of national memory. Postwar West Germans did not re-member the Holocaust all of their own accord, but partly as a response to geopolitical demands within Western Europe and moral challenges from Jews and others around the world. Asians exerted similar pressure on Japanese war memory from the early 1980s through the 1990s and into the new millennium. As post–Cold War geopolitics decreased the dominance of the United States and increased the importance of Asia, Japan was repeatedly called upon to confront its unresolved imperial and wartime past in Korea, China, and elsewhere. In many countries these international factors influenced national memory even in its de-terminedly domestic precincts, a development that seems appropriate for the subject of a world war.

And more than that: over time what I think of as transnational memory began to emerge. For in the end, Auschwitz and Hiroshima did not belong only to those who perpetrated or suffered them but to all who lived in their historical and moral aftermath. Neither the Holo-caust nor the atomic bombings could—or should—be encompassed by one or another particular national rendering of their cause or signifi-cance. On the contrary, Holocaust memory challenges genocide everywhere, and Hiroshima memory confronts nuclear warfare past and future. In this regard, it can be said that the "comfort women,"[1] whose past finally came into memory during the 1990s, were at the same time becoming part of a transnational memory with social, legal, and moral consequences that transcended national or cultural borders. How contested national memories of wartime brutality could be trans-formed into larger, more humane legacies for the world as a whole is the second question at issue here.

Telling the War

One must however begin at the beginning: when the war stories first were told, not only in words but also in commemorations, monuments, and other tangible and intangible representations that constituted the *Ur*-memory of World War II. These stories arose either during the war or immediately after it, in a time of drama or trauma that made things appear clear-cut, black and white, larger than life. I call them "heroic narratives" because villains and victims were clearly marked in strong storylines, which admitted no ambiguity.[2] Most of these could be reduced to a singularly simple statement such as "Austria was the first victim of Nazism," or "the Japanese were embroiled by their leaders in a reckless war." I think of these as "historical one-liners"—reductive slogans that obliterated context, complexity, and diversity, too. Typically, the nation-state, which had made the war, was elided into "the national people," who carried "the people's war," as it was called in Britain, or suffered the "cataclysm of defeat" as in Japan. Total stories of total war, the heroic narratives projected national unity by effacing experiential difference, creating whole nations of partisans, resistants, antifascists—and above all, victims.

Narratives of national victimization were strikingly commonplace. In West Germany, as one historian described it, "a nation of German victims had confronted a handful of Nazi perpetrators and a multitude of brutally vengeful Communist victors."[3] A mere "handful" of homegrown villains meant that the rest of the people were simply overtaken (in Japanese, "embroiled") by events beyond their control or responsibility. From France to Romania, from Italy to Poland, war stories all over Europe blamed the Germans (together with "handfuls" of local collaborators) for every misfortune. Entire nations of victims populated these stories, which, needless to say, took little account of any victims except themselves. Japanese versions of homefront hardship fit this pattern, domesticating the war by setting the story at home and regendering its victims as female in the figure of mothers in *monpe*, the work trousers worn in wartime.

In every case the immediate postwar context determined the plot of the heroic narratives, whether civil war in China and Greece, political division in Korea and Germany, new socialist regimes in Eastern Europe, anticolonial struggles in Southeast Asia, or military occupation in several places. For Japan, the U.S. role was decisive in three ways, each of which reinforced the victims' narrative and removed responsibility from the national people. First, by renaming the Greater East Asia War as the (Japanese-American) Pacific War, the Occupation helped to conjure the disappearance of the China War, thereby extruding both Asia and continental aggression from the main war story. Second, by trying a "handful" of leaders—but not the emperor—at the War Crimes Trial, the United States aligned victors' justice with victims' justice, underscoring the image of a nation and its emperor misled by errant militarists who had now been duly judged and punished.

Third—and most astonishing—by casting the war in domestic terms, whose causes lay at home and could therefore be addressed by postwar reforms for a "Japan reborn," the Occupation contributed to a nearly total amnesia of empire. Korea, Manchuria, Taiwan, and the rest of the imperial territories were suddenly expunged from the official story of the war, leaving the home islands (*naichi*) populated by an allegedly monoethnic national people dedicated to peace and democracy.

No China War, no Asia, no Empire—based on the heroic narrative of war as a mostly internal affair, Japan was able to embark on the postwar without pausing to attend to the postimperial. Where postwar Britain confronted the loss of empire and France struggled for years to come to terms with Algeria, Japan turned away from its imperial past in Asia into the waiting embrace of the future and of the United States. The neocolonial U.S. Cold War imperium only deepened this memory hole, in that American dominance seemed so absolute that postwar Japanese sometimes felt their situation more akin to a postcolonial than a postimperial experience, while their own empire remained in the limbo of official oblivion.

The blanks in Japan's original war story had counterparts in the heroic narratives of other countries, which everywhere depended on the saliency of silence. The insistence on a single national people, for example, created hierarchies of internal victims that determined who would be excluded from the initial memory. So it was in Europe that among survivors returning from concentration camps, political prisoners received narrative notice while Jews did not. Homefront suffering was frequently recounted, but not that of returning Australian or Polish POWs or Japanese repatriates (*hikiagesha*) from the (about to be publicly silenced) empire. Some silences arose from social and psychological trauma, which made people unable or unwilling to speak openly of their experience: what I call the "effability factor." At times there were things that one simply could not utter, either because social receptivity was lacking or the psychological trauma was too great. Jewish Holocaust survivors, Asian "comfort women," soldiers who had raped and murdered, and Allied soldiers who survived the grisly D-Day landings were not ready to talk of their searing personal experiences in public, and often not in private either. A different kind of silence was generated by the simplistic character of the heroic narratives themselves, which when repeated over the years occluded other possible stories. It may be said of postwar French memory, for example, that remembering the Resistance was long preferable to dwelling on "la guerre franco-française," as the internal divisions during the Vichy period were later labeled. Similarly, the official rituals of war memory in Japan commemorated Hiroshima, which turned national victimization into a mission for peace, while excluding Manchuria, with its specter of brutal and failed empire, from the precincts of postwar public memory.

The telling point about these heroic narratives is not just how simplistic and national they were, but how long they lasted. Despite an ongoing dialectic between the spoken and the silent, the remembered and the unremembered, the early war stories held on—and on, all the more persistent in places like Japan where history appeared to validate the view that the bad wartime past they described had been thoroughly superseded by a better postwar future. Frozen memory, unaltered by time—or so it seemed on the fiftieth anniversary of the end of the war in 1995, when so many countries paraded their old stories along with their old veterans, none more egregiously perhaps than the United States, which repeated its vintage one-liner that "the atomic bombs ended the war and saved American lives." And in China in 2001 Prime Minister Koizumi reproduced a tried-and-true Japanese version of "that war" (*ano sensō*) when he intoned, "by facing our past and reflecting on it, postwar Japan, too, was able to prosper as a peaceful nation."[4] End of story.

Terrains of Memory

It was of course not the end of the story at all, but merely evidence of the durability of heroic narratives. Yet despite the long half-life of these early war stories, the memory struggles of the 1990s showed that changes had indeed taken place in public views of World War II. To understand how this memory change occurred requires some notion of how public memory operated in mass-mediated societies in the latter part of the twentieth century. And the first step toward a notion of the operations of memory is to concede that there is no such singular thing as public memory. At best there are different terrains of memory interacting in a dispersed discursive field, and for analytic purposes at least four terrains must be distinguished from one another.

The first is the terrain of official commemoration, which in the case of war memory generally received the most attention, although I argue that such focus could be misleading. Official memory included all activities connected with the state: commemorative rituals, public monuments and museums, veteran and compensation policies, government rhetoric, and national textbooks in countries that have them. One can read the heroic narratives clearly in the texts of war anniversaries. Indonesia's national story, for example, was expressed in its celebration of August 17 as the date of independence from the Dutch, with no mention of the Japanese Occupation, collaboration, or even such local victims as its own *rōmusha* (forced laborers). France commemorated the "French and Allied" victory over the Nazis on May 8, but for a long time not as enthusiastically as it did November 11, the anniversary of the more unequivocally French triumph in World War I. Politically, of course, the liberation of Paris in 1944 was easier to commemorate than the fall of France four years earlier and the subsequent rise of the Vichy regime. By the 1990s two new dates had been added to the French commemorative calendar, both to mark the deportation of Jews, reflecting a change in a national narrative that now included Vichy and the Holocaust. The United States never changed its focus on remembering Pearl Harbor as the beginning and Hiroshima as the end of its Pacific War. In Japan the annual ceremonies marking the atomic bombings of August 6 and 9 and the surrender on August 15 persisted in marking the end of a war that, in official ritual at least, seemed never to have begun—not on September 18, with the Manchurian invasion of 1931; or on July 7, the beginning of total war in China in 1937; or even, with any commemorative fanfare, on December 7, the date of the attack on Pearl Harbor in 1941.

Official commemoration was always politically fraught, as evidenced in the repeated controversies over national monuments, state museums, and school textbooks. When after two decades Japan's "War Dead Peace Memorial Hall" finally opened in 1999, the war had all but disappeared, not only from its innocuous new name, the Shōwa Hall, but also from its exhibits, which—true to the homefront narrative—thoroughly domesticated the war. The presentation centered on "the hardships of the people's daily life"—mostly *monpe* (those trousers again), pots and pans, women and children, and, as a faint echo of a war somewhere off in the distance, a few *senninbari*, the thousand-stitch belts sewn by women for departing soldiers, and a selection of soldiers' letters home to their families.[5] With domestication, of course, came decontextualization. A different but equally diminishing decontextualization of war afflicted the Enola Gay exhibit at the Smithsonian Institution in Washington in 1995, which after heated public controversy reduced the atomic bombings to a shiny piece of airplane fuselage: no bomb victims, no nuclear age; in short, no history. The decade-long debate about the Holocaust Memorial in Berlin finally ended in 1999 with parliamentary approval of the design, a political resolution reached by avoiding the thorny question of what precise story would be told by the "Memorial for the Murdered Jews of Europe." In each of these instances, the solution to public controversy over memory was simply and simplistically to abandon history, which was just "too complicated" to permit a political consensus.

In most cases the terrain of official memory was held hostage to domestic politics. Political concerns drove out complexity because, as bureaucrats and politicians so often said, history was also "too controversial," which was the reason that Japan's Ministry of Health and Welfare resorted to pots and pans in the Shōwa Hall. Or history should be "left for future historians to decide," as Japanese prime ministers liked to say in the 1990s about such things as whether Japan had fought an aggressive or merely an "aggressive-like" war in Asia. Unless compelled to, official memory shied away from unseemly parts of its own past, from Nazi gold in Switzerland and forced labor in Germany to comfort women in Japan. And even when compelling forces intruded, in no country did official memory change easily. In Japan the decades-long conservative dominance in politics, together with the postwar status quo on which it depended, practically guaranteed the perpetuation of the heroic narrative. So it was in 2005 that Japan commemorated, not the sixtieth anniversary of the end of the war as in most countries, but the "sixtieth anniversary of the postwar" *(sengo rokujūnen)*, emphasizing the old story about a wrong war having led to a prosperous peace. When, from the late 1990s, Koreans and Chinese repeatedly evoked Japan's "history problem" *(rekishi ninshiki mondai* in Japanese) they referred primarily to this terrain of official memory. There, such issues as Yasukuni Shrine, national textbooks, the Nanjing Massacre, wartime biological experiments, the colonization of Korea, and the comfort women suggested that Japan's national war memory had utterly failed to keep pace with the times.

Things looked somewhat different on the second terrain of what I call vernacular memory. In my view, this terrain was by far the most important in many countries, in that much of the memory work occurred there. Indeed, in Japan, the state—by failing to meet the continual memory challenges it faced—effectively ceded the action to society, which, ironically perhaps, took up the cause of war memory with more force and perseverance than in countries like France, where the government addressed war memory as its own political task.[6] Vernacular memory everywhere was a vast domain, its war views abundant, amorphous, and much harder to track than the pronouncements of the state. For heuristic purposes one can look at the production and the consumption sides separately, although they were not in fact separable in practice.

In the decades after World War II, people consumed war memory primarily through popular culture and the mass media. The primacy of visual media had been accelerating since before the war, with mass audiences for photojournalism and movie newsreels. During the war, radio and newspapers remained the dominant media, and popular war novels reached millions of readers in the first postwar decades. But it was the visual media—first photography and film and then television—that both carried war stories and also had the greatest impact on changing public views of the war. Holocaust memory was doubtless the prime case, whether in the photographs of the liberated concentration camps in 1945, the prominence of so-called Holocaust television, or the raft of documentary and feature films, from *Night and Fog* in 1955 to *Schindler's List* in 1993. While there was no aesthetic or substantive equivalence among these and countless other examples, their effect on public memory across generations was undeniable. Japanese audiences reached by the novel and film *The Human Condition* in the late 1950s and early 1960s at least saw a fictionalized version of Manchuria and the brutalities of empire and war that were at the time so steadfastly ignored in the official narrative.[7]

Public opinion polls, which figured on a plane somewhere between the consumption and the production of collective views, could be inadvertently revealing about the workings of vernacular memory. Scholars have suggested that the answers people give to survey questions occupy a kind of middle ground between what they think they *ought* to say and what they might *really* be thinking.[8] The former is likely to be publicly conditioned; the latter personal, more for the kitchen table than the questionnaire. In 1995, for example, 62 percent of Japanese polled thought that Japan's war compensation (*sensō no tsugunai*) was insufficient, and of those in their twenties an even higher 70 percent thought it inadequate. In 2005, 75 percent said that there had not been sufficient discussion of Japan's war responsibility, and more than 60 percent of those in their twenties, who admitted to knowing very little about the war, agreed that the subject of war responsibility deserved more debate. In the same year, while Prime Minister Koizumi insisted on visiting Yasukuni (the shrine of the war dead which includes Class A war criminals in its roster of "heroic spirits"), opinion polls repeatedly showed that more than 50 percent of Japanese were against the visits, most of them for the reason of "consideration of neighboring countries." These opinions indicated both a difference from the government's position and also a transgenerational memory that did not derive from official sources like textbooks or state policies toward comfort women and Asian victims of wartime atrocities.[9]

The question then becomes, how did younger people know that this was the public response expected of them? Most probably, they learned it from the media, which in 1995 were filled with stories occasioned by Prime Minister Murayama's efforts to confront the war and have the government compensate the comfort women. Foiled by politics, Murayama largely failed to realize his objectives, with the result that Japan made international headlines once again for stonewalling about its imperial and wartime past. No doubt either that in 2005 the repeated protests—some violent and in the streets, of people in those "neighboring countries" angry about Yasukuni and Japan's failure to recognize its war responsibility—made a dent in the consciousness of Japanese TV viewers and Web surfers. As revealed in these polls and also in numerous exhibits, television programs, and other forms of popular culture, vernacular opinion not only diverged at times from the official story but people could also be more enlightened about history than they were given credit for. Because such dispersed popular views were both hard to grasp and hard to measure, they did not necessarily register on the public balance sheet of Japanese memory, especially at times when state officials and right-wing revisionists were as vociferous in their past-denying rhetoric as they were in the years since the mid-1990s.

On the production side, the contours of the terrain of vernacular memory were always clearer. That was due to the countless groups dedicated to preserving the memory of their own particular experience and seeking a place for that experience within the larger field of public memory. Many countries, including Japan, developed an entire civil society of these "memory activists," as I call them, who tirelessly lobbied for recognition, compensation, and commemoration—in short, for inclusion in an expanded heroic narrative. They belonged to all political persuasions—Right, Left, and Center—and they represented all manner of war experience: associations of veterans, bereaved families, fallen students, repatriates, POWs, internees, expellees, Holocaust survivors, (Dutch) children of the Japanese Occupation (of the East Indies), and so on. Groups were established to work for and against commemorations, memorials, and monuments; to find and bury the unburied dead (Soviet) soldiers; to conduct oral histories and collect documents; to prove war crimes or to disprove war crimes—all in the good name of memory. Some organizations were active for more than five decades; others formed and then dissolved; still others were founded after the turn of the twenty-first century. Some edited books or made films; others built museums. Thus, even as Japan's official Shōwa Hall evaded the war in every way possible, private peace museums sprang up around the country, while Okinawa, which never shared the mainland's heroic narrative to begin with, had long been strewn with museums devoted to the war in which the Okinawan people had so severely suffered. Even as the right-wing Japanese Society for History Textbook Reform (*Atarashii rekishi kyōkasho o tsukuru kai*) agitated for a retrograde war memory in the late 1990s, the left-progressive Center for Research and Documentation on Japan's War Responsibility (*Nihon no sensō sekinin shiryō sentaa*) was energetically engaged in making precisely the opposite case. The contention of the 1990s arose as often among these civil memory workers as it did between them and the government, making the vernacular terrain by far the most active producer of memory, not only in Japan but in many other societies as well.

The third terrain, that of each individual's personal past, also belonged to the vernacular realm, although in a more private, less overtly organized form. Yet, each person's story was also socially constructed, affected by context, and edited, often unconsciously, over the course of time. Among the "sins of memory" identified by a leading psychologist of the subject, suggestibility refers to the way people weave information from outside sources into their own recollections.[10] Sometimes the information is inaccurate, and sometimes it is experientially true but factually false. The Australian POWs who reproduced visual scenes from the movie *The Bridge on the River Kwai* or the Holocaust survivors who recounted bits from *Schindler's List* were not lying about their experiences as Japanese prisoners in Southeast Asia or victims of the Nazis. They had simply absorbed images from the domain of vernacular memory into the panorama of their personal pasts. Once narrated, and repeated over time, these edited stories often assumed a reality more immediate than the original memory itself, their form sometimes following, as in the case of the comfort women in the 1990s, model narratives established by others who had previously spoken out in public. Changes in the effability factor made speaking out possible, as the wartime generation aged, the context changed, and individuals were willing, even eager, to tell their stories while they still could. Public witness and testimony, private stories told by parents and grandparents, and countless wartime memoirs became a vast repository of personal pasts through which collective memories were both reflected and refracted across the decades.

The fourth terrain is the discourse of meta-memory, which until recent years might not have required separate analytic attention. But once memory itself became the object of intense public debate, the debates *about* memory constituted another field *of* memory, operating as if one step removed from the main arena of contestation. If, for example, one neither knew nor cared about the fate of Polish Jews or the enslavement of the comfort women, controversy in the media about the reliability of witness testimony versus the absence of documentary evidence made it nearly impossible not to learn something about these issues. When investigations in 2001 showed that Poles, not Germans, had massacred the Jews in Jedwabne in 1941, the meta-memory debate over evidence gave way to a new and shocking datum of memory that implicated ordinary Polish villagers in the genocide of the Jews. Similarly, Japanese government denials and revisionist attempts to whitewash official responsibility for military brothels only brought the plight of the comfort women to wider national and international attention. And since the four terrains of memory were never separate, but always interrelated, meta-memory operated together with official, vernacular, and personal memory to create the larger, changing topos of public memory of the war.

Chronopolitics of Memory

But how to account for change in national memory dominated by a tenacious heroic narrative? Considering first its directionality—where memory change came from—I found that the vectors of memory did not necessarily originate in the sites most often associated with the control of social knowledge: not the state, not the schools, and not the media either. With the obvious exception of authoritarian systems, the state—despite its unceasing efforts to keep the narrative reins firmly in official hands—seldom possessed sole control of war memory. Governments worked hard to prevent revisions in official memory, or in the case of a new political regime, to establish the story with a different ideological cast. But the continued insistence on a single national narrative often roused the forces of memory change to press harder against the state's version of the past. Nor were the schools as important in securing the shape of memory as most of us would like to think. All the controversy about textbooks and history curricula notwithstanding, the influence of classroom learning in late-twentieth-century mass-mediated societies was surprisingly limited. Of course, it mattered how the war was taught—or more precisely, how it was not taught—as the heroic narratives were reproduced in national classrooms around the world. Yet surveys repeatedly showed that adults' views of the wartime past were as likely to reflect the latest news or the newest film as the textbook lessons of their youth. And although such results might suggest that memory change could be traced to the media themselves, this conclusion, too, turns out to be something of a mirage. For while it is true that both consumers and producers of vernacular memory often depended on the mass media for communication of war memories, the media were more often the contributing channel—literally, the medium—rather than the prime generative source of changes in public memory.

To simplify a complicated social geometry, I would say that memory change traveled mainly along two vectors: one from outside and one from below. From outside came the pressures of international opinion. Sometimes the pressure was exerted by governments as a political instrument, as Chinese officials did in the Japanese textbook controversy of 1982, and Chinese and Koreans together did in the textbook incident of 2001 and once again in the textbook protests of 2005. Sometimes it was wielded by memory activists in other countries, such as the

Chinese-American groups who took up the cause of "the forgotten Holocaust" in the 1990s, with the result that the Nanjing Massacre once again became the focus of memory controversy within Japan.[11] Among the many international catalysts to memory change over the years was a 1972 study of wartime France by an American historian, which helped to break the long repression of Vichy in French public memory. Another was the iterative dialectic between international judgment and domestic conscience that influenced the evolution of Holocaust memory in West Germany.[12] And approve of them or not, class-action lawsuits in U.S. courts helped to bring official Swiss memory face to face—after half a century—with the wartime facts of looted Nazi gold and unpaid Jewish assets in Swiss bank accounts. In none of these cases—not in Japan, France, Germany, or Switzerland— was memory change ever effected by outside impetus alone. On the contrary, without an array of similarly minded forces inside the society in question, the external catalyst would fall on deaf public ears and die without an echo. But it was equally true that domestic memory workers might toil in vain for decades until some outside challenge created a context in which their efforts to modify the heroic narrative finally met with some success.

These efforts constituted the second vector of memory change, which arose from below: from society rather than from the state, in the terrain of vernacular rather than of official memory, to which it was frequently opposed. Here memory activists played a crucial role, not because of the social power they possessed, but because their commitment to their cause meant that they seldom gave up. For decades victims of wartime injustice—from Japanese-American internees to Taiwanese veterans of the imperial Japanese army—sought restitution or redress. For years those excluded from the heroic narrative worked tirelessly to have their experience written into the national story, whether it was African-American soldiers in the United States or Okinawan civilians in Japan. Even groups that wielded political clout and aligned themselves with official memory, such as veterans' organizations—or in Japan, the Association of War-Bereaved Families (*Nihon izokukai*)—often achieved their goals as much by relentlessness as through special favor of the state. In the case of the Shōwa Hall, the Japan Association of War-Bereaved Families persevered during the lengthy political and bureaucratic process required to get the museum established. Here was a group that was politically potent and important to the conservative regime, which nonetheless had to fight long and hard to get the commemoration it thought the war dead deserved. Similarly, the World War II Memorial in Washington, D.C., for which ground was finally broken in late 2000, received support from the long-standing efforts of veterans and the patriotic rhetoric of politicians. But the Memorial owed its ultimate realization to the ability of these groups to raise enough private funds to cover the construction costs. And their eventual success in collecting upwards of $180 million received no small boost from the actor Tom Hanks, who having discovered the epic appeal of World War II when he starred in the movie *Saving Private Ryan*, lent his public support to the fundraising campaign in the late 1990s. Veterans always interested in commemoration, politicians sometimes seeing electoral advantage in it, and an occasional celebrity coming on the scene at the right moment—such are the operations of vernacular memory that depended on the confluence of energies from below.

The tenacity of memory activists suggests that they did not bring about shifts in the weight of public memory by themselves. For if they had, these shifts would have occurred decades earlier, when many of them began their work. In fact, their effectiveness depended on a conjunction of factors, the most important of which was the political context. Thus, every country had its own "chronopolitics" of memory, in which change in domestic and international politics over time created the conditions for changes in the memoryscape and, sometimes, alterations in the heroic narrative as well. This factor may seem too obvious to mention, but it is often overlooked, especially when comparing different national memories of the war in the terrain of meta-memory.

A case in point is the comparisons between West Germany and Japan that became a staple in the press after the fortieth anniversary of the end of the war in 1985. Two iconic moments of national commemoration sparked the new wave of comparison: the first official postwar visit to Yasukuni Shrine by Prime Minister Nakasone on August 15 and the famous speech of President von Weizsäcker on May 8 declaring the need for Germans to take responsibility for the actions of their forebears. In both Japanese and international media, critics drew a stark contrast between a Germany that was confronting its past and a Japan that steadfastly refused to do so. In terms of official memory, the contrast was accurate indeed, but missing in most instances was any historical explanation of why the operations of memory seemed to work so differently in the two countries.

The reason, in good part, was that Japan and West Germany had a different chronopolitics of memory. In brief summary, official Japanese views of the war began with what I think of as early mastery in the 1940s, resulting in decades of frozen memory that began to show cracks only in the 1980s and signs of slow glacial breakup thereafter. Early mastery occurred because postwar Japan was built on the narrative of a bad past, which the postwar reforms were to correct by undoing, or inverting, the domestic structures that had led to war. Acknowledging the "catastrophic war" was thus the premise of the "new Japan." And since the government, the Occupation, and the people wanted to believe (each for their own reasons) that the transformation was succeeding, the heroic narrative of the wartime past froze in place, becoming the permafrost of the peaceful and ultimately prosperous present. What kept the "from-the-ashes" story intact, however, was not the emergence of a new phoenix but the long dominance of the Liberal Democratic Party in domestic politics and of the U.S.-Japan relationship in cold war geopolitics. The peaceful, prosperous status quo helped to keep the conservatives in power and maintain the founding myth of a postwar Japan successfully severed from its wartime history. Meanwhile, the Cold War further compounded the initial American focus on the Pacific War. For if the China War had disappeared in the original narrative, the United States later declared China itself—"lost" as it was to communism—out of political bounds for the U.S.-Japan alliance. Following a scenario of political convenience, conservatives and Americans together performed the "Pacific Partnership," leaving Asia and the empire outside the sightlines of official memory.

Ironically, the politics of opposition also played a part in the long glaciation of war memory, even as the Left fought assiduously against the freeze. For decades progressives worked to bring issues of war responsibility to public debate and to incorporate China into a story of the "Fifteen-Year War," from the Manchurian invasion of 1931 to the defeat in 1945. Their efforts constituted a steady source of oppositional memory of a sort not seen in many countries, in part because they were not confined to the interests of a particular group of memory activists but addressed the problem as a whole. Yet their insistent critique of the postwar present for being too much like the prewar past unintentionally reinforced the idea of a mythic break in 1945. Of course, the opposition differed from the conservative mainstream in thinking that the break *should* have occurred but had failed to do so. Yet they still pinned their hopes for change, however betrayed by events, on the pivotal date of the defeat. Thus for decades the ground of postwar politics remained solidly based on the conservative notion that the bad prewar past had given way to a better postwar present and the progressive counter-position that that it ought to have happened that way but did not. Both views resonated with the original premise of the heroic narrative of the war.

The chronopolitics of memory in West Germany produced a different pattern, one that moved from an early moderation in the 1940s and 1950s to a fierce generational challenge in the 1960s and 1970s. Unlike Japan, a defeated Germany divided into occupational zones experienced neither a unitary postwar reform nor a blanket mastery of the past. Democratization and the establishment of the Federal Republic, which did not occur until 1949, took political precedence. The national narrative of liberation and "zero hour," so similar to the "Japan reborn" after August 15, did not become a direct blueprint for reform, as it did under American direction in Japan. Public sympathy lay with war victims like POWs and expellees from the East, and Chancellor Adenauer, who avoided the term Nazism, was praised for not dwelling overly much on the recent past. But it was international politics, which in Japan helped to remove Asia from the geopolitical equation, that made the war inescapably central in postwar German foreign relations. Reintegration into Western Europe and NATO required attention to past actions in France and other nations that had suffered German occupation. And while West German politicians may have spoken somewhat vaguely of "unspeakable crimes," they nonetheless supported compensation to Jewish survivors and funds for the new state of Israel. Moderation, in short, did not mean silence, but it did not mean mastery either, even on the rhetorical level of the heroic narrative of all Germans as Hitler's victims.

Awareness of the details of Holocaust crimes grew during the 1960s, not least with the Eichmann Trial of 1961, but the real eruption of West German public memory was sparked by political events. When

the "68 generation" attacked the defects of democracy, calling for revolutionary change, they also accused their parents of having evaded
their responsibility for Nazism and war. So the massive public confrontation with the past began, not during Germany's postwar, which
ended in the early 1950s, but prodded by a new generation in the tu-
mult of political crisis. Generations changed in Japan, too, but—and
this is critical—national politics did not. Japan's "postwar" went on for
decades. The Security Treaty crisis of 1960 in Japan, comparable in
many ways to 1968 in Europe, may have defined a political generation
but it did not upset conservative rule or the U.S.-Japanese alliance, either of which might have caused cracks in the frozen memory of the
war. Equally determined by politics was Chancellor Willy Brandt's famous act of kneeling before the Warsaw Ghetto Monument in 1969, a
symbolic gesture of official memory made to express a new departure
in West German policy toward the East. In this regard Prime Minister
Tanaka Kakuei's pallid remarks on the occasion of Sino-Japanese rapprochement in 1972 reflected a regime of memory formed under U.S.
protection and not yet challenged by geopolitical change in East Asia.

When those challenges emerged in earnest during the 1980s, Japan
faced problems of regional reintegration similar to those West Germany had been dealing with since the late 1940s. Without rehearsing
the detail here, it seems safe to conclude that the late eruption of war
memory as a conspicuous public issue in Japan in the 1990s had everything to do with the fortuitous overlap of Hirohito's death, the end of
the Cold War, and the return of Asia to Japan's geopolitical agenda. No
accident then that the "Asia-Pacific War" made its nomenclatural presence publicly felt in 1995, that the revisionists rose up on their reactionary soapboxes in 1996, and that an unending series of wartime
compensation issues, from comfort women to slave labor, fueled the
fires of public memory throughout the decade and beyond. At the same
time a newly unified Germany revealed a different chronopolitics at
work, one that at first subdued rather than fanned the glowing coals of
war memory. This was partly because the heroic narratives had been
decidedly different on either side of the Berlin Wall, making a suddenly unified memory impossible. East Germans had long told the war,
Soviet style, as an antifascist struggle, which left the Nazis—the fascists
against whom East Germans were said to have struggled and prevailed—responsible for the Holocaust. In the 1990s the hit film

Schindler's List and the controversial book *Hitler's Willing Executioners* thus attracted greater attention in the former West, where Holocaust memory was widely entrenched, than in the former East, where both the domestic and geopolitics of war memory had been so different.[13]

At the same time, post–Cold War regional relations between a unified Germany and Poland, the Czech Republic, and other Eastern European nations were creating new geopolitical pressures on war memory. In this respect, one might say that the international chronopolitics of memory in post–Cold War East Asia and postcommunist Eastern Europe resembled one another in the 1990s. For both Germany and Japan were only then beginning—fifty years after the end of the war—to do the memory work necessary for regional reconciliation. Germany's wartime past in Eastern Europe and Japan's in Asia had long been occluded by the West German and Japanese heroic narratives, both of which had faced toward the geopolitical West during the Cold War. The main difference was that Japanese official memory, which had held its frozen ground practically since 1945, was now being forced by geopolitics to deal with its "history problem" without the base in domestic politics that had been established in Germany since the late 1960s. And so the Japanese government continued to resist, even as international pressure mounted. But this pressure from abroad, which seemed unlikely soon to cease, provided the ever tenacious forces of oppositional memory within Japan with a context for memory change that had long been denied them by conservative politics at home.

Coming into Memory

The comfort women are a case in point. This issue, perhaps more than any other, exemplified both the operations of memory as they unfolded in Japan in recent years and also the broader legacies of new transnational memories of the war. Indeed, the increasing prominence of the comfort women in the 1990s represented a coming into memory that challenged heroic narratives in more than one country and even unsettled the time-dishonored male stories rationalizing the link between war and sexual violence.[14]

To speak of coming into memory does not mean that the existence of comfort women was unknown, unspoken, or forgotten in the decades since the war. Far from it. The women and most of the soldiers may have remained silent in public but none, to be sure, *forgot* their experiences. Nor did public discourse shy from mention of the comfort stations. In literature and film, including the much-seen *The Human Condition;* in critical exposés from the 1940s through the 1970s, of which Senda Kakō's writings are the most quoted but by no means the sole examples; in Diet debates in the 1960s about relief for war victims—the comfort women were no secret, but (unlike the biological warfare Unit 731) a datum of open social knowledge from the beginning.[15] Coming into memory, then, refers to something more than breaking silence or revealing hidden truths. It is rather an assault on the heroic narrative, an effort to acquire a place in the publicly recounted war story. Achieving such acknowledgment is never easy, always contested, sometimes flat-out denied. Yet, as with the Holocaust in Europe, which came into memory in this wider sense only in the 1960s, at some point although contestation continued, outright denial was no longer credible. After that, despite the efforts of the deniers and the resistance of the heroic narrative, the comfort women became part of the public story, still contested but ineluctably present in the public domain.

As hard as it had been to confront planned genocide in Europe, it was harder still for the comfort women to come into memory in Asia. In contrast, the horrific criminality of the Japanese Imperial Army's biological experiments by Unit 731 in China gradually received public, official, and finally, even legal acknowledgment with considerably less protestation than did the system of military prostitution. The reason for this remarkable fact was nothing peculiar to Japan. As institutions for managing sex, military brothels everywhere—and in some form they existed almost everywhere—were seldom openly discussed outside the military and were often denied, or covered up, by the armies that organized them. Whether British, American, Japanese, or German, the state found it ideologically and morally inopportune to be seen by its citizens to be in the prostitution business.[16] Militaries variously justified the brothels in terms of protecting soldiers against venereal disease; defending the local population against rape; fulfilling male sexual needs; and, in Nazi Germany at least, preventing homosexuality. This "rational" wartime policy not only treated women as servile sexual objects, but also exploited poverty, race, and class, whether in commercial military prostitution or sex slavery. For such women to claim a place in public memory was more than difficult: it was—and had been for centuries—impossible.

How then did the comfort women come into memory? Here in brief is how it happened, according to my analysis of the operations of memory. For obvious reasons, military brothels had no place in the heroic narrative, nor did prostitutes and sex slaves figure in the original hierarchy of war victims. In the female chapters of the war story, flag-waving patriotic women metamorphosized into mothers in *monpe*, while the repatriates raped by Soviet troops in Manchuria were dismissed and dishonored. (Their German counterparts in Berlin at least received some measure of public assistance.) If such Japanese victims evoked little sympathy, the comfort women, most of whom were Korean, were doubly excluded, once by gender and once more by the oblivion drawn over race and empire. Their absence was reinforced by the effability factor, which kept the surviving Asian women and most (though not all) of the Japanese soldiers who used them from speaking about what the women had endured and the men had done. But there was also a kind of context blindness at work, whereby military brothels were accepted as a male necessity of war, making them morally invisible to Japanese and Americans alike. It probably never occurred to the Allies at the Tokyo tribunal to prosecute practices that they themselves found customary. (The Japanese tried in Batavian courts for forcing Dutch women POWs into prostitution had violated Western racial boundaries, and it was the racial transgression that counted more than the sexual exploitation.) Thus began the decades during which comfort women appeared as part of the natural history of war, mentioned but without any acuity of attention.

Such attention was first paid in the terrain of vernacular memory—always the crucible of memory activism—in this case by women's groups galvanized by feminism and contemporary gender issues. In 1986 the Japanese artist and activist Tomiyama Taeko exhibited her *Umi no kioku* (A Memory of the Sea), a series of paintings and drawings whose strikingly ghostly images evoked the sufferings of Korean comfort women.[17] At a 1988 conference on sex tourism held in Korea, Japanese and Korean participants heard a paper by the feminist academic Yun Chung Ok on her research on Korean comfort women during the war, part of the wider international context of concern with sex tourism at the time.[18] Soon women's organizations both in Korea and Japan took up the issue of the comfort women. The failure of governments, in Japan, Korea, and the Philippines, to respond on the terrain of official memory to the plight of the surviving women further provoked the activists. Only after women's groups had created a public space for them could the former comfort women come forward and speak of their personal past, the effability factor having at long last been altered not only by age but also by the support of other women.[19] The support of men contributed too, including the Japanese lawyers who represented the Korean and Filipino women in their class action suits against the Japanese government, scholars like Yoshimi Yoshiaki who unearthed the documents that made it impossible for the Japanese government to maintain its blanket denial of state involvement, and Japanese activists in international NGOs who joined Korean women in keeping the pressure on the United Nations during the 1990s. If women activists owed their strength to gender concerns, these Japanese men derived their commitment from long years of steadfast progressive opposition to official war memory. But without the Koreans and certainly without the women, the progressives alone would not have made the difference.

And without the cross-border links among memory activists, the issue might have remained a local outcropping of the vexed postcolonial relations between Japan and Korea. But the 1990s was the decade of burgeoning transnational NGOs, among which women's groups figured prominently. From 1992 on, a series of solidarity conferences to support the comfort women were held in Seoul, Tokyo, and Manila, transforming their cause into a genuinely transnational Asian effort. At the Fourth UN World's Women Conference in Beijing in 1995, where the platform for action called for compensation for the victims of sexual slavery, Asian women were joined by Western feminists, Asian Americans, human rights activists, and international law experts. A year earlier the International Committee of Jurists in Geneva had published a report entitled "Comfort Women: The Unfinished Ordeal." In Beijing one of its authors asserted the right to compensation under international law, arguing that Japan's position on the issue was "an affront to all women around the world."[20]

By the mid-1990s transnational NGO activism had led to the floor of formal international organizations. A series of three influential UN reports to the Commission on Human Rights treated the forced prostitution of comfort women as "military sexual slavery"—criminal violence against women, which was not solely of local or regional relevance but a clear transgression of fundamental human rights, a violation of international law, a war crime, and a crime against humanity.[21] Meanwhile, the International Labor Organization condemned Japan's military brothels for violating the Forced Labor Convention of 1930. As the International Criminal Tribunals for the former Yugoslavia and Rwanda began to try individuals for the sexual war crimes committed during the 1990s, the comfort women system became a referent for legal definitions of systematic rape in situations of armed conflict. In less than a decade memory activists had brought the comfort women to the attention not only of Japan but also of the world.

The media, predictably, played a role, not only in what I call the consumption side of vernacular memory but also in generating the activism. Rosa Maria Henson, the first Filipina to come forward with her story in 1992, did so after hearing about other former comfort women on the radio. And the broad network of transnational activism throughout the decade utilized print and broadcast media, films, and increasingly the Internet to get their message across to one another and to the public. The early surge of media attention came as former comfort women bared their painful personal pasts in individual testimony in the early 1990s, while Japanese officials issued their habitual denials. A survey of coverage in the *Asahi* newspaper showed a peak of 622 mentions of military comfort women (*jūgun ianfu*) in 1992, with roughly more than half as many in each of the subsequent six years. In 1995 the government established the Asian Women's Fund—the response in the terrain of official memory—which, however, deflected state responsibility by making the compensation a private rather than a governmental gesture. This unleashed a wave of critical comment at home and in Asia, where numbers of former comfort women refused the gesture precisely because it avoided acknowledgment of state responsibility.[22] Then, after 1996, came the attacks from the Right by the so-called liberal revisionists, who were enraged by the attention to the issue of military prostitution and especially by the appearance of the comfort women in middle-school textbooks.[23] Their high-profile polemic only entrenched the comfort women more deeply in Japanese public discourse. As the press highlighted the acrimonious debates over the validity of their testimony and claims for compensation, the comfort women increasingly appeared in the terrain of meta-memory as well. There they became the focus for debating the nature of public memory itself: which should take precedence, the voices of the victims or the documents of the state? Because the question had no simple answer, it further fueled the controversy.[24] Meanwhile, Japanese sex slavery was growing in media presence in other countries, too, thanks largely to three contemporary concerns: gender and human rights, compensation for wartime grievances, and—in Asian and Western eyes—Japan's perennial inability to confront its imperial past.

The vectors of memory change thus came from outside—from Asia, transnational movements, and international institutions—and from below—from victims, women's groups, feminists, human rights workers, and others who constituted a dynamic civil society of memory activists, both in Japan and elsewhere. Two points should be underlined. The first is that the comfort women gained their place in public consciousness because of efforts conducted almost entirely in the terrain of vernacular memory. Without memory activists, the terrain of individual personal pasts would not have been opened to public view; without memory activists, the terrain of meta-memory debate would not have contributed to the growing awareness of the comfort women. And without the media, from newspapers to the Internet, all the memory work on behalf of the cause would have ended like the proverbial tree falling in the forest with no one to hear it. This means that the terrain of official memory, which usually receives the most attention, is often the least important in accounting for memory change or in making such change happen. State responses to the comfort women, even in Korea, lagged behind the activists at every turn, and the Japanese government continued to bring up the rear, resisting the forces from outside and from below with all its sclerotic might. But the history of memory suggests that Japan's official memory will be unable to resist forever, now that everyone, from Japanese high-school students to members of the new International Criminal Court, both know about—and remember—who the comfort women were and what they suffered at the hands of the wartime imperial state.

The second point relates to the diversity of the terrain of memory activism itself. Their common concern with the issue of the comfort women did not mean that the activists shared a common cause. On the contrary, different people had different agendas, some determined by national context, others by political or social commitment. Their language varied with their objectives. The Korean groups used the term *Chŏngsindae* (the euphemistically named Volunteer Labor Corps), both to emphasize the aspect of colonial coercion and also to avoid the current issue of prostitutes (called comfort women, *wianbu*) around U.S. military bases in South Korea. Presenting the comfort women as the victims of imperialism aligned the campaign with engrained Korean hostility toward their former colonial ruler, giving it greater public presence than a mere "women's issue" might have received. Korean feminists also had to draw a fine line between calling for compensation for wartime grievance and a broader protest against the entire "Confucian" patriarchal system, with its abiding "androcentrism," a word frequently used in Korean scholarly discussion of the comfort women.[25] Japanese and American feminists made analogous, but different, links to contemporary gender discrimination in their own societies, including such issues as sexual harassment, domestic violence, and rape.

Human rights and international law experts used the term "sex slaves" because their main concern was to remove legal impunity for state-sanctioned sexual violence against women. In the words of Gabrielle Kirk McDonald, the former presiding judge at the Yugoslav Tribunal in The Hague and, later, the presiding judge at the mock Women's International War Crimes Tribunal in Tokyo in 2000, "states cannot, through their political agreements and settlements, ignore or forgive crimes against humanity committed against individuals."[26] This argument intended no less than to shift the ground of sovereign immunity that had so long protected states (and heads of states) from legal prosecution. In the immediate background stood Pinochet of Chile and Milosevic of Serbia, not Hirohito of Japan. But when the mock tribunal in 2000 judged Emperor Hirohito guilty of "both individual and superior responsibility" for "knowing participation in a criminal system which cultivated and sustained a system of rape and sexual slavery," judges and prosecutors invoked the legal argument of "chain of command" that is currently undergoing change in international criminal law.[27] Thus the Hirohito of the International Tribunal was not exactly the same as the "emperor system" denounced by sympathetic Japanese counterparts, for whom the term connoted a vastly larger historical universe of oppression.

Activists in the Asian diaspora approached the issue differently again.

Korean-American and Korean-Canadian women took aim at the double discrimination of race and gender, their views of the comfort women animated by their own experiences of ethnic and gender identity in North America. In the celebrated novel *A Gesture Life*, a (male) Korean American explored the delicate ambiguities of diasporic identity in a Korean resident of Japan who had served in the Japanese imperial army and later emigrated to the United States, repressing both his Korean origins and his disturbing memories of the brutality of Japan's wartime comfort stations. Not unlike the younger generation of German novelists who recurred to a Holocaust that had happened before their time, the author used the cruelty of the military brothels to shed light on the human condition, its ordinary flaws and extraordinary evils.[28] Such concerns resonated with the stories of the former comfort women themselves, but they did not originate in the same place. The elderly Korean "grandmas" and Filipino "Lolas" who courageously came forward spoke instead from deep personal suffering and from their often expressed hope "to see justice done before I die."[29]

Thus the memory activists pursued the cause of justice for the comfort women, sometimes in concert with one another, but often with different goals. This diversity was one reason for their impact, for no single locus of engagement could have generated as effective a public presence as these crisscrossing networks of commitment. That most of the activists were women, animated by gender concerns and feminism, also made a huge difference. In many places they worked outside the established opposition groups that were dominated by men and devoted to canonical protest issues. Consider the rueful remark of a male member of the Peace Studies Association of Japan (PSAJ), that when it came to the issue of wartime sexual slavery, "it can be said in all honesty that the PSAJ has contributed nothing."[30]

But the surge of women's activism did not by itself account for the advent of the comfort women into memory in the 1990s. Chronopolitics also played a critical role. In domestic politics, democratization in Korea from the late 1980s unleashed the forces of civil activism, providing women a political opportunity denied them under the dictatorship. Just as in Taiwan, the Philippines, Indonesia, and, later, East Timor, subsequent shifts in political regimes sometimes hindered, but more often helped the memory cause. Not that political leaders naturally favored discussions of military brothels, but as candidates for office, they could no longer ignore them. Whereas Philippines President Corazon Aquino had dismissed the issue out of hand in 1992, her successors, Fidel Ramos and Gloria Arroyo, were forced at least to mention the claims for apology and compensation in diplomatic encounters with their Japanese counterparts. In Japan itself, the brief interregnum in Liberal Democratic rule in the mid-1990s permitted the comfort women a moment of official prominence under the coalition government led by the socialist Prime Minister Murayama. And when the Liberal Democratic Party reasserted its recidivist brand of memory politics after 1996, opposition politicians kept the matter alive in the Diet. By the end of the decade even cabinet spokesmen began (however faintly) to admit, for example, that the Asian Women's Fund had not resolved the problem after all. Distribution of what the Fund called "atonement payments" (in official translation) was discontinued in South Korea, Taiwan, and the Philippines in 2002.

In the United States the identity politics of the 1990s impelled Chinese-American efforts to pass legislative resolutions condemning Japan for its war crimes. In 1996 the Department of Justice added sixteen Japanese to the more than 60,000 Nazi war criminals on the "watch list" to deny entry into the country. In 1997, a proposed congressional resolution called on Japan to make apologies and reparations for its victims, including "the Korean comfort women." In 1999 the California state assembly passed a similar bill, initiated by a Japanese-American assemblyman who had little choice but to respond to Chinese-American activists among his constituency. Thus the currents of domestic politics in each country carried the comfort women issue beyond the reach—and sometimes out of the hands—of the women who had worked so hard to make the cause known.

In chronopolitical effect, however, the currents of geopolitics were even more decisive. The end of the Cold War brought new pressures on Japan from Asian nations, as the "history problem" became an agenda item in bilateral relations with China, Korea, Taiwan, and elsewhere. Pent-up postcolonial hostility in Korea forced a postimperial confrontation, as the coercion of the women in the "Voluntary Labor Corps" came to represent the broad spectrum of colonial oppression visited on Korea by imperial Japan. Of course, some leaders were more forceful than others—Kim Dae Jung of South Korea, for example, who initiated compensation payments to former comfort women from the

Korean government after he came to power in 1998. But none of the Asian governments was forceful enough in the eyes of the activists, as Filipino politicians allowed Japanese economic aid to the Philippines or South Korean leaders permitted the jointly sponsored Japan-Korea 2002 World Cup to mute their calls for justice. Still, the Asian Women's Fund became a political issue nearly everywhere, with Asian governments responding to it in accord with their diplomatic agenda of the moment.

Beyond the realm of regional geopolitics, there is little doubt that the systematic rape that accompanied the ethnic cleansing in Bosnia in the early 1990s also worked to bring the comfort women to prominence in international discourse. As efforts intensified to define rape as a war crime, the Japanese "comfort stations," which had not been the object of prosecution at the Tokyo Trial after the war, were linked to the Bosnian "rape camps," whose perpetrators it was argued must now be prosecuted in the international tribunal for the former Yugoslavia. The grim horrors of the sexual violence in Bosnia and Rwanda helped to bring the forced prostitution of the Asia-Pacific War from the past to the present, and from Asia to the world.

Comfort Women and the World

It had taken fifty years, in Ueno Chizuko's words, to change the "shame of women" into the "crime of men."[31] In the process of coming into memory, the comfort women challenged not only the heroic narrative of Japanese victimization but also the age-old story of the "needs" of men at war. The comfort women had become what I think of as a traveling trope: a reference to a particular and gruesome memory, which resonated with human experience in other times and places. Rather than diminishing the specificity of the particular past, such deterritorialized memory enlarged it. Like the Holocaust, the comfort women were now part of a newly transnational memory of World War II. And as the Nazi Holocaust gradually became the referent for the surpassing evil of genocide, the Asian comfort women signified the end of the long invisibility of wartime sexual violence against women. Theirs was a legacy for the world to reckon with.

The legacy had several aspects. Memory activists—the Korean Council for the Women Drafted for Military Sexual Slavery, the Asian

Center for Women's Human Rights in Manila, The Violence against Women in War Network-Japan, the Women's Caucus for Gender Justice in New York, and many others—made the comfort women count in the international campaign for "women's rights as human rights" in the years following the Vienna Conference on Human Rights in 1993.[32] This included abandoning the traditional language of earlier provisions protecting the "honor" and "dignity" (and, in Korea and other places, the "chastity") of women, since this language seemed to imply that the dishonor belonged to the rape victim rather than to the rape perpetrator, or to the women forced into prostitution rather than to their official procurer, what one scholar labeled "the state as pimp."[33] Instead of evoking some male-determined feminine honor or dignity, such practices as sex tourism, trafficking in women, military prostitution, rape, and other instances of sexual violence were now being redefined as violations of innate human rights—not the rights of women but the rights of humankind.

One concrete outcome of this redefinition was the epoch-making indictment—and conviction—for rape as a crime against humanity in the Yugoslav Tribunal in The Hague in 2001. According to one legal scholar-activist, this landmark development resulted from a combination of transnational NGO pressure and women judges in the Yugoslav and Rwanda tribunals. But it also owed its success to the example of "unprecedented industrialization of sexual slavery" in Japan's comfort stations, which demonstrated that "the rape of women, as booty or as the reward for the penultimate expression of the norm of masculinity, is also an integral part of the arsenal of war." The stories of the comfort women thus played a role in the process by which, in the course of the 1990s, sexual violence in war finally lost its invisibility in international law.[34] This new norm of gender justice carried over into the statute for the International Criminal Court signed in Rome in 1998, which named rape, sexual slavery, and enforced prostitution both as war crimes (Article 8) and as crimes against humanity (Article 7). Such statutes would not in themselves prevent the brutalization of women, but the recognition of gender violence in the same category as torture and genocide was indeed a legal and moral watershed, one unthinkable and unthought in earlier times, even as recently as fifty years ago.

Another legacy of the Asian comfort women for the world was the exemplary effectiveness of transnational activism in making their

claims for memory and justice. Activists worked across political borders, including the one between North and South Korea. They crossed
moral divides, with cooperation not only among the countries of the
victims but also with activists from Japan, the perpetrating nation, and
eventually from many parts of what is now called global civil society.
Of course, like all war memory, nationalism colored much of this activity, as the national people of the heroic narrative were challenged by
national women and their stories.[35] The postcolonial animus of Korean
activists suffused their charges against "the Japanese," melding even
their feminist colleagues into a single homogenized Japanese villain, as
Ueno Chizuko found to her chagrin in Beijing in 1995.[36] Japanese
sometimes reacted the same way, feeling insulted, for example, by UN
criticism of Japan, which they took to be Korean-inspired. And Chinese Americans often lumped all Japanese into one essentialized national perpetrator of war crimes. The idea of a whole nation of perpetrators showed no more historical discrimination than that of a whole
nation of victims—both were national, simplistic, and inimical to understanding.

And yet, many of these groups at least made the transnational effort,
and even their failures bequeathed lessons for what I would call a better
activism, which would seek common ground—in this case on behalf of
gender justice past and future—while maintaining a sensitivity to
different national, social, and historical contexts. Such sensitivity is
what Western feminists often lacked in their judgments of Asian societies, what Korean women sometimes missed in their interactions with
women from the Philippines or Indonesia, and what Japanese progressives could lose sight of in their concern with debates local to Japan.
The legacy of a better activism would be a transnational memory that
both recognized the specific grievances of the comfort women and also
made their experience a referent for preventing similar sexual violence
in other times and places.

Another legacy related to the place of the individual in the collective
memory of war. The lawsuits filed by comfort women in Japan and,
more recently, in the United States demanded recognition, apology,
and compensation for what they had suffered as individuals. Not their
nation or their gender, but their person was at issue. So it did matter
whether they were kidnapped and gang-raped as young virgins—the
so-called model story told by many former comfort women; whether

they chose prostitution willingly; and whether, having chosen sex work or not, they were prevented from escaping from the brothels when they tried to. Male psychology also mattered—not on some generalized collective level but in terms of the individual capacity for brutality and violence. Such topics have yet to be adequately addressed in public memory, which tends not only toward the national but also toward the collective, as if all women were either mothers in *monpe* or whores for sale and all men were soldiers with sexual needs to be satisfied for battle. As long as Asian comfort women were treated as a single group with similar stories who were spoken for by others, however well meaning, the lessons of individual actions had yet fully to be learned.

And since responsibility, too, is both collective and individual, until the experience of the comfort women was both woven into Japan's war stories and also embedded in views that individual men and women have of the way they ought to treat one another, social memory would remain deficient. The most one can hope for from the brutalities of twentieth-century wars is that they be collectively remembered on the one hand and individually repudiated on the other. Redressing the wrongs of the past is only a first step toward making the future a better place to be.

～ 3

Living Soldiers,
Re-lived Memories?

Japanese Veterans and Postwar Testimony
of War Atrocities

DAQING YANG

ON AUGUST 15, 2002, the most important day of annual war commemoration in Japan, TV Asahi aired a special program on the Nanjing Massacre. Hosted by the popular anchor Kume Hiroshi, it introduced a collection of testimonies by some hundred Japanese veterans
who had fought in the battle of Nanjing in the winter of 1937–38.
These testimonies, published in a book on the same day, were the result of four years of painstaking efforts, largely by one female Japanese
elementary school teacher named Matsuoka Tamaki. Under pseudo-
nyms, the veterans spoke about the massacre of surrendered Chinese
soldiers and civilians, as well as instances of rape and looting committed by Japanese soldiers in the fallen city.[1] Not surprisingly, the veterans' testimonies about the Nanjing battle immediately produced an
outcry from those who pointed out inconsistencies and factual errors.
Above all, the critics were particularly furious with a leading national
TV network that featured the book and inclusion of the topic in such a
popular program.[2]

   This episode raises some interesting questions for the study of war
memory in East Asia. Testimonies by war veterans, like testimonies of
survivors and victims, do not belong to these individuals once they become public. They can be claimed by multiple groups with stakes in
this contest. Moreover, if we assume for a moment that such testimonies have some impact on the shaping of collective memories of

war, then one must also look beyond national boundaries.[3] This episode is also a reminder that testimonies of wartime atrocities are always challenged, almost always publicly and sometimes even in an international context.

This chapter explores the varieties of veterans' testimonies in postwar Japan in connection with the ongoing debate over the Japanese atrocities in Nanjing. Once assigned to near oblivion, the event has become arguably one of the most contested historical topics in East Asia. The contours of the Cold War and post–Cold War were significant shapers of the change in historical contestation over the atrocities. The early 1970s, which saw the reopening of formal diplomatic relations between Japan and China, one of the most significant changes in the Cold War's East Asian dynamic, also saw a resurgence of interest, fueled by the Left, in Japanese reconsideration of the Imperial Army's record in China. The post-1989 era, marked by the end of the Shōwa era in Japan, the Tian'anmen confrontation in China, and the global ending of the Cold War, caused yet another significant reconfiguration of the memory of wartime. To better understand the dynamics of collective memories of such a war atrocity, however, one needs to go beyond studying such general trends. I propose to focus my examination on the veterans' testimonies and their changing audience over time and space. This is not to assume that the various "communities of memory"—the veterans, their audience in Japan, and later in China—are homogeneous groups. By paying attention to individuals in relation to various groups, however, such an approach helps us better understand the shaping of and contest over memories of war in postwar Asia.

Veteran Memories in Postwar Japan

The current popularity of veterans' testimonies and reminiscences notwithstanding, their voice was rather muted in the immediate postwar years. At the time of Japan's surrender, there were seven million men in uniform in Japan and overseas. Close to two million Japanese soldiers had been killed—in battle, from sickness or malnutrition, or in postwar detention, compared to a half million civilian losses, mostly as a result of Allied aerial bombing.[4] Given the unprecedented defeat and devastation—not to mention the foreign occupation of the country for the first time in its history—the once almighty military institution itself came under attack as being responsible for bringing on a national calamity. Many former military men became targets of blame. A few top-ranking officers were put on trial as war criminals by the victorious Allies. Most of the discharged veterans—a not insignificant segment of the population—faced difficulty reestablishing themselves materially in a war-torn Japan. All of this must have been a source of enormous agony. A few did speak out. As one angry veteran lamented in an article published in a local Youth Corps *(seinendan)* newsletter, those who fought in the war now suddenly came to be considered militarists and war criminals responsible for the suffering of the Japanese people. Indignant at the tendency in post-surrender Japan to embrace "imported ideas" and to reject all things Japanese, the twice-enlisted veteran expressed his fervent support for the Imperial system as the only embodiment of the Japanese spirit.[5]

Almost as soon as the war was over, many discharged veterans regrouped into what came to be known as *senyūkai*, or war veterans associations, whose formation peaked in the 1960s. Senyūkai were formed on the basis of various units—ships, school class, and military units—and their goals included mourning dead comrades and finding a sense of belonging and support. Increasingly, senyūkai also became a venue for veterans to share their wartime experience. As one Japanese sociologist noted, although individuals could recall past experience and thus reinforce self-identity in isolation, such recollection became more vivid and concrete while meeting with old comrades. As a result, they increasingly spoke among themselves in organized forms and compiled institutional histories of their units. However, senyūkai provided not only a venue to reencounter with the past as it was experienced, but also an opportunity to give new meaning and shape to that experience. While many recalled war experience as tough and miserable, a few also remembered army life as one of the best times of their lives.[6]

How did Japanese war veterans speak out about their experience in World War II? What did they expect of the audience—especially those born after the war—in postwar Japan? Since reminiscences of war experience, unlike other reminiscences, were often met with disdain, veterans were divided among themselves as to whether it was desirable or possible to pass on their experience to the next generations. One study in the 1980s showed that only a small minority (11.5 percent) had no desire to communicate their experiences. "It is necessary to leave future generations the record of war as facts of history," one senyūkai organizer noted. "However, we don't want to say anything to a society that has forgotten the war. This would only make us miserable." Nearly half (48.3 percent) wanted to speak but found it perhaps impossible to be understood; another one third (32.4 percent) wanted to try regardless of the obstacles. One organizer of an army senyūkai complained of the difficulty of even sharing war experience with close family members including his wife, as it would not produce an "echo."[7]

An increasing number of veterans did speak to the general public and found receptive audiences. As historian Yoshida Yutaka noted in his book on war memories in Japan, the early 1950s saw the emergence and increasing popularity of writings by former military men. The former participants rode the boom of the so-called senki mono (war accounts), initially written by officers. A few, such as Tsuji Masanobu or Hattori Takushiro, wrote about wartime exploits without any trace of reflection on their own responsibility. The same was largely true with NCO authors who contributed the bulk of writings in popular journals: they emphasized the bravery and sense of duty of Japanese soldiers. The notable characteristic of these testimonies is their often-shared anger at top-ranking officers. Later, many of the rank-and-file joined in, writing with melancholy about their wartime sufferings.[8] In this sense, what was spoken inside groups like senyūkai became linked to what was increasingly shared with the outside. While many aspects of war experience were spoken about, there were also areas of silence, most notably in regard to war atrocities.

Given the culture of mainstream veteran groups such as the senyūkai, it is perhaps not surprising that the only group of veterans who spoke out as perpetrators of war atrocities was a fringe group. The Association of Returnees from China (Chūgoku kikansha renrakukai, abbreviated as "Chūkiren") was established by Japanese veterans released by the People's Republic of China (PRC) and repatriated to Japan in the mid-1950s. While in Chinese custody, they had gone through "thought reform" aimed at producing admission of guilt in exchange for leniency.[9] Such efforts seemed to have had a lasting effect with quite a number of them, although almost all produced written affidavits while in China. In 1957, Kōbunsha, a subsidiary of the publishing giant Kōdansha, published some of the affidavits as *Sankō* (Burn All, Kill All, Loot All), a Chinese term referring to the Japanese army's ruthless strategy against communist-led guerrillas in north China. The book was based on "literary-style renditions of concrete facts of their own crimes from an objective perspective." As the first postwar Japanese publication of first-person accounts of Japanese army brutalities in China, the book caused a sensation.[10] Although the 1937 Nanjing Massacre was not a subject of the book, reactions in Japan were symptomatic. Following pressure from conservative commentators and veterans—a member of a right-wing group even physically attacked the publisher's office—the publisher declined to bring out a second printing. It was not until the 1970s that pacifist groups like the Sokka Gakkai published books that featured testimonies of veterans who revealed Japanese atrocities overseas.[11]

For every veteran who spoke out, many remained silent, at least in public, about their wartime experience. Silence did not equal amnesia, however; memories, though not shared, were not necessarily lost. Some chose to speak to their closest family members, others literally on their deathbeds. Japanese psychiatrist Noda Masaaki described one such veteran who passed a note to his daughter days before his death, requesting an inscription on his tombstone: he had served as an NCO in the Japanese military police in China during the war. Having no excuse for his behavior against the Chinese people, he wanted to make a sincere apology.[12]

Veterans' voices never became prominent in postwar Japanese society, for they always had to coexist or compete with voices of A-bomb victims, bereaved families, and others. By the 1960s, high economic growth, among other factors, precipitated a spreading sense of anxiety among the war generation about the "weathering" *(fūka)* of the war experience. As Yoshida points out, such a process was by no means a "natural" result of time but was facilitated by political and social conditions. The Cold War ideological confrontation between communism and the "free world" not only came to frame much of the discourse in postwar Japan, as it did as elsewhere; but the political reality of the Cold War, separating Japan from one of its main victims—China—further contributed to the reorientation of postwar Japan's war memories.

Whatever the motivation of bearing witness in public, veterans' testimonies gave the impression of authenticity and proximity to war, an attribute largely absent in the civilian population removed from the battlefront. As time went by, the direct experience of war became increasingly rare in a population increasingly born after the war and pre-occupied with peacetime pursuits. The sudden emergence of an Imperial Japanese Army soldier named Yokoi Shoichi from the jungles of the Philippines in 1972 also set off a mini-boom of popular interest in wartime experience in Japan.[13] Perhaps more importantly, America's war in Vietnam and Japan's diplomatic normalization with China helped make Japanese war atrocities in China a current and contested issue.

Azuma's "Battle Journal": Veterans and the Debate over the Nanjing Massacre

Widely reported in the West during the war, Japanese atrocities in Nanjing in 1937–38 had become a symbol of wartime excesses of the Japanese military.[14] At the military tribunals in Tokyo and Nanjing after the war, five Japanese officers, including General Matsui Iwane, who had headed the Japanese forces in the Nanjing area, were put on trial. From the beginning, testimonies concerning the events in Nanjing encountered a highly divisive context in court. The war crimes trials were essentially the first public occasions that demanded evidence either in support of or refuting the prosecution's account of the "Rape of Nanjing." A few Japanese veterans testified on behalf of the defendants; perhaps not surprisingly, hardly any provided testimony for the prosecution. The only exception was Major General Tanaka Ryūkichi. Though not a participant in the battle of Nanjing, he provided crucial testimonies to the prosecution incriminating General Matsui and a number of other high-ranking Japanese officers.[15] These trials resulted in the death penalty for the accused Japanese officers. In the verdict on Matsui Iwane, the military tribunal provided a succinct description of the Nanjing Massacre as

a long succession of most horrible atrocities committed by the Japanese Army upon the helpless citizens. Wholesale massacres, individual murders, rape, looting and arson were committed by Japanese soldier . . . The orgy of crimes started with the capture of the City on the 13th December 1937 and did not cease until early in February 1938. In this period of six or seven weeks thousands of women were raped, upwards of 100,000 people were killed and untold property was stolen and burned.[16]

In the next decade or so, a few former officers published testimonies that challenged the verdicts of these postwar trials, directly or otherwise. Virtually no Japanese veterans publicly affirmed the occurrence of atrocities in Nanjing. However, things began to change in the 1970s. By then, the Vietnam War raised public awareness in Japan of the brutality of modern warfare close to home. Moreover, the Cold War confrontation in East Asia was changing, symbolized by Sino-American reapproachment and Sino-Japanese diplomatic normalization in 1972. A "China boom" ensued in Japan, producing laudatory accounts of socialist China as well as soul-searching about Japan's wartime deeds. On the eve of Sino-Japanese diplomatic normalization, journalist Honda Katsuichi of the *Asahi* newspaper visited China to collect testimonies of Chinese survivors of Japan's wartime atrocities and published them in his newspaper and as a book.[17] The reports by Honda, who had already become well known in Japan in part because of his coverage of the Vietnam War, created a huge sensation in Japan. It was largely in reaction to Honda's introduction of the Chinese testimonies that writers like Suzuki Akira turned to Japanese veterans in order to question the veracity of these accounts from China as well as the verdicts of the war crimes tribunals. Suzuki, who was too young to fight in the war, met with several former officers who spoke about the chaotic circumstances under which thousands of Chinese POWs were killed, raising doubts about the established account of a planned massacre in Nanjing.[18]

Suzuki's essay, published in the popular monthly journal *Bungei shunjū* under the title "The Phantom of the Nanjing Massacre" and later awarded a prize for nonfiction writing, sparked what became know as the "great debate on the Nanjing Massacre." Others soon joined, including prominent commentator Yamamoto Shichihei. Yamamoto and his allies in *Bungei shunjū* accused Honda and the *Asahi* newspaper of embracing socialist China. Despite the changing Cold War atmosphere between Japan and China, the Yamamoto-Honda debate carried the distinctive mark of residual ideological hostility. There was more than ideology here, however. Yamamoto recalled his own experience in the Imperial Japanese Army (though not in China) and dismissed the "Hundred Men Killing Contest"—a key event related to the Nanjing Massacre—as physically impossible given the fragile nature of the Japanese sword, among others. Echoing earlier fears of the "weathering of war experience," Yamamoto pointed out that, "as the number of those with experience of the military and battlefield become fewer and fewer, accounts that clearly look like fiction are being offered to the public as 'facts' by writers without any such experience." Naming his book *The Japanese Army inside Me (Watashi no naka no Nihon gun)* to emphasize its basis in his own direct experience, Yamamoto underscored the urgency of veterans' memories.[19]

> Our generation had the crime *(zaiseki)* of waging a war. Of course individuals may have different explanations for that. However, even with these explanations, if our generation does not correctly pass on our experience to future generations, then we have additional crime that cannot be explained.

By the early 1980s, the controversy over Japan's history of war and colonialism had come to the forefront in Japan, symbolized by the reaction in its Asian neighbors in the 1982 "textbook incident," when the Japanese government was reported to have toned down descriptions of Japanese wartime actions. The visit to the controversial Yasukuni Shrine by Prime Minister Nakasone Yasuhiro in 1985 sparked further waves of protest from China and Korea. During this period, the dominant ideological confrontation between communism and capitalism was gradually replaced by a reawakening of nationalism in Asia. Japanese war crimes came to be viewed not so much a product of Japanese imperialism, but increasingly as a reflection on the Japanese nation as a whole.

In this heightened atmosphere of the "debate over the Nanjing Massacre" and other controversies over World War II, veterans' testimonies became sought-after commodities. Ara Ken'ichi, a businessman-turned-nonfiction writer, contacted sixty-seven officers and journalists who had been in Nanjing, and was able to interview about half of them. Ara confidently advanced the proposition that if all Japanese participants in the Nanjing battle gathered their testimonies, historians would have the most authentic history of the event.[20] Kaikōsha, the fraternity association of the prewar army cadet school graduates, sent an urgent request to its 18,000 members for eyewitness accounts that could disprove the "so-called Nanjing Massacre."[21] Unemoto Masami, who participated in the battle of Nanjing as a junior officer, was a firm believer in the innocence of the Japanese army and a driving force of the project. He received more than one hundred replies and edited them into an eleven-part series in the Kaikōsha journal under the title "Battle History of Nanjing Based on Testimonies." While many indeed testified to have witnessed no incidents of atrocity in Nanjing, a number of its members offered testimonies that confirmed their existence. One former staff officer under Matsui, then in his late 80s, estimated that some 120,000 captives were killed in the Xiaguan area along the river under orders of another staff officer, although he later modified the figure to "no less than tens of thousands." Veterans' memories, as it turned out, could not be easily harnessed even by veteran groups themselves. Katokawa Kōtarō, an editor of Kaikōsha's journal who had been an army cadet at the time of the Nanjing battle, publicly admitted that "there was no excuse for such massive illegal executions," and stated that "as someone related to the former Japanese Army, I have to apologize deeply to the Chinese people."[22]

Enter Azuma

Other Japanese veterans offered their own testimonies as evidence of atrocities. A few spoke at public meetings organized by citizen groups and talked to reporters. Of all who spoke out, either confirming or denying the atrocities in Nanjing, no one attracted more attention and controversy in Japan (and subsequently in China) than Azuma Shirō.

Born in 1912 in a family of two sons near Kyoto, Azuma graduated from the prefectural middle school—no small achievement at the time. In 1937, he was conscripted into the army (3rd Company, 20th Regiment, 16th Division) and fought in Nanjing and other parts of China. Impressed with Azuma's writing style and gripping tales in his numerous letters sent from the front, his village friend suggested publishing them as writings by soldier-writers in the battlefield, along the lines of the famous Hino Ashihei.[23] Azuma declined. Wounded and discharged in 1939, he returned to Japan and began preparing a wartime journal based on his own memos as well as letters to his village friend. In 1943, his work was cut short when he was called back and fought in China until the Japanese surrender in 1945. Repatriated to Japan,

Azuma was not happy with the postwar atmosphere and penned the angry letter to the local Youth Corps cited earlier. But he managed to pick up his life, marry, raise a family of five, and continue the family business of running movie theaters that became quite successful. He did not seem to have time to think about the war. In a sense, his silence across the postwar decades is as telling as his outspokenness since the late 1980s.

Azuma's coming out was told, rather sympathetically, by Ian Buruma, who interviewed him at home in 1992.[24] On July 7, 1987, at a public symposium organized by a citizens' group commemorating the fiftieth anniversary of the beginning of the Sino-Japanese conflict, 75-year-old Azuma went public with two other veterans who participated in the battle of Nanjing. They testified about instances of army atrocities against the Chinese people in Nanjing and elsewhere. Azuma described witnessing his comrades killing a Chinese family outside Nanjing for no apparent reason. Matsuda Rokusuke, one of the other Japanese veterans who spoke at the gathering, admitted to killing several hundred captured Chinese soldiers with machine guns on the banks of the Yangtze River. He later said he feared that he would have to go to hell for this.[25]

The occasion of the symposium aside, it is not clear what motivated Azuma to speak out at that time. There seemed to be personal reasons: he recalled that shortly after being taken into custody in China after the war, a Chinese officer who was a survivor of the Japanese massacre in Nanjing did not seek revenge because of Chiang Kai-shek's policy of being magnanimous with Japan. Ian Buruma has noted that Azuma was no pacifist, but wanted to tell the war "as it was." Interestingly, although he was largely silent about his wartime experience before 1987, this was not Azuma's first postwar role in memory-making. He had been a member of the senyūkai of his regiment, taking part in its annual gatherings and exchanging correspondence with other members. Several years before, he had contributed a short article based on his journal to the semi-official history of his own regiment.

By the late 1980s, the quest for new evidence about the controversial Nanjing Incident was in full swing, producing a booming publishing industry on the subject. A number of key documents were unearthed in Japan, such as the diary of high-ranking officers such as Lieutenant

General Nakajima Kesago. Diaries by ordinary soldiers, however, were not yet common.[26] Sone Kazuo, a veteran of the Nanjing battle, turned his experience into something of a publishing success, authoring three books on the subject in one year. However, it was soon found out that Sone had misled the readers about part of his military experience.[27] Questions were also raised about Azuma. As it later turned out, while Azuma indeed had brought back many items from the battlefield, he was not able to provide the "battlefield memo" that formed the basis of the wartime journal he completed sometime in 1940–41. Strictly speaking, therefore, the Azuma diary was a memoir written during the war, with the help of some notes. Moreover, although his "wartime diary" was hailed as evidence of Japanese aggression, a closer look reveals some contradictions. For instance, his journal showed a visceral contempt for his company commander, who, among other things, had warned against molesting Chinese women or purchasing goods from vendors in a forbidden area. Nevertheless, excerpts of Azuma's journal quickly appeared in several of the growing number of publications on the controversial subject of the Nanjing Massacre. In December 1987, shortly after his first public testimony, part of his wartime journal was published under the title *Our Nanking Platoon: The Nanjing Massacre According to a Conscript*.[28] Utilizing Azuma's journal and other sources, Shimozato Masaki serialized the "hidden history" of atrocity committed by the 20th Regiment in the Japanese Communist Party newspaper *Akahata*. Azuma's journal was also included in a collection of historical documents concerning the 16th Division and the Nanjing Massacre, issued by the same publisher.[29] After this public exposure, there was no turning back.

The Azuma Trial in Japan

Azuma's public testimony and subsequent book in 1987, while welcomed by many, met with fierce condemnation from some. He received many letters of support but also a great deal of hate mail, even death threats. He was forced to leave the fraternity group of the 20th Regiment.[30] Azuma's troubles did not stop there. On April 14, 1993, a suit was filed against him in a Tokyo court.

In his entry of December 21, 1937, Azuma had described how his platoon leader put a captured Chinese man in a mail bag, poured gasoline from a nearby overturned automobile, and set the bag on fire. He then tied a hand grenade to the bag and pulled the string before throwing the bag into a pond. The subsequent explosion killed the hapless Chinese. As it turned out, the platoon leader, who was accused under a pseudonym in Azuma's book but appeared with his real name in two other publications, was still alive. With the support of his comrades, he filed a libel suit against Azuma alleging that the episode was physically impossible and that it was fabricated by Azuma. The publisher, known for its books on Japanese wartime atrocities including those based on Azuma's journal, was also named a defendant.

Support for the former platoon leader came from various quarters, including some of the usual suspects who had long challenged the occurrence of a massacre in Nanjing. Azuma's former company commander, who was also alive, reportedly tried to intervene to have Azuma retract his statement so as to avoid the suit, not least to avoid the breach of harmony among the senyūkai. He failed, but his efforts may explain the five-year delay between the publication of the books and the lawsuit. Some of Azuma's critics also pointed out that the platoon leader, despite being vilified by Azuma, had in reality liked China and had visited the country six times after the war and met with visiting Chinese delegations to Japan. In contrast, Azuma had never set foot there again until 1987.[31]

In April 1996, the Tokyo District Court found Azuma and his codefendants guilty on the ground that the atrocious incident described in his published journal was not credible, and ordered Azuma and his codefendants to pay 2 million yen each to the plaintiff and to issue a public apology. Azuma and his lawyers immediately appealed the ruling. Azuma, too, had supporters in Japan, including citizen activist groups and some progressive lawyers. A few months after the ruling, they formed a group with the explicit purpose of supporting Azuma in the lawsuit, headed by Yamanouchi Koyako, a woman in her early forties.[32] The group subsequently visited China in search of new supporting evidence.

None of these efforts seemed to have mattered. On December 22, 1998, the Tokyo Higher Court rejected the appeal by Azuma, although it reduced the fine to 500,000 yen each. Interestingly, the date of the ruling was postponed from the original November 26, amid speculations that it was intended to avoid poisoning the atmosphere of the state visit by Chinese president Jiang Zemin (who had postponed his visit from August to November due to severe flooding in China). The change of date, argued the critics, showed the politicized nature of the court system in Japan. Perhaps more telling was the fact that when the verdict was announced, some of the plaintiff's supporters unfolded a banner at the press conference with the words "Fabrication of Nanjing Massacre Defeated!" *(Nankin gyakusatsu netsuzō saiban shōri)*, a notion that some in the media quickly exploited. Needless to say, the thinly concealed glee of the massacre deniers only emboldened right-wing elements and irritated Azuma's supporters. Days after the ruling, a right-wing youth entered Azuma's publisher in broad daylight, destroying furniture and office equipment to vent his anger.

Although many of the supporters on both sides saw the suit as a contest between two opposite camps on the issue of Japan's war memory of the Nanjing Massacre, in one sense, the suit also highlighted the conflict of memory among veterans. Whereas Azuma insisted on the accuracy of his wartime writings, his platoon leader denied he was even in the city on December 21, 1937, the day of the alleged atrocity. Later he maintained he had no recollection of his whereabouts.[33]

The Azuma Trial and a Transnational Memory Spectacle? Azuma in China

By the late 1990s, Azuma was no longer a total stranger to Western audiences. In addition to Ian Buruma's book, Azuma also appeared in the documentary film *In the Name of the Emperor*, in which he emphasized he was fighting in China as "the emperor's soldier." He also recounted the common wartime practice of "peeking at the private parts" of Chinese women—often a prelude to sexual assault—in a matter-of-fact manner, an indication to some of his lack of remorse.[34] But it was in China that Azuma achieved the status of a celebrity Japanese veteran.

By the time he appealed the first ruling in 1996, Azuma's name was already known in China, because of the extensive Chinese media coverage of the case. Azuma first visited China in December 1987, shortly after his public testimony, to atone for his crimes in the newly built memorial in Nanjing on the fiftieth anniversary of the fall of the city. He later made several visits to gather evidence for his appeal. To substantiate Azuma's claim, the Chinese located maps from the time indicating the pond opposite the then Supreme Court building, as Azuma had written in his journal. They showed that the Chinese mail bag in 1937 was indeed large enough to fit an adult, unlike the smaller Japanese mail bags. At his request, they also conducted a live test gauging the timing of a Chinese grenade explosion, which had been much disputed in Azuma's court case. To further solidify such evidence to be submitted to the court of appeals in Japan, the local Public Notary in Nanjing certified the test results as authentic.[35]

Azuma's diary covering the entire war years was published in Chinese translation.[36] Many Chinese historians emphasized the value of Azuma's diary as crucial historical evidence. "As we know," one historian noted, "it is no easy task to reveal and establish a truth of history *(lishi zhenxiang)* so as to receive international recognition and attention. It must be based on numerous historical facts that have been verified." In this regard, Azuma filled a major gap in the documentation of the Japanese atrocities in China: the testimonies of perpetrators which have been lacking, in contrast to those of Chinese or third-party witnesses.[37] In 1998, Chinese historians published a book entitled *The Azuma Suit and the Truth of the Nanjing Massacre*, a compilation of day-by-day activities of Japan's Sixteenth Division (to which Azuma belonged) in the Nanjing Massacre.

Perhaps the single most influential event was a popular TV show that featured Azuma on two consecutive episodes. The popular program *Shihua shishuo* (Tell It as It Is) on national television invited Azuma and a few other Japanese to its studio in April 1999. The program was entitled "Memories of War." In the first episode, Azuma spoke about his own frame of mind from his arrival in China in 1937. In particular, he described an incident in which he killed three Chinese peasants in the Luwanfeng Village in Heibei Province, something "he could not even tell his wife and children." Azuma's testimony was followed by supporters of Azuma from Japan on the trial and the state of historical education. Azuma's daughter spoke about the fact that her father named her "Kazuko" in order to pray for peace (*kazu*, same character as *wa* as in *heiwa*). In the second episode aired a week later, Chinese survivors related their sufferings. The show, reportedly watched by upwards of 100 million viewers in China, generated considerable impact. The Chinese host received hundreds of letters.[38]

Azuma's act of repentance was generally well received in China, as was his willingness to speak about the Japanese war atrocities he had witnessed. On one of his visits, he brought with him his battle-worn Japanese flag, complete with the numerous signatures collected before he was sent off to the China front—a popular practice during the war. He donated the flag and other war memorabilia to the Nanjing Massacre Museum as tokens of his repentance. The fact that Azuma was supported by many Japanese, including those who traveled to China with him on numerous occasions, was not lost on their Chinese hosts.[39] Azuma's repentance not only reinforced the belief that Japanese troops indeed committed atrocities against the Chinese people; it also fit the official line that the Japanese and Chinese people are capable were reconciliation on the basis of a "correct view of history."[40] Some 70,000 signatures were collected in China on Azuma's behalf, asking Japan's Supreme Court to hear his case. Within a few months after the trial, Azuma himself embarked on two speaking tours in China and was invited to speak in the Philippines by the overseas Chinese community there.

Transnational Fallout?

The 1998 court ruling against Azuma came on the heels of the visit by President Jiang Zemin to Japan, during which he demanded a written apology from the Japanese government similar to the one recently given to the Korean President Kim Dae Jung. But Jiang did not get what he asked for. Worse, he was seen as lecturing the Japanese, including the emperor, on the history problem. Jiang's visit added a negative spin to the history debate between Japan and China. Perhaps as a result, the Chinese government strongly protested the 1998 court verdict that rejected Azuma's appeal. Shortly after the Tokyo Higher Court ruled against him, a Chinese Foreign Ministry spokesman twice commented on the ruling. After Japan's Supreme Court refused to take up Azuma's appeal in 2002, the same spokesman as well as China's Foreign Minister protested.

They were protesting both the court's ruling and the activities of Nanjing Massacre deniers in Japan. On January 23, 2002, the day after Azuma's appeal was thrown out by the Supreme Court, a symposium with the title "A Thorough Examination of the Nanjing Massacre—The Biggest Lie in the 20th Century" was convened in the hall "Peace Osaka" in that city. Widely reported in the Japanese and Chinese media, the gathering was seen by many Chinese as evidence that the deniers were gaining strength in Japan. Assemblies were held in various Chinese cities protesting the Osaka event. To calm things down, Japan's foreign minister Kōno Yohei made a statement affirming that "it is an undeniable fact that the former Japanese army killed non-combatants and committed looting after entering Nanjing." Kōno's statement was "duly noted" by the Chinese government. With this state intervention, further fallout from the Azuma trial and other developments seemed to be contained for the time being.

This was not the case with the popular reactions in both countries, however. Understandably, Chinese historians reacted to the Japanese court rulings with alarm. The newly founded Center for the Study of the Nanjing Massacre at the Nanjing Normal University organized a symposium on the Azuma case, attended by more than thirty people, eighteen of whom read papers on various aspects of the trial and the Nanjing Massacre. In the wake of the Azuma trial, Chinese publications and activities about Azuma and his legal battle increased.[41]

The second episode of the on-camera discussion featuring Azuma in the Chinese TV program became confrontational and emotional. Mizutani Naoko, a Japanese graduate student of history at the Renmin University, challenged Azuma about the ambiguities in his court testimonies as to what he actually saw, heard, and did in Nanjing. Further, she criticized another Japanese participant for being too critical of the history education in Japan and argued the Nanjing Massacre was in fact featured in all Japanese textbooks. She also criticized the audience as well as "experts" in China for not really understanding present-day Japan and not caring to know the facts about the Nanjing Massacre including the number of Chinese victims. Some Chinese in the audience were outraged by her posture. To prevent further escalation, the host of the program decided to cut some of the most inflammatory remarks on both sides.[42]

Chinese reactions to Azuma and his trial, in turn, produced further reactions in Japan. The clash of views in the TV studio was prominently reported by the conservative daily *Sankei* newspaper. Mizutani herself wrote in the journal *Sekai*—a Left-leaning monthly—about her frustration with the huge gap between Japanese and Chinese views on Azuma and history in general.[43] As Azuma's popularity rose in China and elsewhere as a courageous Japanese confronting the dark past, however, he seemed to be gaining further notoriety in Japan: Azuma was not only condemned by conservative "revisionist historians" and nationalist commentators, he was also shunned by many of the people who had laboriously sought to uncover Japan's wartime excesses, a point Mizutani emphasized in the TV discussion. Conspicuously absent among his supporters were the academic historians. Relations between Azuma and Honda Katsuichi—the former *Asahi* reporter who had done much to expose the Japan's wartime atrocities, also seemed strained.[44] Only a few citizens' groups stood by him.

Thus the Azuma testimony turned into the so-called "Azuma phenomenon"—his great popularity in China in contrast with his less than trustworthy reputation in Japan. As with the development of Chinese nationalism in modern times, Chinese reaction to the Azuma case was to a large extent a reflection of the perception of present-day Japan. To the Chinese audience, the Azuma court case revealed the "growing influence of the progressive elements among the Japanese people, but also that Japan's right-wing forces still command powerful influence, even over the Japanese government and the judicial branch." To some extent, such concerns on the part of the Chinese were justified by media reports that Azuma's accusers in Japan included many who were active in the Nanjing Massacre denial movement. To many Japanese, however, the Chinese (over)reaction to the Azuma trial confirmed another stereotype—that there is no freedom of speech in China and simply demonstrates that ordinary Chinese do not understand contemporary Japan, especially its separation of judicial power from the executive branch. Such a view seemed to confirm that the Chinese were simply being emotional and not ready to accept conclusions based on pure academic research.

Veteran Testimonies and Communities of Memory

The late French sociologist Maurice Halbwachs wrote that

> the individual participates in two types of memory—individual memory and collective memory. He adopts a quite different, even contrary, attitude as he participates in one or the other . . . In particular, the individual memory, in order to corroborate and make precise and even to cover the gaps in its remembrances, relies

upon, relocates itself within, momentarily merges with, the collective memory.[45]

Halbwachs' observation about the relationship between the individual and the collective in memory formation is confirmed by this brief case study here.

Over the years, Japanese war veterans came to have their testimonies heard by an increasingly wider audience. There is no question that the shift from the early postwar decades preoccupied with recovery and Cold War confrontation to the post–Cold War era of rising nationalism in Northeast Asia defined the changing frames of remembrance. Whether as individuals or as groups, Japanese veterans also contributed considerably to shaping postwar memories of the battlefield. At the same time, their memories were reshaped by the shifting frames of remembrance as well as by the various groups they were associated with, including the mass media. At a time when fewer and fewer of them are still alive, it can also be expected that the quest for such an increasingly scarce commodity as veterans' testimonies would intensify.[46] Highly motivated individuals like Matsuoka Tamaki are the most recent example of this effort. Largely through their dedication, these individuals have occasionally replaced historians as the facilitators in veterans' memories. The news media in both Japan and China have also had great influence in giving prominence to certain veterans.

A brief examination of veterans' testimonies raises questions about the problematic relationship between history and memory that has increasingly come under scrutiny. In addition to their appeal to the general public, historians have found the oral history of participants invaluable in filling the gaps in documentation—many in the case of Japan's war owing to massive destruction. Even testimonies by the rank-and-file, while limited in their range of observation, shed light on the conditions of the discipline and morale of the fighting men as well as their interaction with the enemy population. Like other kinds of testimonies, however, veterans' testimonies of war are never the "raw material" one might expect. As Joan Scott has pointed out, what we commonly assume as "original experience" is in fact interpreted evidence.[47] This is certainly true with oral history, collected long after the event and sometimes for specific purposes.[48] Although Azuma's journal was essentially based on his recollections during the war, it also posed a difficult question for historians. It is noteworthy that one Japanese scholar who praised Azuma's book as "portraying the true conditions of war of aggression" admitted that she did not know whether they belong to truth or fabrication given the possibility of additional materials.[49] In a rare commentary, historian Yoshida Yutaka noted the contribution of Azuma's journal mainly in terms of bucking the trend of avoiding the subject of Japanese atrocities by most Japanese veterans but refrained from commenting on the veracity of Azuma's specific claims.[50] In January 2006, Azuma Shiro died of cancer at the age of 94. He never retracted his claims.

The Azuma case also testifies to both the possibility and the peril of a transnational "community of memory" about World War II in East Asia. The end of the Cold War has greatly facilitated transnational movements of people, goods, and information. Transmission of memories across national boundaries, through personal contact, translation, and mass media, has become increasingly common. Personal visits by Japanese to China, especially to sites of wartime Japanese atrocities, have been taking place regularly. Matsuoka and other Japanese have been to China specifically to collect testimonies of the victims. A popular Chinese book was based on the author's own encounters with a half dozen Japanese veterans while he was a student in Japan.[51] Chinese scholars have participated in numerous symposia in Japan, and a number of Chinese victims and survivors have come to Japan to bear witness at various public events. Japanese works, including veterans' testimonies, have appeared in Chinese translations, while a number of Chinese publications have been translated into Japanese.[52] Films made in China on Japanese atrocities, such as *Nanjing 1937*, have garnered attention in Japan, though often as a result of incidents such as rightwing harassment.

The impact of such transnational movements of people and ideas on the memory of war is ongoing and hard to assess. They created a much needed linkage that breaks down the strictly national boundaries of memory. For all the negative fallout from the Azuma phenomenon, it has also sparked much agony and self-reflection. It has been analyzed in a series of thoughtful essays by Sun Ge, a Chinese scholar trained in intellectual history, which was subsequently translated into Japanese.[53]

As Sun Ge points out, with a domestic trial in Japan shaking the emotions of the Chinese people for the first time, the Azuma episode demonstrated the "possibility of mutual acceptance of the emotional memory concerning the war."[54] At least one thoughtful letter from the Chinese audience of the TV debate expressed sympathy with Mizutani and dissatisfaction with the emotional outburst from the Chinese participants in the televised debate. Paradoxically, by highlighting the deeper schisms between the memories of war in Japan and China, the Azuma case, by bringing about more thoughtful critiques from both Chinese and Japanese writers, demonstrates the shallowness of much of the so-called "collaborative research" between Chinese and Japanese scholars.[55]

Different communities of memory are likely to have different standards of truthfulness—something akin to Foucault's "regime of truth." In a way, the Azuma case illustrates different "regimes of truth" regarding the history of the Sino-Japanese War. Whereas Chinese scholars tend to place great emphasis on the overall character of the war as Japanese aggression, often neglecting "details," a tendency among Japanese historians is their seeming obsession with verifiable details, either ignoring or paying *pro forma* attention to the "big picture."[56] Chinese historians see as their mission to defend above all the "truth of the war," and in this regard Azuma's journal and confession as a whole has the ring of truth. As a result, the details of the specific incident, though much disputed in Japan, are not questioned by most Chinese historians. Similarly, a number of photographs of alleged Japanese atrocities in China, while discredited or questioned in Japan, still command undisputed credibility in Chinese publications and museum exhibits. To historians in Japan, this amounts to the lack of respect for empirical research. To adopt an overused analogy, the Chinese view tends to dwell upon the forest whereas the Japanese gaze often focuses on leaves.

There is much discussion about a new geopolitical framework that has yet to emerge to replace the Cold War confrontation in East Asia. The idea of an East Asian community is garnering increasing interest and support among many in the region and beyond. Conflicting memories of the past, however, remain a major stumbling block to its realization. To negotiate between different communities of memory, whether between different groups within a society or different societies, can bring about discomfort or even misunderstanding. It is through reflection over such discomfort and misunderstanding, however, that we may discover the clues eventually leading us out of this predicament.

∿ 4

Kamikaze Today

The Search for National Heroes in Contemporary Japan

YOSHIKUNI IGARASHI

SINCE THE FORMAL INTRODUCTION of kamikaze missions during the Asia-Pacific War, the young pilots who manned the suicide missions have been widely represented in Japanese culture. Although postwar Japanese society held the military responsible for the war's disastrous outcome, the kamikaze pilots' short military careers and their ultimate sacrifice dissociated them from the negative images of the Japanese military. Their deaths were read as the inadvertent proof of their sincerity and their lack of interest in worldly gain. Most early postwar accounts offered sentimental portrayals of the kamikazes' lives before their final attacks, casting the young pilots as heroic figures who sacrificed their lives for a larger cause. A number of postwar Japanese films that portrayed kamikaze followed suit.[1] The climaxes of the films center around the young protagonists' departures for their death missions, while their cinematic narratives explain the motives for the kamikazes' actions to postwar viewers. Like numerous postwar representations of the kamikaze in postwar Japan, the films insist that the pilots did not die for the sake of the emperor, but for their family, friends, and the larger national community.

In postwar remembrance, the deaths of the kamikaze pilots were crucial not only in framing their individual lives, but also in signifying the nation's trajectory toward defeat. The nation vicariously died its death, so to speak, through the self-deaths of the young pilots. The stories of the kamikaze served as an ideological apparatus that encapsulated war memories within wartime while simultaneously allowing them to surface in popular postwar representations. Their deaths thus secured the boundary between the war and the postwar. Those who survived their missions violated this boundary and became the object of moral disdain in postwar society. The popular term *tokkō kuzure* (degenerate special forces) not only referred to the moral decay of the ex-kamikaze pilots who became lost to drinking, womanizing, and fighting after the war, but also intimated a general disapproval that they survived. Kamikaze pilots should have died, if not for the sake of the nation, at least for the story of the nation.

Even in the 1990s, many still sought to complete the nation's story through the kamikaze pilots' death, as seen in Kobayashi Yoshinori's *Sensōron*.[2] Much like early postwar representations, recent versions tend to focus on the pilots' selfless sacrifice for a larger cause. Yet the films produced in the 1990s and after struggle to render the narratives of the kamikaze relevant to the viewers, the majority of whom have no personal memories of the war. For example, the 1995 film *Winds of God* is a notable example that attempts to convey the immediacy of the war to the postwar generation through a new cinematic narrative. After a traffic accident, the two protagonists slip back five decades and find themselves among a group of kamikaze pilots in August 1945. Although they discover life inside and outside of the military in 1945 to be completely alien, they eventually adjust to it to the degree that one of them participates in a kamikaze mission. Through the time warp and the protagonist's death, the film insists that the audience accept the deaths of the kamikaze as their own generation's loss. Yet the story of the modern kamikaze's death is neatly contained in the film's representational space: the film presents it as a theatrical play within a film. By returning to the dark space of the theater where the pair performs a comic act, the film's final scene relegates the encounter with the past to marginal, dreamlike memories and safely brings the audience back to the peaceful world of postwar society outside the theater. The stark contrast between the inside and the outside of the theater spatially signifies the deep chasm between the war and the postwar. The death of a comedian-turned-kamikaze effectively forecloses the narrative of the kamikaze that the film intends to intertwine with postwar society and thus confirms the unbridgeable gap of this chasm.

The end of the Cold War, and the consequent reconsideration of Japan's relationship with the United States and its East Asian neighbors, meant that the idea of the "postwar" had to be rethought. In many ways, the continuing gap between the war and postwar remained (and remains) a constant in the shaping of Japanese society. Although discourse had been much freer since 1945 in Japan than in, for example, China or Taiwan (two other societies considered in this collection), the Cold War had frozen or else downplayed discussion of many aspects of Japan's prewar imperial history. The post-1989 moment, marked by the death of Emperor Hirohito, saw the end of the Shōwa era happen just at the moment when global and regional realignments caused by the end of the Cold War allowed a new contrast between those aspects of the postwar that were remembered in new ways and those that were treated as continuous with the pre-1989 interpretation.

The 2001 film *Hotaru* (Fireflies) attempts to fill the idea of an unbridgeable gap between war and postwar by insisting that war is still an integral part of postwar society. Rather than focus on the deaths of kamikaze pilots, the film foregrounds the postwar lives of those who survived the Asia-Pacific War, including those who participated in suicide missions. It also points to Japan's unresolved colonial legacies by acknowledging the presence of Koreans among the kamikaze pilots. The film is a belated effort to reestablish the link between the war and the postwar through revisiting what postwar Japanese society has refused to accept—the traumatic effects of the war on postwar society. In bringing the story of the kamikaze closer to the audience, the majority of whom were born after the war, the filmmakers aim to locate the war legacies in the postwar. Thanks to Toei's strong marketing, the film had a respectable gross profit and the audience generally responded favorably to its treatment of war memory. In comparison to Hollywood's war spectacle *Pearl Harbor*, also released in 2001, the Japanese filmmakers' efforts appear far more sophisticated and sincere in depicting the living memory of war. The film is laudable in its efforts to locate traumatic war memories in the everyday life of postwar Japan.

Yet the film's representational strategies never fully grapple with the enormity of war trauma. The film invokes war memories and postwar struggles to deal with them only to announce that the postwar—the period burdened with war memories—is finally over. Being surrounded by the beauty of nature and others' goodwill, the war generation silently waits its turn to exit the story. The filmmakers' conscientious efforts in the end reproduce—rather than rewrite—the narrative that culminates in death. The deaths that occur more than four decades after the war's end conclude the postwar struggle with its war memories. Furthermore, although the film may be a response to recent discussions of Japan's colonial legacies (e.g., Korean forced laborers, "comfort women," discrimination against Korean residents in Japan), the film's central concern with the Korean kamikazes' patriotism in effect aestheticizes and silences the painful memories of colonial subjects. In the end, the film dehistoricizes individual war experiences in order to repackage them as an easy-to-consume aesthetic symbol—fireflies. I offer my reading of *Hotaru* in this chapter not merely to critique its "failure" to accomplish finally a critical rewriting of the kamikaze narrative, but to discuss postwar Japan's desire at the turn of a millennium to foreclose its war story once and for all.

The Second Deaths of the Kamikaze

In the opening sequence of *Hotaru*, the news of Hirohito's death in 1989 sets the film's narrative in motion. This framing presents a reconciliation with the wartime past as primarily Japanese business, despite the film's references to Japan's colonial legacies. The end of the Cold War—the disintegration of the political system that had helped to silence some aspects of Asia-Pacific War memories—registers foremost as the death of the monarch. Hirohito's death was indeed a personal event for those who experienced the war in Japan: for example, many leftist activists who suffered political persecution at the hands of the wartime regime desired to outlive Hirohito simply to gain some vindication. The end of his reign released complex emotions about Japan's wartime past, and the film attempts to capture them within a new narrative that ultimately reconciles the present and the past.

The news of Hirohito's death reaches the ex-kamikaze pilot Yamaoka Shūji and his wife Tomoko, who lead a quiet life in a fishing village in Kagoshima, the southernmost prefecture in mainland Japan. Shūji has little to say about the emperor's death. Even after a request from a news reporter, Shūji refuses to ponder the event. Whatever emotional difficulty he experienced as a kamikaze survivor in the postwar has been buried in silence. Yet another death forces him to confront the buried memories of war. Fujieda Yōji, another survivor from Shūji's kamikaze squadron, commits suicide shortly after the emperor's death to rejoin the fallen kamikazes. The monarch's death announces the end of a turbulent era, with which Fujieda and his generation strongly identified. For more than four decades both Shūji and Fujieda have retired into their respective private lives: Yamaoka has worked as a fisherman and Fujieda as the manager of an apple orchard. The emperor's death brings their lives into a shared space once more and for another, final time, even though they fail to meet each other in person again.

The film establishes the parallel yet shared lives of Shūji and Fujieda by using TV coverage of Hirohito's funeral procession as a pivotal image. In preparing his death march into the winter mountains, Fujieda watches a telecast of the imperial funeral procession. The film then cuts to the living room of Shūji's house, where a television set shows the procession while Tomoko brushes her hair (Figure 4.1). The solemn music that accompanies the procession continues without a break in the background. Fujieda and the Yamaokas are brought back to the coeval space of the nation through the TV image of the imperial death. Fujieda's life is about to expire in the mountains and Tomoko's health is on a steady decline (in the scene, she complains about the dialysis that she has to have on that day). After visually superimposing Tomoko's ailing body onto a spectacular volcanic cloud from Mt. Sakurajima, the film cuts back to Fujieda's solitary death march. Both scenes intimate a strong association between nature and death. In this sequence, the media image of the emperor's death ushers in the end of human time (Shōwa history) and a return to nature.

The film's spectacular depiction of nature serves as a larger framework that encompasses and simultaneously belittles the human's emotional struggles with history. The cinematic narrative is punctuated by nature that is burdened with symbolic deaths. Fujieda chooses Mt. Hakkōda in Aomori Prefecture as the site for his suicide, a site associated with the tragic death of 199 infantrymen during their winter training in 1902.[3] A screen full of cherry blossoms leads the audience to the scene of Fujieda's funeral. Since wartime, the ephemeral lives of the cherry blossoms have been associated with the young lives lost in Japan's war, including those of the kamikaze pilots. Mt. Kaimondake, the mountain that the kamikaze pilots leaving Kyūshū used as the last

Figure 4.1. Yamaoka Tomiko (Tanaka Yūko) in her domestic space. In *Hotaru,*
directed by Furuhata Yasuo. Produced by Takaiwa Tan, Toei Co., 2001.

landmark to check their navigation course, appears in key scenes of the
film. Hence, instead of being innocent, the natural landscape that appears in the film is filled with the presentiment of death.

The female body of Tomoko also serves as an extension of nature in
foreshadowing death. Although the couple learns that Shūji's kidney
can be transplanted to her, she steadfastly refuses any medical intervention, and resigns herself to die in the near future. The film does not adequately address why she refuses the operation. The gap in the narrative suggests that her body belongs to a chapter of history that is about
to close (and return to nature). When her death grows imminent, Shūji
finally tells her the final words entrusted to him by his superior in his
kamikaze squadron, her former fiancé who died in his mission. The
words that express his love for his native land, Korea, as wells as for
Tomoko, unleash the feelings and emotions that she long managed to
bury in her daily life. Yet Tomoko never articulates her own emotional
anguish—she stands only as a marker of a tragic death much like other
natural symbols in the film. Tomoko expresses her struggle with the
past through her silent tears.

While Tomoko embodies the nature to which all historical memories are supposed to return, other female characters serve different
functions in preserving and resurfacing the memories that have been
buried in Yamaoka Shūji's quotidian life for so long. Through their mediation, the kamikaze pilots' masculine identity acquires a feminine
quality. This association with femininity is crucial to the film's por-

trayal of the pilots as young innocents who were dragged into the war by larger forces. Because of women's perceived distance from political power and actual war operations (they allegedly suffered the disastrous consequence of the war without participating in Japan's military operation), their hardship was dissociated from Japan's wartime aggression in the postwar popular imagination. Numerous films in the immediate postwar years portrayed the suffering of ordinary Japanese through the perspectives of mothers and widows. The 1993 kamikaze film *Gekkō no natsu*, similarly assigns a female character the role to recollect and recover the memories of the two kamikaze pilots. Like mothers and widows in many postwar films, the pilots are coupled not with masculine aggression but with feminine forbearance toward their cruel destiny.[4]

Yamamoto Tomiko, the owner of an eatery frequented by a number of kamikaze pilots at the Chiran Army Airbase, is the proprietor of the kamikaze legacies in *Hotaru*. She was their mother away from their home. She remained in town running the same establishment even after the war ended and the surviving pilots had returned to their respective homes. Before his suicide, Fujieda visits Chiran with his granddaughter and runs into Tomiko. Through their conversation, the film informs the audience that Tomiko was instrumental in building a Kannon temple to honor the deceased pilots; thus, it establishes her as a keeper and transmitter of the kamikazes' memories. Furthermore, Tomiko insists on her spiritual ties with the kamikaze through a fantastic tale of a pilot who she claims reappeared as a firefly. Tomiko tells Fujieda's granddaughter the story of Lieutenant Miyagawa who returned after his death. After having been forced to fly back to the base because of engine trouble, Miyagawa told Tomiko in his depressed state that he would surely succeed in ramming into an enemy ship in the next mission: as proof of that, he would return as a firefly. A day after Miyagawa departed for his mission, a firefly flew into Tomiko's eatery. Tomiko and the other pilots were convinced that the insect was Miyagawa.[5]

By transforming the pilot into an ephemeral insect, the film exorcizes the entire kamikaze mission of its aggressive, male identity. The light it emits signifies the pathos of Miyagawa's wish to be among his fictitious family even after his death. The pilot joins his buddies for one last time in the domestic space of Tomiko's eatery. Rather than celebrate the success of his mission, the other corps members desperately cry out his name as if to prolong their final moment with him. Fireflies do not kill: they merely live their short life without disturbing the surrounding environment. In narrating her story in tears, Tomiko makes sure to add that the entire mission at Chiran terminated six days after Miyagawa's death. The timing of his death—his life made no difference to the outcome of the war—helps to project the kamikaze pilots' image as victims facing the invincible forces of history. Fireflies return as a convenient substitute for the cherry blossoms whose short-lived beauty came to connote the kamikaze pilots' ephemeral (thus nonaggresive) lives in the war and postwar. The cherry blossoms were all gone after early April, while the flickering lights of the fireflies were at their peak in June when Miyagawa departed for his final mission. (That Fujieda's funeral takes place during the height of cherry blossom season asserts the symbolic equivalence between the two.) Tomiko's story about Miyagawa's reincarnation also prepares for the final resolution of the tension between the past and the present in the film's conclusion. Forty-five years after Miyagawa's death, another pilot returns as a firefly, this time, not to prove his successful mission, but to tell the Japanese audience that postwar Japan's struggle with its war memories is finally over.

Fujieda Yōji's high-school-age granddaughter, Masami, is another female character who plays a complex role in the film's effort to transmit war memories. While Tomiko stands as a representative of the older generation burdened with the weight of the past, Masami functions as a medium through which the older generation comes to terms with its memories. Masami is a trickster figure that cuts through the impasse between the war and the postwar generations. After Fujieda's funeral, Masami discovers the notebook left by her grandfather that contains a draft of the letter he never sent to Shūji. The notebook is almost destroyed by Masami's parents, who try to conceal the connection between their father's death and his experience as a kamikaze pilot. Masami saves it by convincing them that she will keep it to herself and travels alone, without informing her parents, to Kyūshū to hand-deliver it to Shūji. The notebook explicitly explains the motive of Fujieda's death: he can finally end his struggle with the past and die to join his war buddies. Masami, whose name is transcribed with the characters that mean truth (*shinjitsu*), protects the truth from and simultaneously conveys it to the postwar society that has long deplored the war and its war memories. In the second half of the film, Shūji finally sheds his disciplined, self-imposed silence and confides to Masami, in the open field where his airbase used to be, the feelings he had on his final mission. The masculine character silently endures painful memories (like so many characters that Takakura Ken played in the past), while Masami's androgynous figure assists him to come to terms with his inner feelings and emotions, a realm traditionally deemed as feminine. For those who have seen the 1999 film *Poppoya*, which was produced by the same director, Furuhata Yasuo, and stars Takakura Ken, this narrative is familiar. Much like in *Hotaru*, a mysterious, young female character enters into the older male protagonist's life (she turns out to be an apparition of his dead daughter) and serves as a catalyst for his emotional reexamination. The young female character gently confirms the life of the older man by embracing his memories. The war generation thereby bypasses the postwar generation all together (e.g., Masami's parents who tried to destroy Fujieda's note) and hands its memories down to the new post-postwar generation. The young female character's liminality (she has no strong geographical or historical associations with postwar society) allows this transmission of memories to take place beyond the confines of postwar society.

Masami is also a visual double of the Korean kamikaze pilot, Kim Songjae (Second Lieutenant Kanayama), who died in his mission. The film's narrative revolves around the absent presence of Kim and the sense of guilt that the Japanese protagonists have felt for surviving the war while Kim did not. The film signifies the passing of time by pairing young and older actors in the roles of Fujieda, Shūji, and Tomoko in the war and the postwar segments (Tomiko is an exception: Naraoka Tomoko plays her in both the war and the postwar segments of the film). The symmetry of the war and the postwar is broken by Kim's absence; yet Masami arrives at Chiran as his female stand-in for Kim Songjae in the postwar. Her facial features, with short hair and large sparkly eyes, resemble those of Kim (Figures 4.2 and 4.3). Her young, innocent smile perfectly mimics the young pilot. Kim Songjae returns to the postwar through the figure of Masami to urge Tomiko, Shūji, and Tomoko to confront and reconcile with their past.

The resemblance overwhelms Tomiko when she gazes at Masami's face in the farewell ceremony in which Masami presents a bouquet to

Figure 4.2. Lieutenant Kaneyama/Kim Songjae (Ozawa Yukiyoshi). In *Hotaru*, directed by Furuhata Yasuo. Produced by Takaiwa Tan, Toei Co., 2001.

Figure 4.3. Fujieda Masami (Mizuhashi Takami). In *Hotaru*, directed by Furuhata Yasuo. Produced by Takaiwa Tan, Toei Co., 2001.

Tomiko. As she realizes her physical ability has become limited, she decides to retire to a nursing home. A number of people gather to bid farewell to the "mother of kamikaze," and Tomiko in her brief speech perfunctorily urges the attendees to remember and to continue to talk about the kamikaze pilots. Masami's presence, however, disturbs the courteous gathering where war memories are supposed to recede quietly into the background with Tomiko. Taking a close look at Masami's face, Tomiko seems taken aback and begins to talk about her own guilt in sending the young pilots on kamikaze missions:

> Just like this. I deprived the young and wonderful people of their dreams. I sent them off, saying "for the sake of the nation, congratulations, congratulations." I killed them. Real mothers would not tell them to die. No matter what happened, even if they had to abandon their own country, they protect their children.

As she speaks, she keeps her eyes on the teenager, placing her hand on Masami's shoulder. Yet she does not talk to Masami: she talks through her to the other attendees. Masami turns into the shadow of the kamikaze pilots whom Tomiko saw off on their missions. Tomiko breaks down in tears, showing the raw emotions that the past still triggers.

By making Tomiko suddenly admit her own wartime guilt, the film refuses to participate in the unproblematic celebration of the kamikaze's sacrifice. Although the wartime experiences return to the postwar in a somewhat more honest shape, her emotional elocution creates other problems. In actuality, mothers did not necessarily shield their sons from death in wartime Japan. Many did indeed encourage their sons to support Japan's imperial war as soldiers. Through insisting on the innocence of genuine motherly love (as opposed to Tomiko's nationalistic one), Tomiko projects the images of the pilots (the products of true motherly love) who are once more betrayed. The scene thereby confirms the persecuted status of the pilots in wartime Japan. Wartime society not only collectively failed them but also pressured the "young and wonderful" into accepting their missions "for the sake of the nation."

Through the visual tropes of nature and femininity, the film attempts to reintroduce and reintegrate the fragments of the wartime past for the postwar audience. The cinematic narrative confines the war in which Japan fought against the Allied Powers within the domestic space of Japan. The figures of the enemy have disappeared: Japan in the postwar fights the battle against its own demon—its war memories. The kamikaze pilots died for the sake of the nation and their sacrifice laid the foundation for postwar Japan, therefore, postwar society is obliged to keep their memories alive. The film applies this construct of domestic space also to Japan's former colony, Korea, without any compunction, forcing it to accept the Japanese resolution as its own.

Yamaoka Tomoko was going to marry the Korean pilot, Kim Songjae (Second Lieutenant Kanayama). However, the film refuses to explain why Kim volunteered to be a kamikaze or to offer any depiction of how he might have grappled with his ethnicity within the imperial army. Kim speaks of his true mind when he entrusts the parting words to Shūji and Fujieda:

> Tomo-san. I will go on a mission tomorrow. Thank you. Thanks to you Tomo-san, I was truly happy. I will surely sink an enemy ship. However, I will not die for the Great Empire of Japan. I will go on the mission for my family in Korea, for Tomo-san, with the pride of Korean race. Long live the Korean people. Long live Tomo-san. Thank you. Please live a happy life. Forgive my selfishness.

Although Kim Songjae's final words are full of historical irony, their meaning is not the primary concern of the film. Kim's cry, "Long Live the Korean People" in *Hotaru* turns him into a single-minded nationalist, erasing the complex ideological terrain that surrounded the colonial subject.[6] The audience is invited to understand Kim as a strict analogy: he is much like the conscientious Japanese youth at the time. The only difference is that he sacrifices his life for Korea, while the other kamikaze dies for Japan.

Shūji finally tells Kim Songjae's words to Tomoko after more than four decades of silence and asks her to come to visit Songjae's bereaved family in Korea. The sequence in which Shūji and Tomoko meet Songjae's family is framed within a narrative of conflict and eventual reconciliation, which is problematic since it offers an easy way out of the historical conflicts between the two nations. The film ultimately insists that the reconciliation will be there when "they" accept and understand this tragic death as "we" do. When Shūji and Tomoko arrive at the family residence of the dead Kim Songjae, they are rejected by the male family members. Their exchange makes it clear that their anger defines their Korean identity. The film marks two irreconcilable national positions to dramatize the subsequent resolution of the tension between them.

The Korean men seem to accept Shūji's words in the end, but not Kim's memento, a miniature Korean folk mask. When Tomoko offers it, they fall into silence, tacitly rejecting her. A female character in a wheelchair, Kim Songjae's aunt, breaks the awkward silence by accepting the memento and welcoming Shūji and Tomoko into her house. Through this sequence, the film characterizes the women as less constrained by nationalist ideology and thus better able to embrace the past. They are bonded in the presentiment of their own deaths: the matriarch with her ailing body accepts the overture of reconciliation by another ailing female character. Their femininity in declining health serves as a counterbalance to the masculine national pride that separates the two nations. Kim Songjae's nationalist pledge to sacrifice himself for his people and his family's nationalistic rejection of Songjae's death as a kamikaze are resolved through the understanding between Tomoko and Songjae's aunt.

Through the sequence in which Shūji and Tomoko visit the grave of Kim Songjae's parents (there is no grave for him) at the end of their trip, the film reveals its ideological contours: it claims that respect for the dead will overcome the unfortunate history between Korea and Japan. After their visit to the gravesite, Tomoko notices a firefly *(hotaru)* flying in the winter air. The film demands that the audience accept the firefly as Songjae precisely because it defies realism—it appears in broad daylight and the ground is covered with snow.[7] As the title implies, fireflies serve as the key representational tool to establish an immediate link with the wartime past and the dead. But, unlike Lieutenant Miyagawa's return, which is filled with pathos, Kim's reincarnation is completely devoid of emotion. By letting the firefly return in broad daylight, the filmmakers deny the innermost thoughts of the pilot. As Fukahori Michiyoshi insists, kamikaze pilots often faced their own desire for survival in the darkness of night, while accepting the public persona of stoic hero in the light of day.[8] Kim Songjae's return to his homeland after more than four decades shows no signs of attachment to the lives that he left behind. There is not even a hint of the dark agony that he may have experienced over his fate during sleepless nights. Kim returns not to express the emotional turbulences that he experienced as a Korean kamikaze pilot but to show that he holds no grudges against his Japanese friends and, by extension, against Japan.

Kim Songjae's return to his hometown as a firefly in order to approve and celebrate the Yamaokas' visit temporarily arouses but subsequently resolves the emotional anguish of Songjae's family. Kim's return is visible to Yamaoka and Tomoko alone, for his mission is to complete a Japanese drama of death and reconciliation. Nobody else witnesses his return to his homeland. Even the couple's Korean interpreter is absent from the scene. His return is staged for the Japanese audience alone. Once the emotional drama concludes, Korea is reduced to a scenic countryside detached from all historical and geographical specificity. Nature functions once again as a way to bury the past: Korea and its colonial past, much like the scenery of the countryside, serve only as a stage where Shūji and Tomoko can finally relieve themselves of the burden of the past. What appears to be the film's postcolonial sensitivity turns out to be a disguise for the desire to represent Japan's colonial history exclusively as a Japanese drama.

The colonial conditions under which Koreans lived are buried under the film's aesthetic representations of war. As part of its war effort, the Japanese war regime forcefully conscripted as many as 1.5 million Koreans for physical labor under cruel conditions in mainland Japan, including the construction of a Kyushū airbase near Chiran used for kamikaze missions. A local resident recalls his experience as a first-year junior high school student mobilized to construct the Kanoya Navy Airbase, which served as a kamikaze base, in Kaseda.[9] He and his classmates worked among hundreds of Korean conscripts, a number of whom died from typhus. Although their bodies were buried locally, the location of the burial site is long forgotten and those who supervised the operation do not wish to talk about it. Korean soldiers in the Japanese military were often subjected to physical and mental abuse because of their ethnicity. The Korean kamikaze pilots were no exception in receiving maltreatment. Yet there is absolutely no sign of colonial tension in Kim Songjae's kamikaze corps. The Japanese and the Koreans seem to transcend ethnic boundaries when facing the common destiny of death.

The film is an effort to recuperate memories that have been buried in silence for more than five decades. However, the film conjures up war memories only to repress them: the unmitigated understanding between the dead and the survivors that the film finally arrives at encourages the audience to leave the postwar period and its war memories behind. The end of the postwar sends the colonial memories that haunted the period to oblivion. Thanks to the forgiveness of the deceased, the audience is allowed entry into a land of bliss where the ghosts of war and colonialism no longer disturb their conscience. The film suggests that Tomoko dies shortly after the trip to Korea. In the final sequence of the film, Yamaoka witnesses the burning of the ship that he named after his wife—a symbolic cremation of Tomoko and his own memories. He is overcome by his emotions and cries, but the expression on his face belongs to a man who has no regret about his life. He is ready to join the dead and to foreclose the history of the war generation.

The film projects a closure to Japan's postwar history on the screen. But the sentimental ending unintentionally reveals the film's excessive efforts to tie all the historical elements into a neatly organized narrative. The film's conspicuous design works against the filmmakers' desire to naturalize Japan's postwar history. The film is so determined to project a reconciliation with the past that it sacrifices its realism. The firefly in the winter air turns the film's entire narrative into a fantastic fairytale that undermines the film's historical claim. In the end, it demands that the audience make a leap of faith and accept what is projected on the screen in its totality.

Selling Kamikaze

At the national level, *Hotaru* was very popular. For example, the film was voted the tenth best film of the year in 2001 by the readers of the biweekly, *Kinema junpō* (the best film was Miyazaki Hayao's *Spirited Away*).[10] Readers of Kinema Junpō wrote in their favorable reactions to the film; and the film critic, Satō Tadao, contributed a rave review of the film, insisting that it registers not a sentimentalism but a genuine regret toward Japan's colonial past.[11] *Kinema junpō*, which ran a prerelease series on *Hotaru*, was also eager to report that Korean viewers gave favorable responses to the film.[12] The film appears to have succeeded notably in domesticating the kamikazes' legacies in Japan but also in cleansing postwar Japan's guilty conscience toward its former colony, Korea.

The domestication of the kamikaze, in which *Hotaru* fully participates, also helps to commercialize their images. The effects of this
commercialization are perhaps most manifest in the small southern
Kyūshū town, Chiran, whose historical connection with the kamikaze
pilots is a valuable tourist attraction. Despite its remote location from
the major Japanese cities, it has grown into a Mecca of kamikaze image
seekers. The commercial success of the film has brought more opportunities to merchandize the image of the town and of the kamikaze.
However, what is for sale in the town of Chiran is not the image of the
kamikaze per se (their deaths are too sacrosanct to be given monetary
value) but substitute images that reduce the kamikaze's historical reality to aesthetic signs.

The kamikaze pilots' deaths (and lives) are enshrined as sacred facts
in the Peace Museum for Kamikaze Pilots, dedicated to the 1,036 pilots who departed from the southern Kyūshū airbases, including the
Chiran Army Airbase, for their final missions over the Okinawan wa-
ters. The museum has its origins in the town's efforts to build the
Kannon temple to memorialize the deceased pilots for their "sublime"
dedication to the nation.[13] After the war, several generals who had been
responsible for devising and executing the kamikaze attacks led the effort to create Kannon statues to honor the kamikaze for their sacrifice
for the nation.[14] One of the statues was housed in the temple built by
the town of Chiran in 1955 with locally raised money. Parts of the do-
nation were eventually used to construct a building that displayed the
pilots' mementos, which the town expanded into a Peace Museum in
the mid-1980s as part of "a special town building project." The town's
efforts to differentiate itself from other local communities by tapping
into its historical legacy of the kamikaze paid off handsomely: the museum is now the town's biggest tourist attraction.[15] Along with the gardens of former samurai residences, the museum is one of the stops that
tourist buses make on their southern Kyūshū sightseeing routes. Each
year, about a half million people visit the facility, which stands at the
site of the former Chiran Army Airbase. (In the film, Fujieda Yōji and
Masami visit the museum.) The solemn space of the museum urges
tourists to become temporary pilgrims seeking the meaning of the
kamikazes' deaths. The main focus of the museum is to humanize the
pilots through the displays of their photos, writing, and personal belongings.[16] The visitors are invited to return to 1945 and glimpse the

moments before the pilots' final missions. In their personal struggles with imminent death, the young pilots appear as tragic figures inside the display cases of the museum. The Peace Museum is a space where one is invited to encounter death (and appreciate life) at a safe distance.

Once outside the museum, tourists face the peaceful quotidian life of a small town. The cars and buses that have brought them there immediately take them to another destination out of town. Many who visit the Peace Museum pass through the small town that lacks the amenities that other neighboring tourist destinations offer. The local business interests try to take full advantage of the large number of visitors to the Peace Museum as well as the popularity of the film *Hotaru*. By promoting the more market-friendly images of the fireflies and the local woman who narrated the story about them, the film seems to have provided the means to reconcile the town's two seemingly incompatible imperatives: to protect the kamikaze's revered images and to merchandize them.

These substitute images are available for consumption at another "museum," built in the same year the film was released. The original owner's family reconstructed the eatery that the pilots had frequented and that later became the model for Yamamoto Tomiko's establishment in the film. The building is denoted as the Hotaru Museum, dedicated to the local woman, Torihama Tome, who took care of the pilots during the war, much like Tomiko in the film, and told the stories about them (including the story in which Lieutenant Miyagawa returned as a firefly) to the local people as well as to the media in the postwar. The film producers attempt to complicate the relationship between Tomiko and the deceased pilots through the scene of her farewell gathering. However, her complicity in the wartime efforts in the film is completely absent in the interior of the Hotaru Museum, which sparsely displays objects, photos, and information panels that present Torihama Tome as the proprietor of the kamikazes' memories. Her personal association with the pilots appears to render her the moral authority to speak about them. (Ishihara Shintarō, presently the governor of Tokyo, was among the prominent figures who visited Chiran in the 1980s to listen to what Tome had to say about the kamikaze pilots.) Although the museum tries to emulate the somber effects of the Peace Museum, it is not a space where one contemplates the kamikazes' lives and deaths. Tomi's motherly figure transforms the

Figure 4.4. "Auntie Kamikaze's Inn." Chiran, Kagoshima. (Photo by the author, May 2003.)

kamikazes' ghastly memories into images that are much easier to consume.

Tome's images are for sale in the nearby Tomiya Inn, which was built on the lot adjacent to the original eatery in 1952 to accommodate the bereaved families of the pilots visiting Chiran. The inn's business has been dependent on the town's historical claim to the kamikaze and on the Peace Museum's increasing national eminence since the mid-1980s. Tome's granddaughter-in-law, who runs the inn, is more than willing to speak about Tome's larger-than-life dedication to the pilots and the communities.[17] Although Tome may indeed have been as wise and conscientious as her relative and other defenders claim, the images of the kamikaze's mother in the quotidian sphere of life (her belongings are preserved in a special room upstairs) similarly encases the pilots' lives in a domestic space. The figure of a fictive mother not only domesticates but also helps to commercialize the image of kamikaze. At the entrance of the inn is a three-piece shop curtain *(noren)* with the name Tomiya written on the two outside pieces. The centerpiece features a pictorial representation of Hamashima Tome who stands against Japan's rising-sun national flag. The writing over her reads: "Auntie Kamikaze's Inn" *(tokkō obasan no yado)* (Figure 4.4). As one walks into the inn, one sees the same visual image presented on a panel screen except that the writing on it describes Lieutenant Miyagawa's return as a firefly: "After saying 'Auntie, I will come back tomorrow, as a firefly,' Lieutenant Miyagawa went on a mission and came back as a firefly." Another shop curtain with the same sentence covers a window on the staircase. The interior walls of the small lobby are covered with photographs and information panels describing Tome's life and her eatery. On the table across from the check-in counter lie souvenirs for the guests. There are towels that reproduce the image and the sentence on the screen, as well as keychains with a metal piece in the shape of a diminutive Torihama Tome. Tome's title on the key chains is: "The mother of the kamikaze" *(tokkō no haha)* (Figure 4.5). Tomiya Inn is certainly not the only place that tries to take advantage of the film's commercial success. There are advertisement posters in the town for sweet bean pastry and an alcoholic beverage, both of which were named "Hotaru" (firefly).

Figure 4.5. "The mother of the kamikaze" for sale. Chiran, Kagoshima. (Photo by the author, 2003.)

The name given to the food items highlights the chasm between the pilots' lives and deaths during the war and the everyday life of the present. The visitors to the Peace Museum for Kamikaze Pilots, who are reminded of the tragic end of the kamikaze through their images and writings, safely return to the quotidian life, where they are urged to consume but not contemplate the kamikaze. The film *Hotaru* assists this domestication and commercialization of the kamikaze. By deploying local memories (which were already being nationally recognized though other media), *Hotaru* authenticates its historical claim. The national prominence of the film in turn gave credence to the local tale of fireflies and the woman who spoke about them. In this circular relationship between the local and the national, the figures of the kamikaze disappear or are literalized as museum pieces. Devoid of historical content, the kamikazes are reduced to symbols that circulate in Japan's cultural market.

An Insect Is Sometimes Just an Insect

Also published in *Kinema Junpō*, Yamane Sadao's essay is critical of the filmmakers' assumption that they are capable of sufficiently capturing historical reality through the medium of film: they deploy historical information to give their work an appearance of historical reality in order to enhance its sentimental value. Yamane also emphasizes that, through the powerful images of the famous actor Takakura Ken, who played Shūji, the film transforms painful personal experiences that are often difficult to articulate into a communal tale that can be easily shared.[18] Although Yamane's criticism points out the film's problematic relation with historical reality, his voice belongs to a minority that maintain a critical distance from the film's representational tactics. Yamane's review of *Hotaru* is also perhaps too short and cryptic to effectively resist the film's ideological appeal.[19]

The nonfiction writer Ishimaru Gen-show counters the film's effects better in his nonfiction work, *Kamikaze* (2001), though he does not directly address the film. Through descriptions of his own fantastic encounter with a former kamikaze pilot, the book humorously renders the author's criticism toward the overtly sentimental treatment of the kamikaze, while insisting that the dead, whether humans or insects, have no monopoly over the meaning of the kamikazes' deaths. Ishimaru detests the oppressive weight of the kamikaze tales that define the proper way to narrate the kamikaze's life and experiences. Although the pilots were afraid of death and mired by worldly concerns, their more human struggles have largely been absent within the postwar discourse on the kamikaze. Ishimaru's book tries to bring the larger-than-life images of the kamikaze back to human scale by foregrounding ordinary aspects of their lives—their fear of death and their sexual drive. Ishimaru's use of colloquialism is a calculated move to bring the kamikaze closer to contemporary readers' experiences and to emphasize that the kamikaze were ordinary men who happened to find themselves in an impossible situation.

The final chapter of Ishimaru's book revolves around the interview that he conducts with a kamikaze survivor and his wife in Kyushu. Ishimaru and his driver are lost in the mountains on their way to the interviewees' house. After trying for hours, they are driving in the mountains where dusk turns to pitch dark. A firefly suddenly appears in front of their car, and the driver decides to follow it as he mentions the myth of the kamikaze and the fireflies. Amazingly, the insect leads them to a small house tucked away from the mountain road. At this point of the book, Ishimaru seems sympathetic to the myth. Yet it turns out that this episode prepares for an irreverent ending to the book.

As his interview with the couple nears its conclusion, the wife of the kamikaze survivor suddenly notices a firefly fly into the room. Given the strange way in which his driver has found their house, and the feeling of empathy he has toward the ex-kamikaze's tales, the writer is almost willing to accept the connection between the fireflies and the deceased kamikaze pilots. It is a beautiful sight. The wife begins to talk about the myth, which the film *Hotaru* has helped to popularize. Ishimaru then makes an awkward discovery that the insect that she points at is not a firefly, but actually a moth. It shines from the reflection. Obviously the wife cannot tell the difference because of her weakening eyesight. After a moment of thought, Ishimaru internally settles the issue though a Buddhist-like egalitarian view of life:

> It doesn't have to be a firefly! There is no way that being a "firefly" is correct and being a "moth" is wrong. Be it a firefly or a moth, they are both living creatures! The aestheticization of kamikaze stories, and the deification of kamikaze pilots are absolutely

wrong. We are also mistaken if we believe or are convinced that kamikaze pilots must be reincarnated as fireflies, something beautiful, and must not be born again as earthworms, moths, water skippers, or such creatures . . . Therefore, I've got no problem that the bug that flew through the window was actually a moth.

The moth, as it finished greeting us all, flies over to a wall in a dark corner and rests its wings. It looks like a plane that has just made an emergency landing. It is a really tiny insect that is not good at flying a long distance but tries to live to its full capacity.[20]

While rejecting the aestheticization of the kamikaze legacies, Ishimaru accepts that there is something that connects the dead to the living. What he questions is the aesthetic hierarchy that naturalizes the value of the kamikazes' sacrifices. It is the arrogance of the living that assumes that the kamikaze must be reincarnated as a beautiful insect. Many pilots were forced to make emergency landings on their way to Okinawa, unable to complete their mission because of their outdated, ill-conditioned planes. Their anguish in surviving the missions was incompatible with any aesthetic representation. Perhaps the unimpressive appearance of a moth is appropriate to the struggling life and death of the kamikaze.

Ishimaru, who attains an internal peace through this religious mediation, experiences another turmoil as the wife performs an unexpected act. As she is about to see the party off, she finds the same moth that she has earlier mistaken as a firefly at the doorway. Realizing that it is just a moth, she squishes it with her fingers. After the initial surprise and confusion caused by her unexpected behavior, Ishimaru finds this baroque moment wonderful, since it transforms his own sentimentalism into a farce. Realizing what has happened, he suddenly feels that he is living and enjoying his life. This final scene literally squishes the insect that naturalizes the kamikaze tales, and thus lifts the moral burden, or the ascribed way to relate to the dead kamikaze, from him. The episode of the squished moth appropriately concludes Ishimaru's book. In his mind, the act that kills the moth also squishes the beautiful tale of the kamikaze/firefly that reduced the kamikaze experiences to the moment of their death. The kamikazes' experiences are valuable to him not because of the way in which they died but because of the way in which they lived and desired to live under brutal conditions.

Ishimaru's writing insists that there is no one proper way of understanding the multivalence of kamikaze tales. The film *Hotaru* offers a reading that is noticeably different from the preceding cultural representations of kamikaze in that it emphasizes the second death of kamikaze in Japan in the 1990s, after the death of Hirohito. The deaths do not occur in 1945, but belatedly arrive in the late 1980s and 1990s. The filmmakers acknowledge that the postwar may have been dominated by a heavy silence but were not devoid of war memories. *Hotaru* is an attempt to surface what was repressed in order to conclude the postwar through listening to the voices of the survivors. But, the film still anchors its narrative in deaths: war memories are dug out only to be reburied. The postwar experiences of the survivors are portrayed as mere shadows of the war and war deaths, and postwar history as a struggle with the past that ends with the deaths of the protagonists. They all heroically accept their deaths, which define the cinematic narrative of *Hotaru*. Death also concludes Ishimaru's tale. This death, however, which accidentally falls through the chasm of its discursive meaning, undermines the imaginary unity between the living and the dead. The dead moth reminds the reader that the meaning of death, even that of "heroic" death, emerges only through the living's act of interpretation.

~ 5

Lost Men and War Criminals

Public Intellectuals at Yasukuni Shrine

ANN SHERIF

WHEN FORMER VICE PRESIDENT Richard Nixon visited Japan in
1953, the Japanese government suggested Yasukuni Shrine, where Japanese war dead are enshrined, as part of his itinerary. Although it is
customary for foreign dignitaries to pay tribute to the war dead of their
allies, Nixon refused the invitation after he learned of Yasukuni's central role in State Shintō and militarism.[1]

In wartime Japan, soldiers in the imperial military left for the front,
having been taught that brave sacrifice on the battlefield would earn
them a place as *kami* (deities) at Yasukuni. Nixon's refusal to go to Yasukuni prompted the Japanese government to plan the construction of
Chidorigafuchi National Grave for the Unknown Soldiers, a secular
memorial where the remains of soldiers who perished on the Asian
continent are buried.

Half a century later, however, Chidorigafuchi greets few mourners,
and cowers in the shadow of tall buildings constructed on its perimeters.
Although the prime minister and the imperial family visit occasionally,
Chidorigafuchi is abstract, cold, and lacking in symbolism of mourning
or national memories. In contrast, Yasukuni Shrine, though once rejected by an American vice president, and cut off from direct government funding since the time of the Occupation, has flourished. Perhaps
more than any other site in Japan, the shrine has, throughout the
postwar era, been the focus of debate about Japan's culture and role in

the international community. Domestically and internationally, many constituencies have asserted their views on issues surrounding Yasukuni Shrine, which include the separation of religion and state, Japan's lack of resolution about its imperialist and militarist past, and the control of the memories of war and sacrifice for the nation. Here, I focus on the career of Etō Jun, a public intellectual who was prominent in the Yasukuni controversy during the 1980s and 1990s.

The end of the Cold War marked a turning point in the uses of Yasukuni Shrine. During the Cold War, progressive organizations and citizens argued that the Japanese government should cease in its support of a religious institution that had functioned as an integral part of Japan's imperialism and militarism in the first half of the twentieth century. Despite the provisions in the postwar constitution for separation of church and state, conservative forces, including the ruling Liberal Democratic Party (LDP) and the main organization of bereaved families, persisted in pushing for government support of the shrine because of the need to honor those who died in the "Greater East Asian War" in a manner consistent with what they regarded as the continuity of Japanese culture. Thus, the public debate during the Cold War focused primarily on defining Japan's imperial and militarist past under the postwar peace constitution, because there was, for official purposes, no present or future war at issue. The post–Cold War system, however, presented Japan with the jolting—some would say reprehensible—prospect of becoming a nation capable of waging war.

Post–Cold War Japan faces new challenges in defining its place in the international community. As a close ally of the United States, Japan found itself compelled during the first Gulf War to make a public shift away from its long-standing posture of military nonintervention. This was not, however, such a drastic shift as the image of popular peace-loving, democratic Japan suggested. Since the mid-1980s administration of Prime Minister Nakasone Yasuhiro, a frequent visitor to Yasukuni, LDP-led administrations pushed through the revival of the rising-sun flag and the national anthem as officially approved symbols of the nation, and pressed for official visits to Yasukuni. Despite bitter complaints from other East Asian governments, Prime Minister Koizumi Jun'ichirō persisted in visiting the shrine. In 2006, one of Koizumi's final acts as prime minister was his official visit to the shrine on August 15, the anniversary of the end of World War II, in proud defiance of domestic and international criticism. Though the government's actions may seem initially a mere manipulation of national signs, these policies and practices were also intimately linked to reforms in the educational system (both strict government control of textbooks and curriculum and the compulsory use of the flag and national anthem in school functions).[2]

Seemingly in response to criticism from China and Korea about his visits to Yasukuni, Prime Minister Koizumi developed a new interest in plans for yet another government-supported memorial for the war dead. Yet, as the Koizumi regime's dispatch of Self-Defense Forces to Iraq suggests, the new facility may not be designed to mollify the anger of the victims of Japan's past deeds, or to affirm the postwar peace constitution. For whom would this new memorial be built? Those who die in Japan's future wars?[3] Some critics regarded such policies as part of a long-term project to transform Japan into a "nation that wages war" (*sensō o suru kuni, tatakau kuni*).[4] Tighter control of school curricula, combined with the linking of Japanese national and cultural identity with war at evocative sites such as Yasukuni and the manipulation of potent symbols such as the flag and anthem, would create citizens not only willing to die for their country, but also willing to vote for the repeal of Article 9 of the Japanese Constitution, which bans Japan from waging offensive war.[5]

Although there are those in the United States and Japan who have urged the remilitarization of Japan since soon after the end of World War II, one should not underestimate the alarm with which progressives and even mainstream organizations and individuals in Japan regarded this move to toss out the peace constitution, and Japan's special place as an advocate for peace in a war-torn world. China and Korea, among other Asian countries, also expressed great concern at the prospect of a remilitarized Japan, in large part because Japan has never really made amends for its imperialist militarism during the first half of the twentieth century. In the post–Cold War era, Yasukuni Shrine increasingly stood as a symbol of Japan as future warrior, rather than as a symbol of a defeated nation insistent on honoring its martial past.

Etō Jun and Yasukuni

In a pluralistic society with an active public sphere such as Japan, we must take into consideration not only the state's role in fashioning memories of war and the nation, but also that of other significant "agents of public memory."[6] Japan's vigorous debate about Yasukuni Shrine was carried on in the mass media, and featured influential "outsider public men" such as Etō Jun (1932–99).[7] A literary critic and political advisor, Etō played an important role in the rancorous public discourse concerning Japan's war responsibility and Japan's relations with the United States and Asia, especially in the aftermath of the Cold War. As part of the unresolved controversy over Japan's national identity and future political course, Etō appreciated the uses of the media, the importance of literature, and the weight of personal emotions and the individual in the national work of public mourning.

From the 1950s until his death in 1999, Etō questioned the dominant notion that Japan's democratic postwar politics and culture represented an unproblematic liberation from an irredeemably evil past, with Nobel Prize novelist Ōe Kenzaburō as one of his principal opponents. It was not the wrongdoings of the Empire of Japan that he refuted. Rather, Etō singled out for criticism the means used by the Allied victors to make Japan anew as well as American hypocrisy about its own righteousness.

No Memories of the Glorious War

The triumphalist narrative of World War II, which describes the United States as morally and politically righteous both in the means and outcome of its battle with the evils of Axis fascism, dominates American public memory. Despite—or perhaps because of—the contentious debates and widespread protest over the Vietnam War, the media and popular imagination have understood America's World War II as a "Good War," often without a touch of irony. U.S. presidents have compared subsequent American military engagements with World War II as a means of elevating and justifying their mission. In the face of this powerful discourse, coupled with growing U.S. military and economic might throughout the Cold War and even greater hegemony afterwards, governments and citizens of former Axis nations have been compelled to construct coherent narratives of their discredited past and to seek moral and political redemption.[8] Germany, defeated and fully discredited in World War II, has engaged in meaningful critique of the moral and political meanings of its fascist history.[9]

Japan, in contrast, still engages in public and contentious debate, largely because the state and certain sectors of the populace have been reticent about disavowing the imperial militarist past. These continuing conflicts over Japan's collective memories of the first half of the twentieth century, moreover, have resulted in troubled relations with other Asian countries and in enervating domestic controversy. The battle over Yasukuni Shrine in Tokyo, where dead combatants from Japan's modern wars are enshrined (including Class A war criminals from World War II), reveals most vividly the nature of this entangled and unsatisfactory narrative of Japan's past.[10] Since the end of the Cold War, China, Korea, and other Asian countries have been increasingly vocal about reparations and war crimes, bringing to harsh light the contradictions of war and memory in Japan. The increasingly likely possibility of Japan's remilitarization and constitutional revision exacerbates these debates over Yasukuni, which have grown in prominence since the end of the Cold War.

Before examining Etō's role in advocating for Yasukuni, I will consider the space and meanings of the shrine itself, and especially the museum on its ground, because Etō's opinions on the significance of Yasukuni resonate in many ways with the place. Although many citizens, intellectuals, and the media utterly reject Etō's views of Yasukuni and of Japanese culture, there are many, including the powerful forces in the government, who rely on respectable intellectuals to articulate certain visions of Japan's culture and morality.

Faces of the "Glorious Dead" at Yasukuni

The imposing, monumental structure of Yasukuni Shrine, its towering torii gate, and the adjacent Yūshūkan Museum form an integral part of the Tokyo's landscape. Bordering on the moat that surrounds the imperial palace, Yasukuni sits on prime real estate in the middle of the city. The central shrine buildings contain no images or icons visible to the public. The Yūshūkan Museum, however, features not only examples of the machinery of war and empire (from train engines to Zero airplanes) but also photographs, hundreds of black-and-white portraits of the war dead. In three galleries, these photographs, arranged edge to edge, cover panels on the walls. The Yūshūkan pictures show the faces of the young men (and a very few women) in an attempt to humanize the now-enshrined deities, *Yasukuni no kamigami*.[11] Visitors see the war dead as alert and alive, dressed in their uniforms and caps, not bloodied and dismembered on the battlefield. It is these perfect, very young men who have been lost, and who, the museum suggests, have returned to Yasukuni. The lost men appear as clean and unscathed as the fighter planes, tanks, and anti-aircraft guns that occupy the other rooms of the museum.[12]

For one young soldier, who died on April 10, 1945 in the battle of Okinawa, the museum displays an elaborate bride doll given decades later by his 84-year-old mother, for he died a single man.[13] In one sense, the inclusion of this bride doll at Yasukuni recalls the common practice in historical museums of showing personal belongings in order to bring the large movements of history down to an individual scale, and to evoke feelings of empathy in the viewer. To offer another example, the well-known display of a schoolgirl's lunch box at the Peace Museum in Hiroshima accomplishes these goals, and also suggests the ways that total war reached beyond the battlefield and invaded everyday life. On examining the battered, charred metal lunch box, the viewer assumes correctly that the owner of the box perished in the A-bomb blast. There is no photograph of the girl's face. The Yasukuni bride doll differs in its effect on the viewer in an important way: not only is there a photograph of the young man, but the existence of a bridegroom is also assumed. He would be one of the apotheosized "glorious war dead," waiting in a mysterious realm for his bride. Wartime rhetoric encouraged this understanding of the fate of deceased combatants: comrades in arms pledged that they would meet again at Yasukuni. Even in the 1980s, the elderly mother who donated the doll, four decades after her son's death, remembered him saying proudly to her as he left for the front, "the next time you see me will be at Yasukuni."[14]

If the main shrine appears a repetition of expected shrine architecture, and suggests little about the unique status of Yasukuni as the principal shrine of the cult of the war dead, the Yūshūkan museum is lavish in its presentation of every type of fighter plane, suicide torpedo, and tank the dead combatants may have ridden in; of maps detailing every path and byway they may have trod upon and every front where they may have fought; of every kind of uniform they may have worn; of every cannon, rifle, and anti-aircraft weapon they may have fired.

As presented by this museum, war arises not from politics, greed, or diplomatic failures, but from Japan's glorious warriors and their honorable history. The first two galleries educate the visitor about "Japan's Martial History" (samurai armor and swords) and "The Heart of the Military Man" (poems on the topic of war by emperors ancient and modern), as if military affairs could be detached from other aspects of society and culture, as art, as honorable code. The Yūshūkan's evocation of a link between the samurai past and ancient Shintō is clearly anachronistic. The claim, however, can be traced back to the late-nineteenth- and early-twentieth-century project of constructing a modern tradition of Bushidō, the way of the warrior, and, furthermore, of linking it with the nation's modern military establishment.

In the museum at Yasukuni, other rooms detail Japan's involvement in its modern military conflicts: the Meiji Restoration, the Sino-Japanese War, the Russo-Japanese War, World War II, the "China Incident," and the "Greater East Asian War." That this museum's coverage extends only back to the mid-nineteenth century reminds us that Yasukuni Shrine is a modern institution, invented for the purpose of enshrining the war dead from these conflicts. From the Meiji period through 1945, State Shintō evolved as part of the formation of the modern nation-state and the empire. The emperor-as-god, in whose name soldiers died and whose deified ancestors formed the imperial lineage, symbolized the fusion of religion and state. Those who perished in Japan's modern wars were promised the status of "heroic spirit" as a result of enshrinement in Yasukuni, which became the sole site of the new cult of the war dead.

Yasukuni thus should not be considered a site of tradition in a sea of modernity. Rather, the Yūshūkan affirms the idea that State Shintō (up to 1945) was as an integral part of Japan's modernity: in Harootunian's words "the rearticulation of a religious memory in institutional form constituted a condition of modern, secular society, not a rejection of it."[15] Indeed, Hardacre reminds us of the modernity of Shintō as a centrally organized practice: "in an institutional sense, Shintō has no legitimate claim to antiquity as Japan's 'indigenous religion,' however frequently the claim is made."[16] Further complicating the status of Shintō is the attempt on the part of the various constituencies to identify Shintō as a non-religion, in order to circumvent the constitutional separation of religion and politics. The official visits of prime ministers to the shrine, as well as tacit government support for this costly and centrally located museum and in its glorification of war, highlight the refusal of the LDP-led government to invest in a secular memorial for the war dead that would present the lessons of "their sacrifice and suffering" and the causes and horrors of war.[17]

After the war, the Occupation severed the financial and official political ties between the government and Shintō shrines, both by Occupation directive and in the postwar constitution. However, over the half-century and more since the Occupation, a combination of constituencies, including the Shintō priesthood, bereaved family association *(Izokukai)*, and the LDP-dominated government has tried persistently to revive various types of official state support for the shrine.[18] The shrine and its allies claim that Yasukuni and Shintō itself are "non-religious." Defenders of the Shrine have attempted to define it broadly as an aspect of Japanese culture.

Attempts to regain government support for the shrine have long met with public criticism and lawsuits, based on the constitutional separation of church and state, and plans to make the government financially responsible for the maintenance of the shrine have failed. The efforts to renew the official bonds between state and shrine became especially controversial when it was revealed that Class A war criminals, executed after the Tokyo War Crimes Trials, had been enshrined at Yasukuni in 1978 and, furthermore, that Yasukuni defended these men as heroes who had been falsely accused of criminal acts on the world stage. Despite the failure of Yasukuni promoters in courts of law, however, the older vision of the shrine's symbolic meanings and uses still, surprisingly, retains cultural viability for significant segments of the public and the state. The Yūshūkan Museum especially reveals the conservative aim of reviving "prewar State Shintō's symbolism."[19] As suggested by the museum's anachronistic use of Imperial Japan's phrase, "The Greater East Asian War," the historical narrative presented on the shrine's grounds extols Japan's empire-building and militarism in the first half of the twentieth century.

The Postwar, Literature, and Myself

A brilliant literary and cultural critic, Etō defined the postwar as an "age of loss." Although he was a university professor, Etō found a broad audience for his views of the postwar period by his constant presence in the media. Part of Etō's acute sense of loss stemmed from his nostalgia for what he saw as the origins of Japan's modernity in the Meiji period, a pattern of thinking linked to his life-long study of Meiji novelist and intellectual Natsume Sōseki, as well to as his own formerly prominent family.[20] Etō also articulated the concept that postwar Japanese discourse had been rendered a "closed linguistic space" (the now famous phrase, *tozasareta gengo kūkan*) by the Occupation and especially by its censorship policies and practices.[21] He accused the Occupation, and Japan's dependent relationship on the United States, of irreparably warping Japanese discourse and robbing Japanese writers of autonomy and authenticity.[22] Etō found a broad audience for his critique of America's long and forbidding "shadow," especially in the 1970s and 1980s as the strength of the Japanese economy encouraged the ideas of "Japan as Number 1" and the "Japan that Can Say 'No'." He lived in the United States, traveled widely in Europe, and had long relationships with many American scholars. An authoritative amateur historian and political commentator, Etō carried out research on the Occupation and censorship in Washington, D.C. archives. Despite his intimacy with the United States, over the course of his career, Etō's "search for a real 'Japan' imagined against the mirror of America" took on an increasingly "essentializing and ominous tone."[23]

For nearly fifty years, Etō manipulated with great skill his position as an "outsider public man," so that his words were, without fail, prominently featured in the media and critiqued in academic circles. His friends and enemies included thinkers of every stripe. He wrote about great men (though few women) and debated with prominent intellectuals and writers. After Etō's death in 1999, major cultural and political figures of the day made public tributes to him.

Since the 1950s, critic Karatani Kōjin points out, Japanese writers have been compelled to foster a public persona, to "live publicly, and die publicly," precisely because of the participatory democracy decreed by the victors. They were also faced with the dilemma of reconciling the contradictions between their public and private selves.[24] Under a capitalist democracy, the writer needed not only to sell himself in the media, but also, as a celebrity citizen, to have an opinion about public affairs. Certainly Etō, perhaps even more than his contemporaries Ōe

Kenzaburō and novelist and politician Ishihara Shintarō, succeeded over the five decades of his career in living and writing as a public person. Etō made his private self into his public self, exploring his family history; his travels abroad, and, perhaps most significantly, his deeply felt emotions, in full view of his readers and the media. His publications during the final year of his life exemplify this fusion of the personal and the public. He wrote an intensely personal book called *My Wife and Myself,* and an essay about official visits by prime ministers to Yasukuni Shrine and the shrine's connection to Japanese culture.

While Etō's sad final years may suggest a cranky old man with marginal political opinions, he was in no way an anomaly. Some younger literary critics, such as Katō Norihiro, also advocated for Yasukuni and expressed stridently nationalistic views during the 1990s. Etō created a distinctive brand of nationalism by fashioning an affective field that emphasized individual psychology and empathy, and that validated a melancholy sense of loss as the fate of Japan after its defeat and Occupation, a Japan that did not resolve those traumatic events and thus did not develop a healthy nationalism.[25] Over the course of his career, Etō explored large political and social issues, but always with a personal voice and with an emphasis on emotion. One important sign of this validation of the personal was a series of texts that include the phrase "—*to watashi*" (—and I/myself). As Tanaka Kazuo notes, in the titles of these well known essays from the 1960s and 1970s, Etō juxtaposes "I" with words and concepts with which *watashi* is not usually paired: formidable opponents (or companions?) such as literature, the United States, and "the postwar."[26] The unexpressed title of many of the other texts he wrote subsequently might well have been "Japan and Myself," always a work in progress.[27]

The "I" of the titles is the "I" that frequently voices its distress over this "age of loss" (*sōshitsu no jidai*).[28] What had been lost? Many things, all connected with the defeat, and the Occupation, and, to a lesser extent, the capitalist consumerism of prosperous Japan. But most of all, Japan lost its sense of certainty, authority, and national pride. In Etō's imagination, the age of his grandfather—the Meiji period—was a time when Japan determined its own destiny. The affective field that he offered to readers was one in which I/you felt loss deeply and on many levels. In addition to these "personal tales," Etō devoted himself to scholarly studies of Occupation period censorship, the postwar surrender and constitution, provocative essays about U.S.-Japan relations, and compelling literary criticism.[29]

Much of Etō's admiration for the supposed cultural authenticity of Meiji found its roots in his deep knowledge of literature, especially the career and texts of the greatly revered and still widely read novelist Natsume Sōseki. Part of Etō's admiration for the early-twentieth-century writer arose from a shared conviction about the importance of literature to the nation. Sōseki also had broadly social concerns, such as the potential abuse of power and the meanings of individualism for his age. But Sōseki was a man who, after living in Europe around the turn of the century in order to study English literature, discovered that his voice belonged to Japan, that his place was in molding a new, modern Japanese literature. Etō's own journey to America in the 1960s similarly solidified his pride in Japanese literature and criticism. Even before he went to Princeton, Etō railed against contemporary Japanese critics for their denigration of Japan's sense of morality and of the country's literary past and present. In response to claims that Japan's postwar literature was no more than entertainment and Japanese morals were flimsy, Etō responded emphatically that literature had a social and ethical role, and championed the works of contemporary authors whom he saw as contributing to postwar society.[30]

With his contemporary, novelist Ōe Kenzaburō, Etō shared this conviction about the social significance of literature, reading, and criticism and the responsibilities of the writer. Yet Etō and Ōe expressed profoundly different understandings of the postwar democracy and late capitalist society of which literature was a part. It is illuminating to recall the contrast between Etō's view of the postwar as an "age of loss" and Japanese literature as having been victimized and derailed by the Occupation, and Ōe Kenzaburō's celebration of postwar democracy and literature.[31] Etō, while supporting democracy and the rights guaranteed by the postwar constitution, perceived a loss of control and authenticity as a huge sacrifice that should be acknowledged and dealt with. The contradictions that he had witnessed in U.S. society in the 1960s—including violent racial strife and Kennedy's assassination—made him question the victor's righteous rhetoric of equality and liberty. In contrast, Ōe recalled his childhood pride upon hearing the words of his teacher: Japan was the country chosen for democracy and the renunciation of war. With those words, Ōe's feelings of humiliation and inferiority in the wake of Japan's defeat were transformed into a flush of superiority and joy.[32] The positions of these two literary figures, in turn, echoed larger intellectual debates about the significance of Japan's postwar society.[33]

Redeeming Lost Men

If Ōe considered himself found by democracy, then Etō counted himself among the lost. Certain habits of thought that characterized Etō's career as a successful critic help to explain his idiosyncratic stances—including his support of official prime ministerial visits to Yasukuni. Although Etō was utterly thorough in his inclusion of factual evidence and long quotes from texts as evidence to prove his opinions, his narratives also depended on ellipses. He piled up text after text about collective memory in the postwar and the war dead, but wrote little or nothing about the horrors of the empire, the uses of State Shintō in wartime, or the agony of battle. Wielding his deep knowledge of literature and literary theory, Etō managed to turn arguments away from the military and political and, when it suited his purpose, emphasized the cultural instead. So too, in his writings on Yasukuni, he explained the controversy as not political, but literary, spiritual, and cultural in nature.

A central trope in Etō's literary criticism is the lost man: a man caught up in historical circumstances beyond his control and thus disoriented and uncertain of his identity. His writings about Yasukuni share this concern because they imagine Yasukuni as a final resting place for the dead, the Japanese soldiers otherwise lost between the unforgiving world of the living and an otherwise undefined world of the dead. I can find no phrase in Etō's writings that corresponds precisely to lost men, but the image is evident in both his writings about prewar and postwar literature.

When he addressed literary works written after the war, Etō focused his praise on the characters in the postwar fiction of Kojima Nobuo, Yasuoka Shōtaro, and Endō Shūsaku. With the defeat in 1945 and regime changes of the Cold War decades, the men featured in their novels included shameful fathers, confused and alienated sons, men haunted by nightmares of the war and growing up in the days of empire.[34] These characters, all lost men, felt estranged from the bright promise of the postwar, as did Etō. These fictional men were disoriented and found scant comfort in the democratic project. As an influential critic who wrote constantly for newspapers and many widely circulated journals, Etō championed these postwar novels from the 1950s through the 1970s.

One of Etō's initial motives for writing may have been to resuscitate lost men, as is evident in his debut essay on Natsume Sōseki that appeared soon after the end of the Allied Occupation, when the critical establishment was engaged in the project of defining a new literary canon for the postwar era. It now is difficult to imagine that Sōseki, a novelist and critic whose face graces Japanese currency, would ever have been in need of rescue. Yet Etō wrote incessantly about Sōseki as a means of ensuring that Sōseki and his skepticism about the project of modernity would never be lost. Sōseki was erudite, cosmopolitan, and a profound thinker, but he was also, in a sense, an innocent, having died before the Russian Revolution and the most obvious abuses of Japanese militarism and expansionism.[35] Like Etō, Sōseki regarded literature as central to the life of the nation.

Absolving the Dead's Sin

In Etō's imagination, this constellation of images of lost men was not restricted to literature, but also includes the war dead at Yasukuni Shrine. From the 1970s, Etō increasingly questioned the shift from what he defined as the Japanese narrative of the relationship between the living and the dead to "someone else's" narratives. Etō's quest to find lost men—the dead—found expression in his pronouncements on Yasukuni Shrine, but also related to practices in print culture and the mass media.

For example, Etō advocated literature and journalism as proper sites for remembering the war dead:

> Why is it not acceptable for Japanese to tell stories *(monogatari o kataru)* about that war in accordance to the perspective of the Japanese side? Is it because Japan lost the war thirty-four years ago? Must the people of the defeated nation eternally chant the praise of the supreme commander and presidents of the victorious na-

tion? If that is the case, by whom will the spirits of the many Japanese who died in that war be remembered? It is acceptable to have a special place in our memories for those who died in Hiroshima and Nagasaki. May we not remember the other dead as well? And who decided that it would be this way? There are those who heap scorn on our efforts to remember, but who do they think granted them the authority to do so? If this [suppression of memory of the war dead] is the rule in contemporary literature and journalism, then the situation is not merely that of suppression of free speech. It is the crushing to death *(assatsu)* of literature.[36]

Note Etō's metaphoric evocation of literature as a living thing, threatened always by the movements in larger society. In his thinking, literature, as the narrative of a people, was of even greater significance than freedom of speech. Etō found a way to bring literature into discussions of politics and diplomacy, as is shown by this quotation from his 1979 essay on Japan's diplomatic relations with Vichy France and free France during World War II. In this essay, Etō wrote as an amateur historian, an identity gained through his own extensive writings about the Constitution, diplomatic relations, censorship, and politics, as well as through the relentless public debates in the media with other intellectuals and writers. On face value, it is difficult to dispute Etō's challenge that Japan should find an acceptable means for public remembrance of all who died in the war, not only the privileged victims of the opening shots of the nuclear age.[37] Many readers, however, heartily disagreed with Etō's claim that only one "Japanese way" of remembering exists, as they also resisted conservative initiatives to narrow narratives of history through manipulation of textbooks and the popularization of pro-militarist, anti-Semitic or anti-Korean diatribes in the medium of the comic *manga* (as in the case of Kobayashi Yoshinori). Yet, part of Etō's ability to hold his readers' attention, no matter their political beliefs, came from his constant appeal to the vitality of the literary field.

Given the widespread outrage, both in Japan and abroad, against public visits by Japanese Prime Ministers to Yasukuni Shrine, the central locus of war memories, it might come as a surprise that Etō could defend such regressive modes of remembering and public mourning. Japan is a nation where patriotism has, until the post–Cold War era, been often equated with the extreme right-wing fringe, and nationalism itself is often suspect. Other intellectuals of Etō's stature pressed hard for a clear reckoning over war responsibility. They condemned the Cold War silencing of the transgressions of Japan's imperial past, especially those arising from its fusion of religion and the state, as embodied by the never-purged Shōwa emperor and the official state visits to Yasukuni Shrine. In the end, Etō turned out to be one of the central agents condoning the ministerial visits, and he contributed to reinforcing a particular understanding of the link between the living and the dead.[38]

In the eyes of many, he ended up on the wrong side of the debate. Unlike the fringe ultra-right-wing activists who donned pseudo-military uniforms and gathered at Yasukuni, or rode around in trucks, loudly haranguing Tokyoites about "love of the country" with bullhorns, Etō dwelled in the center of culture, politics, and especially the media, and was much appreciated as a literary critic. Until his death, he published constantly, hobnobbed with powerful politicians, and maintained his reputation as one of the postwar's most distinguished literary critics.

Neo-nationalism and Shades of Conservatism

In 1999, the year of his death, Etō's essay "The *Kokoro* (heart, essence) of Mourning for the War Dead" (hereafter, *Kokoro*) appeared in a book entitled *The Prayers of Yasukuni (Yasukuni no inori)*, designed to commemorate the 130th anniversary of the founding of Yasukuni Shrine. In this brief piece, prominently featured on the first page of the book, Etō justified the practice of public visits by prime ministers to Yasukuni Shrine, but did not allude to the controversial nature of the practice.

The essay reveals the blindness and insight that enabled Etō to advocate for Yasukuni as the premier and righteous site of memory for post–Cold War Japan. Though brief, the essay is a distillation of Etō's later thought, which he sought to communicate with the public. The publication and marketing of the volume in which "Kokoro" appeared indicate the extent to which Etō's message figured in the mainstream of public discourse. The book *Prayers of Yasukuni* is a collection of photographs of the shrine and its precinct, as well as of the contents of the war museum Yūshūkan. The volume also contains text describing the

history of the shrine and the visits of distinguished visitors, both foreign and Japanese. The shrine kiosk, located directly across from the
main shrine structure and on the path to the Yūshūkan, stocks the
book, as does the gift shop inside the museum. In contrast to most
books about Yasukuni, which are published by the Shrine itself, *Yasukuni no inori* was produced by a mainstream publisher and aimed at a
broad audience.

This was not Etō's first foray into studies of Yasukuni, for he
coedited an anthology of essays about the shrine in the mid-1980s with
the right-wing scholar Kobori Keiichirō.[39] Published at the height of
the furor over Prime Minister Nakasone Yasuhiro's 1985 public visit to
Yasukuni, the 1986 anthology attempted to bring a historical perspective to Yasukuni and its ties to government in the postwar era.

Unlike Kobori, whose dubious claims to scholarship include participation in the Nanjing Massacre denials, Etō, while long labeled a conservative, retained a degree of ambiguity in his ideological stance.[40] He
had little to say about the war itself, neither defending nor extolling the
militarism of the empire. Instead, he aimed at making the national loss
into something personal, in the form of the now decades-deceased war
dead. He also linked affect with bereavement—a process surprisingly
absent from the Yasukuni formula. Not coincidentally, Etō's long career as a literary critic was central to the way he defined nationalism.
By keeping in mind Etō's intellectual path as a critic, his conviction
that literature, as an integral part of civilization, has crucial social functions, and his role as an "outsider public man" (who was very close to
the inside), we can better understand his motives for writing on behalf
of Yasukuni, and the effect that his prose might have on the broad read-
ership he sought to reach. For the shrine, in turn, a contribution from
Etō to a volume in honor of the shrine's anniversary lent legitimacy in
the form of the tempered humanism of a distinguished critic.

The Emperor's Poem, or Mourning the War Dead

In his 1999 essay, Etō offers a sweeping definition of what is most important to the Japanese people, in particular the relationship between
the living and the dead in Japan. He does not allow that many fellow
citizens differ in their views on culture and on life and death. Perhaps
we can see his assertions as the crankiness of an old man, a man in

mourning for his wife, and increasingly infirm himself. As did Auden, Etō seemed to feel a need for the certainty of institutional structures late in life. The many readers who knew Etō's work from the mass media, however, would see this essay as consistent with the discourse he had created over the decades. To a broad swath of readers, whether conservative or progressive, Etō remained a writer whose words and ideas mattered, whether one agreed or not with his quest to assuage feelings of loss, and to redeem lost men even if it meant ignoring history.

Kokoro commences with a bold assertion:

> That which the Japanese people value the most, that which the Japanese people feel dearest to their hearts, is the Japanese way of life. This is something that the continuity of the country called Japan has constructed from the time of the *Kojiki*, the *Nihonshoki*, and the *Man'yōshū*. in this are accumulated our memories as individuals and our memories as a *minzoku* (a people).[41]

The essay is structured around simple yet profound pairs of difference: Japanese culture/American culture; Japanese culture/Christianity; the living and the dead; American views of the dead/Japanese views of the dead; the emperor/citizens; and individual memory/ethnic memory. It is striking that he does not mention any other Asian countries. Etō's essay is a meditation on certain large themes: memory, literature, lost men, the living and the dead, the Constitution. His straightforward style and the tight structure of his writing help to explain why readers might find his arguments convincing.

From the beginning of his essay, Etō emphasizes literary texts, in keeping with his view of the centrality of literature in society. Some of these texts function as the markers of historical time and as reminders of origins and aesthetics. Specifically, the ancient nation-founding myths in the *Kojiki* and the *Nihonshoki* indicate the beginnings of written history, and, for Etō, the starting point of the continuity of Japanese culture. These mytho-histories also describe the sun goddess Amaterasu, and the lineage of the imperial family. The *Man'yōshū*, the authoritative eighth-century poetry anthology, contains numerous poems composed by the emperors of old. By citing these particular premodern texts, the critic recalls the early modern and modern construction of a literary canon centered on ancient texts that valorized the imperial lineage (the histories), as well as the poetry of the *Man'yō* age that linked the emperor, and writing itself, with powerful masculinity and virility, rather than the supposedly feminine aesthetics of later Japanese court poetry.[42]

For Etō, *Man'yōshū* poetry communicates profound messages about the relationship between the living and the dead. He chooses to quote a classical poem composed by Kakinomoto Hitomaro (fl. ca. 680–700), who, though not an emperor, was one of the most brilliant of the anthology's poets:

Sasanami no	Though the inlet
Shiga no oowada	At Shiga in Sasanami
Yodomu to mo	Waits calmly
Mukashi no hito ni	Will we ever again meet
Mata mo awameyamo	The people of old?
(MYS, 1:31)[43]	

The speaker of the poem employs poetic place names as a means of suggesting Ōtsu, an ancient capital founded by Emperor Tenchi in 667, only to be destroyed in 672 by fire and battle. In its evocation of the passing of an age and a place, the poem is perfectly consonant with Etō's constant refrain of loss of something important in the past. On another level, Etō finds in this poem an evocation of what he calls a Japanese concern for the repose of the dead (*tamashizume*, or the contemporary term *chinkon*). This religious reading of the poem is not his idiosyncratic interpretation, or a product of canonical interpretations of the classics. Rather, Etō attributes the reading to the renowned ethnologist and folklorist Origuchi Shinobu (1887–1953), who was similarly intent on "considerations of identity and social solidarity" and a search for the "eternal essence" of Japan, as Harootunian has noted.[44] By citing a secular source (an ethnologist), Etō avoids mentioning Shintō or the priesthood. He uses Origuchi's words to articulate the religious aspect of the poem: "the poem includes the intent (*i*) to calm the spirits of the dead who had dwelled in the ancient capitol located in Shiga." Etō does not need to explain the parallel between the suggested meaning of Hitomaro's poem and the ritual of Yasukuni, the purpose of which is to ensure the repose of the spirits of the war dead (*chinkon*). In this passage, Etō projects the religious meanings of the shrine onto the literary text, and conflates religion and literature as inseparable manifestations of Japan's culture.

This identification of Shintō with Japanese *culture* is a characteristic both of modern institutional Shintō and the interpretations of prominent ethnologists such as Origuchi and Yanagita Kunio. These thinkers, and Yanagita in particular, "argued that the native religious system was an irreducibly Japanese inflection because the spirits of the dead always returned to the 'native place' to watch over their descendants from their 'unseen' mountain perspective . . . This idea conferred significance on the life of the living and offered the necessary bonding for community relationships."[45]

Of the thousands of poems in the *Man'yōshū*, Etō purposely chooses a verse that suggests both historical place (*Ōtsu* and *Shiga*) and literary place (the *utamakura* or poetic place name Sasanami), and one, furthermore, that he describes as a landscape poem "extremely rich in descriptive power." Etō also calls on the reader's modern sense of landscape and visual culture: "The landscape that Americans perceive is a landscape visible only to the living. However, the landscape that Japanese people see is different. From ancient times in Japan, there have appeared landscape poems that relate to the repose of the spirits of the dead."[46] Later in the essay, Etō relates the phenomenon of the common gaze of the living and the dead to the land, culture, and traditions of Japan, and to his novel view of the constitution. Note that the living and dead do not necessarily see each other, but together they look out upon the landscape—the land and nature that constitute the place called Japan.[47]

Ethnologist Yanagita had decades earlier emphasized the importance of the Japanese land in the union of the dead and the living, even in the postwar era: "the spirits resided in the national soil forever, [Yanagita] wrote; the belief that they did not go to a distant place had been deeply rooted since the time of antiquity and had persisted continuously down to the present . . . place became an object of worship" due to the identification of locality and deities.[48] Doubtless, Etō found inspiration in Yanagita's emphasis on a "veneration of the *kami* bonded to the household, village, and place" as, in the postwar especially, Yanagita sought a notion of "sacred place" that would remain viable despite the demise of the State Shintō.[49] Unlike Yanagita, however, Etō has little use for the

village. The consummate urbanite, he elevates the entire land of the
nation to the status of sacred, and the entire population of Japan, urban
and rural, as the descendants. In this way, he is able to expand the eth-
nological identification of locality with deity (in the service of ensuring
social solidarity) to the nation-state, and, by implication, to Yasukuni.

Ritual and Critical Thinking

The *Kokoro* essay, with its quotes from classical poetry, references to
canonical literature, and transformation of the constitution (as I will
explain below) is a digested version of a lengthy essay called "The Gaze
of the Living and the Gaze of the Dead" *("Seisha no shisen to shisha no
shisen")* published in 1986, at the height of the Yasukuni controversy
over Prime Minister Nakasone's official visit to Yasukuni and his cabinet's decision to cease such visits in the wake of criticism from China
and other Asian nations. In 1984, as public debate over Yasukuni
mounted, Nakasone formed a fifteen-member advisory board to consider the Yasukuni issue. Etō was invited to join the board, whose
members included both supporters and critics of government involvement in the shrine.[50]

In his 1986 essay, Etō reports on his participation in the advisory
board, and expresses his disappointment that its numerous meetings
focused almost exclusively on constitutional interpretation, and especially Article 20 of the Constitution, which stipulates the separation of
religion and state. In Etō's thinking, discussion of the question of official state visits to Yasukuni should include cultural issues as much as the
law. By culture, Etō refers to both literature and systems of belief. As in
the much shorter *Kokoro* essay, he quotes poetry and also emphasizes a
proper relationship between the living and the dead. It is in these practices, he writes, that Japanese culture dwells, not in interpretations of a
legal document. Commenting on a poem censored during the Occupation, he asserts that the poem has been rendered "the corpse of a
poem" by the censors. The chronotrope (*toki kūkan*, his translation of
Bahktin's term) that the poet attempted to evoke in his writing has
been extinguished by the censors, so that all that is left is a "mere
corpse of time-space, the only linguistic space that the occupiers are
willing to recognize. It is reduced merely to physical space, and is no
longer a linguistic space where literature or religion can survive."[51]

Etō clearly wrote the 1986 "Gaze" essay in reaction to contemporary social events, and his claims take on a historical tinge barely evident in the 1999 *Kokoro* essay. For example, in the earlier text, he presents the following as evidence for his claim (made in both essays) that Americans have a different concept of the dead from Japanese: not only do Christians believe that the dead leave this world to be with God, but in the 1986 *Challenger* space shuttle disaster, the United States did not even attempt to recover the bodies of the dead astronauts. Never mind that not all Americans are Christians, and there may have been no remains to retrieve after *Challenger* exploded.

While the *Kokoro* essay presents the dead in a dignified, somewhat abstract manner, and mostly in association with the memories and needs of their descendants, in the "Gaze," Etō is out and out haunted by the war dead. He reports sitting in the Prime Minister's Official Residence during one of the litigious advisory board meetings about Yasukuni and feeling that the "eyes of the war dead were staring down at us." Then he takes on a shamanistic role, virtually speaking for the dead:

> I could not help feeling that I could hear whispers of their voices, saying, "What are these people doing? Why are they having these trivial arguments? Why do they not feel a need to pray for us? Wouldn't it be the most natural thing in the world for the Prime Minister, as representative of the people of Japan, to visit Yasukuni Shrine and bow to us there? Whether he comes to bow or not, we, as the spirits of Yasukuni, are watching over the living as they pass their days. What wasted desiccated souls they have! It is so sad."[52]

Etō's seemingly irrational vision only makes sense in light of the passion with which he had sought, for decades, to give voice to those he thought had been silenced unfairly by the Occupation. One text for which he campaigned with particular passion from the 1970s and 1980s was Yoshida Mitsuru's epic poem *Senkan Yamato no saigo* (The End of the Battleship *Yamato*).[53] Yoshida, a survivor of the mammoth battleship *Yamato*, composed his epic poem in memory of his many dead comrades, but the SCAP (Supreme Command for the Allied Powers) censors banned the poem as nationalistic and glorifying war. In the 1970s, Yoshida, a bank employee and a Christian, contacted Etō about the censorship of his poem. Etō took it upon himself to research the poem in U.S. archives, and to publish the poem and commentaries. His exploration of Occupation censorship also led him to the censored text of ethnologist Yanagita Kunio's *Ujigami to ujiko* (Tutelary Dieties and the Shrine's Community). The marks and comments of the SCAP censors on Yanagita's text allowed Etō to imagine alternatives for the spiritual landscape of the postwar.

The Constitution and Myself

In both essays, Etō defiantly redefines Japan's constitution. For a man who had written a book and many essays about the postwar constitution, this is not an easy conceptual leap. Or perhaps it is precisely Etō's decades-long obsession with the constitution as a legal document that allowed him to transform it into something entirely different, and to make it his own. Transforming the constitution into something other than a document brought by aliens also helped Etō to find a place for the lost men to belong, and to assuage the feelings of loss.

In the 1999 text, Etō uses the word "constitution" three times, each time slightly differently. He pointedly employs the English word "constitution" rather than the Japanese term *kenpō*, in order to remind the reader that the document originally came about through the auspices of the Allied Occupation forces.

How does Etō change the meaning of the constitution in the 1999 essay? Initially, he refers to the constitution as an instrument, as the means by which the nation "determines its attitude toward the war dead, as in the case of official visits by prime ministers to Yasukuni." Despite his indirect reference to the Japanese constitution's articles on the separation of religion and state, Etō clearly also has in mind another understanding of the constitution: a constitution not as a document that lays out laws and principals, but rather an "accumulation" or a synthesis of "culture, traditions, and customs." While this transformation is so sudden that it seems akin to magic in the "Kokoro" essay, the earlier "Gaze" essay offers a clear definition of what Etō means by the word constitution: "the OED offers the 'make up of the nation' as one definition of the word 'constitution.'" He also denigrates the document called the Constitution of Japan as "something hastily drafted, in six days and six nights, by the twenty-five U.S. military officers."[54] In addition, he condemns debates over constitutional interpretation as "inconsequential" in comparison to the question of the proper way for the living to treat the dead.

On second mention, his transformation of the externally imposed constitution from a legal document to the accumulations of memories and culture itself becomes starkly clear:

> As Professor Origuchi noted, it is not the case that the living alone are physically conscious of the landscape. The dead, at the same time, are looking at that scene. The spirits of those dead and living interact, and only then do the land, culture, and traditions of Japan come into being *(seiritsu shite iru)*. That is Japan's constitution. In short, if a time comes when we no longer think of the dead, Japanese culture will cease to exist. I will also consider the continuity of the nation. That continuity implies the continuity of that country's culture, as well as that country's receptivity *(kanjūsei)*. In order for the living to live life to the fullest, they must always be thinking of the dead.

Etō's concept of constitution thus ranges far beyond the 1946 American-authored constitution. Perhaps Etō alludes to Edmund Burke's (1729–97) conservative notion of society as "a partnership not only between those who are living, but between those who are living, those who are dead, and those who are to be born. Each contract of each particular state is but a clause in the great primeval contract of eternal society."[55]

After having redefined the constitution as a "way of life," Etō relates it to the Emperor: "Lastly, [one aspect of] Japan's way of life is the practice of the emperor and the people joining together as one to mourn the war dead, which in itself is based in Japan's constitution." In this way, Etō uses narrative to imagine a place for lost men.

Ethnicity and Narrative

To Etō Jun, literature offered the possibility of creating an authentic narrative of one's own. He saw literary genre as universal, but also as form that had the capacity to communicate origins, ethnicity, and culture, which inevitably differed among peoples. Long before he focused on Yasukuni, he frequently invoked literary concepts as a means of clarifying dilemmas of contemporary society:

Since ancient times, many peoples *(minzoku)* around the world have survived by discovering the story of their own trials and suffering, and by constantly reaffirming these stories. The epic poetry transmitted down through the generations of these various peoples would often tell of maritime adventures and battles. This was because ocean voyages and wars share many features in common with life as experienced by people living in groups. However, none of these peoples has ever assented to borrowing a tale told by another people and living within the framework *(waku)* of that story. In the instance of a story of a different origin being incorporated, along with the people who transmitted it, into a different group of people, there would always be [a means] of identifying and integrating that story and its teller. Except when a people became extinct or scattered, none of them ever tried to substitute the narrative of another people for their own. Indeed, in some cases, the story of a people who have vanished survives beyond them, by virtue of its own power as narrative. [For example,] long after the glory of the Heike clan disappeared from the earth, *The Tale of the Heike* is still told. The Celtic people fostered the Arthurian Legends even after they spread to the British Isles, Ireland, and Brittany.

If epic poetry functions as a means of discovery and affirmation of ethnic identity for the collective, then the history of the novel *(shōsetsu)* developed as a project of discovery and affirmation of individual identity. A hero in the genre of fiction is not a character who gives a performance of a self-image created by someone else. Rather the hero of a novel is someone equipped with the courage to encounter his own true self, no matter how despicable a figure that may be. On occasion, the novelist also attempted to search deeply within the [collective] memory of the epic poem for the links that connect the discovered self and the whole. In other words, literature must be a project of searching for the figure of the self *(jiko)* that connects the singular to the whole, all within the space of a single language.[56]

In this passage from a 1979 essay on Franco-Japanese relations during the war, Etō thus creates an extraordinary fusion of diplomatic history and discussion of literary genre. As an agent of memory in this broad debate over Yasukuni, Etō contributes a new formulation of Japanese culture by inserting literature into the existing mixture of religion, ritual, politics that has, for more than a century, characterized Shintō's part in the modern state. State Shintō claimed the status of "non-religion" or "supra-religious entity" partly because the shrines were responsible for state rituals. Until 1945, many in the Shintō priesthood pushed for recognition that Shintō "had a public character and stood outside the sphere of religion." The lack of a clear consensus about the status of Shintō was compounded because the prewar public had an awareness of the shrines as the site of "large-scale rites of state" as a result of extensive coverage in the newspapers.[57] This ambiguity concerning the status of Shintō has continued into the postwar era, despite the fact that both the Occupation and the postwar Japanese government ruled that shrines are legally classified as religious institutions. In postwar court cases and Diet bills aimed at reviving government support for Yasukuni, the LDP and the Izokukai, among others, claimed that "its service to the nation should place it above being classified as a religious institution."[58]

Etō's writings about mourning the war dead serve to complicate further the question of the status of the shrines. In addition to the fact that he does he not invoke the category of religion, he makes comparisons that suggest a seamless identification between culture and religion in the Japanese case. For example, he contrasts Christian views on the dead with Japanese views, as if Japanese had a uniform approach to mourning (regardless of the multiple influences of Buddhism, Shintō, and Christianity). Even more novel is his conflation of ethnology and literature, social science and art, as shown by his invocation of Yanagita Kunio and Origuchi Shinobu in the interpretation of classical poetry.

The Emperor's Pain

In addition to his equation of religion with Japanese culture and fusion of literature with ethnology, Etō also situates the words and actions of the Shōwa emperor as significant and acceptable markers of collective memory. His 1999 essay is notable for its utterly casual inclusion of the emperor. For a political figure whose death a decade earlier had given rise to considerable soul searching about war responsibility, the Shōwa emperor is reborn, in Etō's essay, without sin, as the postwar emperor, who, though now human, retains "older associations of divinity and authority."[59] Fast becoming a lost man, the emperor is redeemed by Etō as he returns him to the originary moment of the postwar:

> By what means do the bereaved families of the war dead remember the end of the war? Most likely, they hold in their memories the Emperor's Broadcast to the Japanese People on Surrender [August 15, 1945]: "The thought of those officers and men as well as others who have fallen in the field of battle, those who died at their posts of duty, or those who met with death [otherwise] and all their bereaved families, pains our heart night and day. The welfare of the wounded and the war sufferers and of those who have lost their home and livelihood is the object of our profound solicitude." Such is the basis for official visits to Yasukuni Shrine . . . In the postwar, the Shōwa Emperor attended the ceremonies in memory of the war dead, and repeated, each year, "This still pains our heart." For this reason, the bereaved families, as well as all Japanese people, feel that His Majesty has remembered us, and attend the services at the Budōkan . . . [One aspect of] Japan's way of life is the practice of the Emperor and the people joining together as one to mourn the war dead, which in itself is based in Japan's Constitution.[60]

Etō's claims in 1999 seem anachronistic, even willfully blind to the decades-long vigorous debate over collective memory and national identity. At the same time, they fit perfectly with the long-term project of conservatives in the postwar to "keep the aura of an archaic experience before the population" and furthermore to indulge in "repetition, to deny the passage of historical time and the irretrievability of the past . . . a return of the repressed, now out of time and place, a temporality stripped of its historical markers."[61] His emphasis on the practice of paying respects to the enshrined deities at the shrine, furthermore, lays emphasis on ritual. This move also encourages flight from history and politics. As Hardacre writes, ritual "has no contrary and . . . hence cannot be directly challenged by rational argument," and it therefore "discourages critical thinking."[62]

The Future Dead

During the last phase of the Cold War when Japan attained unprecedented levels of economic growth, Etō presented himself as the hero who would rescue Japanese culture from "someone else's story"—specifically the hegemonic American narrative. In one sense, the post–Cold War essay *Kokoro* is the distillation of Etō's quest to find a place for all the lost men—the war dead, the bewildered bourgeoisie of postwar fiction, and Etō himself. His writings position literature as the site for the living to engage with the dead, as a solution to long-lost masculinity.

Etō excluded from his version of the "Japanese way of life" and memory many of the narratives of other publics: the veterans' postwar testimonies about the Nanjing atrocities, the wartime persecution of oppositional thinkers and activists by the imperial government, as well as the postnational visions of progressive activists. Both versions of his essay on the war dead imagine a Japanese cultural landscape made up of the dead, who are both needy and vocal. Etō invites the living to engage in archaic ritual in order to appease and comfort the dead. The Cold War–era essay of 1986 recognizes the urgent voices of both critical neighbors in Asia and dissenting country people, and suggests the vibrancy of public discourse in a debate over national identity and memories of war. Sitting at the center of the debate, Etō hallucinates what he has long written about: the dead, he feels, speak directly to him. In contrast, Etō's post–Cold War essay of 1999 presents a hermeneutically sealed, timeless fusion of poetry, imperial pronouncements, and the now silent yet still lost dead. His essay previews the visitor's experience at the Yasukuni museum, with its panels of calligraphic poetry, photographic containment of the dead, and even a bride doll to help us envision a strange wedding.

All the vigor and passion of the public debate over Yasukuni transpired under the umbrella of Article 9 of Japan's "peace" constitution. It is astonishing to remember that, during the half-century of Etō's project of finding prayers for lost men, no Japanese participated in or died in direct combat. Deaths of course did continue—tens of thousands of *hibakusha* perished from radiation sickness; some war criminals were executed. Many died of old age.

By 1999, when Etō wrote his final essay, Japan would seem to have joined the victors in the Cold War. We can only speculate about what

Etō, who has now joined the dead, would think about the post–Cold War, post–9/11 precedent-breaking deployment of Japan's amply equipped Self-Defense Forces to Iraq, and the surprising possibility of new Japanese war dead. But this also raises the question of how Japan's future war dead will be mourned. Will enshrinement at Yasukuni await them? What will the many publics say? What will the neighbors say, now that Japan is on the side of the coalition that plans for certain victory, as it imagines to have had in World War II, in its holy war on terrorism.

～ 6

The Execution of Tosaka Jun and Other Tales

Historical Amnesia, Memory, and the Question of Japan's "Postwar"

HARRY D. HAROOTUNIAN

As LONG AS I'VE BEEN INVOLVED in the study of Japan's national history I can't recall a time when Japanese were not reminded of the "postwar" (*sengo*) or reminding everybody else that they were still living it. It seems that they, like those of us with a professional interest in the country, have lived a permanent postwar that shows no sign of ending. Several generations of Japanese have grown old and even passed away since 1945 and have known no other description of the temporality of their lives than the permanent eclipse of the postwar. If this seems like a strange way for a society to define itself—and it must since the Germans and the Italians have long abandoned this chronological marker to describe their present—consider what it means for Americans who are currently engaged in a war on terrorism that cannot possibly ever end and where the population will forever live under the tyranny of color-coded alerts and anxiety fueled by the administration and a complicitous media. While there are obvious differences between a society that prolongs a relationship with a war it fought and lost and one that is locked in a never-ending struggle with an unseen and unknown enemy, there is still an interesting symmetry that needs to be spelled out. It is important, and possibly instructive, in any case, to figure out why Japanese insist on seeing themselves bonded to a postwar, just as it will be meaningful to understand why Americans wish now to exist in a time of war that has no chance of ending and moving on to its aftermath, a postwar. What desire or need would persuade Japanese to house itself permanently in a temporality marked by a relation to the war's end? Some writers have proposed that Japan, after the war, was caught up in the gaze of the United States and incorporated into its hegemonic system to forfeit whatever autonomy the country once possessed.

Incorporation offered both security and recovery under American domination, and subordination bought the promise of forgetfulness and memory loss of the past immediately before the war and the last moment Japan had acted autonomously, however disastrous the result. It is interesting to pair this loss of national autonomy with the demand for personal autonomy as a condition of political subjectivity and political personality modernizers like Maruyama Masao and others called for in the years immediately after the war. The reason for national amnesia stems, no doubt, from more complex sources and probably has more to do with how the participants in postwar Japan, especially politicians and intellectuals, sought to remake their world through what might be called an act of historical repetition that insisted on the identity of the present with its prewar past and the desire, reinforced by the Occupation, to continue the socioeconomic endowment that had been fixed since the Meiji period and had figured in the very fascism and imperialism that drove Japan into its conflict with the United States. This meant, as we shall see, actually remembering some things as a condition of forgetting others.

With Japan, the slide into the temporality of a permanent postwar seemed to be linked to a process of self-victimization that stemmed from a combination of convictions that blamed the military and the prewar state for starting war and the American decision to end it by bombing Hiroshima and Nagasaki with atomic weapons. This explanation required accepting no responsibility for bringing about the war and the depredations in Asia since it was the work of the state and the military. The devastation and deaths caused by the unprecedented deployment of nuclear weapons meant that Japanese had suffered more than their Asian victims. Some postwar thinkers even believed that an absence of rationality in prewar Japan brought on the "madness." At the same time, the population was punished by American weapons of mass destruction that exceeded anything the Japanese had done in Asia. But the really consequential effect is the silencing of the immediate past which might have helped explain the events and forces that propelled the Japanese into war. Silencing a specific past worked to elevate the moment of defeat ending the war with Japan. Such "eventfulness," scaled to the Holocaust itself, required only the act of mourning to sustain and continue the portrayal of self-victimization into an endless future. In its operation, mourning for loss continues in the present, represses the past, and brackets the future, which will be different only when and if the grieving ends and the present is finally permitted to become the past.

War and its aftermath intensified a fateful partnership between Japan and the United States that reached back to the mid-nineteenth century and guaranteed that the two countries would hereafter be bonded together as permanent allegories of each other. It is reasonable to suppose that living in the time of an interminable postwar means only that Japan has the longest living population in the world and this is all they have known. It may also suggest that clinging to a perpetual "postwar" was merely Japan's way of dealing with the Cold War. But the "postwar" didn't disappear in 1989 with the collapse of the Berlin Wall, as its content was too embedded in the nation's modern history and its memory of the modern that exceeded the geopolitical limits that had figured the Cold War. It is important to recognize that for so many Japanese, now reaching over several generations, the military occupation that inaugurated the postwar blanked out both an understanding of those aspects of the modern past capable of explaining the conjunctural events leading to war and, with few exceptions, the searing experience of wartime itself. According to the critic Kato Norihiro, a determined voice in contemporary discussions who has spoken up against the whitening out of history, only a few writers "remembered" the wartime and actually vocalized their thoughts about the experience of living through it. Even after the United States officially ended the military occupation in 1952, succeeded by the Japan-U.S. Security Treaty keeping American troops stationed in Japan, Japanese believed they were still living in the time of the postwar well through the decades of the 1960s and 1970s when the country had, in fact, achieved global economic prominence. In that time, the idea of the postwar was nourished and given a renewed lease on life by a new nationalism promoted by writers like Etō Jun, who condemned the United States for having exceeded the terms of the Potsdam Treaty ending the war and its declaration of "unconditional surrender." In Etō's thinking, nothing in the original document authorized subsequent American censorship, which presumably had stilled critical values and choked native sentiment. In many ways, Etō's argument prefigured later denunciations of the military occupation as a form of neo-colonization rather than democratization, introduced a new conception of what Japan had forfeited as a consequence of its modernization, and announced the permissibility of a new nationalism. Under this critique the time of the postwar—continuing subordination to the United States—fused with the timeless precinct of the colony with no chance of ever becoming a postcolony. Despite Etō's appeal to a new(er) nationalism, premised on Japan's willingness to break its dependence on the United States and end the postwar, the argument went a long way to disputing the claims associated with America's democratization of Japan, the putative result of "embracing defeat," but demonstrated persuasively the dire consequences of America's divergent path. This critique still remains muted among non-Japanese accounts of the Occupation, especially those that still wish to see America's "helping hand" as a decisive force in reshaping postwar society. What these narratives all seek to disguise is the obvious fact that the Occupation sought to remake Japanese the archipelago, without any justification other than imperial design, into an island of Dr. Moreau. To ensure the lasting success of this "experiment," American soldiers have been continuously stationed in Japan and Okinawa since the end of the war, now almost sixty years, to become permanent tenants of the landscape.

During the late 1980s and 1990s, critics like Kato further amplified this argument with the insistent complaint that the United States had effectively denied the Japanese the right to mourn for their own war dead. This refusal, coupled with the charge of censorship, not only sustained the status of *sengo* as a colonized temporality and encouraged forgetfulness but actually distorted and "twisted" Japanese in such ways as to permanently alienate them from themselves and their history. At the same moment Japanese were being told they were living a disfigured and deformed existence there appeared an aggressive and virulent call for a total revision of history textbooks and thus an overhauling (and an inverting) of the prevailing conception of history to show the nation that Japan had not been responsible for the war. According to this new narrative, the putative depredations in Asia were overstated

and exaggerated and accusations of having started the war in Manchuria (1931) and enlarging it in China (1937) had, in fact, been put
forward to displace the real reasons prompting Japan to fight to maintain its own security and independence. (In all fairness, narratives produced outside of Japan, especially by Americans of the modernization
persuasion, also deemphasized the immediate prewar era of the 1930s
and the role played by fascism, a word that seems to have been pro-
scribed in Japan's historical lexicon.) But this was simply a super-
scripting of a history that clearly revealed Japan's agency in waging an
imperial war in Asia. Among the most eloquent and courageous voices
living through this turbulent time who were willing to bear witness to
the nation's involvement in the events leading to war and speak out
against the fascist state in the 1930s, many were already silenced by the
time Japan's "postwar" agony began. The very events that later "historical" revisionists sought to invert, discount, and diminish had driven
many of its most vociferous critics to early deaths and the memory of
their intervention to the blankness of historical amnesia.

The Darkness of the Lived Moment

In the autumn of 1945, not long after the surrender papers had been
signed on the *USS Missouri*, the leftist philosopher Kakehashi Akihide
recalled how he had heard the news of the death of two prominent
philosophers who had been earlier imprisoned—Miki Kiyoshi, who
had died in prison six weeks after the war ended and Tosaka Jun, who
died a month before it terminated. Shocked by news that Japan would
be deprived of two of its leading thinkers, whom all believed would
play dominate roles in shaping forthcoming discussions after the war,
Kakehashi was particularly dismayed by the personal loss of his friend
(and comrade) Tosaka and why there seemed to be so little information
concerning the fate and last days of the most brilliant and original
Marxist of the prewar years. With others bearing similar testimony,
Kakehashi wondered why Tosaka was so rapidly forgotten while the
memory of Miki and his imprisonment was immediately restored to
public memory in 1945. In the ensuing months, Miki's achievements
and accounts of his heroic last days won widespread sympathy from a
war-weary population and in whose prison death they undoubtedly saw
their own tragic sacrifice. Miki's last philosophic testament, "Philosophic Notes," a permanent reminder of war, brutality, and senseless

destruction, was published in 1946 and became an instant bestseller, along with the "autobiography" of the older Marxist Kawakami Hajime.

The success of these works by two thinkers—both of whom had been Marxists at one time in their careers—attested to how their examples had captured the popular imagination in a time of despair and hopelessness surrounded by signs of ruin and destruction everywhere. In subsequent narratives of postwar Japan, produced in Japan and elsewhere then and now, no mention has been made of the solitary figure of Tosaka Jun, whose conditions of imprisonment led directly to his death at the age of 48 years and constituted nothing less than an act of state execution. Unlike Miki, Tosaka left no last testament of his prison years, only his prewar oeuvre, no final meditations on religious figures like Shinran or philosophic reflections since he was incarcerated in circumstances that explicitly prohibited him from reading and writing and in a space so constricted that it barely allowed him to turn around. One recalls the figure of Antonio Gramsci rotting in a fascist jail in Italy but who was still permitted to read, which he did prodigiously, and write, to which the posthumously published "Prison Notebooks" now stand as one of the great monuments to his spirit and intellect. Tosaka was left to dehydrate in an airless cell not much larger than a cigar box. Miki Kiyoshi, who had been Tosaka's friend and unofficial mentor, and who had assisted Tosaka when he lost his university position, was still a prominent figure in official circles until his untimely imprisonment. Perhaps the most active member of Prime Minister Konoe's brain trust, the Shōwa Kenkyukai, and certainly its most powerful thinker, Miki had put into practice his philosophic convictions in a number of brilliant policy papers on the current situation and its world historical meaning. By the time of the Pacific War, Miki's theories on "cooperativism" and "Asian capitalism" were bordering on fascism, even though he always distanced himself from this description. But the inhuman incarceration of Tosaka was designed to silence him completely, since it was obvious he would not recant like so many of his contemporaries, and thus aimed to obliterate his memory altogether from the past he had lived as present with which his work constitutes a painful record of struggle.

There is, then, an interesting symmetry between the prewar state's desire to silence Tosaka permanently and the erasure of his memory, and powerful critique from postwar historiography and discourse. This act of silencing worked to actually eliminate Tosaka's powerful presence in the 1930s—his brilliant rethinking of Marxism as a philosophy of the everyday, his scorching critique of the complicity of liberalism and fascism, his fearless assessments of the contemporary situation, and his tireless leadership of the *Yuibutsuron kenkyukai* (Materialism Study Society). While the prewar state sought to still his denunciation of "Japanism" and "archaism" as the forms of fascism that prevailed in Japan, the postwar order succeeded in repressing his account of how liberalism had been implicated and even complicit in producing prewar fascism. If the former managed to finally silence him, the latter destroyed the memory of his critique so thoroughly that it was literally forgotten and resulted in removing his absent presence from all subsequent discussions. All we have left is a book of reminiscences published in the 1970s of philosophers and friends and a badly edited and incomplete collection of his writings from the same period. Not even the Japan Communist Party, which came out of the war momentarily authoritative owing to its earlier "scientific" assessment of the predictable perils of monopoly capitalism, remembered Tosaka as one Marxism's leading lights in the 1930s, its most original thinker and committed martyr. The reason for this silencing undoubtedly derived from Tosaka's long-standing critique of nationalism and the nation-state form which many of his contemporaries had simply taken for granted as an unproblematic category and the Japan Communist Party in the postwar period would enthusiastically embrace in its campaign to win popular political support.

In the immediate postwar years Japan seemed determined to resuscitate the figure of prewar society, by distancing it from its explicit militarism and imperial aspirations. But the erasure of Tosaka also entailed diminishing the memory of what Ernst Bloch once described as "the darkness of the lived moment,"[1] which meant obliterating the world Tosaka and others inhabited and struggled to the point of giving up their own lives in order to prevent the fascism that finally drove the country into a ruinous imperial war, in other words, the darkness veiling the "unmastered Now: and its unopened future."[2] What is so important is how their moment was bracketed and even repressed in accounts concerning the postwar Occupation and the subsequent recovery. It is necessary to recognize how, during the 1960s and 1970s, the prevailing approach to understanding Japan, which saw in it a showcase of successful modernization, was fused with the Occupation at the cost of forgetting the experiences of the 1930s prior to war and reconstruction. It was complicity with this revival that the liberalism of postwar thought seemed ready to supply.

To be sure, this "recovery" was assisted by the U.S. military, especially with its decision to retain the emperor and not try him as a war criminal, and preserve the structure of the imperial household which in time would become the dominant model for social organization, despite the putative dedivinization of imperial authority. But the same army of occupation that actively supported the retention of Japan's central social and political institution—emperor and court—was also convinced that its transubstantiation into a symbol of national unity would reinforce the guarantee of future demilitarization promised by Article 9 of the Constitution and the pledge to renounce war. Under these circumstances it seems somewhat ironic to condemn the military occupation as an instrument of neocolonialism. This is not to say that the United States played no role in refiguring postwar society and contributing to the reinstatement of prewar political culture. Yet, it is important to recognize that in spite of long-standing complaints that the United States robbed the Japanese of their true history, it is difficult to overlook the fact that apart from Article 9—now under siege—much of what the Americans did during its occupation and even after enhanced the Japanese determination to make their own history according to a design derived from a prior experience rather than the alien dictates of a colonizing army, even though the Occupation looked upon Japan as a social laboratory and the temporality of defeat as a window of opportunity for "experimentation." What I mean is that postwar Japan constituted, on its own, what might be called a "second coming" or repetition, in a different register, of historical fascism and its desire to remove social conflict and secure social harmony in order to make capitalism work better. What the concept of a "second coming" suggests is a theory of historical repetition that sees it both as an overlay of a "first coming" (the prewar), the coordinates of state and society still filtering through as signposts for the postwar present. What came to be known as "postwar thought," principally the discussions of modernizers who sought to install a proper political subjectivity and personality in the postwar, assisted by institutional policies of the Occupation, represented their present according to relations of resemblance and contiguity with the past seen as forms of association. It mattered little if the past—a former present—was actually lived or imagined since the desire for repetition was subordinated to the requirements of simple representation.

In this operation, "repetition was subjected to a principle of identity in the former present (the past) and a rule of resemblance in the present one."[3] Nothing better dramatizes the force of this theory of historical repetition than the declaration that war's end provided a second chance, implying an improvement of the past or the subtraction of its regressive elements and the retention of the emperor and the imperial house and the desire to maintain a fictive "historical continuity" between the present and the distant national past. The imperial court's relocation in postwar society continued to reflect prewar arrangements, ideological sentiment, and the political primacy of the state, which ruled as an imperial bureaucracy. One of the fateful questions never asked by occupation enthusiasts who supported the preservation of the imperial house was whether there could be an emperor without an empire. Perhaps this empire would now be reconstituted as a temporal rather than simply a spatial order, an immense, unseen temporal imperium presided over by the emperor (who was once a "manifest deity") whose presence symbolized not only a fictive national unity but rather the unity of intergenerational links of ancestors stretching back from the present to origins. What remained to remind Japanese of this unseen domain was the continuing practice of imperial time—an imperial reign naming an era and marking its passage—that existed alongside world standard time.

What the repetition and its reliance on analogy managed to conceal is the vast difference between the conjuncture of the 1930s and its postwar successor. Tosaka's generation faced a complex context that combined world depression, militarism and fascism at home, and imperialism abroad. Throughout the decade there was widespread agreement among thinkers and writers that they were living in a time of historical crisis set into motion by accelerated capitalist modernization. World depression simply supplied the momentary occasion to prompt thoughtful people everywhere to identify the vast social, economic, and political contradictions capitalism had unleashed but had until recently successfully contained. The historical watermark of this crisis was the production of discourses on culture (and art) that constantly sought to reshape a relationship to politics and in a temporal and spatial configuration where the lived contradictions seemed to be more sharply etched into the fabric of Japanese life. It could also be found in the manifest ruptures, discontinuities, unevenness, and observably different temporalities that coexisted uneasily with each other to define the modernist moment. Japan shared this moment with other industrializing societies and their colonial proxies: a recognition of a crisis that put into question a perceived separation between modes of cognition and the necessity of finding adequate and lasting forms of representation. For the Japanese the dilemma was expressed in controversies over the real, art for art's sake and "pure literature" that tried desperately to secure unification of the fragmented domains of modernity by either making everyday life into art (culture) or art into everyday life (politics). With capitalism, concepts like culture, representation, and modernity were rapidly recruited to supply mediation in a sociohistorical environment marked by the ceaseless production of new forces of production and social relations that could end only in furthering division and conflict.

Nowhere were the issues of capitalist modernity and the resulting problems for representation more intensely engaged than in discussions that sought to shape a modernism founded on an identification of the concrete over the mediations of the commodity form and social abstraction that inadvertently put into question its relationship with fascism. The quest for lasting and stable forms of representation capable of arresting the fragmentation produced by the ever-changing world of the commodity and the proposed reunion of everyday life and art constituted an illusive fantasy (the Romantic Yasuda Yojuro's project of "irony") and the common ground of modernism and fascism alike. What modernists and fascists shared was the recognition of the impossibility of representing an historical object or set of events that are already mediated by social abstraction and that prevents seeing them as they really happened, at the same time they are witnessing the withdrawal of those fixed forms of representation from other, prior modes of existence. In other words, where capital confronts its other, so to speak, representation becomes an irresolvable problem since it faces the twin demands of capital's reason on the one hand and the claims of a prior culture of reference on the other which, like receding echoes, was retreating steadily into a remaindered world of irrationality and ghosts. In interwar Japan, the time of modernism, a dominant modern discourse on aesthetics, committed to the concrete and immediate, aspired to displace a politics imbedded in abstract exchange that spoke directly to fascism's own distrust of contemporary politics since it had already announced a verdict on all political attempts to break the logic of reified existence. Yet, such an appeal to art presumed to be more than an adequate replacement for politics by "granting to the masses" the gift of expression in order to keep social relationships based on private property unchanged, to dissuade them from demanding the right to abolish property relations. But the endpoint of this effort to revise the relations between culture and politics by instating the former in the place of the latter was to promote, as Miki Kiyoshi advised, *techne*, technology, which quickly translated into making war. This technological harnessing of war, according to Walter Benjamin, was at the heart of imperialism and colonial violence which invariably disclosed the "discrepancy between the enormous means of production and their inadequate use in the process of production (in other words by unemployment and the lack of markets.)"[4] While Benjamin foresaw imperialist war as an "uprising of technology" that seeks to compensate in "human material" for the "natural material" "society has denied it," it also demonstrated the truism that there can be no consideration of imperialism without one of fascism and the reverse.

Both modernism and fascism thus found each other in the common struggle to find a mode of representation capable of mastering the fundamental abstractness of what really happens. Ultimately, both were obliged to appeal to some form of presentation and performance that promised relief and escape from the constraints of socially abstract mediation and the relentless fragmentation of life. With fascism there was the attempt to get out of politics altogether, but not the state form, since it was anchored in representational categories by appealing to the unity of folk community as a natural order. It is important to recognize that modernism, for the most part and despite its familiar dislike of the market, and fascism rarely entertained the possibility of eliminating capitalism and its reliance on private property in their combined effort to resolve the question of representation. It was this refusal, according to Tosaka, that linked fascism and the Japanist ideology to what he called cultural liberalism (and its own commitment to maintaining the regime of private property) and the desire to recover an aura—archaism—no longer available.

The Bourgeois Subject and the Good Japanese

Postwar thought (as it was named) could congratulate itself for believing it had found a way of avoiding the excessive forms of "ultranationalism" and fascist ideology that disfigured prewar society by subtracting them from the political equation and occupying the vacated space with an emphasis on theories of subjective autonomy, political ethos, and responsibility. But this theory of a second start was based on a misrecognition of the thirties conjuncture and an inflated investment in the powers of a heroic bourgeois individualism gendered as male. Its greatest mistake was to think it could wish away fascism as an historical moment and aberration that had passed now that Japanese (and we, I must add) had lived through its inaugural forms. Despite the promise of social democrats (the so-called modernizers or party of the enlightenment gathered around Otsuka Hisao, Maruyama Masao, and Kawashima Takayoshi) to formulate a conception of society based on a rational, autonomous, and responsible subject, the putative site where meaning is produced, capable of making informed decisions, as if its absence among the prewar masses had caused the war, postwar Japan seemed to overlook the problematic of the 1930s that had sent both modernism and fascism on its joint mission to resolve the aporia of representation. Many of the most active participants in these discussions concerning the shape of postwar society during the occupation years looked to their present—the *après guerre*—as a second chance for liberalism. The desire to restore a truer liberalism or a liberal order where one allegedly had not existed or had been aborted before the postwar risked bringing back its already proven penchant for accommodation which Tosaka's critique had earlier identified and warned against.

At the heart of the postwar repression of this prior critique was its rewriting of the text of the enlightenment. Just as Tosaka had perceived a kinship between liberalism's affirming culture and the formation of a Japanist—fascist—ideology, he had also produced an elegant defense of the promise of rationality and critical science for the masses. Tosaka had seen in the space of everyday life the site for this new scientific knowledge fused to the common sense of the masses. (It is important to note that while this move paralleled Gramsci's own valorization of common sense at about the same time, the apparent confluence was coincidental but perhaps a constant produced by the conjuncture). Enlightenment meant critical knowledge for the masses, whose common sense, already founded on the basis of experiencing a daily life that had been only incompletely colonized by the state and dominated by its bureaucratic apparatus, was thus already prepared to receive its promises of liberation. (Tosaka had actually conceived a project that would design an encyclopedia of knowledge for the masses.) Hence, the irony of the postwar forgetfulness, what Etienne Balibar once described in another context as the "absence of memory,"[5] was that it worked to reinforce the claim of an enlightenmentism serving the requirements of capitalist modernization as it was being presently redefined by modernizers and liberals, but that ultimately was realized by the one-party state. In fact, it is difficult to dissociate many of these postwar modernizers from the state, since as academics at places like Tokyo and Kyoto universities they were already civil servants. Moreover, it is important to suggest that many also saw a connection between the state and the planned modernization conceived and implemented by "scientific" managers. So great was the momentary popularity of "enlightenment" that one thinker (Shimizu Ikutaro) even wrote a book years later advising "to forget the enlightenment," while another (Tsurumi Shunsuke) attributed excessive Westernization to it in the course of Japan's modernity.

The "enlightened" modernizers of the early postwar monopolized the enlightenment conception of rationality even as they watered down its critical force to meet the requirements of instrumental, situational, and pragmatic necessity serving a newly established liberal democracy and its "autonomous" political subject. In other words, enlightenment was immediately put to the task of serving the present, as it was, and remained indistinguishable from its immediate demands. What the "party of the enlightenment" managed to accomplish was a lasting inversion of the goal of a critical practice that had induced people like Tosaka to embrace the ideals of science and rationality as exemplars capable of arming the masses in their effort to improve their everyday lives and guarantee its continued separation from the nation-state and its desire to colonize it. Where Tosaka saw in science a means of constructing a critique against the state and the liberal order, against an affirming culture and the academic philosophy "grounding" it, the postwar modernizers promoted a program of enlightenment as necessary to figure an autonomous individual, expectantly responsible and informed and thus positioned to resisting, unlike the prewar masses, the lure of voluntary submission to irrational claims of authority.

It was, I believe, this identification of masses with the irrational that prompted postwar intellectuals to locate rationality not in the everyday but in the state and its political leadership. But they clumsily betrayed their distrust and fear of the masses (a product of prewar socialization) and failed at the same time to conceal a conceit traditionally accorded to the intellectual elites. In Maruyama, they had found a brilliant defender of the primacy of the state and the crucial role played by "free-floating" and "unclassed" intellectuals like himself who, because of the position they occupied above the crowd of classes and their accompanying claim to political neutrality, was best situated to supply the kind of disinterested "scientific" leadership and planning demanded by the new political society. Unless the masses were led by a managerial elite of experts and specialists, resembling both Max Weber's and Karl Mannheim's (the latter a favorite in Maruyama's program) scientific planners now grafted onto the figure of philosophic leadership imagined by Yoshino Sakuzo for a fledgling social democracy in Japan in the 1920s, there could be no second chance and the promise of a new beginning.

Significantly, Maruyama Masao, perhaps the most forceful proponent of this view and in whose thinking echoes of Schmittian state theory reverberated, made a hero of the Meiji pamphleteer Fukuzawa Yukichi and his pragmatism as the model for a second start, fully aware that he represented the polar opposite of the subaltern masses and the political and economic aspirations of their own common sense. Where Tosaka, in short, saw the enlightenment as a way out of capitalism and liberalism, postwar thought made it a condition of the modernization of the Japanese state. If Tosaka, like Gramsci, privileged a common sense embedded in everyday life as the knowledge base of the masses, the postwar "enlighteners" replaced it with the authority of the average as crudely expressed in the fetishized principle of consensus, which derived its force from what counted and what was visible as against what was not and had been left out.

For Maruyama, the new start supplied the opportunity for exercising the application of greater scientific rationality, especially as it was to be exemplified in a scientific management dedicated to rational planning. By contrast, Tosaka had invested this rationality in the "common sense" of the masses, in the lived everyday, as against the state's propensity to assimilate it. The difference was a crucial one since the state represented the site of the non-everyday which Maruyama and the modernizers now wanted to reinstate as the locus of rational planning and leadership. It is important to observe that Maruyama, especially, was fastened to the rule of continuity (and contiguity) with the past and even declared early in the postwar that on this score he had not changed his thinking since the prewar period. His avowed desire was always to rid society of the irrational but Nakano Toshio has recently called into account the question of this unchanged "problem consciousness."[6] In fact, Nakano manages to cast doubt on the veracity of Maruyama's self-assessment by suggesting that during the war Maruyama, according to his testimony, changed from a commonly held view that saw the emperor as the principal of rulership that authorized a system of governance *("ichikun banmin")*. Years later he confessed that "liberation from the strong spell" of the emperor system "was a serious thing for me."[7] But it must also be said that Maruyama never wavered from a conviction that envisaged the emperor, despite the putative change to symbolic status, as the principle (and thus, principal) of national unity. Under the sanction of this conception of legitimacy, he promoted an arrangement whereby prewar liberalism was accommodated to the new postwar constitution.

By the same measure, others in the postwar would seek to carry forward an understanding of the problematic of representation capable of securing immunity from both capital and history. The critic Kobayashi Hideo expanded on a position developed earlier in the prewar discursive hot house on politics and culture and provided a firm link with the past with the publication of his great work on Motoori Norinaga in the 1970s, which aimed to show how language (Japanese) imbricated native cognition—*mono no aware*—and had thus already escaped the fateful division between representation and the represented for performance and presentation. Kobayashi had already distinguished himself in the 1930s with his powerful defense of "pure literature" against the noisy claims of all kinds of realism. Moreover, he was also on record for having leveled a powerful attack on historicist narratives of progress (Marxian and non-Marxian) for a conception of everydayness that signaled a sense of enduring commonness exemplified in classic literature that brought to light the constant presence of affect and emotionality. At this point, his thinking converged with that of Tosaka, inasmuch both, for vastly different reasons, eschewed historical narratives that occluded and diminished the lived reality of everyday life. But their paths soon diverged over the content of everydayness, with Tosaka insisting on the primacy of the now-time of the working class and Kobayashi looking to an aesthetic found in an indeterminate past. In contrast to Tosaka Jun's masses living in the material now, Kobayashi looked to writers like Shiga Naoya and Kikuchi Kan and their portrayals of the solitary self in an everyday life removed from the social nexus as models of concreteness and commonness echoing the classics of the past, even though it was clearly embedded in the world of the present. What their examples signified was art's disavowal of the constraints of temporality altogether in the pursuit of a timeless aesthetic free from both historical accountability and an order driven by the identity between the rational and real. The writer Mishima Yukio carried this message to the level of grand spectacle but not before figuring a relationship and reunion between art and politics, expressed in a noncommodified emperor who remained outside of history, not bound by it, but who was still capable of entering and crucially remaking it (as a work of art) in the image of a politics no longer anchored in reified forms of representation. Still others would emphasize how Japan, because of the Occupation, had been forcibly cut off from its true past and made to forget it in order to live a deception.

At the same time, the state, which had never gone away despite its associations with the prewar past and war, reappeared with even greater force than before (now as the locomotive of democracy). In its new avatar, it seized control of the everyday that Tosaka identified with the streets and masses and saw as a sanctuary that had not yet been fully colonized by national socialization (state ideology) and dominated by bureaucracy to resituate it in the home, now enclosed and shielded from publicity and even removed from the center, as the early housing projects like the suburban *danchi* clearly dramatized. The "modernizers" who formulated "postwar" thought constructed a narrative founded on "protecting the constitution" and its entailment of a liberal political subject capable of informed and responsible conduct, exercising the rights it granted and supporting its guarantees. Even Maruyama (in an article on the Meiji political journalist Kuga Katsunan) worried about the "future prospects" of the new constitution and "progress" and rising above the "steep precipice" Japanese confront that are greater "today" than ever before. The problem was exacerbated by the unresolved contradiction between the retention of an emperor absolved of war guilt and the establishment of sovereignty in the people.

For his part, Tosaka, as early as 1925, had called attention to how political party cabinets rooted in the Diet constituted a first step toward fascism. Tosaka had fixed the existence of the universal suffrage empowerment and the selection of party cabinets as the mechanism that enabled fascism by failing to prevent its formation, what he described as a "type of fascism that employs the Diet" and named as "constitutional fascism." The analysis became part of a more complex account that identified as a "mistake" the view that was made to see constitutional fascism as liberalism. Here, Tosaka proposed that what he was describing as "constitutional fascism," despite expressing close kinship with liberalism, is a phenomenon that gives birth to militaristic or "direct action" fascism. "But in our times," he added, "any kind of substantial liberalism is an illusion we must avoid." What he was pointing to was the fallacy of envisioning "senior statesmen of the court" as a sign of substantive liberalism when they represent nothing more than a constitutional fascism that trades on a misrecognition that they, as liberals, are actually at cross purposes with the fascism of "direct action."[8] With the effacement of Tosaka's memory, it is no accident that "modernizers" in the postwar ignored the logic of this argument against "constitutional liberalism" since it collided with their own affirmation to protect the "imperial constitutional system" as a condition for actualizing national unity.

If the immediate postwar years were flush with signs of renewal and the hope of realizing what Maruyama Masao described as a "second chance," the years after the early 1960s, announced by the mass demonstrations protesting the U.S.-Japan Security Treaty, saw the optimism fold into the timeless politics of the Liberal Democratic Party (LDP) version of liberal democracy and modernization, which itself collapsed the future into a endless present at the moment Japan's economy headed for global supremacy. While the putative dreams of social democracy and the heroism of rational subjectivity were said to have vanished in the din of shrill pronouncements promising higher standards of living, greater opportunities for domestic consumption in such campaigns as "My Home-ism" aimed at stuffing the cramped but private spaces of middle-class apartments that had become the ideal domain of everyday life, unlimited economic growth and the conceits of exaggerated rational bureaucratic planification calling for the end of all politics (and thus conflict), the repetition of the "second coming" of capitalism now fully under way resulted from as much the complicity of modernizers and their fellow travelers as the state and the single party that commanded its ruling heights. If the much heralded policy of "high economic growth" *(kodo seicho)* worked to ensure the permanence of single-party control (massively assisted by the United States, to be sure) it also inaugurated a modernizing process of Japanese society on an installment plan (economy and production first, consumption and culture later) that promised to complete the unfinished business of the prewar. But it was founded on the realization of a modern order whose reality proved to be an unintended counterfeit version of what postwar thought had originally envisaged but eventually accommodated as consistent with its fundamental convictions—a modernization program guided by the state that celebrated capitalism by first privileging production for export and consumption at home in the final instant. The repetition and liberalist desire to remove the masses (whom they distrusted and feared) and everydayness from the calculus of a proper and rational political agenda opened the door for the state to resocialize the former into dutiful workers and relocate the latter from the streets to the home and firm. By overinvesting in the promise of bourgeois individualism and rational political responsibility, postwar modernizers, in the eyes of conservative critics, were associated with continued Americanization (the specter of the Occupation) and invited the charge that an enhanced material lifestyle was merely the sign of a defeated status and thus the price Japanese were made to pay for having allowed themselves to be colonized, physically and spiritually, and forfeiting their true identity.

With the repetition came the echoes of the older debates concerning representation that modernism and fascism had struggled to resolve in the prewar in new and more muted registers, even though the earlier battles were not summoned. Yet neither modernism nor fascism, as such, ended with the war, as current historical accounts dramatize with depressing regularity. Some Japanese have proposed that the advent of "postmodernity" in the 1970s signaled the final death of modernism and modernity, while LDP single-party "democracy" was made to appear as a resolution of the aporetic status of political representation. What "high economic growth" permitted was a fusion of state and market on a scale never before reached, based on the constitution of a new subject position (the selfless, dutiful worker) promoted by the Ministry of Education's program for national socialization in the schools, called *Ningenzo kitai sareru* (Making the Ideal Image of the Human) or what we might call the 'Good Japanese.' The principal effect of this fusion was to make way for the ultimate assimilation of everydayness into the nation and the final suturing of the social into a seamless political totality, improving on what Max Weber once described as the "bureaucratic domination of everyday life." This was undoubtedly the goal of Prime Minister Ohira Masayoshi's ambitious plan of the late 1970s looking forward toward the twenty-first century to prepare for a new "age of culture" that would succeed an age devoted to economic recovery and establish what planners called a "holonic society." A virtual aestheticizing of capitalism, this theory of modernization sought to locate the mystery of Japan's global economic success in the recesses of its peculiar premodern cultural endowment (reworking the Weberian argument for Western Europe) and affirm the "Japanese Thing" and what it meant to be uniquely Japanese. It should be pointed out that the Ohira plan, recommending a restructuring of the archipelago into "garden cities," described its purpose as a "conquering of modernity," that intentionally aligned itself with both the wartime conference calling for an "overcoming of the modern" as the solution to all of the problems resulting from Japan's modern history and unintentionally bonded with postmodernists who drew their authority from the same source as they announced the end of modernism and modernity.

In other words, the response to the momentary success of "high economic growth" and the fading vision of society postwar thought envisioned for a new Japan prompted some thinkers and writers, already discouraged by the call to action during the struggle over the security pact in the early 1960s, to support a diluted modernism or nationalism. Still others, perhaps reeling from the impact of income doubling and the failed aspirations of collective action, turned to embracing forms of what was described as "abstract denial" (postmodern discourse) as compensation for the sense of a discredited contemporary reality. The apparent success of LDP policies paradoxically induced a search for ways of getting out from under the strains and hardships such policies had inflicted.

One theory offering release that surfaced for a short shelf life advocated a turnover from an industrial to an information society, from an emphasis on manufacturing for export to one committed to services and domestic consumption. But this repositioning of consumption over production only reflected a seriously diminished inflection of modernization that often slipped into postmodern cynicism. By the same token, the ambitions of Japanist discourse were revitalized by appeals to "great nationism" and calls for the "internationalization" of Japanese society in the late 1980s. This move increasingly advocated a new and often arrogant cultural nationalism that invited "new conservatives" and vestigial modernizers to cohabit the same nationalist discourse. With the dimming of the postwar vision and its abiding faith in a "second chance" to achieve a true(r) democratic order, the status of the modern was unhesitatingly put into question. Criticism settled on laying responsibility for Japan's current circumstances—1970s and 1980s—and misfortune at the doorstep of modernity itself, while the reformulation of an idealistic Japanese ideology demanding the fulfillment of the "Japanese Thing" and satisfying the clamor to "conquer modernity" surfaced as leading principles to reconfigure contemporary society just before the bubble began to burst in the early 1990s. Here, it is possible to recognize a contrast between what was called "contemporary thought" and "postwar thought," with the latter now designated as an historical moment that had passed (and was past), while the former was now identified with a living and endless present.

Despite the desire to tease out differences between these two categories, they shared more than mere historical resemblance and kinship inasmuch both constituted attenuations of liberalism and remained locked in a pervasive present. Liberalism, it might be recalled, constituted the avowed "foundation of social thought" after the war, as it did before the war, and embodied a predisposition toward Japanism and nationalism, already noted by Tosaka, that forged proximal or contiguous relationships with all those efforts that deceptively tried to overcome the modern in the name of a truer Japanese identity. Tosaka had observed that because Japan was already an established liberal and bourgeois social order, the culture of representation easily fused with political representation (as a means to avoid representation altogether) in order to secure the stability of both. Political practice, limited to determining social relations, was beginning to enlist to its cause meanings from the domain of mytho-culture (not history) to risk forfeiting the productive but conflict-bound nonidentity between culture and politics. With others in that time of crisis, he recognized that an effective politics must respect the asymmetry between a limited politics and an expansive culture. Moreover, Tosaka also saw exactly how the partnership between liberalism and fascism led to the cancellation of politics by offering the prospect of cultural rather than political identification promising to rid society of conflict. In other words, he was able to presciently see how modern liberalism, what he called a practiced cultural liberalism, easily opened the way to Japanism and fascism, how a commitment to rationality and modernity could lead to its repudiation in the promotion of an irrational and ahistorical archaism and its program for saving an exceptionalist cultural endowment by overcoming the modern.

Epilogue: Pastless Present/Endless Everyday

What, then, seemed to have occurred in the long night of the postwar, through the 1970s and 1980s and even beyond was, I believe, a revival of the logic (the repressed?) that had earlier authorized an alliance between liberalism and Japanism into a dominant common sense which, according to early postwar discourse, should have been eliminated with the war. As for the everyday that had held out so much promise for Tosaka and his generation, it lost its slight claim to sovereignty from the state. Since the beginning of the postwar, it is necessary to recall, the state had targeted the everyday as the site for domestic consumption which, once its placement was relocated from street to household (that is, apartment), had by the 1990s thoroughly colonized it with commodification and overtaken its capacity for liberation or, at the very least, semi-autonomy.

By the 1990s and the beginning of the new century, the fabled Japanese political economy—the dream of modernizers—was still stalled by a mountain of bad loans, bureaucratic inertia, overpriced domestic cost of living, dependence on the American market, and the bankruptcy of political vision produced by "single-party democracy." The much-vaunted male, bourgeois subject and its capacity to produce meaning so venerated by postwar thought metamorphosed into what the pop sociologist Miyadai Shinji has envisaged as a body that acts like a malleable and changeable environment (perhaps an exhausted echo of Watsuji Tetsuro's conception of "climate and culture" *[Fudo]*) that has no inner life, as such, and is currently represented by the performance of *enjo kosai* (compensated dating), "parasite girls," *hikikomari*, and other forms of "aberrant" youthful behavior, all products of ceaseless commodification. Although this appeal to sexually prodigious female teenagers is as much the conjuring of male fantasy as it is a datum of social research, or the referral to dangerous children capable of complete withdrawal and/or destructive behavior reflects more the product of overdetermined adult fears for an imagined disciplined and orderly society than a genuine national problem, it does point to the possible formation of new subject positions whose gender and sexuality are diverse and no longer singularly male and whose age limit has been somewhat lowered.

What appears significant in this observation, as it must be for our society as well, is the recognition that the body is no longer the reservoir of the self as such, no longer the sanctuary of the irreducible subject who produces meaning, but simply a site—a "habitat" colonized by commodities and driven by continuous consumption that allows one to get through an "everyday that never ends." With the vanishing of a subject who produces meaning and the installation of an "everyday that never ends" as the body's environment through which passage is navigable only with the assistance of consumption, we have, perhaps, reached the end of Japan's long postwar and its stories about itself and are now in a position to get a faint glimmer of what lies ahead and what for so long had been forgotten. When we look back upon the immense spectacle of postwar Japan, in any case, we must, I believe, read its cultural and political text as a reconfiguration of the knotted history that marked Japan's entry into capitalist modernity. This perspective reveals an unrecognized repetition with difference of what had been so constitutive of the prewar experience rather than either a postmodern departure or a distorted version of an authentic history—a what might have been. Instead of the storied "second chance" dreamed up by liberal thinkers determined to realize a political order that had not been adequately attempted or even existed, the postwar was simply a reiteration in the time of the "second coming."

～ 7

China's "Good War"

Voices, Locations, and Generations in the Interpretation of the War of Resistance to Japan

RANA MITTER

THE IDEA THAT WORLD WAR II was the "Good War" is most associated with the journalist Studs Terkel, even though his use of the phrase was loaded with irony.[1] His oral history of hundreds of memories of that "Good War" is just one of the most prominent ways in which personal experience has come more and more to the fore in explaining the wider cultural significance of that, and other, wars in the Western psyche. The journalist and the writer also appear as new interpreters of war in twentieth-century China: not so much the journalist as news reporter, giving calm, seemingly objective accounts in the third person, but rather the journalist as a new voice in Chinese writing of the twentieth century, the first-person narrator, using reportage not just to talk about some great event, but also to explore the nature of the self and of her or his own relationship to society.

Self-examination emerges often at times of great social trauma. The most famous period of reportage (*baogao wenxue*) in recent Chinese scholarship is the era of "scar literature" in the late 1970s, when writers were given more leeway to deal with the personal traumas of the Cultural Revolution. The writing of Liu Binyan, in pieces such as "People or Monsters?" was clearly an exploration of recent political trauma, but composed in a highly personalized style.[2] The antecedents to that type of reportage, as well as its successors, have been less explored so far. However, one of the most notable phenomena in contemporary Chi-

nese politics, the "new remembering of World War II," to quote
Arthur Waldron's phrase, has given us the opportunity not only to see
how one of the greatest, if not the greatest, traumas in modern Chinese
history has been reexamined in China, but also to trace the links between contemporaneous and retrospective narratives of that war experience, and to examine the way in which the War of Resistance fits into
a continuing exploration in China of issues such as the modern self and
the effects of mass trauma on society, as well as the parts of history, in
the war itself and beyond, that are remembered and forgotten.[3] In particular, it is a central part of China's reorientation of its own war
memory as part of its refashioning of identity after the Cold War. The
binaries and fissures of that decades-long virtual conflict are changing
almost visibly as memories from before the Cold War are resurrected
as part of contemporary identity.[4]

This chapter addresses writing that can broadly be categorized as
"popular" writing on the War of Resistance in post-1989 China. It is
not primarily concerned with another, highly impressive, growth area
in China, which is academic writing on the same topic. For well over a
decade, high-quality research, exemplified by monographs and journals, has presented primary and secondary materials on the war.[5] Even
some areas formerly off-limits, for instance the collaborationist governments that worked under the Japanese, have now been subjected to
scholarly scrutiny in China, although the range of permitted interpretation of those events is still relatively limited. Yet, as in the West, this
type of writing has relatively little direct impact on the reading public.
What the upsurge in academic writing on the war does is to provide
material for a wider, more popular reinterpretation of the War of
Resistance, and the fact that such research has been permitted by state
authorities is part of a sea change in attitudes toward the war experience. Various factors contributed to a significant change in official
boundaries for discussion of the war in China from the mid-1980s: the
desire to woo Taiwan into reunification, the disappearance of the Cold
War motivations for downplaying Japanese war atrocities and stressing
Nationalist ones, and the increasing delegitimation of Marxism in the
post-1978 reform era within China and the post-1989, post–Cold War
era outside it. The most obvious and perhaps startling manifestation of
this change in public culture was the much more positive tone taken
toward the role of the Nationalist government of Chiang Kai-shek in

contributing to the victory against Japan, a victory previously attributed almost entirely to the Chinese Communist Party (CCP). This reorientation could be seen through media such as textbooks, popular films, and large and prominent museums intended largely for school-age children. The conflict between Nationalists and Communists, endlessly recalled during the Mao era, did not disappear in historical discussion; but now it tended to take second place to a narrative that stressed Communist and Nationalist unity in the face of Japanese atrocities and aggression in the 1930s and 1940s. At the same time, Japanese war crimes, most famously the 1937–38 Nanjing Massacre (Rape of Nanjing), and the public projection of China as a victim of bloody Japanese aggression, became increasingly prominent in public culture through the same media. The trauma of events such as the Great Leap Forward and the Cultural Revolution, the latter much discussed in public in the 1970s and 1980s, gave way to China's own "good war" in which noble Chinese patriots, Communist and Nationalist, fought against Japanese devils.[6] It was an earlier shift in Cold War orientations that had begun this process: the recognition of the People's Republic of China (PRC) by Japan in 1972 was the consequence of a shift in global politics that came from the alienation of the Soviet Union from the PRC, and the desire of the United States to be the only major power to maintain workable relations with the two communist giants. Yet while the rapprochement between Beijing and Tokyo meant a warming of relations in one sense, it also allowed the development of a historiography that would lead to a much more confrontational relationship between the two Asian powers after the Cold War blocs finally thawed in the following decade.

The new genre of retrospective writing about the war, just like writing at the time, often tries to generalize experience and understanding of the experience of conflict, even when many factors affect one's point of view: occupation or flight, gender, class, aggressor or victim. It would be too much to claim that the writers discussed in the text that follows speak for an entire generation; the fact that they have chosen or been chosen to make their views public automatically categorizes their work in a certain way. Yet the very fact that they are educated and self-expressive, and write for the public domain, suggests that they are capable of articulating accounts that are intended to have an effect in wider society, and reflect realities that they see there. One notable phenomenon in the West has been the rise, rather than the fall in interest in the world wars as we become more distant from the events themselves, and fewer people remain to recall the events themselves.[7] In that sense, China is catching up with a worldwide phenomenon. World War II becomes a "good war" not just in terms of the cause for which it was fought, but in contrast with what came after: the Cold War and its shades of gray.

After all, Britain and France entered the war because their guarantee to Poland had been called in. The Soviet Union and the United States entered only when Germany and Japan respectively had attacked them first. Other justifications—whether saving the world for democracy, or to prevent the destruction of Europe's Jewish community—came later. Considering that the war failed to save much of the world (certainly not Poland) for democracy, later justifications were often important for contemporary political purposes. The postwar history of the Allied powers also made the events of World War II more powerful in retrospect. The United Kingdom, in Dean Acheson's famous phrase, "lost an empire and failed to find a role"; the United States became entwined in Vietnam and the ensuing "civil war" of the 1960s; and the Soviet Union became a sullen Cold War giant keeping a captive Eastern European empire literally enclosed with tanks, concrete, and barbed wire. For these societies, entwined in the ambiguities and uncertainties of the Cold War, the Battle of Britain, Midway, and Stalingrad provided powerful justification for what they had become. China, of all the Allied powers, had perhaps the most problematic relationship with its past because of its swift move from the Sino-Japanese War to the Civil War; unlike in the Soviet Union, the war against Japan was never able to provide a fount of universally resonant cultural memory.[8]

Yet the Sino-Japanese War has the advantage of being the war, and more widely the trauma, that was most indisputably, among the many that China endured in the twentieth century, not the fault of the Chinese. The civil wars of the Republican era, particularly virulent in the 1910s and 1920s, culminating in the final Nationalist-Communist confrontation of 1946–49; the massive upheavals of the Great Leap Forward and the Cultural Revolution, as well as the constant mass mobilization that underpinned class warfare in the People's Republic: all these were heavily influenced by foreign intervention or in some cases (such as the Great Leap Forward) isolation from it, yet the perception that remains is of Chinese in conflict with other Chinese. Only imperialism provided a (seemingly) uncomplicated pole of aggression and hostility contrasted with which the Chinese can be seen as blameless; the second Sino-Japanese War was both the most recent and most devastating example of that imperialism. In a sense, the renewed interest in World War II in China merely shows China "normalizing" its experience of that conflict, and joining in an increasingly globalized discussion of the war's significance, which grows stronger the further we move away from the events themselves. Two of the authors discussed here, Fang Jun and Fan Jianchuan, speak of the war's international meaning explicitly: Fang contrasts what he sees as Japanese denial of war guilt with German education at all levels of society about Nazism; Fan writes his foreword in Switzerland, whose peaceful history he cites as a model for what China needs.

Writing about War

Here I explore three ways in which contemporary writing about the Sino-Japanese War in the reportage genre reflected aspects both of the politics of the post–Cold War era and ideas that have been important in twentieth-century China more widely. Both genre and images owe a great deal to writing both in the recent and more distant past, but this reportage also reflected officially sanctioned opening of boundaries in areas such as the contribution of the Nationalist government to the war effort. In some areas, these writers pushed the boundaries further than the official discourse must have intended, for reasons of regional pride or anger over the still unresolved legacy of the Cultural Revolution.

The collection edited by Song Shiqi and Yan Jingzheng entitled *The War of Resistance to Japan Through the Pens of Journalists* (1995) is the first case in point.[9] On the fiftieth anniversary of the ending of the war, the People's Daily Publishing Company in Beijing asked sixty-two former war correspondents, many of them former employees of the predecessors of the CCP-controlled Xinhua (New China News Agency), and long-standing party members, to write short memoirs of their period as war correspondents in 1937–45. The most famous, perhaps, was Lu Yi, one of the best known frontline correspondents of the 1930s, who worked for the Tianjin *Da gongbao*.[10] In some ways the collection is rather bland; its accounts, although told in the first person, generally use formulaic and standardized language. Yet the topics discussed in the memoirs are significant in that they include many of the battles and campaigns that took place in the Nationalist-controlled areas of China (such as Taierzhuang and Xuzhou); and beneath the official reediting of the pieces, it is clear that the former correspondents valued the opportunity finally to put the most significant events of their lives on public record.

Much more heart-on-sleeve about the connection between the war and the nature of contemporary Chinese identity are books by members of the postwar generation, who have no personal memories to draw upon, yet express their relationship to the war perhaps far more as personal odyssey in which the war is a vehicle for other ideas and feelings. One prominent example of this is Fang Jun's *The Devil Soldiers I Knew* (1997).[11] Fang Jun was born in 1954 in Beijing, the son of an Eighth Route Army veteran, became a steelworker, and then joined the military and the CCP in 1973. In the 1980s, he studied Japanese at night school and became an assistant in the office of the *Yomiuri Shimbun* and then the Japanese consulate, before going to Japan as an overseas student between 1991 and 1997. Fang had found out that in the early 1990s, there were still 300,000–400,000 living Japanese soldiers who had taken part in the invasion of China, and stimulated by the memory of conversations with his father about the war years, decided that he would interview various of these Japanese "devil soldiers" before they died.[12] His book, a highly personal and emotional account of self-discovery, is shaped through a succession of interviews with Japanese army veterans.

Fan Jianchuan's book title and subtitle indicate sweeping aims. The title, "One Person's War of Resistance," implies a participant's memoir, but the subtitle reveals something rather different: "Using one person's collection to look at a war of the whole nation."[13] It is a variant of the exercise Fang Jun is carrying out in his memoir (Fan tells us his book was specifically inspired by Fang's). Fan is also reconstructing the war experience, but in his case, via the artefacts that he has collected. Fan was born in 1957 in Sichuan, and had been a soldier, a teacher, and an official, before resigning to go into business (as his birth date suggests, this is a true story of the reform era). He has also been a collector of memorabilia since childhood, with a particular interest in the ceramic goods of the Cultural Revolution and the War of Resistance, and his collections of these two are among "the leading examples in the country."[14] He was, in 2000, deputy chairman of the Sichuan provincial collectors' committee. Each short chapter starts with a particular item from his collection—a cup, a helmet, an ID card—and segues into a reflection about the item's significance during the war and in society today. It goes further than Fang Jun in placing the War of Resistance in the context of other traumas such as the Cultural Revolution.

The Sino-Japanese War as Exploration of the Modern Self

One of the ways in which writing about the War of Resistance stands out in the contemporary era is its continuities with tropes and genres that have been important in the shaping of modern China more widely. In this sense, the War of Resistance becomes parallel to events such as the Cultural Revolution or the May Fourth Movement; often important not so much for the objective history of particular campaigns, social phenomena, or events, but rather the classic Geertzian cultural sense; in other words, their meaning within a matrix of interlocking significations.

One area in which these accounts are noteworthy, though it may not be immediately obvious, is in their status as first-person narratives. Autobiography is a genre with its own specific history in China; as Pei-yi Wu has argued, the Confucian tradition militated heavily against accounts that pushed the subjective self forward in accounts of events, deeming such accounts arrogant, self-promoting, and untrustworthy. "Traditional" Confucian autobiography tends to omit such grammatical indicators as first-person pronouns, making it hard to tell which person the account is written in.[15] The May Fourth era of the early twentieth century, influenced by European romanticism, saw writers such as Guo Moruo and Yu Dafu revel in the subjective self and the very non-Confucian exploration of the self as a valid subject in its own right, but by the 1930s, the increasing influence of Marxism as an intellectual worldview as well as the feeling of collective national anxiety about the threat from Japan put paid to much of this individualism for its own sake. Yet this did not prevent journalists and writers, often drawing on the conventions of mass-market fiction, from projecting themselves as personalities via newspaper columns; they did so, however, not in a celebration of themselves, but in the Confucian style of men who, though self-declaredly uneducated, nonetheless had to speak out at a time of national peril.[16] This style did not exist in quite the same way during the high Mao era, particularly after the chilling clampdown of the Anti-Rightist Movement which followed the brief Hundred Flowers liberalization in 1957. It was revived in the "scar litera-ture" era under Hua Guofeng and the early period of Deng Xiaoping's period as paramount leader. Yet its primary purpose at that time was to make use of the official sanctioning of criticism of the Cultural Revolu-tion.

It was not until the 1990s, when Cold War restrictions on discussion of the Sino-Japanese conflict had faded, that the War of Resistance as a whole became a subject of reportage. For someone like Fang Jun, who was only a child at the time of the Cultural Revolution, there is clearly another agenda behind his desire, fifty years on, to explore the war years. The way in which he expresses that desire shows significant nods to the traditions of first-person reportage that had developed in fits and starts in twentieth-century China and owed some of their origins to norms and conventions that were significantly older.[17]

So Fang Jun, in his concluding chapter, addresses the question of why he wrote such a personalized book in the first place. He protests: "I'm not a politician, I'm not an artist, I'm not an educator, nor am I an es-sayist, and moreover, I've never thought of doing such stuff."[18] Earlier, he declares: "I really have no talent for writing . . . If the Japanese were like the Germans, would I still need to write? . . . [Yet] I feel that it is a sort of historical responsibility that is driving me on."[19] Yet despite these protestations, the book is full of literary artifice, used with great skill: to give just one example, the repetitions in the foreword, where he ex-plains why he began to weep when learning of Japanese war atrocities: "My tears were for the humiliation of the Chinese people half a century before; my tears were for the blood shed in struggle by . . . the Chinese people half a century before; my tears were for the heart of a former sol-dier . . . who risked death for his country."[20] He ends the book by an-swering his own question as to why he wrote it: "I hope that our moth-erland will be rich and strong, I hope that our children will be healthy and strong. When it was not rich and strong, when they were not healthy and strong, then we let the Northeast [Manchuria] go, we lost Lugouqiao [the Marco Polo Bridge], we retreated from Shanghai, and the blood flowed in Nanjing."[21] With a nod to the Social Darwinism that has informed most nationalist discourse in China, Fang Jun situates his own personal odyssey very much as part of a wider and praiseworthy agenda in contemporary politics: the fear that neo-imperialism may once again make China vulnerable. Though he is careful to acknowledge students and veterans in Japan who have recognized their country's war guilt—this is a sophisticated book, despite the author's protestations of lack of culture—Fang Jun positions himself very much as part of a current discourse that sees China, even in its current prominent position in East Asia, as always on the verge of victimhood. As James Hevia's chapter in this volume suggests, the post–Cold War moment, shaped by a perceived neoliberal, neo-imperialist discourse, has encouraged the use of historical examples of China's suffering at the hands of foreign powers in contemporary politics.

Similar considerations motivate Fan Jianchuan. However, the link between the personalized autobiography and the wider national agenda is far harder to find in the volume of war correspondents' memoirs. This is perhaps not surprising for a book that emanated from the People's Daily Publishing House, one of the most official voices that one can imagine in contemporary China, and whose editors note in the foreword that the collection is meant to be "the war of resistance through the pens of reporters," not "reporters during the war of resistance," and that several of the pieces were therefore edited in unstated ways to fit this agenda of the topic, rather than the people, being at the center.[22] With its emphasis on material objectivity, the Marxist approach to autobiography perhaps was not so far from the traditional Confucian view that one should not foreground the self too obviously.

The War, Cannibalism, and Culture

As part of his construction of a purportedly unsophisticated literary self, Fang Jun also uses one of the most powerful images in Chinese culture, when he titles his very first chapter "Human flesh dumplings," reporting that in one of his interviews with a Japanese veteran, the old soldier told tales of how he had heard (at second hand) that guards at a certain prison had cooked up body parts of various Chinese prisoners, women in particular, and eaten them.[23]

It is not possible here to go into the question of whether the Japanese did ever eat flesh dumplings. I am unaware of historical evidence that they did, other than in extreme cases of battlefield starvation, and if incidents are documented, horrific and brutal though they are, they must have been intensely rare. Fang Jun, with the disingenuousness that marks the book, claims in the first sentence of that chapter that originally he intended to place this section at the back of the book, rather than at the beginning. In fact he did place it at the start: but why give priority to the one incident in the book that is reported, even by the Japanese veteran telling it, at second hand? Yamashita, the veteran, does not claim that he ate human flesh, but that he had heard that others knew of it being done. Considering how many well-documented atrocities the Japanese did commit in China during the war period, why does this one have such power that it is brought up before the more "mainstream" atrocities reported at first hand elsewhere in the book?[24]

In part, it may well be because of the continuing importance of cannibalism as a recurring theme in Chinese culture, although as a taboo, not a practice to be emulated. In the twentieth century, Lu Xun was perhaps the most famous user of the image in his *Diary of a Madman* (1918), in which the metaphor used by the "madman" for the pervasiveness of Confucian thought in Chinese culture is that of a society where people eat each other, although the image is many centuries old. More recently, and controversially, rumors of cannibalism during the excesses of the Cultural Revolution in deepest rural China have come to the surface since the 1980s, though these reports are emphatically not among those encouraged by the Chinese government.[25] Whether these stories are true or not—and if they are, again, they are surely very rare—they speak to a continuing cultural fascination with and repulsion for the phenomenon of cannibalism.

For Fang Jun, after hearing Yamashita's story, the idea of cannibalism affects his encounter with the Japanese around him in 1991. As Yamashita and he sit together, Fang says he is suddenly revolted by the dumplings they are eating: "I felt that the meat on the plate in my hand was bright red human flesh! . . . I put the plate on the table, and said to the old Japanese devil: 'This is human flesh! Old man . . . I can't make dumplings out of human flesh for you!'"[26] Later, he visits Mount Fuji and hurls accusations at the mountain: Why did it not speak out and tell the truth about this awful phenomenon? This section is stylized and highly literary in its presentation.

Cannibalism is presented here not in terms of a historical phenomenon, but as a means, constructed through an essentially literary mode of writing, through which to look at Chinese society. It is both comparable and in contrast with one of the more notable exposés of cannibalism in recent years, Zheng Yi's *Scarlet Memorial (Hongse jinianbei)*, published in Taiwan after the author had escaped from post-Tiananmen China.[27] *Scarlet Memorial* is a reportage account of the phenomenon of cannibalism in Guangxi autonomous region during the Cultural Revolution, at the most extreme period of internal conflict. Although reportage was instrumental in the reconsideration of the Cultural Revolution during the 1970s and 1980s, *Scarlet Memorial* would simply not have been publishable in China, particularly after 1989. Yet it is a product of the reconsideration of communist society in the wake of the Cultural Revolution, examining, with a May Fourth single-mindedness, the path along which blind obedience had taken China, and laying the blame directly at the feet of the CCP and of Chinese culture and society itself. While literal cannibalism is clearly at the center of the tale, the symbolic and culturally resonant idea of cannibalism, so powerful for Lu Xun and his forebears as well, is clearly what makes the investigation of this particular evil so powerful for Zheng Yi: as he says near the end of his book, "Lu Xun stated in his first short story, 'Diary of a Madman,' that throughout China's history books, we read about nothing but cannibalism . . . I for one believe it. In my opinion, the entire totalitarian Han culture is one of cannibalism . . . Cannibalism was recently pushed to unprecedented extremes by the CCP theories of struggle and dictatorship."[28] Once again, as in the most radical antitraditional May Fourth tradition, cannibalism was used as a means of focusing more widely on trends in China that led to metaphorical, as well as literal, self-devouring.

Not so with Fang Jun's piece, of course. While there is no explicit reference to the May Fourth trope of cannibalism, such an artfully constructed piece of reportage as *Devil Soldiers* is unlikely to have placed "human flesh dumplings" at the very beginning of the book by accident, particularly after the faux-naivete of the opening words of the book proper: "Originally, I planned to put this topic at the end of the book." For both Zheng Yi and Fang Jun, beyond the horror of an incident of cannibalism in its own right, there is a cultural significance to the idea. Yet Fang Jun does not use the cannibalism trope as Lu Xun or Zheng Yi did, to criticize China from within, but instead to find a way to portray China's invaders as ultimately evil, in some way culturally beyond the pale. Although this is clearly at the extreme, the chapter on "Human flesh dumplings" reflects the wider way in which writing on the Sino-Japanese war has been used to reconstruct the twentieth-century Chinese as positive, patriotic figures who are at the same time victims of unspeakable savagery by others, rather than the authors of their own misfortunes. Not that self-loathing is lacking in contemporary Chinese writing: one need only read Wang Shuo's novels to see that. One should also note that neither of these self-presentations is in any objective sense truer than the other; as with their May Fourth counterparts three-quarters of a century earlier, they are responses to contemporary issues in China rather than being wholly reflections of the past. Yet the use of the war against Japan, and Japanese war atrocities in particular, as a means of creating identity using tropes liberated by the end of the Cold War, is very noticeable in this sort of writing.

The Permitted Past: New Boundaries of Interpretation

The meeting place for the league was the National Normal School, and the place where they had asked me to lecture was the school's auditorium. The auditorium could hold over 1,000 people; at 7 o'clock, I mounted the stage, and after the league's leader had introduced me, I gave a special talk on the determination for resistance at the center, and on the words that chairman Chiang had personally uttered in Shanghai, and in Nanjing . . . In their applause and welcoming voices, I saw their warm enthusiasm for resistance to the enemy and saving the nation. Afterwards, all the League members sang inspiring songs about national salvation; their spirit strengthened mountains and rivers, their voices moved the wall-tiles, and it made you very emotional.[29]

This reportage was by Du Zhongyuan, prominent journalist and anti-Japanese nationalist, writing in September 1937, on a visit to Taiyuan where he addressed the local National Salvation League. Two years before, Du had been imprisoned on the order of the Nationalist government for allowing the publication of an article which insulted the Japanese emperor; the magazine he edited, *Xinsheng*, or *New Life*, was a Marxist-influenced voice for the urban unemployed. Now he was one of the biggest boosters for the United Front.

In the early 1990s, Zhang Menghui wrote about his time in wartime Chongqing, when he helped write a national salvation song. A Sichuanese native, Zhang had become editor of the *National Gazette*

(Guomin gongbao) in Chongqing in 1943, and continued to work as a writer and publisher in post-1949 China:

> The voices of the youths in the Nationalist areas grew ever louder. They had not yet gone to the frontline and joined up, but they weren't just sitting there and waiting for victory. They used their strength to the utmost to provide fuel for the fire of the war of resistance. Half a century has gone by. China has gone through massive changes. But the songs of national salvation in resistance to Japan still remain deep in the hearts of us old people.[30]

These pieces, written some five and a half decades apart, are notable for their similarities perhaps more than their differences. Retrospect and romanticism have surely affected the way in which the journalist recalled the events of the early war period. Yet many of the linguistic conventions and the tropes remain the same: the expression "War of Resistance to Japan" was officially adopted early on, and the idea that unity against Japan was constant, enthusiastic, and unquestioned, is explicit throughout.

What is significant, though, is the intervening period between the 1930s and 1990s, when these tropes and ideas, though remaining embedded in the political culture, changed their meanings significantly. The Maoist period forced interpretation away from the Nationalist role in the war, and although the War of Resistance continued to be a memory in popular culture, it took second place to issues of class warfare. Even after the changes in atmosphere of the 1980s, this collection of memoirs continues to stress the CCP's role in the war, and glorify events such as the Hundred Regiments Campaign in which later communist icons such as Peng Dehuai were involved. Yet the publication of the memoirs, officially restricted though they are, does mark a significant change in emphasis. Although most of the sixty-two participants were in fact CCP members or sympathizers before 1949, the geographical spread of the pieces takes in far more of the war period outside the Yan'an base area than was feasible before the 1980s. Furthermore, there are implications throughout the memoirs that the participants are glad to have a chance to speak of matters that they feel have been unjustly ignored in the past few decades. Zhang Menghui, in his conclusion above, takes care to note that however many decades have passed, the events that he took part in during the War of Resistance continue to be significant.

The theme of the link between past and present comes up over and over again: Zhang Menghui's statement is echoed by Ding Fuhai, who ends his piece: "Half a century has gone by, and our country has produced massive changes. But the history of Japanese imperialism invading us, we will never forget! The Chinese people's brave spirit of resistance to Japan will eternally stimulate us forward!"[31] In a rare account from a woman correspondent, Lu Huinian's memoir elevates her wartime experience in gendered terms: "I have done two important jobs in my life," she began: "mothering and news."[32]

Over and over, the writers recall the importance of the war period; while they do not explicitly contrast it with what came in between in the Mao era, the terminology they use, all of which changes little from reports from the 1930s themselves—war to the end, enemy, imperialism—stresses the sheer significance of the events to the shaping of their own lives as well as that of the country, as well as the increasing downgrading of the Mao-era conflict with the Nationalists. Nonetheless, why should such nostalgia necessarily have any significance for later generations? As we shall see, the phenomena of writers such as Fang Jun and Fan Jianchuan show that, for whatever reason, the reclamation of the war against Japan as a "good war," one that justified both the nation and the lives and experiences of those who lived through it, has also shaped the postwar generations who are looking back to the war, not to their own experiences, to find legitimacy in contemporary China.

For instance, Fan Jianchuan's reflections on his memorabilia sum up the essential divide in this way: "On the one side were Mao Zedong and Chiang Kaishek in the camp of resistance to Japan, on the other were Wang Jingwei and Puyi, representing the camp of treachery."[33] Looking at his collection of memorabilia, he notes: "From the few . . . Chiang Kaishek items [I have], we can say they are the proof that he made a contribution to the War of Resistance to Japan."[34] He reflects further on collaboration:

We Chinese often call ourselves descendants of the dragon . . . with Wang Jingwei's . . . type, we gnash our teeth in hatred, and look on them as fleas produced by the dragon. In fact, rather than saying that they are a variant type of the dragon seed, say instead that our Chinese nation closely resembles . . . a group of ants . . . among whom a certain proportion are fleas. The strong proof of this is the 800,000 puppet soldiers who were willing to sell themselves to the Japanese . . . Of all the bad things that happen in the world, half are done by bad people, and the other half are the result of the apathy, indifference, tolerance and even support of people who don't care about the bad people. If those 800,000 puppet troops (and not every one of those puppet troops was a follower of the big collaborators or evildoers) had not produced Wang Jingwei, then they could instead have produced Li Jingwei or Zhang Jingwei; if they had not produced Chen Gongbo, then they would have produced Wang Gongbo or Zhao Gongbo.[35]

On the surface, there is nothing much here that the CCP-endorsed version of the new public memory of the Sino-Japanese war could find fault with. It is worth noting that the very topic of collaboration has been discussed much only in the last decade or so, though there is now a considerable literature about it. Nonetheless, it is still not feasible politically to take an attitude toward the collaborators other than the one Fan puts forward here: namely, that Wang Jingwei's lust for power was such that he was exploited easily by the Japanese.[36] Yet it is not too far-fetched to wonder whether the passage above about ants and fleas is not just talking about the War against Japan, but also about the Cultural Revolution, or other periods during which Chinese society produced "fleas" as well as "ants." The Cultural Revolution, after all, was officially blamed on the Gang of Four, a convenient scapegoating that allowed wider questions about the nature of Chinese society, such as those raised in *Scarlet Memorial*, to go unasked by the CCP.[37] Fang Jun's work moved responsibility for China's crisis strongly away from the Chinese themselves to the imperialist invaders. Although there is nothing explicit in Fan's statement above that contradicts that interpretation, there is a strong hint that something within Chinese society also made it easier for the Japanese to exercise control. And the hint that perhaps the Cultural Revolution is what is meant, though not stated, is made more explicit in a later passage. As we will see below, Fan's work shows how the newly permitted boundaries for interpretation of the war can be exceeded.

Problematic Memories: Forgotten or Forbidden?

Fang Jun and Fan Jianchuan know each other: Fan specifically cites Fang as an inspiration for his own book. The commonalities and differences in the way that they address the revisions in memory of the Sino-Japanese War are revealing. Yet the two works take quite different positions on the importance of the Sino-Japanese War in contemporary Chinese life, even though they deal with many similar topics and tropes, as well as taking a strongly individualistic and personalized stance. In other words, there is no monolithic post–Cold War interpretation of the War of Resistance: we are speaking not of new Chinese memory, but of memories. In a way that is common in Chinese political writing, Fan uses his book to make more critical and self-reflective observations about contemporary Chinese life, but is rarely explicit in doing so, preferring to rely on hint and inference. The boundary between memories that are permitted and those that are frowned upon is often, deliberately, left vague.

For instance, probably because of his family connections with the Eighth Route Army, Fang Jun hews much more to a traditional CCP-driven historiography, which downplays the contribution by Chiang Kai-shek and the Nationalist government to the victory over the Japanese. Fang's father, a veteran of the (Communist) Eighth Route Army, tells him that "the reason that Chiang Kai-shek had to withdraw to Taiwan was that he didn't fight the Japanese." Fang then regrets that he never took the opportunity to ask his father, "If Chiang had begun to fight the Japanese, what then?"[38] One entire chapter (entitled "Your dad was in the Eighth Route Army?") deals with an interview with a Japanese veteran who talks about his respect for this most iconic of communist forces during the War.[39] There are also references that suggest the widening of the agenda beyond the hagiography of the CCP's contribution. One of these is Fang's discovery of the story of the Manchurian resistance leader Ma Zhanshan: "when I left China in 1991, almost all the anti-Japanese heroes whom I had in my heart were CCP people," he notes, but finding out about Ma Zhanshan changed that view; another is the desire of a Japanese army veteran, Kobayashi, to return in Fang's company to Beijing, where he served during the war, and visit the street named after the Nationalist general Zhang Zizhong, who was killed in battle against the Japanese during the war.[40] Yet the fuller discussion of Japanese atrocities, rather than rehabilitation of the Nationalists, is really the major historiographical change that is visible in this account.

In contrast, Fan Jianchuan gives far more attention to the record of the Nationalists, and spends very little time at all on the CCP and the Eighth Route Army. Although Fan's nationalist credentials are strong, his account is strongly flavored by a regional emphasis that is given particular piquancy by its relationship to the War of Resistance: specifically, that the exclusion of the Nationalist contribution from Chinese historiography until very recently meant that Sichuanese contributions to the War, few of which related to the CCP, were also underreported.

So the white sun on the blue sky of the Nationalist flag recurs over and over again among the photographs of the prized exhibits in Fan's collection—for instance, enamelled badges from Sichuan militias and regular troops.[41] Among the heroic tales he tells are of seven Sichuan heroes on the frontline, and of a woman medical orderly named Zhang Shufen, all of whom served in the Nationalist army.[42] Fan reflects on Zhang Shufen's picture, still on her ID card which is now in his collection: she looks determined, he observes. Did she survive? Did she have children? If she were alive now, he muses, she would probably be about 80. And then, the leap from the personal to the general: "If we fought a just war, isn't it correct that we relied on the contributions and sacrifices of millions of soldiers such as Zhang Shufen?"[43] Regardless of their affiliation to one party or another, the "just war" was not just about leaders, but about ordinary people. Studs Terkel would have little to argue with here. The regional element also comes out more strongly near the end, where Fan declares: "Sichuan, you are the strongman who held up the War of Resistance!" and goes on to point out that Chongqing was the center of the nation's resistance during the War: unstated, but heavily implied, is the understanding, Chongqing, not Yan'an.[44] By the end of the book, the nods toward Chiang Kai-shek really become quite explicit, as in the section where Fan declares that the much-mocked New Life movement of the 1930s was not necessarily such a bad idea: ideas such as not spitting on the street or waiting politely in line for buses rather than pushing on board, he says, are sensible enough.[45] In contrast, the CCP and the Eighth Route Army are hardly mentioned. This is a different view of the Chiang regime even from the more tolerant views of the war correspondents or of Fang Jun. It suggests that for Fang and Fan, the War of Resistance has become a good war, but the decision about what was "good" within it is still dependent on the many different positions from which the war can be interpreted. Yet without the ending of the Cold War binaries within Chinese society, such differences could never have been expressed.

Some clue as to why Fan feels it is so crucial to restore Sichuan's contribution, and the Nationalist contribution, to the War of Resistance emerges in the segment where he discusses his most-prized item of memorabilia: oddly, it is one that does not date from the war period at all. The chapter is entitled: "An 'appeal' on an earthenware cup: the fate of a Sichuanese old soldier of the War of Resistance." Fan says of the item: "It's an ordinary earthenware cup, not very old . . . but it's one of the most precious items in my collection of War of Resistance items." The cup has written on it, somewhat misspelled in Chinese: "I only remember the eight years of the War of Resistance. I fought the Japanese, and I took a bullet in my leg. I determinedly fought to the end and never left the line of fire! 15 September 1966."[46]

As Fan goes on to explain, this was written on the cup just a few months after the Cultural Revolution broke out. Under what Fan terms the "red terror" *(hongse kongbu)*, the owner must have come under attack as a Sichuanese former soldier in the Nationalist army whose record now counted against him. The owner, Fan suggested, could not have been well educated, as the relatively short sentences above contain four miswritten characters. He must also have been a soldier in the Nationalist army, not the Eighth Route Army or a local guerrilla force; otherwise he would not have come under attack during the Cultural Revolution.

Looking at this string of characters, I felt saddened and angry. In the eight years of the War of Resistance, he had dodged death and had for many years been considered to have had an honorable experience, and suddenly, overnight, it was considered shameful?! He . . . had no place to appeal, in the political high temperature of that era, the majority of people didn't believe him . . . so all he could think of was to write on this cup, and write down some words from his heart; he was surely sad and angry.[47]

Worse still, Fan wondered, perhaps he was sent down and made the cup while serving a sentence of reform through labor *(laogai)*. But the cup, which Fan makes not only the subject of a lengthy reflection, but also uses as the image for the front cover of the book, suggests strongly that at least a significant part of his interest in the War of Resistance is the way that it provides a "just war" with which to contrast later events such as the Cultural Revolution and the Mao era more generally, which downplayed the importance of the nation and the region.

Conclusion

Fan Jianchuan, in his introduction, observes that his friends regard his collections of memorabilia as somewhat eccentric, and suggest that he should leave such matters to the government. Yet he declares that he finds himself personally connected to these themes, and it is clear that the way in which he uses his collection to make observations about contemporary China do not exactly match the messages of an official institution such as the Museum of the War of Resistance to Japan in Beijing, even if they are not in direct opposition to it.[48] He specifically advocates that "I hope that having read this, my readers will continue to hold to reform and open up, and have determination to enrich the people and strengthen the country."[49] This is not so different from Fang Jun's message after his own first-person journey, in his case conducted via interviews, rather than memorabilia. Yet the shades of gray between the interpretations of just two younger writers who have turned to the memory of the War of Resistance show the way in which state permission to address a previously taboo topic does not guarantee that all those who exploit that permission will respect the same boundaries. Even the more tightly edited and controlled selection of war correspondents' memoirs show an element of self-justification and implied dissatisfaction along with the obedient adherence to the new political norms of interpretation of the war. There is little doubt that the War of Resistance is now China's "good war." Furthermore, in a world where the Cold War definitions of Chinese identity no longer hold, the history of the war plays an important role in redefining Chineseness. But many issues—generation, gender, regional affiliation, experience of the war itself, of the Cultural Revolution, and of the reform era—shape group and individual understandings of *why* that war was "good." The repeated diplomatic disputes over war memory that have marked Sino-Japanese relations in the first years of the new millennium suggest that there is a new hardening of boundaries at work: it remains to be seen whether this will once again hinder the nuanced understanding of the war and its legacy that the region so desperately needed, but was denied, during the Cold War.

~ 8

Remembering the Century of Humiliation

The Yuanming Gardens and Dagu Forts Museums

JAMES L. HEVIA

IN EAST ASIA, the end of the Cold War came in the midst of massive economic transformations that had already begun to rework memory of war and revolution. This was especially the case in the People's Republic of China (PRC), where nationalism, now uncoupled from a socialism that the state itself was rapidly abandoning, moved to the center of official public discourse. At the core of post–Cold War—and post-socialist—Chinese nationalism was the juxtaposition of the achievements of China's ancient civilization to the humiliating military defeats and unequal treaties *(bupingdeng tiaoyue)* imposed on China by Euroamerican powers in the nineteenth century. Now, however, rather than relating the depredations visited upon China to the promotion of a world revolution against capitalism and imperialism, the state's goal has been to integrate China into a global market, while regaining the territories lost to the motherland through unequal treaties. The result has been the reconfiguring of a dominant trope foundational for both the Nationalist Party of Chiang Kai-shek and the Communist Party of Mao Zedong—the century of national humiliation *(bainian guochi)*.[1] No longer represented as an aspect of global class struggle, nineteenth-century Western imperial warfare has instead been repositioned in relation to China's place within a post–Cold War world of American hegemony and neoliberal globalization. China's attention to a war that is not part of World War II, even widely defined, provides an important contrast to the experience of Japan as explored in other chapters in this volume. For Japan, the memory of the "Fifteen Years' War" of the 1930s and 1940s stands absolutely central to contemporary political uses of history. For the Chinese, in contrast, the War of Resistance to Japan (as it is known in China) is clearly a key part of China's remembering of conflict; the long history of China's victimization from the Opium Wars onward means that a much wider range of wars remain in contention in Chinese memory during the post–Cold War moment.

While this shift is evident in a number of domains of contemporary Chinese thought and practice, it is also publicly visible in new museums[2] and theme parks, and at reconfigured historical sites that recall national humiliation. Perhaps nowhere are these processes more evident than at the Yuanming Gardens (old Summer Palace) and the Dagu Forts museums. Built northwest of Beijing by Qing emperors as a refuge from the dust and heat capital, the Yuanming Gardens comprised a vast complex of pavilions, temples, and pleasure palaces. They were almost completely destroyed by the British army in 1860 during the second Opium War (1856–60). The Dagu forts were located on the Bohai gulf, at the mouth of the Bei River, and were designed to protect Beijing and Tianjin from maritime invasions. The forts were attacked and seized by European armies in 1858, 1860, and 1900. Made into national memorials by the government of the People's Republic because they vividly bore the signs of China's humiliations at the hands of Western imperialism, these "sites of memory" have recently been rededicated with new monuments to commemorate the recession of Hong Kong in 1997. Today each in its own way shows distinct signs of metamorphosis, indications of change within a broader context of state-sponsored public memory. Both also display a movement across the twentieth century from history to national heritage, or to the "theme parkization" of the past.

The premise of this chapter is that by tracing the history of sites such as the Yuanming Gardens and the Dagu Forts, and uncovering the palimpsestual layering of meanings evident at each, we can come to understand better the contemporary memory of war and revolution in East Asia. Before proceeding to a discussion of the Gardens and Forts, however, let me clarify the use of the term "sites of memory." I take it from Pierre Nora, who compares such sites to embodied or lived memory. Embodied memory is the kind produced by the ceremonies of a community or a household, and is lived through the taken for granted routines and rituals of social life.[3] In contrast, the sort of memory that adheres to sites, Nora argues, is a product of "a society deeply absorbed in its own transformation and renewal, one that inherently values the new over the ancient, the young over the old, the future over the past." In the place of lived memory, we have national museums, archives, holidays, and official histories; memorial monuments, veterans organizations, and fraternal orders. Each of these sites fabricates a relationship between an ever receding, increasingly disembodied past, and a present in which the inherent value of the new is given precedence.

Central to Nora's argument is the notion that sites of memory rely on a willful intention to remember, a desire to block, through their very material presence, forgetting. This materiality might be understood as providing, on the one hand, an anchor for the present and, on the other, a condensation of the complexities of the past into a singular meaning. Yet, if such willful action is designed to fix meaning through a unitary and unambiguous materiality, the sites themselves, Nora asserts, have a "capacity for metamorphosis, an endless recycling of their meaning, and an unpredictable proliferation of their ramifications."[4]

To put this another way, original acts of will must be repeated if memory is to be regenerated; but when such acts are performed, they are necessarily inflected through a new set of relationships different from those involved in the moment of original constitution. What will be reconstructed as memory can thus be open to alteration and to an infusion of new meaning. It is this double identity—one fixed, the other mutable—that makes sites of memory themselves contingent and changeable, and hence, historical. These general observations about sites of memory are no less the case in a socialist than in a capitalist economic order; no less pertinent to an "authoritarian" than to a "democratic" political structure. In any of these cases, the key arena of expression and contention is invariably the nation. Who gets to define it and under what conditions? How is its past of warfare and conflict to be recalled? In the wake of the Cold War, such questions take on added urgency in the former socialist world as the relation between the nation and the global is reimagined and structurally reconfigured by neoliberalism.

From History to Heritage

It may be useful to begin this discussion with the notion of humiliation itself and the way it has been linked, on the one hand, to European perceptions of their actions in China and, on the other, to Chinese understandings of those actions. At least from the time of the British destruction of the Yuanming Gardens in 1860, Europeans and Americans operating in and on China came to believe that deliberate acts of humiliation were necessary elements for transforming Chinese attitudes toward the Western presence in China. It was generally held that emperors, mandarins, and the common people all had difficulty distinguishing appearances from reality, preferring instead to dwell in a fantasy realm where China was clearly superior to all other countries. Western commentators saw what they considered this singular failure of the Chinese to face up to their own weakness—so obvious to them— to be the core of the China problem and a central element of the Far Eastern Question as it was constituted in Europe.[5]

Few believed, however, that reason and persuasion alone would alter Chinese attitudes; rather, most felt they had to be shocked or awed into a new sensibility. In 1900, Europeans and Americans put this belief into practice by penetrating "sacred" places like the Forbidden City (Figure 8.1), destroying and looting palaces, blowing up Buddhist and Daoist temples, burning sacred texts, and publicly executing, in particularly demeaning ways, perpetrators of violence against Europeans. In this classroom of violence and punishment, lessons were assumed to be learned only when they simultaneously undermined native beliefs and superstitions and clearly demonstrated Western superiority in explicit and understandable terms.

In this early version of psychological warfare, humiliation was seen as a device for stripping away the particular mental processes that made it possible for Chinese to avoid directly confronting reality. The pedagogy of humiliation thereby served to construct more pliable colonized subjects. These techniques for dealing with an imaginary Chinese cultural mind run like a golden thread through British thinking on China well into the twentieth century; they were later readily translated by the U.S. Central Intelligence Agency, for instance, into the psychological elements of "counter-insurgency" warfare from the Philippines to Vietnam.

Figure 8.1. Humiliation of China. From *Leslie's Weekly,*
November 17, 1900.

The lessons taught by the imperial powers were learned by people in
China, but not necessarily in the way they had been intended. In the
immediate aftermath of the Boxer Uprising, Chinese nationalists
coined the term "national humiliation" and used it to rally support in
anti-imperialist and anti-dynastic campaigns.[6] In the first two decades
of the twentieth century, as Paul Cohen recently pointed out, a
plethora of books appeared recounting the humiliations that had been
heaped upon the Qing dynasty and the Chinese people, all of which
demonstrated the pressing need for patriotic Chinese citizens to take
action.[7] In other instances, the sense of humiliation of reformers such

as Liang Qichao and Kang Youwei was reinforced when they saw objects plundered from the Yuanming Gardens on public display in American and French Museums—Liang in New York in 1893, Kang while in Paris a few years after the Boxer uprising. Liang wrote of a sense of shame *(hanyen)*. Kang spoke of a wound that broke his heart *(shangxin)*[8] and led him to form the "Know Our Humiliation Society."[9]

The merging of personal grief and a sense of collective shame appears significant here. It not only provided a rationale for denouncing the Qing dynasty, but also seems to have given an impetus to forms of direct action such as protest demonstrations, and for acts that could eradicate signs of humiliation *(xuechi)*. This was the case, for example, after Germany's defeat in World War I. The Ketteler Arch, the memorial that had been demanded by Germany for its minister slain during the Boxer Uprising, was moved into Zhongshan park in the Forbidden City, and rededicated to Sun Yat-sen.[10]

By the 1920s, national humiliation had been institutionalized as a collective malaise represented and redressed through a succession of memorial days throughout the year. Public institutions such as schools and government offices recognized up to twenty-four such days annually.[11] Occurring two and occasionally three times a month from January through November, National Humiliation Days included the dates of signing the "unequal treaties" and the Boxer Protocol imposed by the Western powers, the dates Chinese territory was leased to foreigners (e.g., Weihaiwei to Great Britain), the dates of protest rallies in which demonstrators were killed (e.g., the May 30th Incident in Shanghai), and the dates on which the armies of foreign powers entered Beijing in 1860 and 1900.[12]

As sites of memory, humiliation days provided a foundation upon which to build a new Chinese national consciousness. The new historical subject, the national subject, whether an individual or a collectivity, would be a strong, pure, self-sacrificing anti-imperialist who would rise above historical shame and reclaim China's sovereign rights. This larger-than-life figure would become the model of the new man and woman who would build socialism in China.

National humiliation and its resulting anti-imperialism played a constitutive role in the Chinese Communists' construction of a new China. The People's Republic was established on a unity forged through liberation *(jiefang)* from the humiliations of imperialism and feudalism. When addressing the First Plenary Session of the Chinese People's Political Consultative Conference on September 21, 1949—just a few weeks before the formal inauguration of the PRC—Mao Zedong entitled his remarks "The Chinese people have stood up!" With this direct bodily imagery, he declared that China would "no longer be a nation subject to insult and humiliation."[13] With the advent of the Korean War and the implementation of the Cold War "Containment Policy" by the United States, such imagery became a staple of verbal and visual propaganda. The human figures visible in the socialist realist genre of artistic representation that dominated Chinese public space for more than three decades stood proudly defiant in the face of imperialist provocations.

Few of the national humiliation days seem to have continued into the PRC era, however. They were replaced by positive holidays marking the triumphs of the road to revolution. Nevertheless, a strong anti-imperialist strain of communist thought, built upon remembrance and transcendence of the century of humiliation, was clearly commonplace in public art, school books, radio, film, and later television. Furthermore, Chinese history from the nineteenth century forward was periodized into two segments, from the Opium Wars of 1840 to 1919 as "modern" history and 1919 forward as "contemporary" history. The year 1919, of course, marks the beginning of the May Fourth era, during which the Chinese Communist Party was founded. It signifies, in other words, that moment in which a mature consciousness linking imperialism and feudalism emerged and with it, a means for overcoming the past.

Within this periodization, Chinese historians, building upon a number of Mao's observations concerning the nature of Western imperialism, sought to transform tales of Qing failures into the narrative of the heroic resistance of Chinese peasants and patriotic officials against the Western onslaught. In the process, martyrs were created—fellow countrymen who gave their lives in the anti-imperialist revolutionary struggle. In the case of the events that are memorialized at Yuanming Gardens and Dagu, Chinese communist historians drew upon the historical record left by British, French, German, Russian, and American participants to demonstrate the savagery and unprincipled nature of the aggression against China. This strong and vocal anti-imperialist strain can be found in the writings of Hu Sheng, whose *Imperialism and Chinese Politics* is probably the best known of the genre outside of China.[14] It is a scathing and sarcastic critique of the Powers, the Qing dynasty, and Chinese bourgeois "collaborators." Filled with quotations from Chairman Mao and stinging attacks on imperial capitalism and its running dogs, this kind of passionate anti-imperialism remained evident to the end of the Maoist era and continued to be disseminated internationally in English and other European languages.

The history that resulted was a counter-narrative to British imperial historiography and the scholars influenced by it. In general, historians in Europe and North America have been critical of this counter-narrative, arguing that historical facts have been shoe-horned into ideological or mythical structures in the service of the party-state.[15] Yet it is also the case that elements of the critical position generated by Chinese historians remain difficult to ignore—they were supported by the documentary record. Their use of that record to bring a bill of indictments against Western imperial powers can be read productively, I believe, as performances of very real defiance, the kind that Frantz Fanon[16] saw as part of a process of unlocking the mental shackles of colonialism and realizing liberation.

Humiliation, a general outcome of Western imperialism and colonialism for the colonized, is here turned into something positive and productive, the impetus for leading the Chinese people and other oppressed peoples of the world to stand up. The feisty language of international class struggle evident in both the Chinese and English versions of these works not only performed a symbolic violence, but also established a site of memory that anchored the PRC present, while condensing the vast record of Sino-Western interaction into a simplified and moralistic narrative, one made all the more memorable by its clear identification of heroes and villains. It also had an effect in Europe and North America, generating a host of anxieties over communist-sponsored revolutions in the "third world," some of which were inspired by a Maoist telling of history.

Coupled to these textual sites of memory were the physical places where the events of the nineteenth century unfolded. While the new state seems to have placed its major efforts on creating museums and public monuments of the revolution, it also used its limited resources to preserve many of the sites that were made meaningful by Western imperial aggression. These were re-inscribed, however, within the narrative of liberation.

Much, if not all of this revolutionary memorialization has changed over the last fifteen years. Although the party-state remains a major actor in producing history, in the post–Cold War era it does so in an altered domestic and global context. No longer the vanguard of a worldwide anti-imperialist struggle, the Chinese state apparatus works now to preserve history under the sign of "national heritage." In this new formation, historical sites that once highlighted the ingenuity and labor of the masses and the exploitation of feudal rulers now deliver other messages. At Chengde, the Qing summer palace located about 150 miles northwest of Beijing, for example, a massive restoration of a number of Tibetan Buddhist temples began in the early 1990s. Gone are references to the toiling masses. In their stead are paeans to the high arts of imperial China, the unity of a multicultural nation-state, and the Communist Party's patronage of Tibetan Buddhism. The restored site has also been elevated onto the global stage—it is one among several other official World Heritage sites, an international preservation project of the United Nations Educational, Scientific and Cultural Organization (UNESCO).[17] As such, Chengde's temples and parks become part of China's entry into the globalizing capitalist era of world-class theme parks.

Here, as in other sectors of activity that link China to the international order of capital, state agencies have sought to remake the PRC along the lines of "global standards." Such efforts range from establishing standards of population quality and mass consumption, to new notions of China's historical contributions to a multicultural world history. While state-sponsored historical preservation is clearly part of a development strategy designed to promote external and internal tourism and perhaps to safely ensconce the feudal *and* revolutionary pasts under the apolitical and sanitized sign of heritage,[18] such activities also have the effect of contributing to a broader discourse on patriotism (*aiguo*, love of country, patriotism) and national pride.

This then is the context in which I consider the Yuanming Gardens and Dagu Forts Museum. Both sites are marked by efforts to "remember imperialism" and to recall "national humiliation," while directly and indirectly embracing contemporary processes of globalization.

Yuanming Gardens Museum

For some years now, the Yuanming Gardens, also known as the Old Summer Palace, has been a work in progress. For much of the PRC period, the ruins of the gardens were used for a people's commune and as a place where professors and teachers from nearby universities could perform the manual labor necessary to alter their class consciousness. While the latter practice ended with the close of the Cultural Revolution, farmers continued to live and grow crops within the grounds of the park. In the early 1980s, however, things began to change. A historical research unit was set up that began to publish a journal in 1981, and a small museum was organized. Among other things in the collection, this museum contained a fascinating diorama of British soldiers looting the Yuanming Gardens in 1860.

By the 1990s, an even greater change was evident. At the same time as the garden and public park was being turned into a somewhat tacky leisure center, including power boats for hire, a "paintball" arena and shooting gallery, and an odd display of "primitive totems" on an island in one of the garden's lakes, historical restoration and museumification were also in evidence.[19] The gardens were reconstituted as a signifier of high cultural art from the past and as a different sort of historical memory text and are now clearly associated with national heritage. There are publications that dwell on the beauties of the gardens, models of each of the buildings, and projects to digitally reconstruct portions of the gardens.[20] In 2001 there were also large open-air posters explaining the artistic merit of the architecture and objects to be found at the site. Once defined primarily through the humiliating absence of grand architecture destroyed by pyromaniac imperialists, the Yuanming Gardens have now become a place dedicated to the aesthetic appreciation of China's cultural heritage.[21] These gestures bring the gardens into alignment with sites like the Forbidden City in Beijing or Chengde as part of China's contribution to world art and architecture.

At the same time, however, attention is still drawn to the British destruction of the palaces. Within the European garden area located in the northeast corner of the park, new commemorative structures were erected in 1997 as part of the official celebration of the return of Hong Kong to China (Figure 8.2). One of these is a long wall bearing fifty-one plaques tightly packed with text that provide a blow-by-blow synopsis of the history of imperialism in China from 1840 through the war with Japan that ended in 1945. Large golden characters next to the first plaque proclaim "Never Forget National Humiliation" (*wuwang guochi*). Nearby is a museum that displays a history of the destruction of

Figure 8.2. "Never Forget National Humiliation Wall,"
Yuanming yuan. (Photo by the author, 2002.)

the palaces. It still includes the dusty and ill-lit 1980s diorama of the looting of the Summer Palace, but also displays numerous records of the occupation of Beijing in 1900. Drawings, maps, and photographs are accompanied by dense textual explanations. Of particular interest is the inclusion of photographs taken by European and American photographers of the Euro-American military campaigns of 1860 and 1900.

Like the citation of Western sources in the early PRC history of modern China, these references operate as a powerful condemnation of imperialism by the imperialists themselves. There is also at least one critical Western voice to be heard, that of Victor Hugo, whose comments, presented in French and Chinese, eloquently condemn the looting and destruction of the Summer Palace.

As if to emphasize this point, the display also contains an important public recognition of a foreign location where some Summer Palace loot is held today (Figure 8.3). On one wall, there are photographs of imperial objects that General Montauban sent to the Empress Eugénie in 1860 for her oriental collection at the Château de Fontainebleau. The pictures are taken from a French guidebook to the collection produced when the Château was restored in the early 1990s.[22]

The presence of pictures from this booklet in the museum suggests a heightened sensitivity to the overt display of Qing plunder in European and American museums, the same museums that had so disturbed Liang Qichao and Kang Youwei at the beginning of the twentieth cen-

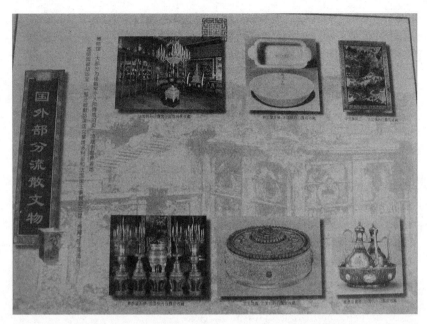

Figure 8.3. Summer Palace plunder in the Château de Fontainebleau, Yuanming Garden Museum display. (Photo by the author, 2002.)

tury. Events in Hong Kong in 2001 reinforced this impression. In recent years,[23] auction houses such as London's Sotheby's and Christie's have sold Summer Palace plunder on the international market, sometimes drawing specific attention to its status as loot by dubbing the auctions "imperial sales." In 2001, Sotheby's and Christie's Hong Kong teamed on an auction sale that included four items from the Yuanming Gardens in a second "imperial sale." Two bronze animal heads (a monkey and an ox) were identified as among the zodiac of twelve animals that made up part of the water clock the Qianlong emperor had commissioned his Jesuit missionaries to build in the European section of the Yuanming Garden.

This sale proved to be the last straw. Outraged, the PRC government formally protested, requesting that Christie's and Sotheby's withdraw the items. When they refused, an unprecedented event occurred—mainland Chinese companies intervened and bought the objects, paying in excess of $6 million for the four pieces, three times the asking price.[24] In fall 2003, one of these pieces was displayed at the Yuanming Gardens.

From the point of view of a number of constituencies within and outside the PRC, the message seemed clear: as reform China reconstructed itself as a modernized nation-state and global power, it could no longer tolerate the flaunting of objects outside China that mark national humiliation.

The Dagu Forts Museum

The linkage between past humiliation and contemporary patriotism is also clearly made at other sites. The Dagu Forts Museum is one such example. Even as the barren salt-flats around Dagu are being transformed into a state-of-the-art container port facility to service north China's export industries, and as coastal summer resort townhouses and high-rise apartment begin to appear all around where the forts once stood, there is nested within and juxtaposed to this new globalized "Chinese modern" a museum of exceedingly modest proportions. It recalls the century of national humiliation.

The forts were destroyed as a condition of the *Final Protocol* of 1901, the treaty imposed on China by European powers and the United States in the wake of the Boxer Uprising the previous year. All that remains today is a walled mound with an ancient gun atop it. Below are a large stone monument, a modest rectangular building containing a museum, and a Korean War–vintage Mig fighter jet, a decaying icon of modern military might occasionally found in public parks and historic sites around north China (Figure 8.4: note the high-rises in the distance). The monument recounts a brief history of the military actions at Dagu and indicates that it was dedicated by the Tianjin municipality in 1997, as part of the celebration of Hong Kong's return. Inside the museum, the historical humiliations from 1840 to 1900 are laid out chronologically. Detailed maps trace the global opium trade of the nineteenth century; diagrams show the military actions at Dagu in 1858, 1859, 1860, and 1900; and heroic paintings of Chinese soldiers depict them hurling themselves at the superior guns of foreign soldiers (Figure 8.5).

There are also reproductions of original documents, including the Treaty of Tianjin imposed by Great Britain following its invasion in 1858, with the most galling passages highlighted in red; a painting of the sack of the nearby town of Tanggu; and Felice Beato's photographs

Figure 8.4. Dagu Forts Museum, showing Mig jet and Memorial. (Photo by the author, 2002.)

of Lord Elgin and General Hope Grant, as well as one of Harry Parkes, over which angry graffiti have been scrawled. In the Boxer section, there are photographs taken by Henry Savage Landor and published in his *China and the Allies*, and others taken by the American photographer and author of stereographic tours of the Holy Land, India, and China, James Ricalton, including the destruction of Tianjin. There is also a photograph that has taken on iconic qualities; it shows a column of Western soldiers marching toward the Meridian Gate *(Wumen)* of the Forbidden City.

Here, as in the Yuanming Gardens at Beijing, visual evidence keeps the imaginary of national humiliation alive, but one may wonder if the same sense of shame and its transcendence that marked the strident anti-imperialism of the first few decades of the PRC still operate today. Anti-imperialist rhetoric pointed, after all, to a fundamental bifurcation of history that was built into the global processes of deterritorialization and reterritorialization wrought by European and American imperial capitalism over the last century and a half.

On the side of the colonized, the era of Western imperialism re-

Figure 8.5. Heroic bravery in a painting at Dagu
Forts Museum. (Photo by the author, 2002.)

mained an open wound that, in the case of China, was to be healed by
socialism and national reconstruction. Moreover, when the history of
Western imperialism was rewritten in China in the 1950s, formal empire was barely in the past—parts of Africa were only then being decol-
onized, and others remained under white rule, while colonial-style
warfare was still much in evidence in Southeast Asia.

This raises the central question posed by the two sites. What are we
to make of the "Never Forget National Humiliation" wall, paintings of
heroic Qing soldiers in the style of a now receding heroic socialist
genre, or the memorial at Dagu? As these sites are engulfed by global
forms of capital and development, by amusement park diversions and
phalanxes of high-rises, what relation do they have to the era of socialist construction and national self-reliance, a time when anti-
imperialism really seemed to matter? To put this another way, how are
we—or contemporary Chinese citizens—to evaluate the new state-

sponsored productions of historical memory in relation to the global-izing forces that are reterritorializing China at the same moment as state socialism is deterritorialized? What, in other words, are these sites of memory being preserved to remember?

At both the Yuanming Gardens and the Dagu Forts museums, the rhetorical force of the presentations points to a technological gap be-tween a "backward" China and a "modernized" West; it also suggests that courage and sheer numbers were not enough to defend the moth-erland. This has been a powerful message that seems to have been ac-cepted by most Chinese people in the post-Mao era. Moreover, this message was part of socialist modernization. Dagu's Mig fighter, how-ever decrepit it seems today, stood as a Cold War–era science and tech-nology answer to the challenge posed by Western imperialism.

Now, however, the Chinese party-state rushes hell-bent toward inte-gration into a global economy that a generation ago was the arch enemy of everything that the PRC stood for. Surely in this process, the authors of official Chinese history are sponsoring more than value-free preservation and heritage, and promoting more than patriotism from the top down. A computer modeling project for the Yuanming Gar-dens and those high-rise buildings marching to the sea that are visible from the mound at Dagu (Figure 8.4) send another sort of message, one inflected now through reform-era opening up and the abandon-ment of state socialism. China can do more than defend itself; it is catching up with the West. The return to the motherland of Hong Kong is situated within this reconstituted nationalism, suggesting the official end of an epoch that began in 1839 with the first Opium War.

Today the site where the forts once stood is part of a huge land recla-mation project, complete with sea-side apartment blocks, high-rise buildings, and a state-of-the-art container port facility to service north China's export industries, it is a site absorbed in its own transformation and renewal, looking toward the future rather than to the past. Cer-tainly the impact of globalization on China would justify such an inter-pretation. But it is also the case that for many older Chinese people, there is a lived memory of a socialist past, of an embodied collectivism. Reform has fragmented, dispersed, and critically revised that past, but it has not yet severed the links to lived memory. Sites like the Yuan-ming Gardens and the Dagu Forts museums may also be caught up in a nostalgia for the clarity and purity of a time when moral certitude was much more easily defined, when warfare was part of lived memory, and when the enemy of the people was unambiguously American militarism and capitalism.

The current configuration of museums and memorials found at the sites discussed here sit, therefore, uneasily beside a memory of a revolutionary and Cold War past, and state involvement in preserving them. At present, such recollections may only articulate with a general sense of unease over the disparities generated by economic reform. If, however, American military unilateralism signals the beginnings of the emergence of a new form of imperial capitalism, then the injunction that introduces the narrative of the century of humiliation at the Yuanming Gardens could disrupt the smug complacencies of national heritage and rekindle a historic memory of the violence that accompanies globalization.

~ 9

Frontiers of Memory

Conflict, Imperialism, and Official Histories in the Formation of Post–Cold War Taiwan Identity

EDWARD VICKERS

IN JUNE 1998, I took a break from my language studies in Taipei to visit the National Palace Museum on the outskirts of the city. Having completed the tour, I had returned to the lobby and was preparing to leave when, without warning, a siren sounded and solid iron shutters descended, blocking off the entrance. "What's going on?" I asked. "Air-raid drill," came the reply. The museum had to be prepared to protect its collections in the event of an attack from across the Taiwan Strait. Only two years previously, the 1996 presidential elections had taken place against the backdrop of Chinese live-fire missile tests in the seas north and south of the island—maneuvers meant to intimidate Taiwan's electorate into backing pro-unification candidates. Like the island as a whole, the Palace Museum operated in the shadow of China's continuing cold war—a conflict featuring its very own missile crisis.

This ongoing standoff between the Republic of China (ROC, as the Taiwanese polity is still officially known) and the People's Republic (PRC) has its roots in the unfinished Chinese Civil War of the 1940s, which in turn was intertwined with the emerging geopolitics of the Cold War world. It is thus perhaps misleading to talk of a "post–Cold War" dispensation in East Asia; Taiwan, like the two Koreas, is a Cold War iceberg that has yet to melt. What has changed, since the demise of the Soviet Union, is the sense that communism as an ideology represents any sort of worldwide menace, and the perception that Taiwan, South Korea, and Japan are front-line bases for the defense of the "Free World." Instead, it is the potential for confrontation between a rising nationalist China and the American superpower that keeps the status quo in the Taiwan Strait frozen—at least for the present.

As socialism has been largely discredited or abandoned in the PRC, the past quarter-century has witnessed a resurgence of official and popular nationalism there (see the chapters in this volume by Rana Mitter and James Hevia). This nationalism has been characterized by a neo-Darwinian essentialization of "the Chinese people" as a primordial, if not entirely homogeneous, unit; an emphasis on national strength reinforced by memories of "humiliation" at the hands of Western powers and the Japanese; and a tireless evocation of the unique glories and splendors of "five thousand years" of Chinese civilization. Above all, there is an insistence on the "one China principle"—committing the regime and the entire "Chinese people" to the sacred task of uniting and defending all territory claimed by the PRC—including, and especially, the island of Taiwan.

As will become apparent from the discussion that follows, there is consequently now little to differentiate the nationalism of the post-communist PRC from that of its Kuomintang (KMT) precursor and rival. The shift from socialism to patriotism as the legitimating ideology of the PRC state has prompted a reevaluation of the historical roles of "patriotic" figures from the Chinese past, including the KMT and its leader, Chiang Kai-shek.[1] Rather than being uniformly vilified, as in the past, Chiang is now accorded qualified praise for his contribution to Chinese victory in the War of Resistance against Japan. However, as far as any relevance for improving cross-Straits relations is concerned, this reassessment has come perhaps twenty or thirty years too late. Since the late 1980s or early 1990s, Taiwanese have been embroiled in a struggle to redefine their own collective identity, as part and parcel of a wider drive to divest themselves of the political and cultural legacy of Chiang and his regime.

It is this struggle, as it relates to an ongoing reevaluation and rediscovery of the Taiwanese and Chinese past, that forms the subject of this chapter. The focus here is on the terrain that has witnessed some of the fiercest battles over Taiwanese identity: the school curriculum for history, and some of the museums, old and new, that have embodied and promoted official visions of the past. In Taiwan, the memory of war stands central to the reconfiguring of national identity, but unlike in Japan and mainland China, it is not so much the Sino-Japanese War of 1937–45 that shapes memory, but competing under-standings of the legacy of two occupations: the Japanese colonial pe-riod of 1895–1945, and the Chinese Civil War, which resulted in a Cold War regime viewed by many indigenous Taiwanese as more "colonial" than its Japanese predecessor. The starting point for this analysis must be the orthodox vision of national identity propounded by the ROC regime after its flight to Taiwan in 1949. For the KMT, the island was straightforwardly and unproblematically "Chinese"— just as it remains today for the PRC authorities. Indeed, the ROC on Taiwan was seen as more genuinely Chinese than mainland China under the PRC, precisely because it defined itself in part by its espousal of Chinese traditional culture in its purest form, unsullied by the con-tamination of communism. The imposition of KMT rule, for which this one-China orthodoxy provided the ideological raison d'être, in-volved the oppression of the "native" *(bentu)* Taiwanese population, epitomized by the infamous "228 Incident." The way in which this in-cident came to be acknowledged in school teaching materials and mu-seums during the democratizing era of the 1990s is considered in the second section of this chapter. However, to understand the gulf that separated, and to some extent still separates, native Taiwanese *(benshen-gren)* from their mainlander compatriots *(waishengren)* who migrated to the island after the Civil War, it is necessary to appreciate differ-ences in the way in which both groups experienced and remembered Japanese imperialism. The discussion therefore proceeds to focus on the role played by memories of conflicts with Japan in the ongoing de-bate over Taiwanese identity. Finally, the changing interpretation of the roles of Dutch colonialists, Ming Dynasty loyalists, and Taiwan's indigenous inhabitants in the island's past is considered briefly.

It is these latter aspects of the Taiwanese past that in recent years have begun to receive particular attention from those wishing to em-phasize the island's distinctiveness from the Chinese mainland, and to promote a new identity for Taiwan as a distinctive "multicultural" community subject throughout its history to diverse cultural and polit-ical influences. However, while this may come as a long-overdue cor-rective to the stifling "one-China" orthodoxy of the KMT, the attempt to dragoon the past into a campaign to construct a new vision of a harmonious, pluralistic Taiwan has involved distortions of its own. Past conflicts are emphasized, downplayed, or entirely ignored in the interests of constructing a seamless narrative that reinforces the desired political messages. For all the intensity of the political controversy between pro-unification KMT "Blues" and pro-independence DPP (Democratic Progressive Party) "Greens," in their approaches to the past and to its political uses, if not in their interpretations of particular events, the two camps perhaps have more in common than either would like to acknowledge.

From "Free China" Fortress to Multicultural Island—Official Visions of Taiwan's Identity

The school curriculum during the era of KMT martial law (up to the late 1980s) functioned as "a massive engine of conquest," whose objective was to transform Taiwan's population into uncritical Chinese patriots. To that end, Mandarin was imposed as the sole medium of instruction and language of public discourse; the *Three People's Principles* of Sun Yat-sen were enshrined as the state ideology, to be taught and examined at all levels of education; and a state-centered narrative of Chinese history, the steel frame of patriotic consciousness, was enshrined in the school curriculum. The production of school textbooks for history, as for all other subjects, remained until the late 1990s the prerogative of the *Guoli Bianyi Guan* (National Office for Compilation and Translation), an arm of the central government.

The main thrust of the official historical narrative is indicated by the opening chapter of the junior *(Guomin Zhongxue)* textbooks. This was an unambiguous statement of Han chauvinism and Chinese cultural superiority, which identified four "special characteristics of our country's history": its length (spanning almost 5,000 years—making China the only one of the world's ancient civilizations to have stood the test of time); the capacity to peacefully assimilate ethnic groups *(minzu ronghe)*—*minzu* on the frontiers were represented as being irresistibly attracted toward the superior culture of the Chinese race; and an "emphasis on propriety" rooted in the Confucian tradition. "Propriety and morality," declared the text, "are the essence *(jinghua)* of our national culture, and constitute the unique characteristics *(dute de xingge)* of the

Chinese *minzu*. The fourth "special characteristic" was "the love of peace":

> The Chinese are a peace-loving, warm-hearted people, whose relations with their neighbours have been governed by their sense of morality, and who have very seldom mounted armed invasions [of neighbouring countries]. Despite possessing a cultural heritage that has been admired and coveted by her neighbours, China has never taken a selfish or small-minded approach to interaction with other states, but has freely shared her cultural inheritance. Japan, Korea and Vietnam are the three countries that have been most profoundly influenced by Chinese culture.[2]

One clear implication of this characterization of Chineseness is to lay the blame for conflict involving China and any foreign state squarely on the latter; if they accepted this vision of China as a supremely civilized and peace-loving power, ROC citizens could conceive of military conflict only as the result of aggression from less civilized powers coveting their nation's wealth and culture. As one of the neighboring countries portrayed as benefiting most from the process of peaceful cultural exchange, Japan's aggression against China from the late nineteenth century onwards was thus seen—apart from anything else—as an instance of gross ingratitude. Meanwhile, campaigns undertaken by the Chinese against other "ethnic groups" within their own borders (defined by the KMT to include Outer Mongolia as well as the rest of the pre-1911 Qing territories) could be represented as missions to "pacify" the outlying regions, whose inhabitants would in time inevitably come to appreciate the benefits of Han civilization. Han colonization of these border regions—including Taiwan—was interpreted as another aspect of the benign process of "assimilation."

By the 1950s, Taiwan's population consisted of the descendants of Hoklo and Hakka migrants from Fujian and northern Guangdong respectively (collectively termed *benshengren* or "inhabitants of this province"), those who had come to the island from the mainland with the KMT after the Civil War (*waishengren*, or "people from outside provinces"), and the indigenous tribes who were largely confined to more mountainous regions. KMT historiography almost entirely ignored these aborigines, while the heterogeneous groups that made up the ethnic Chinese population were seen as members of a single, homogeneous Han *minzu*. As members of this "Han race," the inhabitants of Taiwan were expected to identify with the state-centerd narrative of Chinese history. Taiwan's own role in this narrative was extremely peripheral—until, that is, the narrative reached the point at which the ROC regime decamped to the island in 1949, after which it became the "base for recovery" of the mainland *(fuxing jidi)*.

The KMT account of Chinese history as contained in the school textbooks of the 1950s–80s was in most respects strikingly similar to that to be found in PRC texts of the early twenty-first century—there is nothing in the summary of China's "special characteristics" cited above that would look out of place in a contemporary mainland textbook.[3] What distinguished the KMT texts was the absence of references to class struggle (seen as a principal vector of historical change in the older PRC texts, but far less so in more recent editions), and inveterate hostility toward communism, with the communist victory in the Civil War attributed largely to foreign interference. This consisted principally of the treacherous "Soviet invasion" of Manchuria, just before the Japanese surrender in 1945, which effectively handed this heavily industrialized region over to the Chinese Communist Party (CCP). The Soviet Union's interference, the text claims, continued in the form of extensive aid to the CCP, while the Americans made the catastrophic miscalculation of imposing an embargo on military aid to either side while attempting to negotiate peace. The mainland thus fell under the control of the Communists and became a "vassal state" *(fuyong)* of the Soviet Union. The majority of Chinese were condemned to suffer under this barbaric, alien-inspired regime, and it was left to the ROC Government on Taiwan ("Free China") to keep alive the sacred flame of Chinese civilization.[4]

Taiwan occupies a central role in the narrative only in the final chapter of the pre-1990s senior high school textbook, which concludes with a telling comparison of the achievements of the ROC on Taiwan (economic miracle) and the PRC on the Chinese mainland (socialist basket case).[5] However, reference is made to the island at earlier points in the narrative, principally in relation to the Japanese invasion of Taiwan in 1868, the Sino-French War of 1884–85 and its aftermath, the 1894–95 Sino-Japanese War that led to the island's cession to Japan, and the retrocession that followed the end of the World War II in 1945. All but the last of these events are discussed in the chapter on "The Loss of Vassal States and Frontier Regions and the Leasing of Coastal Harbours and Bays" *(bianjiang fan shu de sangshi yu yanhai gang wan de zujie)*.[6] The Japanese incursion took place after Taiwanese *shanbao* ("mountain compatriots"—the polite term for the aboriginal population) attacked a group of Liuqiu (Okinawan) islanders who had been washed up on the southern coast of Taiwan after a typhoon. This rare allusion to the aborigines implicitly praises their "ferocious resistance" to the Japanese soldiers who were subsequently dispatched to the island.[7] Following this incident, the central government "undertook a thorough investigation of the maritime regions," and accorded special urgency to the task of Taiwan's development. The text describes how the island subsequently became a showcase for "self-strengthening" policies, including the modernization of infrastructure through a program of road-building, the construction of Taiwan's first railway, the encouragement of trade with the mainland and an influx of new settlers. Taiwan's strategic importance was further underlined by the 1884–85 war with France, after which it was elevated to full provincial status.[8]

Despite these various initiatives, the Qing government was finally unable to resist Japanese demands for the cession of the island after defeat in the war of 1894–95. The text emphasizes that, at the negotiations with the victorious Japanese, "China was most of all unwilling to cede Taiwan. The Guangxu Emperor said, 'If Taiwan is lost, then all those under heaven will be heartbroken.'" It goes on to describe how the leading inhabitants of Taiwan, in their determination to resist Japanese domination, established the "Republic of Taiwan" *(Taiwan Minguo)*, while carefully noting that they "declared that once peace had been achieved, they would return to China." Although the Japanese eventually occupied the whole island, "resistance to Japan continued . . . right down until the recovery of Taiwan [in 1945]."[9] Indeed, it is in the section dealing with the aftermath of World War II that Taiwan is next mentioned:

THE RECOVERY OF TAIWAN:

> Since the Jia Wu War [of 1894–95], China had suffered numerous disasters at the hands of the Japanese, and Taiwan had been under her imperial rule for 51 years. But the nationalist revolutionary

spirit of Taiwan compatriots, and their resolve to resist [the Japanese], were passed down from generation to generation. After the success of the Xing Hai Revolution [the Nationalist Revolution of 1911], Taiwan compatriots were greatly encouraged, and the movement to resist Japan reached a high tide, the ultimate goal always being to return once again to the motherland. The aim of the Nationalist Revolution is to strive for the freedom and equality of all the Nation's people. In the midst of the Northern Expedition of 1927, Generalissimo Chiang declared that Taiwan must be returned to China; in 1938, the Temporary National Assembly of the Chinese Kuomintang once more emphatically declared its resolution to liberate Taiwan. It was in part for the sake of Taiwan that China abandoned herself so entirely to the War of Resistance against Japan. Meanwhile, many Taiwan compatriots came to the mainland to join the war effort. After the declaration of war against Japan, all Sino-Japanese treaties became invalid, and the retrocession of Taiwan followed as a matter of course . . . When Japan surrendered, Taiwan compatriots went mad with joy.[10]

The point of all these references is to underline, on the one hand, the solicitous interest in Taiwan taken by the Chinese regime (whether Qing or Republican) and its officials, and their determination to defend it or, once lost, to recover it; and on the other, the steadfast patriotism of the inhabitants of the island, as demonstrated by their determination to resist all foreign oppressors. The import of these messages for students on Taiwan during the Cold War era is clear: the unity and liberty (from foreign/socialist domination) of China are defined as the supreme objectives for all Chinese people, including and especially those lucky enough to reside on Taiwan, the last redoubt of "Free China" (Figure 9.1).

However, the attempt to indoctrinate Taiwan's population so that they would identify with the KMT's "one China" vision evidently met with only limited success. Some of the reasons for this will emerge in the discussion below of memories of KMT repression and Japanese colonialism. In short, by the 1970s tectonic shifts in the geopolitics of Cold War East Asia, namely the rapprochement between the United States and Communist China leading to the ROC's expulsion from the

Figure 9.1. "Zhan Wang" (Bright Prospects). 228
Peace Memorial Museum, Taipei. (Photo by the
author, 2004.)

United Nations and American recognition of the People's Republic,
meant that the KMT vision of recovery of the mainland was more than
ever exposed as fantasy. The evident weakness of the regime's international position—in particular its diminished importance to America—
in turn rendered it more susceptible to internal dissent, particularly
among the growing *benshengren* middle class, who became increasingly
bold in confronting the authorities. The KMT, for its part, perhaps
chastened by the toppling of the authoritarian Marcos regime in the
neighburing Philippines and by unrest in South Korea, and perhaps
also subject to a degree of American pressure, from the late 1980s
proved relatively nimble in responding to pressure for change. Moves
to dismantle the repressive structures of martial law began under Pres-

ident Chiang Ching-kuo, and continued apace under his successor from 1988, the native Taiwanese Lee Teng-hui.[11]

The democratization process that the KMT initiated quickly gathered a momentum of its own, driving the party in directions that made many of its more conservative members distinctly uncomfortable. By the 1990s, Taiwan had been politically (and, to a large extent, economically and socially) isolated from the Chinese mainland for a whole century, with the exception of four short years following the end of World War II. Not only the *benshengren* majority, but also the children of the *waishengren*, had grown up with little knowledge of or contact with the rest of China. Moreover, the lifting of the ban on travel to the mainland in the late 1980s, while it made possible many tearful reunions between elderly *waishengren* and long-lost relatives, revealed more starkly to all Taiwanese the economic, political, and cultural gulf that divided their prosperous and sophisticated island community from the China over the water. As electoral politics took hold in the mid-1990s, the KMT under President Lee thus found itself competing with its new rival, the pro-independence DPP, for the support of a growing majority of Taiwanese for whom the rigid "one-China" orthodoxy appeared increasingly anachronistic and intolerable. There might not be an appetite among the electorate for open confrontation with Communist China over the independence/reunification issue, but there were votes to be gained from policies promoting a "Taiwan for the Taiwanese" agenda that stopped short of demanding outright independence.

Of all the anachronisms that demanded correction, one of the most outstanding was the almost complete absence from the school curriculum of Taiwan-related content. This was addressed by the development of a new course for junior high schools, the *Renshi Taiwan* (Knowing Taiwan) course, consisting of three components with separate textbooks for each: History, Society, and Geography. The course, which was issued to schools in 1997 in the teeth of fierce opposition from pro-unification conservatives, effectively set out a new official vision of Taiwan's identity that radically challenged the KMT's traditional "one-China" ideology. Just as the old textbooks had begun with an exposition of the "special characteristics" of "Our Country" (China), so the new History text for *Renshi Taiwan* opened with a definition of the "special characteristics" of Taiwan:

THE SPECIAL CHARACTERISTICS OF TAIWAN HISTORY

In the course of Taiwan's history, in every period, different forms of culture have always coexisted. Cultural pluralism is one of the outstanding characteristics of Taiwan's history. The pluralism of Taiwan's culture is of course intimately linked to the nature and extent of her relations with her neighbors. In prehistoric times these relations were extensive, as they were in the seventeenth, eighteenth, nineteenth, and twentieth centuries of the historical era. Therefore internationalism is another special characteristic of Taiwan's history. Since Taiwan is an island, her resources are limited, and she has therefore relied on commercial exchange with the outside world in order to supply those products she lacks. Thus Taiwan has always been a base for international trade, and a flourishing international trade is another special characteristic of Taiwan's history.

From the seventeenth century onwards, Han people were plagued by difficulties and dangers, and many sought to escape troubles on the Chinese mainland by coming to Taiwan. They developed relations with the aboriginal peoples, and together they struggled to shape a new territory. This heroic spirit of defying danger, and the spirit of overcoming difficulties, have also become unique characteristics of Taiwan's people. Contemporary Taiwan's cultural pluralism, close international relations, flourishing international commerce, and spirit of struggling against dangers and overcoming adversity are all legacies bequeathed by our past, and we should treasure them and further develop them in the future.[12]

In their eagerness to promote a sense of Taiwanese identity rooted in history, the curriculum developers thus veered toward a vision of primordial "Taiwaneseness" that consciously or unconsciously mimicked the template of the old KMT vision of primordial "Chineseness," even while rejecting the latter's ideological content. Their education appeared to have conditioned them, like their Nationalist predecessors, to define identity in primordialist, ethnocultural terms, and to see history textbooks as instruments for explicit moralization.

One of the key figures in the development of the *Renshi Taiwan* course was Tu Cheng-sheng, who headed the committee that drafted the Society textbook—even more radical in its promotion of "Taiwan-eseness" than the history text quoted above.[13] In 2000, Tu was appointed by the new DPP administration of Chen Shui-bian as Director of the National Palace Museum (a cabinet-level position), and was subsequently made Education Minister in 2004. This museum had been designed in the 1960s to symbolize Taiwan's role as the prime repository of traditional Chinese culture, and the epic journey whereby its treasures (mostly from the original National Palace Museum in Beijing's Forbidden City) had been saved first from Japanese and then from communist depredation during the 1930s and 1940s was celebrated as a kind of cultural Long March. Tu faced the tricky task of transforming this icon of Taiwan's Chineseness into an institution that would serve the DPP's agenda of promoting a sense of Taiwanese identity. The result was a plan for constructing a "Southern Branch Museum," to be built in the town of Taibao and devoted entirely to the Asian treasures in the Museum's collection. Political sensitivity over the pro-independence leanings of the DPP meant that the plan for the new branch was justified in terms of a vague pan-Asianism, though its underlying meaning was nonetheless clear. A museum booklet promoting the scheme declared that the Asian artefacts (mostly objects given as tribute to Chinese emperors by rulers of countries such as Japan, Korea, Vietnam, Thailand, and Tibet) had hitherto been "overlooked." "Taiwan is part of Asia, and China is part of Asia, but we don't understand Asia," declared the booklet, and it was therefore necessary to improve understanding of the history of cultural interaction in the region so as to "promote popular understanding of cultural pluralism and appreciation of different cultures."[14]

The National Palace Museum, like the school history curriculum, has thus become embroiled in the broader controversy over Taiwan's identity, between the supporters of a vision of the island as home to a historically distinctive, "culturally pluralist" Asian community, one-China patriots who remain loyal to the old KMT vision, and those in between uneasy about the politicization of the past by either side.[15] By representing both Taiwan and China as "parts of Asia," the planners of the new Southern Branch Museum are implicitly underlining Taiwan's separateness from "China," in much the same way, and for the same reasons, as some Scottish nationalists have (explicitly) promoted a vision of Scotland as part of "Europe," but not of Britain. Meanwhile, beyond the generalities and euphemisms of this pan-Asian multiculturalism, the challenge to the former historical orthodoxy has involved radical reappraisals of certain key episodes in the Taiwanese past.

The 228 Incident and the Rise of Taiwanese Consciousness

The period since the mid-1990s has witnessed an exponential growth in the number of museums devoted to Taiwanese or local history and culture, particularly under the DPP administration that came to power in 2000. However, one of the first of these new, Taiwan-oriented museums was the "228 Peace Memorial Museum," opened in 1997 while Chen Shui-bian of the DPP (elected ROC President in 2000) was the Mayor of Taipei. The massacre of Taiwanese that took place on February 28, 1947 and the period thereafter had assumed totemic significance for the *benshengren* opponents of KMT rule. Throughout the period of martial law (up to 1987), the KMT regime had refused to acknowledge the atrocities committed then or subsequently, during the "White Terror" *(baise kongbu)* of the late 1940s and early 1950s. However, as Taiwan's democratization proceeded rapidly in the early 1990s, the KMT under Lee Teng-hui sought to put the party's repressive past behind it, thus hoping to diminish the significance of the "228 Incident" as an electoral liability for the ruling party. It was the KMT premier at the time, Lien Chan, who unveiled the 228 Memorial in the Peace Park where the new museum was also situated. At the same time, also under Lien's premiership, the incident was finally acknowledged in school textbooks.

The interpretation of the 228 Incident favored by the more conservative wing of the KMT was summarized in the 1997 edition of the senior secondary history textbook:

> Just after the recovery of Taiwan, as a result of severe wartime destruction, postwar disorder, and economic chaos, large numbers of people became unemployed, everyday life was difficult, and social problems were serious. When Chen Yi (a KMT official from the mainland) assumed the leadership of the Taiwan provincial administration, he was simultaneously the head of the police force and of the army on the island, and even the office of the Central Government on Taiwan was under his orders. In fact, his powers were no different from those exercised by Taiwan's Japanese colonial governors, and this greatly disappointed Taiwan compatriots who had long awaited reunification. In addition, the institution of martial law, the eco-

nomic controls introduced by the government, and the corruption and misbehavior of some officials and soldiers, made the people even more discontented. In 1947, a move to outlaw the private sale of cigarettes sparked conflicts between officials and ordinary people, the "228 Incident" occurred, and many innocent people became casualties. When the Chairman of the National Government, Mr. Chiang Zhong-zheng (Chiang Kai-shek) heard of this, he severely reprimanded Chen Yi and ordered him to cease reprisals . . . Chen Yi was transferred and replaced, the provincial government was reorganized, and the government's declarations pacified the populace. To ease the pain caused by this incident, in November 1990 the Administrative Yuan established the "228 Incident Unit" (*zhuan an xiao zu*), whose remit was to research the incident and establish the historical truth. After President Lee Teng-hui apologized to the families of the victims, the government awarded them compensation and erected the "228 Memorial" to ease (the spirits of) the unfortunate dead.[16]

This account effectively exculpates Chiang Kai-shek, who in this edition of the senior high school textbook retains his status as the national savior. As with the text's greatly expanded section on the "Construction of the Base for Recovery" (*fuxing jidi de jianshe*), the account here attempts to reconcile greater recognition of Taiwan's own history with an essentially unaltered "one China" narrative. Particular care is taken to avoid reference to issues that might inflame *benshengren* animosity toward *waishengren* as a group. For example, no mention is made of the fact that Taiwan's resources were plundered to fuel the anticommunist war effort on the mainland, that most posts in post-retrocession Taiwan went to mainlanders, or that the repression following 228 was directed largely at the native Taiwanese intelligentsia, the leading critics of KMT authority on the island, whom many KMT officials saw as tainted by their Japanese education. Finally, by seamlessly moving from the account of the incident itself to the measures taken over forty years later to commemorate and compensate the victims, the text gives the impression that historical closure has been achieved, and overlooks the persistence of political repression down to the 1980s.

However, it was the significance of the 228 Incident as a symbol of *benshengren* resentment against the whole apparatus of KMT repression that gave it such potency as a rallying cry for pro-democracy activists from the 1970s onwards. This aspect of the incident is explicitly recognized in the *Renshi Taiwan* texts—indeed, beside receiving extensive coverage in the History volume of the course, the incident and the events leading up to it are the only historical episode to also receive extended treatment in Tu Cheng-sheng's Society volume. Here, a section with the heading "We Can Reform Society" (in a chapter entitled "The Taste of Democracy") begins with an account of the 228 Incident, noting that it "was a serious setback to the Taiwanese democracy movement."[17] It goes on to describe how this movement persisted, despite further persecution during the White Terror, through to the *Tang Wai* movement of the 1970s and 1980s, the *Meilidao* Incident of 1979, and finally the establishment of the DPP in 1986. The text studiously avoids inciting resentment against *waishengren* or the KMT, and explicitly promotes a pluralistic vision of "Taiwaneseness," but its view of the significance of the 228 Incident to the movement for Taiwan's democratization nonetheless chimes with the interpretation put forward in the DPP's electioneering literature (Figure 9.2).[18]

The publication in the same year (1997) by the *Guoli Bianyi Guan* of these two rather different accounts of the island's history (in the senior high and *Renshi Taiwan* texts) could be seen as epitomizing the much-vaunted "pluralism" of Taiwanese society. This was not a pluralism that implied much tolerance across the ideological divide, as witnessed by the acrimonious controversy that greeted the launch of the *Renshi Taiwan* course.[19] Just as Taiwan played little more than a walk-on role in the traditional KMT narrative of the Chinese past, so—to the outrage of KMT conservatives—China featured little in the account of Taiwan's past in the *Renshi Taiwan* texts. *Renshi Taiwan* represented not simply an attempt to rectify the lack of coverage of Taiwan's past in the school curriculum, but also a conscious nation-building project aimed largely at underlining the island's distinctiveness from the Chinese mainland. In this respect, it differed markedly from the contemporary drive in Hong Kong to incorporate local history into the school curriculum there. Hong Kong's history was filtered through the prism of one-China political correctness in much the same way as Taiwan's history had been during the KMT's martial law era.[20] By contrast, Taiwan's curriculum developers were relatively free to construct a historical narrative that appealed to, as it sought to reinforce, the emerging popular sense of Taiwanese identity.

But who could be Taiwanese? For decades the *benshengren* opponents of KMT rule had used the label *Taiwanren* to define themselves—the KMT's *waishengren* elite were by definition from "outside."

Figure 9.2. The spark that ignited the 228 Incident: An exhibit in the 228 Peace Memorial Museum, Taipei (note the cigarette cartons, bottom left). (Photo by the author, 2004.)

The 228 Incident, as the most infamous atrocity perpetrated by *waishengren* against *benshengren*, had tended to crystalized this ethnic divide more than any other issue.[21] Thus, while addressing the incident in a more open manner was crucial to any reconciliation between the *waishengren* political elite and the former victims of KMT repression, continued exploitation of it for political ends by anti-KMT politicians might prove socially divisive.

Although the 228 Peace Memorial Museum in central Taipei was constructed while Chen Shui-bian was Mayor of the city, the funding and management of the museum was originally the responsibility of the "Taiwan Peace Foundation," an independent, though DPP-affiliated, group.[22] Chen and his DPP municipal adminstration wanted to avoid perceptions that the museum was a party-political project (even though they might otherwise continue to invoke the 228 Incident for party-political ends). The establishment of the museum was predictably interpreted by some KMT conservatives as a politically inspired move designed to appeal primarily to the DPP's core supporters, but the exhibition narrative, like the content of the *Renshi Taiwan* texts, does not go out of its way to demonize the *waishengren* as a group. Instead, in the manner of the Hiroshima Peace Memorial Museum in Japan, the 228 Peace Memorial Museum (the similarity in the names is not coincidental) dwells on the tragedy of this particular event as an instance of the general folly of war.

In the case of the Hiroshima Museum, the focus on Japanese victimhood distracts from the issue of Japan's responsibility for the Pacific War, and thus arguably obstructs rather than facilitates reconciliation between Japan and the victims of her wartime aggression.[23] However, in the case of the 228 Incident, the victimhood of the native Taiwanese appears less ambiguous, and therefore acknowledging their suffering in the 228 Museum and in school texts perhaps contributes less problematically to the process of reconciliation between *benshengren* and *waishengren*. Moreover, one of the key figures in pressing for a 228 Memorial Museum was a second-generation *waishengren* university professor, and other *waishengren* have been actively involved in events to commemorate 228.[24] The year after the museum opened, Chen Shui-bian lost the Taipei mayoral election to the KMT's Ma Ying-jeou, another second-generation *waishengren*. In 1999, Ma wrote in the foreword to the museum's yearbook, "We believe that in commemorating 228 we should adopt an objective yet sympathetic and understanding attitude towards this profoundly influential event. At the same time, commemorating 228 ought to be the right and duty of all the people of Taiwan, and not the prerogative of a few politicians."[25]

By the time that Ma wrote this, however, the political meaning of 228 was already changing. The emphasis on "peace" in the 228 Memorial Museum, and the determination expressed in the exhibtion text to ensure that no similar atrocity should ever happen again, was directed primarily neither at the *waishengren* nor at the KMT. For all Taiwanese, *benshengren* or *waishengren*, the threat to peace in the mid-1990s (and thereafter) came not from any prospect of renewed internal repression, but from the People's Republic of China. During the 1996 presidential election, Peng Min-min, the DPP's presidential candidate, made this explicit, declaring, "The February 28 Incident only proves that Taiwan must not unify with China, otherwise an even worse historical disaster would take place."[26] The incident has come primarily to symbolize the importance of protecting independence and democracy for all the island's inhabitants—both native Taiwanese and "new Taiwanese" of *waishengren* extraction—from the threat of another mainland takeover.

Establishing the Roots of Taiwanese Multiculturalism: From Japanese Colonialists to Aboriginal Ancestors

A sense of Taiwan as a society fundamentally distinct from that of the People's Republic, and a determination to defend this distinctiveness from a new mainland threat, have involved not only a reimagining of the 228 Incident; they have also given rise to a drive to project this sense of independent "Taiwaneseness" back into the remote past. This aspiration is common to many societies—newly independent or seeking independence—where insecurity over national identity seems to strengthen the urge to locate the roots of the nation in distant, or even mythical, antiquity. In the Ukraine, for example, the desire to construct a national genealogy distinct from that of Russia prompted some nationalist scholars to propound the bizarre theory that their nation was descended from the biblical armies of Gog and Magog.[27] The mainstream discourse of "Taiwaneseness" may not entertain quite such outlandish notions, but the urge to project backward the values of contemporary society is frequently evident in the treatment in textbooks and museums of key historical episodes.

The period of Japanese imperial rule is one aspect of Taiwan's history that has been subjected to a long-overdue reappraisal since the early 1990s, evident in film and literature before its influence reached school curricula. However, newer school texts focus less than their predecessors on the theme of resistance to Japanese rule and more on the social, economic, and educational developments that took place during that period. These were entirely ignored by the previous textbooks, which portrayed the postcolonial era of KMT rule as the era of rapid modernization; by contrast, *Renshi Taiwan* highlights Japan's contribution to the island's economic development, the establishment of a modern education system, and the extent of Japanese influence on social mores.[28] At the same time, the books draw attention to the repressive aspects of Japanese rule, such as the intensive program of "Japanization" that took place in Taiwan (as in Korea) after 1937, and the conscription of more than 200,000 Taiwanese men into the Imperial Army during World War II (a sensitive subject entirely ignored in the old textbook cited earlier, which instead claimed that "patriotic" Taiwanese fought on the Chinese side against the Japanese).[29] Nevertheless, the books were praised by the right-wing Japanese cartoonist Kobayashi Yoshinori in his controversial 2001 book *Theory of Taiwan* for their "balanced" and "objective" treatment of the period of colonial rule.[30]

This acknowledgment of the significance of the Japanese period for the island's economic, social, and cultural development is one aspect of the new vision of a culturally pluralist Taiwan. Further segments of this multicultural tapestry are the periods of rule by Dutch colonialists and the Ming loyalist, Cheng Cheng-gong (or Koxinga), who brought his forces to the island following the fall of the Ming dynasty, evicting the Dutch in the process. Koxinga's eviction of the foreign colonialists and his occupation of Taiwan as a base for loyalist Ming rebels opposing an alien regime on the Chinese mainland had been celebrated by the KMT for the obvious parallels with their own position. In 1961, a monument—now sadly neglected and decayed—was erected in honour of Koxinga the (Chinese) "national hero" *(minzu yingxiong)* at the spot near Tainan where he landed in 1661. A Koxinga Museum was opened in Tainan itself alongside the old Koxinga temple, celebrating his patriotic exploits (Figure 9.3).

The interpretation of the Koxinga regime and its Dutch predecessor

Figure 9.3. The commemorative obelisk erected in 1961
at Lu Er Men, the site of Koxinga's landfall in 1661.
(Photo by the author, 2004.)

was very different in a 2003 exhibition at the National Palace Museum:
Ilha Formosa: Taiwan's Emergence on the World Scene in the 17th Century,
conceived by Tu Cheng-sheng. According to Tu, Dutch colonization
came at a time when "Taiwan did not fall under the jurisdiction of any
country,"[31] and was a "major trading point for private merchants" from
many countries. He wistfully speculates that "if . . . the Dutch had
stayed on, Taiwan may have gone through a long period of European
colonization and become an independent country in the 20th century,
pretty much like what happened to Australia or New Zealand."[32] That
the Dutch did not stay on was of course due to Koxinga, whose "sea
trader" (or pirate) father, "Nicholas Iquan," was baptized a Catholic,
and whose mother was Japanese.

This sanitization and domestication of aboriginal heritage is epitomized by the slogan at the front of the Shihsanhang exhibition guide:

"Our territory—our past" *(zade tudi—zade guoqu)*. The aborigines, once ignored and despised by the KMT regime as by most of their Han compatriots, now play a central role the founding myth of a multicultural Taiwan. Their Austronesian ethnicity—emphasized in all the new museums—definitively distinguishes them from the mainland Chinese, and thus the more that Taiwan's majority Han community can associate itself with the aboriginal heritage, the more they can convince themselves and others of their own distinctiveness from the Chinese of the People's Republic. Thus in 2004, designated by the DPP government as "Visit Taiwan Year," the national tourist board adopted as its logo a cartoon image of an aboriginal child with a feather head-dress, and the slogan "Naruwan" (an aboriginal word that none of my Taiwanese acquaintances were able to translate). Meanwhile, recent years have witnessed a new fashion among many Taiwanese for tracing their family histories back to aboriginal roots—a fashion reflected in the astonishing assertion made in 1997 by a Taiwanese scientist that "the majority of Taiwanese are descendents of Austronesians (60%)."[33]

Conclusion: The New Taiwanese Nationalism—A Primordialist Pluralism?

The celebration of a "culturally pluralist" Taiwan within a diverse, pluralist Asian region has become a mantra of official cultural and educational policy under the DPP regime, serving to distance the island culturally and historically from the Chinese mainland, and functioning as a euphemistic substitute for explicit assertions of Taiwanese independence. The changing shape of Taiwanese identity is intricately linked with the end of the Cold War in Asia, and the conflict between the Kuomintang and Communists in its old, ideological formulation. The changing memory of two experiences, Japanese imperialism and the Chinese Civil War, make Taiwan's collective memory in some ways highly comparable to those in China and Japan (see Hevia's treatment of the Opium Wars in contemporary Chinese discourse, or Igarashi's treatment of movies about kamikaze). Yet in other important respects, the connections between conflict and memory in Taiwan are entirely specific to that society.

For instance, Taiwan's aborigines have benefited in many respects from the increased attention and respect they have received since the 1980s, but the price appears to have been an appropriation of their heritage to underpin the construction of a new Taiwanese identity. In this approach to Taiwan's prehistory, there is perhaps more than a shade of the KMT discourse of peaceful Han "assimilation" *(minzu ronghe)* of minority nationalities. The Taiwanese of the "Green" camp may have comprehensively rejected the Nationalist historical narrative, but the old historiographical assumptions and the underlying moral outlook appear to have struck deeper roots; "the Taiwanese people" have replaced "the Chinese race" as the subject of a narrative whose moralizing bent is in many respects strikingly similar. The Taiwanese, like the Chinese in their old textbooks, are depicted as a peace-loving people, whose ethnic origins and essential moral characteristics (including "pluralism") are traceable to a primordial past, and who have been the victims of past conflict and oppression, but never its perpetrators.

Bentu Taiwanese side-step their historical victimization of the island's indigenous population perhaps primarily because it jars with their own self-image as victims of oppression, most recently at the hands of Chiang Kai-shek's KMT. The moral significance of national victimhood was in turn a key theme of the KMT narrative, which saw Western imperialist depredation succeeded by Japanese invasion, culminating in a stab-in-the-back for Chinese nationalism from a foreign-assisted communist revolution. Meanwhile, Chinese nationalist historiography (in both its KMT and CCP variants) has consistently overlooked, or interpreted away, instances of conflict between Han Chinese and "minority nationalities" such as the Tibetans, just as the history of conflict between Han settlers and aborigines is still generally overlooked in Taiwan. However, whereas in China "minority nationalities" are peripheral distractions from a historical narrative centered on the "Han race," in contemporary Taiwan the aborigines have become increasingly central to a new nationalist narrative. Though Taiwan would seem to be a quintessential instance of what Ernest Gellner termed a "nation without a navel,"[34] many Taiwanese seem intent on appropriating their aboriginal heritage as a sort of prosthetic national navel.

If Taiwanese nationalism possesses any umbilical connection of this sort, it is arguably to the Chinese cultural heritage that has been the dominant influence on local social mores and beliefs, including those concerning the nature and role of history. Nevertheless, it is hardly surprising that many of those who value their independence from China most highly fight shy of acknowledging the full extent of this Chinese influence, and seek to emphasize instead the extensive involvement of other cultures in the development of a pluralistic Taiwan—a strategy pilloried in China's state media as *Wenhua Taidu*, or "Cultural Taiwanese Independence."[35] While post-socialist China has laid claim to the essentialist ethnoculturalism that the KMT previously championed, and has—like the KMT before it—sought to encompass Taiwan within this homogenizing and totalizing vision, Taiwanese from the "Green" camp have clearly been tempted to counter this vision with a discourse that in some respects mimics, even while it rejects, the essentialism of "one-China" nationalism.

Even so, any family resemblance between Taiwanese and Chinese nationalist historiography—at least as embodied in school texts and museums—should not distract from the fact that pluralism and democracy do indeed characterize contemporary Taiwan, as witnessed by the openness with which controversies over history textbooks, new museums, and interpretations of the island's past more generally have been conducted in the local media. Moreover, that this is so undeniably does have much to do with Taiwan's openness to commercial, cultural, and educational interaction with Japan, the West (particularly America), and the wider world during the latter part of the twentieth century, although it is misleading to portray this openness and pluralism as essential characteristics of "Taiwaneseness" traceable to the primordial past. To do so, after all, might be taken to imply that openness, pluralism, and the democracy that is their concomitant are characteristics somehow alien to "Chinese" culture—a line of argument popular among apologists of the CCP regime on the mainland, but which the case of Taiwan, insofar as it is a Chinese society, spectacularly disproves.[36] Its late-twentieth-century transformation, and the rise of a new national consciousness that this has entailed, refutes the kind of genealogical determinism that informs official CCP historiography—as the Harvard-educated Taiwanese scholar, Wang Ming-ke, argues in his 1997 monograph *Hua Xia Bian Yuan* (China's Frontiers):

We have no way of predicting how (or whether) the Chinese and the communities on their frontiers will in the future unite or divide, nor the effects that this may have on the wider world. However, what we can be sure of is this: while the unification of the [Chinese] state may be achieved through the use of bombs and missiles, no unification of national sentiment will be brought about by military force. Moreover, to respond to [differences in] historical memory by seeking to apportion blame, rectify [interpretations], and engage in struggles and disputes is less worthwhile than attempting to understand memory in terms of the context that produces it; only this kind of understanding can help to resolve the causes of the disputes over identity that underlie these historical controversies.[37]

~ 10

The Korean War after the Cold War

Commemorating the Armistice Agreement in South Korea

SHEILA MIYOSHI JAGER AND JIYUL KIM

THE END OF THE Cold War and the transition to democratic rule in South Korea in the early 1990s did not lead to the reunification of the Korean peninsula.[1] But the collapse of European communism had a profound impact on the domestic politics of that country in the 1990s and beyond. In particular, the politics of democratization fueled new and competing reinterpretations of the past, and the memories of a brutal civil war that had sustained South Korea through the Cold War period underwent a marked shift for reasons rooted largely in the present.[2]

We are here concerned with the reconfiguration of history in South Korea after the fall of the Berlin Wall in 1989 and the collapse of the Soviet Union in 1991. While the Cold War continues in outward form on the Korean peninsula as a standoff between the two Koreas divided at the 38th parallel, this tension masks an undeniable change that has taken place within South Korean society with regard to its memorialization of the Korean War. After the West's "victory" in the Cold War, the South Korean government and public have been forced to draw a line under the historical narratives that had sustained their nation since the Republic of Korea's (ROK) founding in 1948. Under the authoritarian regimes that led South Korea into prosperity during the Cold War period, the Korean War was used to create support for the state's national security and economic policies. The dynamics of democratic transitional politics since 1989 have forced the South Koreans to re-think this history in light of North Korea's demise, in order to accommodate a new understanding of the war that might promote a peaceful reunification of the two Koreas.

Despite South Korea's "victory" in the Cold War (accentuated in the global media by images of starving North Korean children), the Korean War has proved unincorporable into this "victory narrative" in large part because it was impossible to fashion a narrative of triumph when the need to create a unified vision of the Korean nation was more pressing. Moreover, it was no longer tactful to recall the horrors of the war in detail when the focus of concern was to end the war and all the unpleasantness attached to it. This required a new treatment of the war as a family "tragedy" to be followed by rites of "reconciliation."

One of the showpieces of the new historical revision is the War Memorial complex in Seoul. Originally conceived and planned under the Roh Tae Woo (No T'ae-u) administration (1988–92), the Memorial—a museum and park compound more than 20,000 square meters in size built in downtown Seoul—opened its doors in 1994 with additional structures added on in succeeding years. The War Memorial is a fascinating microcosm of the way in which some threads of South Korea's treatment of its wartime experience have changed over the years, initiating what we call a "post–Cold War" narrative of the Korean War. Following the election of opposition leader Kim Dae Jung (Kim Tae-jung) (1997–2002) as president in 1997 and the transition to multiparty liberal democratic politics, another structure was added to the compound to commemorate the fiftieth anniversary of the armistice signing on July 27, 2003. The Korean War Monument, the first of its kind in South Korea, is representative of a second and more recent trend in South Korea, what we term "post–Korean War" historical revisionism, which redefines Korea's wartime experience by commemorating the tentative *end* of the war. By inspiring a tacit "forgetfulness" of the actual brutality of the war, the Korean War Monument's primary purpose is to inspire a new pan-Korean nationalism and peaceful coexistence of the two Koreas.

The role of the United States is central to these changing narratives. The idea of South Korea as a victim state began to emerge at the same time as the rhetoric of Korea as a major power, ready to take its rightful place among the advanced nations of the world. Following their successful co-hosting of the 2002 World Cup, South Koreans have become increasingly confident of their nation's international status. At the same time, growing resentment of South Korea's "client status" vis-à-vis the United States has led South Korean leaders to question the continuing logic of the U.S.-South Korean alliance that was forged during the Cold War. As was the case of radical anti-Americanism fostered by student dissident groups in the late 1980s, the idea of Korea as a victim state was transformed in 2002 into popular form following the accidental death of two schoolgirls caused by a U.S. military vehicle. Commemorations of Korea's newest "victims" became an unexpected source for the creation of a new nationalism, inclusive of both Koreas, against a common foreign foe. Riding the wave of anti-Americanism into the Blue House in 2002, Roh Mu Hyun was able to make use of this anti-American feeling to fuel a pan-Korean nationalism whose aim is to overcome the legacy of the wartime past and secure a permanent peace on the Korean peninsula. This new focus on ending the Korean War through the promotion of national reconciliation and peace was, moreover, markedly evident in South Korea's nonchalant reaction to North Korea's nuclear test on October 9, 2006. Despite the UN Security Council's punitive sanctions on North Korea, the pervasive view among South Korea's new nationalists was that resolution to the ongoing crisis would still be best resolved through engagement and dialogue, a position that put South Korea's leaders, once again, sharply at odds with the United States.

The "Continuous War" Paradigm: South Korea and the Cold War

The history of South Korea is itself a Cold War creation. The Cold War dominated South Korea's historical course from its birth in 1948 to the end of authoritarian rule in 1993, a period coinciding almost exactly with the beginning and the end of the Cold War. Conceived by the United States as a key component along with Japan, of a northeast Asian bulwark against communism, South Korea was inextricably intertwined with U.S. interests and policy. At the same time, South Korea's status within the structures of American containment created great opportunity for economic growth, prompted by massive aid from the United States. It was only after the Korean War that the South Korean economy became fully incorporated into the world capitalist system. Moreover, its definition of prosperity, security, and legitimacy was profoundly penetrated by the perceived necessity of maintaining a "continuous war" against communism in general and North Korea in particular. Especially under the military regime of Park Chung Hee (Pak Chŏng-hŭi) (1961–79), the "continuous war" against communism facilitated the momentum for "continuous development" aiming toward ever-greater prosperity, security, and legitimacy. Choi Jang-jip (Ch'oe Chang-jip) has noted that "the wartime experience and the suffering left in its wake were articulated and rearticulated through the ideological apparatuses of the state to control the language, set the parameters of common discourse, and to produce and reproduce the anticommunist worldview that was immediate and real. The political terrain was rearranged by the terror of war, and anticommunism achieved a hegemonic hold over civil society."[3]

South Korea was not only dominated by the regional Cold War waged by the United States; it also appropriated and mobilized the Cold War for its own nationalistic purposes. In this domestic project, too, the United States was a key historical agent, for it was the source of legitimacy and material largesse. Nationalism "became transformed into a statism that privileged anti-communism over unification."[4]

The positive uses to which the wartime experience was put thus turned the "continuous war" with communism and North Korea into powerful sources of domestic mobilization for the legitimacy of its government's economic and national security policies. Park Chung Hee and his military successors skillfully shaped the nation's collective memory of the Korean War by using the power of the state to refine and manage this grand narrative. North Korea's record of intransigence and provocations further legitimized the "continuous war" paradigm. This collective memory, together with the state's increasingly tight control of South Korean society as a normal consequence of "wartime" mobilization, created a new social and cultural environment for Park's national "revolution." This process was especially apparent between 1967 and 1969, a critical period in Park's overall vision of South Korean economic development and modernization in that it marked the end of the First Five-Year Economic Development Plan (1962–66), which, by exceeding all goals, established the basis for South Korea's economic independence and growth. More importantly, the success of the First Five-Year Plan instilled a sense of national self-confidence, and laid the groundwork for implementing the Second Five-Year Plan (1967–71), which was designed to achieve the cherished goal of economic autonomy through export-oriented heavy industry.

But the success of the First Five-Year Plan also seemed to have brought with it, according to Park, a level of complacency and "slackening of the national fervor," that compelled him to call for a "renewal" of the national spirit in conjunction with the Second Five-Year Plan. Indeed, Park's "Second Economy" *(che yi ŭi kyŏngje)* movement, kicked off in 1967, was the first of a series of spiritually oriented social mobilization and moral suasion campaigns designed to keep the Korean people on track and focused on economic development.[5] He explained the meaning and purpose of the "Second Economy" movement this way in December 1967:

> What is the meaning of the term? If the term, First Economy, is allowed to indicate what is meant by the commonly used term, economy, that is, visible matters such as production, construction, and export, the Second Economy can be adopted to mean spiritual construction, in other words, the invisible economy . . . No matter how much we produce and export, our economy cannot grow if our people are wasteful and run after luxuries . . . If our spiritual posture slackens—in other words, if we neglect the Second Economy—our nation as a whole will become wasteful and run after luxuries, thereby degrading its best characteristics, no matter how much we produce and construct.[6]

Park's nation-building campaign was given a boost by a series of North Korean provocations between 1967 and 1969 that Park used to evoke the threat of a second Korean War to instill a sense of urgency in developing military and economic power to forestall or prepare for such an eventuality. Typical of Park's exhortations is the passage from a speech he gave in April 1968 at the activation ceremony of the Homeland Reserve Force, which conjured up the image of another Korean War to convince South Koreans that they must not let up in the task of national reconstruction:

> Now is the time for us to discard our indulgence in idle ease and apparent peace . . . Kim Il Sung [Kim Il-sŏng], and his followers, . . . are madly pursuing war preparations . . . In prepara-

tion for an all-out war, they have devised partisan warfare, and a commando force . . . By dispatching these guerilla forces *en masse* . . . the Communists attempt to create . . . unrest and stir up confusion . . . while eagerly awaiting a good opportunity for another Korean War.[7]

Park's ending slogan in this speech, "fight while working and work while fighting," one he used in many other public messages that year, emphasized the link between preparing for defense against the North Korean threat and the pursuit of economic development and modernization.[8] Economic development not only meant a better life, but also salvation from another Korean War.

It would be misleading, however, to characterize Park's treatment of North Korea as monolithic and unchanging. The depiction of the North Korean "enemy" and "threat" actually underwent a two-stage evolutionary process during the Park years. During the 1960s, North Korea was primarily conceived as military-economic competitor with whom South Korea had to "catch up."[9] By the 1970s, however, the image of North Korea changed to one of a desperate challenger of South Korean existence that was rapidly running out of time before it permanently lost the military option for unification owing to South Korea's rapid economic growth. Even as Park began to undertake what appeared to be a comprehensive campaign in the early 1970s to establish dialogue with the North for eventual peaceful unification, the latter's rejection of Park's overtures was interpreted in terms of North Korean leadership's failure to give up on their irrational goal of communizing the peninsula through war:

In the course of the South-North talks, we took the position that both sides should endeavor to build up mutual confidence by solving easier and more practical problems first, and thus to remove gradually the barriers between the South and the North by expediting many-sided exchanges. We believed that such an approach would best serve to make the talks productive, and to accelerate the process of peaceful unification. *On the contrary, North Korea not only rejected our reasonable demands and realistic proposals, without working toward eliminating the causes of mutual distrust between the south and the north, but also continued to make absurd asser-*

tions, which might endanger the security of the Republic of Korea. Due to
this obstinate attitude of the North Korean side, no progress was made in
the dialogue, and South-North relations reached a point where mutual
distrust seemed about to deepen, and tension to further increase . . . In-
deed, it is owing to our perseverance and sincerity that the South-
North dialogue has barely kept in existence. North Korea has
shown no sign or sincerity about normalizing the South-North dialogue, but has newly engaged in provocative acts against five islands off the west coast which belong to out territory. The North
Koreans have recently introduced a large number of various new
weapons for surprise attack. They have also built new naval and
airbases in areas near the armistice line. *Thus they have been bent on*
preparing for another war.[10]

These characterizations of North Korea as "absurd and obstinate"
and bent "on preparing for another war" allowed Park not only to
maintain a demonized image of North Korea, but also to invoke it to
partly justify a radical restructuring of the constitutional order, the
Yushin (revitalization) reforms in late 1972 (the other important element of the rhetoric of justification was to maintain the spiritual momentum for political and economic development).

The question remains why Park initiated a dialogue with North
Korea in 1972 in the first place when the image of a demonized North
Korea that had been cultivated throughout the 1960s already served his
nationalist purposes. The root causes for the dialogue with North
Korea derived from major transformations of the global web of Cold
War ties which had a particularly keen impact on South Korea and
were cause for serious concern over its security. A series of diplomatic,
military, and economic events and actions between 1969 and 1973
seemed to signal a new era, one that was far more ambiguous and dangerous for South Korea. These included the 1969 announcement of
President Nixon's Guam Doctrine and its draw down of the U.S. presence in Asia and the 1970 decision to withdraw one of two U.S. divisions that had been maintained in South Korea even at the height of
the Vietnam War; the end in 1971 of the Bretton Woods system that
had stabilized international currencies since 1944; the 1973 oil shock
caused by sharp increases in OPEC prices; the perceived failure of the
United States in Indochina when it withdrew from Vietnam in 1973,
an effort to which South Korea had contributed 50,000 soldiers since

the mid-1960s, a force second in size only to that of the United States; and President Nixon's rapprochement diplomacy to normalize U.S. relations with North Korea's two key allies, China, which had become a nuclear power, and the Soviet Union. Park's reaction to these developments was that South Korea could no longer rely solely on its erstwhile ally, the United States, and had to formulate a new policy toward the North, in order to prevent a second Korean War that would destroy all the gains of the previous decade:

> As for the recent developments in the international situation, it may be said that the era of Cold War . . . came to an end . . . Judging also from a series of events witnessed in this part of the world, it seems unlikely that unification can be attained within a short period of time . . . These international trends give rise to a most serious problem in the history of our nation: . . . how to pursue national unification in the face of the stark realities of [the] international situation.[11]

The failure of the 1972 North-South initiative was followed by a series of provocative North Korean actions that only heightened the sense of war fears in the South while further reinforcing the "irrationality" of the North. These included the assassination attempt on Park in August 1974 that killed his wife (the second such attempt after the North Korean commando raid in January 1968), the discovery of invasion tunnels under the DMZ in 1974 and 1975, and the thirtieth anniversary of the founding of North Korea in October 1975 which North Koreans identified as the year for unification of the peninsula under communism. Repeated rhetorical evocations of the North Korean threat, combined with North Korean actions, made it possible for Park to justify the radical *Yushin* reforms, which essentially insured his permanent rule.

> If we are strong, they [North Korea] will offer to negotiate. If we seem weak, they will always challenge us with force. Therefore, we must accelerate the build-up of our national power through national consensus and total security. This is the basic objective of the October 1972 *Yushin* reforms, which I believe is the only way to achieving our national task [of unification].[12]

By intent and design, and supported by North Korea's provocations, Park was able to portray an intransigent and demonized North Korea on which to base his authoritarian actions in the name of urgent economic development and national security while exhorting the people to ever increasing efforts at national construction and constant vigilance against the possibility of another Korean War.

South Korea and the Post–Cold War: The War Memorial

Efforts to revise the "continuous war" narrative of the Korean War, especially the demonization of North Korea, began during the mid-1980s following the brutal suppression of the Kwangju Uprising in May 1980 by Park's military successor, Chun Doo Hwan (Chŏn Tu-hwan). The magnitude of state violence, and the complete devastation of the democratic forces in South Korea after the uprising, drove young dissident intellectuals to search for the origins of their predicament. The domestic challenges to the state's legitimacy and the "continuous war" narrative that had sustained the South Korean government throughout the Cold War were influenced as much by internal forces as by global changes. In the wake of the nation-wide pro-democracy demonstrations of June 1987, then president-elect Roh Tae Woo was forced to respond to the changing situation. On June 29, 1987, amid national jubilation, Roh accepted the demands of the opposition and agreed to hold direct presidential elections, which, because of a split in the opposition party, he won.

One of the first things that the new Roh administration (1988–92) set out to do was to normalize South Korea's relations with the Soviet Union. *Nordpolitik*, as the policy was known, came to mean economic penetration in socialist bloc countries and the South's predominance over the North in a changing international climate. Prodded by South Korea, the Soviet Union was transformed over the next two years, according to Don Oberdorfer, "from godfather, superpower guarantor, and economic benefactor of North Korea to partner and in some respects, client of South Korea."[13]

These events, which came on the heels of South Korea's global coming-out party during the 1988 Seoul Olympics, provided the pivot for South Korea's new initiatives toward North Korea. Roh's drive to establish relations with the allies of North Korea, as reform efforts swept over communist regimes in the Soviet Union, China, and

Eastern Europe, was calculated to alter their strategic alignments with the Korean peninsula and so induce North Korea to join the international community.[14]

It was during this climate of reform that the reinterpretation of history became an issue in the leadership. During the Cold War, the continuous war paradigm, the national struggle against communism, and the North Korean threat had shaped South Korea's image as a developing state under siege. In the era of reform, and particularly with the collapse of European communism after 1989, the leaders turned their attention outward onto the world stage, confident in South Korea's status as a global economic powerhouse. The stark contrast between a rich and powerful South Korea and an impoverished and isolated North Korea could no longer support the continuous war narrative. But the problem for South Korea's leaders was how to fashion a narrative of triumph that would also leave the open possibility for peninsular reconciliation. A new story of the Korean War had to be constructed, one that would mobilize South Koreans in "tacit forgetfulness" of North Korea's "criminal responsibility" for the war, while simultaneously holding North Korea accountable for the nation's family tragedy.

The new interpretations of the war are strongly visible in the War Memorial complex, one of the showpieces of Roh Tae Woo's presidential legacy (Figure 10.1). Whereas Cold War narratives of the war had placed the North Korean invasion and brutality at the center of the story, precisely in order to *prevent* the wounds of the war from healing, the new narrative is engaged in what might be called collective forgiveness. The Cold War, which ended in victory for South Korea (although it did not "end" the Korean War), ended in bitterness and humiliation for the North Koreans. It therefore proved impossible to fashion a narrative of triumph that would foster reconciliation between the two Koreas. "Forgiving" North Korea's wrongs by incorporating them into a narrative of pan-Korean familial tragedy allowed South Koreans to exclude the negative aspects of the war while commemorating the war as a national calamity for both sides.

Planned and conceived during the Roh administration, its construction was authorized by top-level figures, including Roh Tae Woo, Choi Gap-sŏk, and Paek Sŏn-yŏp (the latter the paradigmatic hero of the Korean War).[15] Built in Yongsan-gu adjacent to the U.S. Eighth Army base in the center of Seoul, the huge memorial compound includes a

Figure 10.1. War Memorial, Seoul. (Photo by the authors, 2002.)

museum as well as an outdoor exhibition area, concessions stands, and a small amusement area for children. It first opened its doors in 1994 and has since become a popular destination for school field trips. The Memorial complex is arranged in eight main sections: the Memorial Hall, containing the busts of national war heroes from the fourth century to the Korean War; the War History Room, which features relics from the prehistoric age, the Three Kingdom era (third to seventh centuries), Koryŏ (918–1392) and Chosŏn dynasties (1392–1910); the Korean War Room, which houses various displays on the background and history of the Korean War; the Expeditionary Forces Room, which features Korea's involvement in Vietnam, the Gulf War, and Somalia; the Armed Forces Room, which contains materials pertaining to the history and development of the South Korean military services; the Large Equipment Room, which features military equipment used by both North and South Koreans during the war; the Korean Defense Industries Room, which contains materials related to the history of South Korea's defense industries, and finally, the Outdoor Exhibition Area, which displays large-scale armaments used during the Korean War and postwar era, as well as the *Statue of Brothers* and a replica of the *Stele of King Kwanggaet'o*. The monumentality and the inculcation of nationalism are closely connected in the War Memorial, where reverence for war heroes is linked to a largely mythical Korean military tradition that has come to serve as the "master subject" of nation.[16]

Notably absent are any depictions of the brutal struggle between the North and South Koreans which was the fundamental narrative during the Cold War. While the Korean War room provides a standard overview of the historical events of the war, its treatment of North Korea's role is largely abstracted from the brutal history of that conflict. Indeed, one of the striking features of this exhibit is its downplaying of anti–North Korean rhetoric. While the exhibition clearly leaves no doubt which party instigated the war, the intent was, in the words of the museum's guide, "to quickly get over the fact that the Korean War was an act of provocation by North Korea."[17] Instead, the viewers are presented with a chronological history, illustrated by dioramas and photographs of wartime destitution and poverty, to illustrate the tragedy of the conflict, not its brutality.

There are no bloody battle scenes, or any reference to known North Korean atrocities committed during the war. The successive purges of South Korean sympathizers after Seoul was occupied by the North Korean People's Army (NKPA) in June 1950, for example, and the executions of both American and South Korean prisoners of war are nowhere to be found. The previously publicized execution of an estimated 5,000–7,000 South Korean civilians, 40 American soldiers, and 17 South Korean soldiers during the last days of the NKPA occupation of Taejon in September 1950—an event highlighted in the history books of the previous military regimes—is also missing.[18] The revenge killings of thousands of old men, women, and children of the families of South Korean policemen, government employees, and soldiers shortly before the NKPA abandonment of Seoul in October 1950 are not here either. Nor is mention made of the mass graves outside Mokp'o, Kongju, and Hamyang, discovered by U.S. and South Korean forces after the UN retaking of these cities following the In'chŏn landing.[19]

In a war that had been particularly remembered for its viciousness, the dioramas and photographs used to illustrate the wartime experience now engender tacit forgetfulness made possible by focusing on universal themes of wartime suffering, dislocation and poverty. As the internal War Museum exhibition manual relates:

A tragedy without comparison in world history, the Korean War had neither victors nor losers. Although it inflicted incalculable cost in human lives and material damage, there was no recompense for such sacrifices and the only thing that was achieved was a restoration of the *status quo ante bellum*. There must never be a repeat of a tragedy like the Korean War.[20]

Paul Fussell has described the standardization of language in the discourse of war in post–World War I Britain and in particular, the provision of a ritualized, stylized language which was employed to overcome the horrific reality of war and render it publicly transmissible and binding rather than repulsive.[21] Rana Mitter has described something similar in his analysis of the War of Resistance Museum and the "new" remembering of the 1931–45 Sino-Japanese War in Beijing.[22] The War Memorial, too, is saturated with language of this sort, with the word "sacrifice" replacing the word "death," and soldiers being referred to as "heroes" and "martyrs" whose "spirit of national self-defense" has "protected the nation throughout the ages." By subsuming the memory of this conflict into a greater national struggle ongoing since ancient times, the War Memorial abstracts the Korean War experience into a larger story of heroic overcoming of adversity.

The Korean War martyrs are remembered in relation to a long line of similar historical "martyrs" who have sacrificed themselves in defense of their country. This theme repeats itself in the Hall of Heroes (Figure 10.2) with its sculpted busts of famed patriots since ancient times. National history is told in flashback: here, Koguryŏ's struggle against the Sui Chinese in AD 598 becomes the "ancestral" predecessor of Yi Sun-sin's sixteenth century struggle against the Japanese and South Korea's recent struggle with North Korean Communists. In this way, the War Memorial becomes the repository of *all* of Korea's past and future. By positing Korea's "ethos" of national resistance throughout the ages, the War Memorial lays claim to a defeated North Korea while embracing the North in the name of a common history. The notion that Korea's martyrs (who are linked to South Korea's struggle against communism) have "protected" the nation since time immemorial reveals the Memorial's attempt to privilege South Korea as the legitimate and authentic Korea, which speaks on behalf of the

Figure 10.2. Hall of Heroes, War Memorial, Seoul. (Photo by the authors, 2002.)

nation's *entire* patriotic history. The inclusiveness of this heroic narrative of timeless struggle masks the distinction between the North and South Korean soldier, since the sacrifices made by South Korean war martyrs are connected symbolically to Korea's heroes *before* the division and *before* the war. Indeed, the link made between Korea's ancient wars and the Korean War, along one historical continuum of nationalist struggle, evokes a *common* past that could unite the two Koreas in shared remembrance of a tragic war that must never be repeated.

Yet, the war that must never be repeated came dangerously close to being repeated in 1994. Just as the War Memorial was preparing to open its doors to the public, the first nuclear proliferation crisis of the post–Cold War period began to unfold on the Korean peninsula. As the Cold War thaw was transforming into a new post–Cold War freeze, Kim Young Sam (Kim Yŏng-sam), the former opposition leader who had joined the ruling party in 1990, became the first civilian president in 1993. When North Korea declared that it would withdraw from the Nuclear Non-Proliferation Treaty on March 12, 1993, Kim reacted angrily, charging that the "North Koreans were trying to buy time to finish their nuclear project" and expressing hope that the United States "would not continue to be led on by North Korea."[23] As tensions began to mount, Washington proposed a deal: North Korea would freeze its nuclear program in exchange for two proliferation-resistant light water reactors and a supply of heavy fuel oil.[24]

The signing of the Agreed Framework on October 21, 1994 put a temporary end to the international tension that had been building since 1991 over North Korea's nuclear program. But North Korea was back in the news in 1995, this time making an unprecedented appeal for international aid to cover a food shortage brought on by bad weather and poor harvests. Reports of widespread famine and malnutrition led the Kim administration and other world leaders to believe that North Korea was on the verge of imminent collapse. After alternating between a hard-line stance against the North, calculated to bring about its demise, and backing a conciliatory approach aimed to bring about a "soft landing," Kim Young Sam shifted powerfully to the hard side. Not only was Kim Young Sam's government unresponsive to UN and humanitarian appeals for food aid "it also sought to dissuade others from providing aid."[25]

But North Korea's imminent collapse failed to materialize. It was in the context of continuing tensions in North-South relations that Kim Dae Jung, who was elected in December 1997 as South Korea's first president from the opposition party, attempted to reorient his government's policy toward its northern neighbor. Domestically, the ascendancy of the Kim Dae Jung administration marked a period of economic crisis and reform. The story of the near collapse of the South Korean economy after the 1997 Asian financial crisis and the economic miracle of South Korea's recovery from that crisis does not need retelling here. What does bear repeating is that it was in this seesawing climate of political and economic reform during the late 1990s that Korean history once again became hugely contested. On taking office in early February 1998, Kim dramatically declared an end to the vindictive politics of the previous administration.[26] One of his first acts was to pardon the two former presidents, Chun Doo Hwan and Roh Tae Woo, who had been sentenced to jail on corruption charges (Chun was also sentenced to death for his role in suppressing the 1980 Kwangju Uprising but this was later commuted to life imprisonment). Kim Dae Jung also made the unprecedented move to erect a Memorial Hall in honor of his former nemesis, Park Chung Hee, the man who had persecuted Kim throughout his early political career (the Memorial Hall was never built, however, because of the controversy surrounding Park's legacy). In the new era of reform and forgiveness of the past, a new dialogue about the war began to emerge that reflected both change and continuity from earlier versions.

"Post–Korean War" South Korea: The Korean War Monument as Peace Monument

In an article on Tiananmen Square, Wu Hung describes what he sees as the complex relationship between memory and event. "Memory, though invisible and hidden, bridges separated events into a continuous process" so that with every new and momentous event, like the death of leader or a national crisis, the memories associated with a particular Memorial change, while the Memorial itself often assumes a new identity.[27] Hung discusses this process in his analysis of the Monument to the People's Heroes in Tiananmen Square. Whereas the Monument was originally erected to announce the birth of Mao Zedong's revolutionary China, its meaning gradually changed over time so that by 1989, it had assumed an altogether different identity, one that now opposed the Chinese Communist Party and the "revolutionary China" that Mao had created.

Something similar has also occurred to the War Memorial in Seoul. This transformation, however, signified not so much a change in the Memorial's overall meaning as simply a *shift* in emphasis. While the theme of national reconciliation and peace had always been present throughout the War Memorial, the narrative of South Korean "victory" over the North is an equally dominant theme.[28] The reunification message was predicated upon South Korea's "forgiveness" of the North—and was premised on the idea that the two Koreas would reunite under the South which was the authentic and legitimate Korea whose prosperity presented a clear contrast to the poverty-stricken, isolated, and totalitarian North Korean state.

The *Statue of Brothers*, located on the left-hand side of the Memorial complex, represents this message of reconciliation and triumph explicitly (Figure 10.3). The enormous discrepancy in the size between the two figures shows how the "forgiving" embrace of the larger and stronger South Korean soldier of his weaker and smaller North Korean brother in a rhetoric of family "reunion" could also be written to show the "defeat of communism and the victory of South Korean democ-

Figure 10.3. The *Statue of Brothers*, War Memorial, Seoul. (Photo by the authors, 2002.)

racy."[29] The notion of national rebirth, symbolized by the cracked base in the shape of an ancient Silla tomb mound, evokes ideas of hope, birth, and national renewal (the Silla Kingdom unified the peninsula in the seventh century). Rising out of the tomb, a reunified peninsula is reborn again as a nation of brothers, although the South Korean elder brother is more powerful and hence more legitimate.

These themes of competition and victory are, however, absent from the newest monument to be added to the War Memorial complex (Figure 10.4). Unveiled during the commemoration ceremonies of the fiftieth anniversary of armistice signing on July 27, 2003, the Korean War Monument represents a significant departure from themes of triumph that characterized Roh's *Nordpolitik*. In fact, the 2003 commemorations of the Korean War became the source for the construction of a new pan-Korean nationalism based on the idea of a *shared* experience of national tragedy, the memorialization of which would contribute to a lasting peace on the peninsula.

The era of reconciliation in contemporary Korean affairs, which

Figure 10.4. The Korean War Monument, War Memorial, Seoul. (Photo by the authors, 2002.)

began with Kim Dae Jung's ascendancy to political power in 1998, has seen a multitude of new interpretations of Korean history. These stretch from a positive appraisal of Park Chung Hee's presidency (which became widely known as the "Park Chung Hee syndrome") to new understandings of North Korea as fellow sufferers of a tragic division.[30] This view legitimized the Sunshine Policy of Kim Dae Jung who named his new diplomatic efforts toward North Korea after Aesops' fable, "The North Wind and the Sun."[31] Rejecting the premise of previous South Korean presidents that only a hard-line approach would make the North more conciliatory, the essence of Kim's policy was to separate politics from economics, in order to permit South Korean companies to do business with North Korea without regard to political differences. The impact of this approach, according to Kim, would be felt gradually as North Korea was penetrated and influenced by the liberalizing influence of an economy integrated with the global economy. In time, it was hoped, North Korea will have liberalized enough to make a more open relationship or even unification with South Korea possible.[32]

This policy brought about a marked change in South Korean assessment of the wartime past, of which the Korean War Monument (here-after KWM) is just a part. The focus of this wide-ranging revision is on *ending* the war and thus moving beyond the conflict toward achieving a permanent peace.

The shift from remembering the start of the war (June 25) to com-memorating its provisional end (July 27), the dating of the armistice, signaled a new nationalist strategy of memory-through-forgetting. What is "remembered" here is the armistice and the fact that North and South Koreans are one people; what is forgotten is how and why the war began. In the words of Cho Hŭi-yŏn, an activist and history professor working on behalf of the new "peace" movements that have sprung up in South Korea in recent years, "the history and future of the Korean peninsula must now be interpreted from a 7-27 perspective rather than the 6-25 perspective." The former, according to him, "refers to the reinterpretation of Korean history and future in peaceful terms, while the latter involves a conflictual interpretation that repro-duces the Cold War structures of inter-Korean conflict."[33]

This message of "future peace" through the celebration and com-memoration of Korea's ageless "unity" is a theme that also appears in the KWM, conveyed explicitly by this message displayed in a small ex-hibition area at the base of the structure:

> Peace is not a valley squeezed between peaks of war. The barbed wire fence [DMZ] that divided us has become an oasis of green life, and the blood that had flowed on the battlefield has become the flower petals of our souls. Look! Even out of the Korean War's half century of pain there is a forest of prosperity full of trees of dazzling freedom and love.

At the center of the KWM is the June 25th Tower, which represents, according to the guide manual, a "new beginning." Molded in the combined form of a slim bronze dagger (*sehyŏng tonggŏm*) that "sym-bolizes the eternal history and martial spirit of the Korean people" and that of "a life giving tree, which symbolizes the prosperity and peace of the Korean people" the Tower symbolizes "the rise of the Korean people from the ashes of war while also representing both the spirit of martialism and an image of peace."[34] The Tower, which marks the be-ginning of the war, was also supposed to demonstrate its end, a promise made to future generations that the fraternal war "will never happen again." As the Fiftieth Anniversary of the Korean War Commemoration Committee put it, "the erection of the war monument is a testament to the promise of eternal peace to our descendents."[35]

The use of the Korean slim bronze dagger as the centerpiece of the KWM is significant, because, as the archaeologist Hyung Il Pai has noted, "it has become the diagnostic marker for the appearance of the earliest 'Korean' race, which is equated with the Yemaek people, who supposedly migrated from somewhere in Manchuria around 1000–700 B.C. into the Korean peninsula."[36] Among Korean nationalist historians, the slim dagger stands as a racial marker of a "distinct prehistoric Korean archeological culture."[37] A unifying symbol of the ancient past, its combined form as a "life-giving tree" also connotes the nation's future rebirth. Like the *Statue of Brothers*, situated near the KWM, the idea of national rebirth through the peaceful reunification of the peninsula is a common theme. In the case of the KWM, however, there are no allusions to a South-North struggle and reconciliation. What is commemorated is the suffering of war and the struggle to overcome it through the shared memorialization of a common (ancient) past. This common past is represented by the Stone Wall, which "symbolizes the Korean peninsula" and upon which are etched copies of prehistoric Korean rock drawings, signifying Korean unity. To get to the heart of the KWM, one must descend into the Stone Wall area and enter beneath the Stone Bowl "that seemingly supports the tower" and that "holds the spirit of the Korean people and their desire for unification." In these layers of symbolic meaning, the Stone Wall, the Stone Bowl, and the June 25th Tower all express hope for the rebirth of peace among brothers that union would bring.

It is significant, then, that the *Statues Defending the Nation* that surrounds the bronze dagger is the only place directly referring to wartime experience (Figure 10.5). The thirty-eight figures—an allusion to the 38th parallel—represent "peoples of all social standings who collectively overcame the difficulties of the war" and symbolize "both the suffering and pain of the Korean War and the noble spirit of self-sacrifice and martial self-defense possessed by our martyrs."[38] While specific to South Korean soldiers, who lead and help the people to overcome the war, "our" martyrs is also a reference to a long line of historical martyrs honored throughout the War Memorial for their sacrifices for the nation in other wars. The KWM thus commemorates

Figure 10.5. Statues Defending the Nation, War Memorial, Seoul. (Photo by the authors, 2002.)

the Korean War as one in a long line of historical wars in which the Korean soldier was called upon to defend his country. The ambiguity of the June 25th Tower reiterates this message, for there is nothing *specific* about the events of 1950–53, since what is being represented by the bronze dagger and life-giving tree is "the eternal history and martial spirit" of the Korean people. The Korean spirit of national self-defense, represented by the South Korean soldier but also indirectly incorporating the North Korean people as part of the nation's common legacy, is the center of commemoration.

Like the War Memorial, the UN participation in the war is significantly marginalized in the KWM. Placed on the stairwell leading downward from the Stone Bowl to the Stone Wall, the twenty-one poles, "symbols of the 21 participating nations," are almost invisible from the entrance of the War Memorial. Their invisibility matches the striking visibility of the bronze dagger that rises above the thirty-eight statues, announcing Korean unity and future peace (Figure 10.6). The *particularity* of the Korean War experience is subsumed within a general narrative commemorating the "spirit of national self-defense."

Figure 10.6. The Korean War Monument, War Memorial, Seoul. (Photo by the authors, 2002.)

The KWM's seemingly political neutrality about the war is intended to make possible proclamations of the honor of the veterans who served while expressing a *shared* vision of pan-Korean unity and peace. With this monument the South Korean veterans can affirm their pride in having served their country while also affirming that their service was part of a larger legacy of Korean national self-defense that has existed since time immemorial.

The KWM's placement between the *Statue of Brothers* (to its west) (Figure 10.7), which sits on a Silla Kingdom tomb, and the *Stele of King Kwanggaet'o*, the great king of Koguryŏ (on its east) (Figure 10.8) is thus significant. Silla's ancient territory roughly correlates with the boundaries of contemporary South Korea while North Korea now occupies the land of the ancient northern kingdom of Koguryŏ. North and South Korea, like the ancient territories of Koguryŏ and Silla, meet together under a united symbol of shared "Koreanness"—the ancient bronze dagger and life-giving tree—of Korea's eternal past and its eternal (unified) future. No longer separated nations, the KWM recalls

Figure 10.7. Statues Defending the Nation and the *Statue of Brothers*, War Memorial, Seoul. (Photo by the authors, 2002.)

a time *before* the division, and even *before* the Three Kingdom period itself.

Where the War Memorial was the first officially sanctioned narrative in this new interpretation of the war, popular history aimed at a mass audience soon followed. One such topic has been the alleged massacre of Korean civilians by American soldiers at No Gun-ri (Nogŭn-ri) during the early days of the war. When the Associated Press first broke the story in September 1999, it stirred considerable controversy in both the United States and in South Korea.[39] The report, which received a Pulitzer Prize in 2000, and the restraint removed by the end of military rule in South Korea, have resulted in the creation of a wealth of new works by respected South Korean historians devoted to uncovering what they have termed "the hidden history of the war." Indeed, in this genre, formerly off-limit topics have now been written about extensively, including new research on South Korean and U.S. responsibility for mass killings of civilians and political prisoners during the war.[40] The topic of alleged U.S. wartime atrocities has created an in-

Figure 10.8. Statues Defending the Nation and the *Stele of King Kwanggaet'o,* War Memorial, Seoul. (Photo by the authors, 2002.)

dustry of new historical works devoted to reexamining the relationship between the U.S. and ROK governments during and after the war.[41]

The end of the Cold War, democratization, and the reconstruction of wartime memory in the 1990s have meant that the perception of the U.S. role has undergone considerable reevaluation by South Korean lawmakers and historians (with a dramatic shift in perception from its role as savior from communism to perpetrator of war crimes). Demands for justice on behalf of No Gun-ri survivors fed into a popularized narrative of the war that began to emerge during the 1990s: that of South Korea as victim of the United States. As an editorial in the *Han'guk ilbo* (October 2, 1999) put it:

> Now that the victims in the tragic event have proven to be innocent civilians by all witness and documents, Washington had better admit and apologize for the mistaken killings and agree to the victim's justifiable call for redress. At the same time, it is imperative for our government to take sincere measures to meet the victims' demands without further delay [. . .] Everyone should

bear in mind the historic lesson that must be learned from this incident that attempting to cover past wrongdoings or mistakes is tantamount to committing a more intolerable crime.[42]

The attack on innocent Korean civilians and their victimization fed into the old image of Korea as victim, not only of Japanese colonialism, but also of an *entire* history of foreign aggression. (Not surprisingly, it was also during this period that the Korean government demanded a formal apology from Japan on behalf of the Korean "comfort women"—Korea's most visible victims of World War II—who were forced to serve as sexual slaves for the Japanese military).[43] It is this history of victimization and Korea's simultaneous triumph over it that the War Memorial and the KWM commemorates. The *Statues Defending the Nation* in the KWM are configured so as to show both the adversity faced by the Korean people, depicted on each end by the frail and pathetic poses of an old man and woman, and their triumph over this adversity, symbolized by the strong and masculine figures of the Korean soldiers. These powerful and triumphant figures lead the people by embodying the nation's "spirit of national-self defense" against the foreign foe.

The controversy surrounding the No Gun-ri incident thus reinforced basic themes of the War Memorial—not of anti-Americanism of which there is no hint—but the narrative of Korean victimization and (eventual) heroic triumph. Through a "strategic forgetfulness" of the brutality of the war (and memories of North Korea's role in that brutality), the KWM sought to re-remember the war by invoking a familiar narrative of victimization from which the two Koreas would eventually emerge triumphant.

Peace Politics and Anti-Americanism

In order to bring about a new Northeast Asia, a structure of peace must first be established on the Korean peninsula. It certainly is most unfortunate that the peninsula still remains the last legacy of the Cold War of the 20th century. In the 21st century, we have to change the peninsula into a land that sends out the message of peace to the rest of the world.

~ *President Roh Mu Hyun, Inaugural Speech, February 25, 2003*

While the fiftieth anniversary of the armistice signing was officially being commemorated at the War Memorial grounds on July 27, 2003, South Korean lawmakers were putting together a bipartisan proposal to make July 27 a day of "pacifism" or "peace."[44] The new shift in the commemorative culture of contemporary South Korea devoted to the memory of the war's tentative end marks what one political commentator has termed the "creation of a progressive peace system between the two Koreas."[45] Cho Hǔi-yǒn has noted that the end of the Cold War and the concomitant improvement of inter-Korean relations have necessitated a reconsideration of the armistice and the Cold War logic that supported it: "While the armistice must be observed since it is the only international agreement that provides for the suspension of military hostilities [on the Korean peninsula], it must now give way to discussions that foresee the formation of a progressive peace system between the two Koreas and the conclusion of a peace treaty."[46]

Among the many new peace movements that have emerged in recent years, the "Organizing Committee for the 50th Anniversary of the Armistice on the Korean Peninsula" held a peace rally at Imjingak near Panmunjǒm, also on July 27, 2003. The principal aim of the rally was, according to its organizer, to bring about the "consolidation of North-South cooperation and national collaboration" through the creation of a "pan-national anti-war peace movement" that would become "the center of East Asian and global peace movements around the globe."

> The current suspension of hostilities and the extension of that volatility has led to the current tragedy of having to worry about a second Korean War in the year 2003 which marks the 50th anniversary of the armistice [. . .] The armistice [suspension of hostilities] is an abnormal state of affairs which must be resolved so that "a permanent termination" of the war can be realized as soon as possible.[47]

The Committee consisted of seventy-six civic organizations that have sprung up in recent years, including the Alliance for Unification, and the Pan-Korean Alliance for Reunification. Expressing concerns over "the nuclear tensions between the US and the DPRK," the Committee urged the following measures:

First, normalization of U.S.-DPRK relations through the freezing of nuclear programs and concluding a non-aggression pact;

Second, the suspension of arms build-up on the Korean peninsula and Japanese militarism;

Third, consolidation of North-South cooperation and national collaboration;

Fourth, the creation of a transnational [global] anti-war peace movement.[48]

Similar forums were held throughout the month of July. On July 26, for example, in cooperation with The Korea Society, the Peace Committee held a "Korean Peninsula Peace Forum" at Yŏnsei University (sponsored by the Han'gyŏrae Foundation for Unification and Culture) whose aim was to promote "themes of anti-war and peace." Like other open forums commemorating the armistice anniversary, the call to finally "end" the Korean War in order to achieve a "permanent peace" on the Korean peninsula was imbued with distinctly anti-American overtones. The participants of the July 26th Korean Peninsula Peace Forum agreed on two overriding principles, "first, Korea must become fully aware of the hegemonic nature of the U.S. that brought about the nuclear crisis as well as the instability of the armistice; second, it must overcome the crisis by cooperating with anti-war movements at the global level."[49]

In another July 29 conference hosted by the Solidarity for Peace and Unification of Korea, entitled "Citizens Solidarity for Peace and Unification and the Lawyers for a Democratic Society," also at Yŏnsei University, participants were asked to come up with proposals for "revising the U.S.-South Korean Mutual Defense Treaty in a more 'autonomous' manner." Like other civic organizations devoted to achieving the "peace and prosperity" of the two Koreas, the United States has become the focus of intense criticism for having been "the direct cause of the series of crises on the Korean peninsula since the 1990s."[50]

While anti-Americanism is not new to South Korea, what is new is that anti-American sentiments appear to have spread into almost all strata of South Korean society, ranging from elite government policymakers and intellectuals to members of the middle class and the younger generation.[51] According to a recent public opinion poll, 63 percent of South Koreans have an unfavorable opinion of the United States and 56 percent feel that anti-Americanism is growing stronger. Another recent poll revealed that more South Koreans find the United States a greater threat to their national security than North Korea.[52] While the sources of tensions are many, it is the changing perceptions of North Korea that have had the most profound impact on U.S.-ROK relations in recent years.[53]

At the core of the U.S.-ROK alliance is the presupposition of a common North Korean threat. It was the Korean War that led to the signing of the Mutual Defense Treaty between the United States and the ROK in October 1953, and for nearly half a century the Cold War and the common memory of the war bound the United States and South Korea in a common mission to defend the nation against another North Korean invasion. But while this threat no longer appears credible to the younger generations of South Koreans, Americans, recovering from the trauma of 9/11, regard the North Korean regime as a rogue state, intent on pursuing nuclear weapons in defiance of international agreements and widely proliferating arms and missiles. Whereas the Cold War continues in the United States under the guise of the new "war on terrorism," it has irrevocably "ended" in South Korea. The disastrous U.S.-ROK summit in March 2001 and George W. Bush's denunciation of North Korea as part of an "axis of evil" in his State of the Union Address on January 29, 2002, reveals the fundamental disjuncture between the American hard line and the South Korean engagement policies toward North Korea.

Popular anti-American sentiments in South Korea helped Roh Mu Hyun to win his way into the Blue House in 2002. Indeed, in February 2003, Yun Yŏng-kwan—the ROK foreign minister and who was subsequently pushed out for his pro-American policy stance—caused consternation in Washington for allegedly preferring a nuclear North Korea to a collapse scenario.[54] Although he later denied that this was the policy of the Roh administration, his statement was widely taken as illustrating Roh's "ostrich pacifist approach"—that is, that a military solution to the conflict was unthinkable.[55] Roh's perceived "coddling" of the North further raised eyebrows in Washington after his August 19, 2003 apology to North Korea for the burning of a North Korean flag that had taken place at a small anticommunist rally. The August 15 rally to commemorate Korea's liberation from Japanese occupation at the end of World War II had attracted about 7,000 people, most of whom were elder church members and Korean War Veterans. As the conservative journalist, author, and well-known critic Cho Gap-che remarked about the apology, "our soldiers will be confused now where they should aim their rifles."[56]

It was in this climate of what we call "post–Korean War" politics that the reinterpretation of South Korea's relationship with the United States became an issue and helped to bolster a pan-Korean nationalism rooted in Korea's self image as victim. In this new narrative of the Korean War, the Korean past informs the present, not just the period of so-called "American neo-imperialism," but also Korea's *entire* history of struggle against the foreign foe. Achieving peace and ending the Korean War meant not only overcoming the armistice and the Cold War logic that sustained the old order by creating a "progressive peace system between the two Koreas," but also linking Korea's record of resistance against foreign aggression to serve as a lesson for the present. Herein lies, perhaps, the deeper meaning of the KWM's "Bronze Sword and the Life Giving Tree": the commemoration of the spirit of the two Koreas' *shared* "spirit of national self-defense" against an ongoing threat of foreign invasions and would-be oppressors. These images highlight the other side of Korea's posture as a former great power that had been able to resist invaders in the past. This nationalism resurrects the duality of Korea as victim and hero: not just centuries of (shared) national victimization experienced at the hand of foreign invaders, but also Korea's (shared) triumph in overcoming these challenges to their national sovereignty. As one leader of the so-called new peace movements put it, ending the Korean War depends upon "the shift from a passive conception of peace [a mere exclusion of war] to an active conception of peace which [must be] based on the perception that true national reconciliation cannot transpire under imperialist conditions and the presence of foreign troops."[57] Pan-Korean nationalism necessitates the expulsion of the foreign enemy—in this case the United States—to facilitate the commemoration of a "shared national spirit" that would finally end of the Korean War and bring about the peaceful reunion of the two Koreas. In this reinterpretation of history,

North Korea's past transgressions are "forgotten"(and forgiven) in order to foster a new nationalism, inclusive of all Koreans, by finding a common enemy to oppose (Japan and the United States).

It is in this context that we must understand the national furor that arose over the accidental deaths of two Korean schoolgirls caused by two American soldiers on June 13, 2002 (Figure 10.9). Two middle school girls were going to a birthday party in Ŭijŏng-bu, located just north of Seoul, walking along the edge of a two-lane highway. A convoy of U.S. armored vehicles belonging to the 2nd Infantry Division was also on the road. Two armored vehicles had already passed the girls, who were walking on the pavement because there was no shoulder. They had their heads down and their fingers in their ears to block out the noise. They were run over and killed. The driver of the armored vehicle that killed the girls, the third or fourth in line of the column of military vehicles, did not hear the vehicle spotter warning him about the girls' presence because of a faulty headset. It was a tragic accident.

Figure 10.9. Anti-American demonstrations in front of the American embassy, Seoul. (Photo by Donald N. Clark, 2003.)

While the deaths and the later acquittal of the U.S. soldiers responsible for the accident created a national furor in South Korea, spurring a wave of anti-American protests and an outbreak of conspiratorial theories, ranging from reports that the soldiers had killed the girls on purpose to charges that the soldiers had laughed off the incident, what interests us here is how the tragedy became entangled in the thickets of memory politics. The deaths were linked to South Korea's "neo-colonial" status that fed into the image of Korea as victim.

Illustrating this popular anti-American feeling, the pop group *Uri Nara* released a hit song shortly after the incident entitled "Arrest Tank" to protest the acquittal in a U.S. military court of the two American soldiers responsible for the accident. "If no soldiers were responsible," the song goes, "then at least their armored vehicles should be arrested before they leave Korea."[58]

In direct and obvious ways, the deaths of the two schoolgirls became connected to a whole array of issues related to Korea's history of colonialism under Japan that played upon the trope of a violated motherland that must recover from foreign occupation to achieve its former greatness (independence and reunification). The deaths became symbolic of South Korea's "client status" under the United States, and demands to revise the Status of Forces Agreement (SOFA) created a popular constituency in South Korea for arguing that foreign "imperialists" were once again trampling upon the sovereignty of the Korean nation and impeding the path of national unification. Even the otherwise conservative Grand National Party lodged a petition to demand a revision of the SOFA. "The aggressive U.S. policy has forced South Koreans to change their perception of what an ally is," said Rep. Kim Wŏn-ung of the Grand National Party. "In the past, a country that helped deter war here was an ally. But now, only those who contribute to promoting inter-Korean peace, reconciliation and unification should be considered our ally."[59] Connecting the deaths of the girls with South Korea's "client status" and American efforts to "impede" the reunification of the peninsula, the invocation of a common enemy (the United States) has been used to foster a new nationalism, inclusive of both Koreas. Indeed, riding the wave of popular anti-Americanism, then presidential candidate Roh Mu Hyun stated just days before the close of the extremely tight presidential race that he might favor neutrality if war ever broke out between North Korea and the United States, an extraordinary statement coming from one of America's closest allies.[60] As an editorial of the *Chungang ilbo* put it:

> The cry for an independent foreign policy that began with the Roh Mu Hyun government is not a temporary whim. It is not the product of the personal beliefs of the president but the reflection of a political flow that has been given power for the first time in our political history. *In some ways, it is natural for Koreans, who have achieved the most successful democracy and market economy in Asia, to desire an independent foreign policy.*[61]

The deaths of the two schoolgirls became a vehicle for re-remembering and forgetting a host of issues related to colonialism, war, and the division of the peninsula. The intensification of memory and identity struggles in South Korea in recent years, exemplified by the Korean War Monument and the new commemoration of July 27th as a day of pacifism and peace, was part of the growing search for an alternative view of the war years, including new interpretations of U.S.-ROK relations. Attempts to rewrite North Korean history back into one of shared and ongoing national struggle and triumph over foreign adversity (the "spirit of national self-defense") that was crystallized in the planning of the War Memorial, and later highlighted in the Korean War Monument, reveal the growing desire for the "normalization" of relations between the two Koreas. The new obsession with peace and the highlighting of the armistice agreement as the key event of war commemoration reflect the shift in South Korea's post–Cold War and post–Korean War consciousness from a "war" narrative to a "peace" narrative. This shift has also brought a fundamental reevaluation of U.S.-South Korean relations in the aftermath of the Iraq War and the legacy of the unfinished war that the United States is now seen as perpetuating. This is why former President Kim Dae Jung, in his response to criticism of South Korea's engagement policy following North Korea's claimed nuclear test on October 9, 2006, blamed the crisis squarely on the Bush administration's hard-line policy toward North Korea. "Since 1994, we stressed a package resolution and the Clinton administration positively accepted this. As a consequence, our plan almost bore fruit," he said, "the George W. Bush administration, however, has ignored this and the result is today's failure."[62] President Roh Mu Hyun embraced this assessment, abruptly backtracking on his initial October 9 statement that the engagement policy would have to be revamped, by stating just two days later that inter-Korean dialogue would continue, as would the inter-Korean Kaesong Industrial Complex and tourism to Mt. Kumgang. Nearly 71 percent of South Koreans backed Roh's continued engagement approach in a poll published by the *Chungang Ilbo* following North Korea's nuclear test. In that poll, 70.8 percent polled stated that "dialogue between North and South Korea was the best way to resolve the current crisis."[63] Seoul, along with China and Russia, also refused to support an initial move by the United States and other members of the UN Security Council to adopt a resolution that includes a threat of military action against North Korea for its nuclear test. As the former South Korean ambassador to the United States, Han Sung-joo, put it, "there is a general consensus in South Korea, not only among politicians but also in the general population, that engagement is the right policy."[64] Efforts to finally end the Korean War reveal how pan-Korean nationalism and the current struggle over how to best deal with the North Korean nuclear crisis are intimately caught up in the politics of memory and South Koreans' need to accommodate North Korea both in their past and in their future.

∼ 11

The Korean War

What Is It that We Are Remembering to Forget?

BRUCE CUMINGS

THE FIFTIETH ANNIVERSARY of the presumed end of the Korean War arrived in July 2003, but the two Koreas technically remain at war, which appears unlikely to be resolved anytime soon. The armistice signed on July 27, 1953 stilled the guns, but it brought no formal peace. Instead, the Korean War is one of the longest running conflicts remaining in the world, perhaps the longest in its yearly continuity—even if we have conflicts in the Balkans and the Middle East that have much more ancient roots. The longevity and insolubility of the Korean conflict makes it the best example in the world of how easy it is to get into a war, and how hard it is to get out. American troops arrived in southern Korea in September 1945, and 25,000 of them are still there today, long after the Cold War ended and the Soviet Union collapsed. More daunting, war could come again, and very quickly—indeed a new, perhaps more catastrophic Korean War almost did come again in June 1994, as the result of American worry about North Korea's nuclear facilities. Today, in the aftermath of the war against Iraq, another crisis that could lead to war confronts us.

The difference, of course, between the 1950–53 Korean War and a future conflict on the Korean peninsula is that for the vast majority of South Koreans, North Korea no longer appears to be the major threat it once was. Today, more South Koreans view the United States to be a greater source of potential instability on the Korean peninsula than

North Korea. The dawn of a new post–Cold War era has witnessed not only the relative decline in South Koreans' affinity with the United States; post–Cold War South Korea has ushered in a tide of suppressed memories and hidden truths about the war that have pushed a new generation of South Korean leaders to confront their past in ways that might lead them to finally end their civil war and achieve the peaceful reconciliation of the two Koreas.

A Forgotten War?

The Korean War was clearly a war, but of what kind? A conventional war of aggression was the answer in the 1950s and again in the 1990s: "another Munich" according to Truman, "Stalin's war" according to researchers of Soviet documents unearthed after 1991. All blame goes to the Russians and the North Koreans. This point of agreement requires the war to begin on June 25, 1950, and only then; clearly there was an invasion of the South by the North (the whole world knew that on June 26, 1950), therefore it was an open-and-shut case of aggression. Beyond that Washington-forged consensus, the reigning trope consigns this war to oblivion: a forgotten war. The Korean War is of course forgotten in the United States, if not in Korea where approximately 25,000 American soldiers and 600,000 South Korean soldiers still confront the North's legions. The war's having vanished at home explains the experience of a North Korean official who came to New York in the 1980s on Olympic business, finding that people could barely recall when the Korean War occurred, that cab drivers thought communists ran South Korea (since human rights were so violated), and that Americans were friendly and innocent of the antagonism he expected to find. He rightly called it a form of amnesia, but thought it might be useful in starting a new relationship.

Still, this title is a way to think about the Korean War. By calling the Korean conflict a "forgotten war," we both name it, and we remember it—a paradox: What is it that we are remembering to forget? We do not remember history but particular verdicts, integral to and shaped by the raucous domestic politics of the 1950s. The war is forgotten and buried. But what is the epitaph on the American tombstone? The tombstone has two messages: for the Truman Cold War liberal, Korea was a success, "the limited war." For the MacArthur conservative,

Korea was a failure: the first defeat in American history, more properly a stalemate, in any case it proved that there was "no substitute for victory." The problem for MacArthur's epitaph is that if MacArthur saw no substitute for victory, he likewise saw no limit on victory: each victory begged another war. The problem for the Truman liberal is that the limited war got rather unlimited in late 1950.

So we need another verdict: a split decision—the first Korean War, the war for the South in the summer of 1950, was a success. The second war, the war for the North, was a failure. In this manner Secretary of State Dean Acheson produced a schizophrenic epitaph: the decision to defend South Korea was the finest hour of the Truman presidency; the decision to march to the Yalu occasioned "an incalculable defeat to US foreign policy and destroyed the Truman administration;" this was "the worst defeat . . . since Bull Run" (another interesting analogy). Acheson assumed, however, that the latter happened not to him but to his *bête noire:* Acheson squares the circle by blaming it all on MacArthur, and liberal historiography has squared the circle in the same way. The Korean War happened during the height of the McCarthy period, and it was the handiwork of Dean Acheson and Harry Truman; McCarthy attacked both, and so the experience of the war disappeared in the shaping of the Cold War consensus: Truman and Acheson were the good guys. Cold War debate was almost always between the middle and the Right, the consensus anchored by the McCarthys on one end and the Achesons or Hubert Humphreys on the other. Furthermore, the Korean War is no icon for the conservative or the liberal, it merely symbolized an absence, mostly a forgetting, but also a never-knowing. The result is a kind of hegemony of forgetting, in which almost everything to do with the war is buried history in the United States.

The forgetting perhaps has a deeper reason, one found in the pathological realm of amnesia: as the intimations of American decline multiplied in the 1980s and early 1990s, so did nostalgia for the 1950s. Reagan was the first two-term president since Eisenhower, his smiling persona drew on Ike's public mastery, and the Reaganites made frank comparisons with that quintessentially Republican era. If this rerun had a B-movie and even a Brumairean first-time-tragedy, second-time-farce quality to it for Reagan's detractors, it clearly drew on a wellspring of mass nostalgia for a lost time when American was Number

One. Subsequently Newt Gingrich nominated 1955 as the year when the American Dream hit its apogee. The Korean War is an errant counterpoint to these rosy memories, and so it vanishes.

A rule of this amnesia might be, "all of so-and-so's paintings (or photographs, or books, or cinema) are interesting except those done about Korea." This I found out only by reading the fine print of Picasso's obituary that he did a mural in 1951 in the genre of Guernica, titled *Massacre in Korea;* I decided to put it on the cover of my first book. When I asked a friend if it would be good for the cover, she said "it would be for the Vietnam War, but I don't know if it would be for Korea." Picasso seemed guilty of a curious displacement. It took years of reading to find out that Margaret Bourke-White had her camera eye trained on the unconventional in Korea, literally the "unconventional" guerrilla war in the South, or the filmmaker Chris Marker who produced a marvelous book of photos on North Korea in the late 1950s, or that Marilyn Monroe's career owed in large measure to her being the Betty Grable of the Korean War, "discovered" during its height and nicknamed "Miss Flamethrower."

Journalists reported Korea not just in the McCarthy era, but under military censorship, so for most Americans, the war was a never-known thing. Foreign reporters (usually from the British Commonwealth) covered the war in much more depth and honesty than Americans, with the remarkable exception of I. F. Stone. Reginald Thompson, an Englishman, authored *Cry Korea*, a fine, honest eyewitness account of the first year of the war. War correspondents found the campaign for the South "strangely disturbing," he wrote, different from World War II in its guerrilla and popular aspects. "There were few who dared to write the truth of things as they saw them." Koreans were dehumanized; G.I.'s "never spoke of the enemy as though they were people, but as one might speak of apes." Even among correspondents, "every man's dearest wish was to kill a Korean. 'Today, . . . I'll get me a gook.'" Complete control of the air was achieved within days, and produced a certain atmosphere of indulgence, which no doubt contributed to Korean casualties. As I. F. Stone put it, the air raids and the sanitized reports "reflected not the pity which human feeling called for, but a kind of gay moral imbecility, utterly devoid of imagination—as if the flyers were playing in a bowling alley, with villages for pins." So it is not just a forgotten war, but a repressed, occluded experience, what Nietzsche called *historia abscondita*, what Pierre Macherey called a "structured absence."

Television was in its infancy during the war, and Hollywood constructed Korea in the patriotic, heroic modes of World War II. Because the fit of that genre was so poor in Korea, however, with the exception of Sam Fuller's *Steel Helmet*, there is barely a memorable film among the many produced in the 1950s; the best, like *The Bridges at Toko-ri*, just happen to be set in Korea—it might as well have been the bridge at Remagen. The "structured absence" is none other than the script of World War II itself, for in Korea an American army victorious on a world scale five years earlier was fought to a standstill by rough peasant armies. The one and only classic film of the Korean War is *The Manchurian Candidate*, whose genius was to wrap the Orientalism and communist-hating of the 1950s in the black humor of the 1960s, thus making both palatable; the film allows one to be chic in one's prejudices. The one clear exception to the hegemony of forgetting, the long-running TV series *M*A*S*H*, is no exception because it was a series about Vietnam, once removed to Korea.

Yet the amnesia masks a reality in which we all are a product of Korea whether we know it or not; it was the Korean War, not Greece or Turkey or the Marshall Plan or Vietnam, that inaugurated big defense budgets (the budget quadrupled from June to December 1950) and the national security state, that transformed a limited containment doctrine into a global crusade, that ignited McCarthyism just as it seemed to fizzle, and thereby gave the Cold War its long run. The American split verdict on the Korean War, coming closely on the heels of a failed war to liberate the North, was an agreement to disagree, a stitched-together mending of a torn national psyche; like so many other debates in the United States, it followed the lines first etched by partisan disagreement in Washington. Above all it reflected a compact to forget—a selective forgetting that preserved psychic order. You remember one verdict and forget or condemn the other. Each verdict implies a corresponding amnesia. "Better a mended sock than a torn one," said Hegel; "not so for self-awareness."

In this repression and forgetting there is nonetheless a text of the Korean War, a conventional wisdom, and it is this that resides in the consciousness of most Americans, however consciously or unconsciously (usually the latter). The ubiquitous name for this war in the

United States ("the forgotten war") betrays the emptiness that exists in the American mind about the nature of this war. It is daunting to learn that the first usage of this term came in 1951,[1] two years before the war ended, but after it had entered a phase of trench warfare along what is now the demilitarized zone—and therefore rarely occupied the front pages of American newspapers anymore.

Likewise, as early as 1973 Martha Gellhorn found that the whip-hand of history regarding the Vietnam War was held by the party of forgetting. "Consensual amnesia was the American reaction, an almost instant reaction, to the Vietnam War," she wrote; television reinforced the forgetting by maintaining "a respectful silence" after 1973, even though this new "forgotten war" was not yet over.[2] Galloping along in amnesia's wake was the party of revision. The first was prerequisite to the second; by 1980 Ronald Reagan campaigned on the position that Vietnam had been a "just war." But that war had been, to use Alexander Solzhenitsyn's metaphor, an iron crowbar of history that descended upon and branded an entire generation. Thus the parties of forgetting and revision have had to contend with the party of memory, which fundamentally distinguishes Vietnam from Korea in the United States.

The 1990–91 Gulf War was the first war fought in the interest of forgetting. It was, for President George H. W. Bush, a war to "put Vietnam behind us." A new war bursting suddenly upon the world in the dog days of August, it was the first clear-cut case of major aggression across international boundaries since World War II. Nonetheless when Americans joined it, its conduct still interrogated a memory. That memory offered up the following lessons: never again, a war fought "with one hand tied behind our backs." Never again, a war blamed on American soldiers, making them unwelcome back home. Never again, a victory on the battlefield lost in the living room. If this judgment was reflexive, the opposition to that Gulf War was reminiscent. Nostalgic for Vietnam, it never transcended that experience. The opposition played out its own "lessons," founded in Third World innocence and First World malevolence. In my view, none of these lessons bear up under scrutiny. The Gulf War was fought for very different reasons by Bush and his advisors, and it was by no means "another Vietnam." But the presumed lessons have weight as representations, pitched for the media and the television. Thus our third paradox: the Gulf War was fought against a remembered war, with the party of forgetting hoping to bury it, the party of remembering hoping to revive it.

Iraq was the perfect surrogate for the party of forgetting bent on wiping out a "Vietnam syndrome" that had hampered America's global policeman role for twenty years, and that (or so the Pentagon thought) had its origin in the living room. An ironic reversal took place, in which the antiwar cry of the 1960s, "no more Vietnams," became the battle cry of the 1990s. The "lessons" of Vietnam had a television or celluloid tinge to them. When George Bush said we won't fight this one with one hand tied behind our backs, he implicitly harked back to Rambo: "Are they going to let us win it this time?," Rambo says in *First Blood*, the prelude to his "return to Vietnam." When Bush said the Gulf War would "put Vietnam behind us," he echoed Coppola's justification for making *Apocalypse Now*. Thus stubborn, recalcitrant memory propels an unnecessary war to necessity.

If Saddam Hussein's Iraq served Bush's amnesiac purposes, it was a poor surrogate for Ho Chi Minh's Vietnam—as war protesters understood immediately, because they tend to be sincere people. Hardly a thing could be said on Saddam's behalf, he had no constituency in the United States, Iraq was far more threatening than Grenada or Noriega's Panama, something truly important was at stake (hegemony in the Persian Gulf), and so the war became a surrogate for the wars the United States could not win in Vietnam and Korea—a victory without cost, interrogating the past and preparing the future. Most remarkable in this respect, however, was General Norman Schwartzkopf, the media's war hero. Several times he told TV journalists that, in his view, there were no experts on the Middle East. None of them knew what they were talking about. Even the Arab experts were wanting, he thought. The epistemology here seems to connote this: even the object does not know itself, so why need I be detained in doing with it as I will? My totalizing subject-position might be affronted by real people, real history, real difference, so why bother? Schwartzkopf unconsciously acknowledged Edward Said's judgment that "the Orient was not Europe's interlocutor, but its silent Other;" a decorated Vietnam veteran, he revealed the emotion Benedict Anderson spoke of, "a rage at Vietnamese 'inscrutability,'" a desire to penetrate an opaque, alien, recalcitrant entity with whom one could not even converse. Better just to forget about them.

A decade later, the scion of the Bush family, a president who lost the 2000 election by half a million votes, chose to posit his reckoning with Saddam Hussein on the post–September 11 "war on terrorism." Saddam was hiding "weapons of mass destruction" and giving the run-around to United Nations inspectors; therefore, against world opinion and a significant American minority, Bush launched a preventive war that, like the first war against Iraq, went quickly to its conclusion. Lost in the claims of victory was the illegality of this war, violating the UN Charter and every precept of war-making by previous presidents. From Polk's attack on Mexico through the firing on Fort Sumter, the sinking of the *Maine* and the *Lusitania*, Pearl Harbor, the Korean War, and Iraq's invasion of Kuwait, presidents who were either bent on war or expecting it to erupt, nonetheless waited until the enemy made the first move. In the preceding months Saddam Hussein was almost catatonic in his desire not to provoke George W. Bush, but the war came anyway—without provocation, without any reasonable threat that Saddam might attack someone else, Bush started a massive war when he could not know what the consequences of that war would be.

Writing in the week that the war ended, what is remarkable is the current amnesia about this prelude to war. Liberal editorialists like those in the *New York Times* recall that they opposed the war, but do not give the reasons for their opposition; ex post facto, they have become concerned that Bush not extend his doctrine of preventive war to Syria, or Iran or North Korea. The memory of this war is likely to be solidified again by the Beltway consensus: a lightning-like triumph, the victory itself overwhelming enough to ensure that might makes right, and to erase the circumstances in which Washington started this war by invading Iraq. And now everyone wonders, is North Korea next, a charter member of Bush's "axis of evil"?

A Civil War

Let's return to Korea: there is still a nagging problem: unlike Saddam Hussein invading Kuwait, or Bush invading Iraq, Koreans invaded Korea. What do we make of that? In the midst of the terrible crisis in December 1950 that ineluctably followed upon the American decision to invade the North, another view was presented: that of Richard Stokes, the British Minister of Works, who intuited this paradox. The

38th parallel decision in 1945, taken unilaterally by Americans, was "the invitation to such a conflict as has in fact arisen:"

> In the American Civil War the Americans would never have tolerated for a single moment the setting up of an imaginery [*sic*] line between the forces of North and South, and there can be no doubt as to what would have been their re-action if the British had intervened in force on behalf of the South. This parallel is a close one because in America the conflict was not merely between two groups of Americans, but was between two conflicting economic systems as is the case in Korea.[3]

Ever since 1950, this civil war analogy has been like a Rumplestiltskin for the official American view: say it and the logic collapses, the interpretation loses its power. But Stokes carried his argument one step further: not just a civil war, but a war between two conflicting social and economic systems. It is precisely that Korean conflict which continues today, with the United States using every resource at its command to support the economic system of the South (even if in somewhat altered form after the $70 billion bailout in late 1997, in return for reforms stage managed by Treasury Secretary Robert Rubin), and the North going it alone after 1991, with an utterly different economic conception—one of manifest and cruelly diminishing returns for the past twenty years, but nonetheless a stark alternative to the South.

I have a simple proposition to maintain: Stokes was right, the longevity of the conflict finds its reason in the essential nature of this war, the thing we need to know first: it was a civil war, a war fought by Koreans, for Korean goals. Koreans know this war in their bones as a fratricidal conflict. If Americans have trouble reflecting on this "forgotten war" as a conflict primarily fought among Koreans, for Korean goals, they should hearken to the great chroniclers of their own civil war. That distant war was the last war to rage back and forth across American territory. Six hundred thousand Americans lost their lives in it, more than the total number of American deaths in all the wars of the twentieth century, from World Wars I and II through Korea and Vietnam. The civil war pitted brother against brother, son against father, mother against herself. Memories of that war lasted so long that a bitter controversy about the flag of the Confederacy that flew over the

South Carolina statehouse only ended in the year 2000. I first went to the South when I was twelve years old, to spend some time with relatives in Memphis, and my shock at seeing segregationist Jim Crow laws in action was only slightly greater than my shock at finding out I was a Yankee—almost a century after the war ended.

Ambrose Bierce once wrote a short story called "An Occurrence at Owl Creek Bridge." Like the late Joseph Heller and his famous novel, *Catch-22*, the recent books by Paul Fussell on his experience in World War II, or the wonderful novels by Tim O'Brien about Vietnam, the realities of the battlefield turned Ambrose Bierce into a specialist in black humor, if not cynicism, about the human condition. Bierce, who was outranked as an American writer a century ago only by Mark Twain, is best known for a handful of short stories—"Owl Creek Bridge," "Chickamauga," "The Mocking-Bird," "Three and One Are One," "An Affair of Outposts"—all of them drawn from his experience in the American Civil War.

Bierce specialized in surprise endings to his stories, ones that drove home a truth about the human nature of civil war: in "The Mocking-Bird," Private Grayrock of the Federal Army, posted as a sentinel, sees something moving in the Virginia woods and fires his musket. Convinced that he actually hit something, he spends hours scouring the area. In the end John Grayrock finds the body, a single bullet hole marking the gray uniform. Inside the uniform is William Grayrock, his brother. (In the course of this sad story, Bierce refers without explanation to the "unconverted civilians" of southwestern Virginia in 1861, who torment John Grayrock's mind in their imagined multitude, materializing from all angles to shoot at him—peeping from behind trees, rushing out of the woods, hiding in a home.) In "The Story of a Conscience" a man commits suicide after realizing that he has killed an enemy spy who once spared his own life, earlier in the war. In "Chickamauga," a soldier dreams so vividly that we believe him to be reunited with his family and kinsmen, but the story ends with the man standing over his mother's dead body, her hands clutched full of grass, beside the burned-out remains of his childhood home.

In the summer of 2000, and for every summer of the previous half century, a soldier named Art Hunter had awakened in the middle of the night with cold sweats, imagining the faces of two old people, a man and a woman, hovering above his bed. These two weathered faces had made his life "a living hell," and when they haunted him in the middle of the night he would get his hunting rifle, go sit on the porch, and smoke a cigarette. In 1991 soldier Hunter finally got the U.S. Government to give him full disability pay for his severe posttraumatic stress disorder, but the nightmares still came to him in his home in the foothills of Virginia's Blue Ridge Mountains.[4]

On September 30, 1999, a woman named Chŏn Chun-ja appeared on the front page of *The New York Times,* dressed as if she were yet another middle-aged and middle-class Korean housewife going shopping. Instead she stood at the mouth of a tall tunnel in Nogun village, down the road from the town of Yŏngdong in South Ch'ungch'ŏng Province, South Korea. She pointed to a hill where, she alleged, in July 1950 "American soldiers machine-gunned hundreds of helpless civilians under a railroad bridge." She and other survivors went on to say that they had been petitioning their government and the American government for years, seeking compensation for this massacre; they had been completely stonewalled in both Seoul and Washington. Meanwhile the article also carried the testimony of American soldiers who did the firing, who said that their commander had ordered them to fire on civilians.[5] Art Hunter was one of those soldiers, firing for hours and days into a white-clad mass of women, children, and elderly people gathered under the railroad bridge.

The Korean War, like our Civil War, had a long gestation and occurred primarily because of issues internal to Korea. That is the basic reason why it has never ended. The civil conflict began not in 1950, but in 1945, with the division of this ancient nation as World War II ended. Within a year two regimes effectively existed, completely at odds with each other; the internal conflict erupted over the nature of these two regimes. It was a conflict fought by political means in the year after Japan's surrender, by violent and irregular means from the fall of 1946 to the spring of 1948, through guerrilla war in the South from spring 1948 to the summer of 1950, and through border conflict along the 38th parallel beginning in May 1949 and appearing to end in December 1949. In 1949 the South provoked the majority of the border fighting, as previously secret documents demonstrate, but the North chose not to fight at that time. Why?

The answer introduces us to the North Korean perspective on this war, a perspective virtually absent in American commentary on the war, at the time and ever since. In the autumn of 1987, I spent a number of weeks in the North, negotiating with them over rights to film and do interviews on behalf of Thames Television of London, and the documentary it was producing entitled "Korea: The Unknown War." "Who do you think started the Korean War?," was the question our interrogators began with. Now I am sure that to prove ourselves unbiased and pursuers of truth, various American conservatives would want us to say, "Why, of course, everyone knows it was Kim Il Sung who started the Korean War!" That would have gotten us a quick escort to the airport (at minimum). Fortunately I was able instead to tell the truth: "It was a civil war, and in a civil war the question of who fired the first shot doesn't matter." This response energized a wiry, elderly man, who had been watching us intently: "It was not a civil war. It was a war of American imperialism waged against the Korean people. For nearly forty years, our party has maintained that position on the war. How do you respond to that?" His eyes had narrowed, his face had turned to stone: so had everyone else's. So Thames producer Max Whitby and I batted our response around for a while, hoping the question would go away.

Shortly the head of their documentary film outfit motioned in my direction and said to one of his aides in sotto voce Korean, "ask that son-of-a-bitch." And then I said that the evidence convinces me that it was a civil war; that it started in 1945 with the division of Korea; that it was fought by unconventional means until the summer of 1949 when the South sought several times to attack across the parallel, but was restrained by American commanders. In 1949 the North was not ready to fight, because its best soldiers were still fighting in the Chinese civil war. In the summer of 1950 those soldiers had returned, and now the North was ready to fight. To my surprise their side exchanged glances, faces softened, and the question was not brought up again. Perhaps they decided just to drop it, or perhaps they thought my answer was the best they were likely to get, from their standpoint. In any case it is the truth.

The Korean War was (and is) a civil war; only this conception can account for the 100,000 lives lost in the South before June 1950 (at least 30,000 of which came amid the 1948–49 rebellion on Cheju Island—as far away as you can get from the North and still be in Korea), and the continuance of the conflict down to the present, in spite of assumptions that Moscow's puppets in Pyongyang would surely collapse after the Soviet Union itself met oblivion in 1991. It is therefore instructive to see what Thucydides, the first philosopher of war, had to say about civil war. Perhaps the most famous line from his book, "war is a stern teacher," comes from the civil war in Corcyra:

> War is a stern teacher. So revolutions broke out in city after city . . . What used to be described as a thoughtless act of aggression was now regarded as the courage one would expect to find in a party member; to think of the future and wait was merely another way of saying one was a coward; any idea of moderation was just an attempt to disguise one's unmanly character; ability to understand a question from all sides meant that one was totally unfitted for action. Fanatical enthusiasm was the mark of a real man, and to plot against an enemy behind his back was perfectly legitimate self-defense. Anyone who held violent opinions could always be trusted, and anyone who objected to them became a suspect . . . [etc.][6]

This a mnemonic for "Korea:" The passage fits the Korean civil war with no necessity to dot i's or cross t's, and it explains the continuing blight on the Korean mind drawn by that war, just like a doctor drawing blood: to understand the Korean War "from all sides" is still to go to jail in the North, and to risk oblivion in the now (and finally) democratic South. It also fits the American Civil War, by far the most devastating of all American wars to Americans, but one that happened long enough ago that most Americans have no idea what it means to have warfare sweeping back and forth across the national territory, or to have brother pitted against brother.

War Is Judged Twice

In the most influential American book on justice in war, Michael Walzer argues that wars are always judged twice: first as to the justice of going to war, and second according to how the war is fought. People can use bad means to fight just wars, and vice versa. He defends the Truman administration's logic of intervention with the following argument: the U.S. response to North Korean aggression was correct because Truman took the problem to the United Nations, which was the legitimate organ of world opinion, and thus of global justice ("it was the crime of the aggressor to challenge individual and communal rights," and the United Nations acted correctly in backing American involvement in the war). In justifying the American invasion of North Korea, however, the U.S. Ambassador to the United Nations called the 38th parallel "an imaginary line." Walzer then comments, "I will leave aside the odd notion that the 38th parallel was an imaginary line (how then did we recognize the initial aggression?)." Walzer leaves this mouthful without further thought, because it is the essence of his argument that Truman was right to defend the 38th parallel as an international boundary—this was his "initial aggression."[7]

Kim Il Sung crossed the five-year-old 38th parallel, not an international boundary like that between Iraq and Kuwait, or Germany and Poland; instead it bisected a nation that had a rare and well-recognized unitary existence going back to antiquity. The counter-logic implied by saying "Koreans invade Korea" disrupts the received wisdom or renders a logical reconstruction of the official American position impossible, even for a political theorist with the rhetorical skills of Michael Walzer. It is also often forgotten that until the rupture of the Tet Offensive in 1968, the same original sin also marked North Vietnam, through the 1964 attack on American ships in the Tonkin Gulf, or the "indirect invasion" which it sponsored via the Vietcong insurgency in the South. The United States had committed no sins in Vietnam, but with its allies was engaged in a collective-security response to aggression. Thus in November 1961 the White House spoke of strengthening South Vietnam against "attack by the Communists," as if they were outsiders to Vietnam, and few in the media questioned the legitimacy of the Cold War premise that American policy sought only to preserve an anti-Communist South against aggression. Vietnam was fought not as "a new kind of war" but as another Korea, with success defined as a permanently divided Vietnam—as the Pentagon's film, *Why Vietnam?* stated in 1965.[8]

When Walzer comes to the *way* in which Americans fought the Korean War, however, he is unequivocally damning: the air war, in which oceans of napalm were dropped long before the excruciating misery of this infernal weapon became a subject of controversy, was not restrained by the dictates of *jus in bello* (justice in war-fighting), and therefore constituted a war crime. In the aftermath of the Chinese intervention Gen. Douglas MacArthur's decided to burn everything in Korea that might serve the enemy, including civilians left behind who served the enemy, whether forced to or not.

As soon as Chinese troops hit Korean soil, MacArthur ordered that a wasteland be created between the war front and the Yalu River border, destroying from the air every "installation, factory, city, and village" over thousands of square miles of North Korean territory. As a British attaché put it, except for the town of Najin near the Soviet border and the Yalu River dams, MacArthur's orders were "to destroy every means of communication and every installation and factories and cities and villages. This destruction is to start at the Manchurian border and to progress south."[9] This terrible swath of destruction, targeting every village in its path, followed Chinese forces right into South Korea: George Barrett of the *New York Times* found "a macabre tribute to the totality of modern war" in a village north of Anyang:

> The inhabitants throughout the village and in the fields were caught and killed and kept the exact postures they held when the napalm struck—a man about to get on his bicycle, fifty boys and girls playing in an orphanage, a housewife strangely unmarked, holding in her hand a page torn from a Sears-Roebuck catalogue crayoned at Mail Order No. 3,811,294 for a $2.98 "bewitching bed jacket—coral."

(Dean Acheson wanted censorship authorities notified about this kind of "sensationalized reporting," so it could be stopped.)[10]

The Hungarian writer Tibor Meray had been a correspondent in North Korea during the war, and left Budapest for Paris after his participation in the 1956 rebellion against communism. When a Thames Television team interviewed him in 1986, he said that however brutal Koreans on either side might have been in this war,

> I saw destruction and horrible things committed by the American forces: everything which moved in North Korea was a military target, peasants in the fields often were machine gunned by pilots who I, this was my impression, amused themselves to shoot the targets which moved.

Meray had crossed the Yalu in August 1951 and witnessed "a complete devastation between the Yalu River and the capital," Pyongyang. There were simply "no more cities in North Korea." The incessant, indiscriminate bombing forced his party always to drive by night:

> We traveled in moonlight, so my impression was that I am traveling on the moon, because there was only devastation . . . every city was a collection of chimneys. I don't know why houses collapsed and chimneys did not, but I went through a city of 200,000 inhabitants and I saw thousands of chimneys and that—that was all.[11]

It is common for Americans to write that Japanese leaders have not yet atoned for their sins in World War II, unlike the Germans, leading to insensitivity to the suffering of neighboring Koreans and Chinese, bland textbook accounts of the war that leave school children in the dark about its real nature, and periodic ritualized apologies that do nothing to suggest that the Japanese feel any true remorse. Yet it is impossible to imagine an American leader apologizing to the North Korean people for the genocidal air war that was mounted against them for three years, and that left hundreds of thousands of civilians dead, if not millions. Even to suggest the idea seems absurd. Yet the North Korea that emerged from the Korean War had birthmarks and deformations that were not merely self-inflicted; the United States maintains a responsibility for the warping of this regime that occurred during the war, and that has continued for decades in the never-ending confrontation mounted against it by the world's greatest power. It is this kind of self-awareness and recognition that can begin the process of reconciliation with this old and determined enemy; in many ways President Kim Dae Jung showed the way in the past five years, refusing to let the distant memories of a vicious civil war deter him from seeking reconciliation with his Northern brethren.

War Is a Stern Teacher: The Return of Memory

The civil conflict in Korea began the day the country was divided, and it continues today. But in the past fifteen years Koreans have developed a strong critique of the American role in that division, and in the War itself. The ferment in the 1980s and 1990s in South Korea prompted a deeply revisionist look at the origins of the Republic of Korea and the Korean War. This work is extensive, and has the following characteristics: first, a concern for the mass of the Korean population, after generations of scholarship only about the elite; second, a harsh look at the role of the United States in the 1940s transition from Japanese to South Korean rule; third, a radical and didactic concern for using the past to criticize the present and shape the future; and finally, not much—or not enough—concern with primary research (although many new sources on the late 1940s have been uncovered by some practitioners of "the new history"). It is a fact, even if it is immodest to say it, that my own work played a part in this new history—stimulating young historians to dig into the past, and stimulating the Seoul American embassy and the U.S. Information Service to import American scholars to refute my work.[12]

Historian Shim Chi-yŏn has produced a number of books on the late 1940s, focusing on the major political parties of the period and greatly increasing our knowledge; he also produced an interesting study on the U.S.-Soviet Joint Commissions in 1946 and 1947.[13] Ch'oe Sang-yŏng's critical study of the U.S. Occupation first emerged as a dissertation at Tokyo University under the guidance of Prof. Sakamoto Yoshikazu; when he returned to Seoul after completing it in the early 1970s, the KCIA read passages out loud from it while torturing him. Now his study is published.[14] He taught at Korea University for many years, and was ambassador to Japan under Kim Dae Jung. Yi U-jae has done excellent work on peasants' and workers' movements in the early postwar period, both on his own and in collaboration with others.[15]

Historians from the southwestern Chŏlla provinces, in which the Left was strongest and that suffered the severest repression in the postwar period, have been particularly active. This work comes from historians like An Chong-ch'ŏl, and novelistic chroniclers of postwar history like Ch'oe Myŏng-hui. (Ms. Ch'oe comes from Namwŏn, a hotbed of rebellion in 1945–50, and the headquarters of the U.S.-ROK guerrilla suppression command in 1949–50. People in Namwŏn not only had strong people's committees but also often supported the North Koreans when they occupied the area in the summer of 1950. When the ROK forces retook the area, they massacred so many people that the living honor the dead in mass ancestor worship, on the anniversary day of specific massacres.)[16]

The previously forbidden subject of South Korea's left-wing people's committees, which emerged in the wake of Japan's defeat and which governed affairs in many counties for months and even years thereafter, has also gotten attention since the mid-1980s with much new information coming available. We now have a remarkable variety of personal memoirs of the local committees, the Yŏsu-Sunch'ŏn Rebellion, the insurgency on Cheju and its draconian extermination, and an extensive record of massacres before and during the Korean War, perpetrated by the Rhee regime, and sometimes by Americans.[17] Very little of this has gotten into English and is generally unknown in the United States, except of course for the July 1950 massacre at Nogŭn-ri. That massacre hit the front pages of American newspapers in late September 1999,[18] as if no one had ever imagined that such things could have happened during the Korean War. In this curious American lexicon, civilian massacres—about which one could read in *Life Magazine* or *Collier's* in the summer of 1950—disappear into oblivion because of a false construction of the nature of the Korean War, never to be mentioned again. They are lost for a sufficiently long time, such that that when they reappear, they counterpoint everything about the received wisdom on this forgotten war.

It takes only a few days in the archives of the U.S. Military Government or the State Department to realize that the Korean critique of Americans for their country's division, the Military Government's suppression of alternative political forces, U.S. support for a succession of dictatorships, and American complicity in political massacres (Yŏsu in 1948, Cheju in 1948–49, the Chiri-san guerrillas, many others like Nogŭn-ri during the war, and Kwangju in 1980), is echoed time and time again in classified reports. In 1949 David Mark, a State Department official, undertook a full review of American policy toward Korea, which echoed many subsequent findings by scholars: Yŏ Un-hyŏng's "People's Republic" and the local committees that it spawned could have been utilized by the United States, because the local organizations were in every county, and only came to be dominated by leftists and communists *after* the American command came out against them in December 1945. This is now history, Mr. Mark wrote; "nevertheless it has set the pattern for political power development in South Korea."[19] The late 1940s were indeed the crucible of Korean politics thereafter.

The fledgling CIA's first biographical study of a foreign leader was done on Syngman Rhee, as were some of its earliest political analyses on foreign governments. South Korean political life, a 1947 report stated, was "dominated by a rivalry between Rightists and the remnants of the Left Wing People's Committees," described as a "grassroots independence movement which found expression in the establishment of the People's Committees throughout Korea in August 1945." As for the ruling political groups,

> The leadership of the Right [*sic*] . . . is provided by that numerically small class which virtually monopolizes the native wealth and education of the country. Since it fears that an equalitarian distribution of the vested Japanese assets [i.e., colonial capital] would serve as a precedent for the confiscation of concentrated Korean-owned wealth, it has been brought into basic opposition with the Left. Since this class could not have acquired and maintained its favored position under Japanese rule without a certain minimum of "collaboration," it has experienced difficulty in finding acceptable candidates for political office and has been forced to support imported expatriate politicians such as Rhee Syngman and Kim Koo. These, while they have no pro-Japanese taint, are essentially demagogues bent on autocratic rule.

The result was that "extreme Rightists control the overt political structure in the US zone," mainly through the agency of the Japanese-built National Police, which had been "ruthlessly brutal in suppressing disorder." The structure of the southern bureaucracy was "substantially the old Japanese machinery," with the Home Affairs Ministry exercising "a high degree of control over virtually all phases of the life of the people."[20]

For the next fifty years, the acceptable political spectrum consisted of the ruling forces and parties of Rhee, Park, Chun, Roh and Kim (Y.S.), and an opposition deriving from the Korean Democratic Party founded in September 1945, led by figures like Kim Sŏng-su, Cho Pyŏng-ok, and Chang Myun. The ROK did not have a real transition to the opposition until Kim Dae Jung's election in 1998, and it did not have a president until February 2003 who was not part of the political divide (and political system) going back to the U.S. Occupation. (Kim Dae Jung got his political start in the self-governing committees that sprouted near the southwestern port of Mokp'o; the Right always used that against him to claim that he was a communist or pro-North, but in fact he made his peace with the existing system in the late 1940s, and was an establishment politician thereafter, however much he was hounded by the militarists.)

Ever since this early and determining point, however, South Korean politics has had a suppressed "third force," with strong roots in the southwest, but a presence all over the country. If we locate these forces on the "Left," we reduce them to the polarized and caricatured constructions of the Cold War, in which any kind of mayhem committed by the Right is insufficient truly to distance them from American support, so long as they remain firmly anticommunist. For decades these political and social forces resided of necessity in the long memories of participants in the local committees, labor and peasant unions, and rebellions of the late 1940s, harboring many personal and local truths that could not be voiced. Suppressed memory, though, is history's way of preserving and sheltering a past that possesses immanent energy in the present; the minute conditions change, that suppressed history pours forth. Thus, in the past fifteen years, Koreans have produced hundreds of investigations, histories, memoirs, oral accounts, documentaries, and novels that trace back to the years immediately after liberation.

The Kwangju Rebellion provoked more anti-American criticism than any event since the period before the Korean War, and an immense outpouring of writing once Chun Doo Hwan was overthrown.[21] The brutal suppression of this rebellion, with American acquiescence if not outright support (acquiescence at the least, in that with American command of the South Korean armed forces, American authorities could not but be involved), was the subject of several National Assembly inquiries in the early 1990s and still gnaws at the heart of the relationship. Its influence is sufficient to lead to continuing demands for the rewriting of centrally vetted school textbooks (for example, the reconstitution of the October 1946 uprisings as a patriotic people's struggle, rather than a treacherous riot).[22]

Koreans have thus been experiencing a cathartic politics, where many suppressed and unpalatable truths have come forth with enormous political force. The new president, Roh Mu Hyun, is the first of the ROK's leaders not to have a recognizable lineage back to the 1940s. His lineage is more recent, to the extraordinary turmoil of the 1980s, when he put his career and his life in danger to defend labor leaders and human rights activists; through marriage he is also connected to a family blacklisted politically for events going back decades. (Roh's father-in-law was a member of the South Korean Labor Party, outlawed under the UN Occupation; he was arrested for allegedly helping the North Koreans during the war, and died in prison.) His electoral victory is inexplicable, however, apart from the turning point that came in 1995–96, in the "Campaign to Rectify the Authoritarian Past" that brought Chun Doo Hwan and Roh Tae Woo into the docket, where they were successfully prosecuted for high treason and monumental corruption. An admirably thorough and honest investigation of the Kwangju rebellion began, Chun's foul dictatorship was completely discredited and he found himself with a death sentence hanging over his head, until President-elect Kim Dae Jung magnanimously pardoned him. Now with President Roh in power, the National Assembly has promised to compensate victims of the suppression on Cheju Island.

All this has strong public support in the ROK. A sophisticated social science analysis by Professor Doh Shin demonstrated deep and widespread support for the cashiering of Generals Chun and Roh: their arrest and prosecution both for their role in squashing the Kwangju rebellion and their *coup d'etat*, and for taking nearly $1 billion in political contributions merited "strong support" from more than 65 percent of respondents in a scientific poll, and over 15 percent said they "somewhat support" these actions. By contrast, there was much more tepid support for punishing the conglomerate leaders who provided the political slush funds.[23]

The Korean tide of suppressed memory and contemporary reckoning with the past has established important truths for courageous people who, after the dictatorships ended, have pressed their case against all odds for years. For scholars, the strong democracy and civil society that emerged from the bottom up in the South, in the teeth of astonishing repression and with very little support from agencies of government in the United States, validates a method of going back to the beginning and taking no received wisdom for granted. I remember how, as a young man working in the U.S. archives, I came across vast internal records of the suppression of peasant rebels in South Cholla in the fall of 1946, the breaking of strong labor unions in the cities, the American-directed suppression of the Cheju and Yŏsu rebellions and the many guerrillas that operated out of Chiri-san in the period 1948–55 (finally extinguished in the joint U.S.-ROK counterinsurgent program known as "Operation Rat-Killer"), and wondered how all this could have disappeared without an apparent trace. Then one day I read Kim Chi-ha's poem, *Chiri-san* (Chiri Mountain),[24] and came to believe that I did not know the half of it:

> A cry
> a banner
> Before burning eyes, the glare of the white
> uniforms has vanished.
> The rusted scythes, ages-long poverty,
> the weeping embrace and the fleeting promise to return:
> all are gone,
> yet still cry out in my heart.

Conclusion: Beyond Good and Evil

From the preface of my first book on the origins of the Korean War to the conclusion of my second, I argued against a discrete encapsulation that would place this war in the time frame of June 25, 1950 to July 27, 1953. This historical construction tells us that all that went before June 25 is mere prehistory, all that comes after is post-bellum. It also presumes to demarcate the period of active American involvement; before June 1950, it is Syngman Rhee against Kim Il Sung backed or controlled by Stalin and/or Mao; after July 1953, it is Rhee against the same people, his fledgling Republic ever under threat. Above all, though, this construction focuses the bright glare of our attention on the question of who started the war, on the presupposition that the correct answer to this question tends to suggest answers to all the other questions. And, of course, throughout the past decade new Soviet documents have also caused historians to focus only on what happened in June 1950. But what is highlighted here obscures all that went before and all that came after, placing it in the shadows of irrelevance. Then you tie up this neat package and bury it for a few decades under the epitaph, *Korea: The Forgotten War.*

In this manner a wrongly conceived and never known civil conflict disappears before our very eyes, as an American construction that only an American would believe; but American *amour-propre* remains firmly intact. In the conclusion to my second volume, I asked the question, what is it we are remembering to forget about the Korean War? And I used a couple of quotations from Friedrich Nietzsche (the greatest student of history and memory), to underline the significance of naming this as the Forgotten War: forgetting, Nietzsche said, is no mere result of inertia: "It is rather an active and in the strictest sense positive faculty of repression." We human beings need to be forgetful; forgetfulness is "like a doorkeeper, a preserver of psychic order, repose and etiquette . . . there could be no present without forgetfulness." Happiness, cheerfulness, hope—they all have as their talisman, a salutary forgetting. The opposite faculty is, of course, *memory.*[25] The preservation of memory is a struggle precisely with inertia: "an active *desire* not to rid oneself" of memories, however unpleasant; a will to memory, a conviction never to forget. Violence is the sternest teacher of the memory, in a human *"mnemotechnics:"* the oldest psychology on earth is that which must be "burned" in: "only that which never ceases to *hurt* stays in the memory."[26]

In this passage, which had profound influence on Freud, Nietzsche might as well have been writing about Americans, an ahistorical people looking toward the future, the frontier, the next new thing, with history and memory passing in the rapidly disappearing wake of the rearview mirror. We as a people are the party of forgetfulness, and a thousand examples come to mind: a "drugstore Indian" still standing amid a pile of ersatz Native American kitsch in the Missoula, Montana airport, with (now) politically correct slogans attached; a President named Bush who, as a bystander to the profound transformations of the 1960s, found it easiest to forget when fully inebriated in his fraternity at Yale; a nation of elderly migrants in Winnebagos, rocketing around the country with who-knows-what memories left in their wanderings (in the 2002 film *About Schmidt*, Jack Nicholson's wife of many decades dies, after which he fires up the Winnebago).

For the party of memory, contemporary Jewry is the best example of Nietzsche's truth—"never forget" becoming the ruling mnemonic for the Holocaust. The Vietnam generation is another good example. What will happen when they die off, however? Who will maintain the memory of that war—that is to say, a *correct* memory of its futility, criminality, and appalling violence? Nietzsche found something he liked to call *historia abscondita:* concealed, secret, or unknown history: "perhaps the past is still essentially undiscovered!"[27] Who knows what will come forward from the past to shake us in the present, to find new truths, and to give future interpretations a new direction. Art Hunter knew the truth of what happened in Nogun village so many years ago, but why did it haunt him? I think it is because a young man on the giving end of a rifle intuits a fundamental human truth about warfare, that the soldier is there to kill, but also to save:

> The soldier, be he friend or foe, is charged with the protection of the weak and unarmed. It is the very essence and reason for his being. When he violates this sacred trust he not only profanes his entire culture but threatens the very fabric of international society.

The author of this moving statement went on to say that "the traditions of fighting men are long and honorable, based upon the noblest of human traits—sacrifice." He was General of the Army Douglas MacArthur.[28]

The restorative truths told by the courageous survivors and living victims of the Korean conflict are fruits of the popular struggle for democracy in Korea; this surge of civil society is also a surge of suppressed information, and would never have been possible during the long decades of dictatorship. This Korean outpouring is also, however, akin to what writers like Ambrose Bierce did for Americans in the aftermath of their civil conflict, penning poignant stories that captured the terrible truths of fratricidal war. Survivors like Chon Chun-ja did something wonderful for Art Hunter, too: by coming forward and telling their stories, they made it possible for him to begin purging himself of a terrible guilt. Now it is high time to take the personal truths of the victims and survivors and turn them into a restorative truth, a requiem for the "forgotten war" that might finally achieve the peaceful reconciliation that the two Koreas have been denied since Dean Rusk first etched a line at the 38th parallel in August 1945.

~ 12

Doubly Forgotten

Korea's Vietnam War and the Revival of Memory

CHARLES K. ARMSTRONG

THE SURRENDER OF THE JAPANESE ARMY and government to the Allies on August 15, 1945 marks an important rupture in East Asian, as well as world, history. But only in Japan is the period since 1945 consistently referred to as the "postwar." In Korea, this period is usually labeled "contemporary history" (hyŏndaesa), more recent in the past than "modern history" (kŭndaesa), the latter generally thought to begin sometime in the nineteenth century. Chinese historiography follows a similar periodization, although in mainland China the break between modern history (jindaishi) and contemporary history (xiandaishi) is conventionally set at the founding of the People's Republic of China (PRC) in 1949. While there are a number of reasons for the difference in terminology between Japan and continental East Asia, one is particularly obvious: for Chinese, Koreans, and Vietnamese, the period immediately following the end of World War II was not a time of peace, but of civil and international war.

Collectively, the renewed civil war in China, the Korean War, and the wars in Indochina constitute three decades of virtually continuous warfare in "postwar" East Asia. This "Thirty Years' War," from the Japanese surrender to the fall of Saigon, is generally studied as three distinct wars in China, Korea, and Vietnam, but in fact the three conflicts were intertwined and mutually reinforcing. This connection was not only geopolitical—the three countries were at the front lines of the

Cold War in East Asia, communist and noncommunist armies confronting one another with the direct or indirect support of superpower backers—but also personal. Hundreds of thousands of Koreans fought in the Chinese civil war, especially in Manchuria, and mostly on the communist side;[1] up to 1 million Chinese People's Volunteers fought alongside the North Korean People's Army in the Korean War; advice and materiel from the PRC were indispensable for the North Vietnamese in their war against the Americans;[2] and, constituting perhaps the least known important connection in this regional warfare, 325,517 Republic of Korea (ROK) forces participated in the Vietnam War to aid the South Vietnamese and Americans. From those forces 5,066 casualties were reported (including 4,650 combat deaths), 8 soldiers were listed as missing, and 5 defected to North Korea.[3]

Viewed regionally rather than nationally, the convergence of postcolonial independence struggles and the Cold War in East Asia can be seen as a contest of two transnational movements, one pro-American and the other communist. Despite their surface similarities, these alliances formed very differently from their counterparts in Europe: whereas the Soviet-led Warsaw Pact and Council for Mutual Economic Exchange were reactions to NATO and the Marshall Plan in the West, the American-led alliances in Asia were a great extent reactions to the perceived success of the communists. The communist regimes that emerged out of these wars in China, North Korea, and Vietnam still exist today, to no small degree because (with the ambiguous exception of North Korea) they were the winners in their civil wars, which in turn were mutually dependent on one another for success.

The ROK venture in Vietnam, like the American war as a whole, was therefore a failure. Despite the public enthusiasm with which the government of President Park Chung Hee sent his troops to South Vietnam between 1964 and 1966, the ROK chose by and large to forget the event. No commemoration marked the return of the last ROK soldiers in the early 1970s, veterans were hidden away, and the event itself was rarely referred to publicly. The only significant deployment of ROK troops outside of the Korean peninsula in the Republic's history, Vietnam became South Korea's "forgotten war." If the Korean War was long forgotten in the United States, Korea's Vietnam War was doubly forgotten. Even though the ROK military comprised by far the largest non-U.S. foreign force in Vietnam—at its peak in 1968, the

Table 12.1. Non-U.S. Foreign Forces in Vietnam

Year	Korea	Thailand	Australia	Philippines	New Zealand
1964	150	—	200	17	30
1965	20,620	16	1,557	72	119
1966	44,566	244	4,525	2,061	155
1967	47,829	2,205	6,818	2,020	534
1968	50,003	6,005	7,661	1,576	516
1969	48,869	11,568	7,672	189	552
1970	48,537	11,568	6,763	77	441
1971	45,700	6,000	2,000	50	100
1972	36,790	40	130	50	50

Source: Robert M. Blackburn, *Mercenaries and Lyndon Johnson's "More Flags": The Hiring of Korean, Filipino, and Thai Soldiers in the Vietnam War* (Jefferson, NC: McFarland & Co., 1994), 158.

50,000-strong Korean contingent was nearly seven times the size of Australia's, the next largest foreign combat force—not a single book has been written in English on the Koreans in Vietnam (Table 12.1). Nor, however, was much of substance written on the subject in Korean until the 1990s. The revival of memories of Vietnam has been an unexpected by-product of both the global and domestic political changes that have occurred in South Korea in the aftermath of the Cold War. The establishment of diplomatic ties between South Korea, Vietnam, and China that occurred in 1992, the end of military rule and the inauguration of South Korea's first civilian president, Kim Young Sam in 1993, wrought revolutionary changes in the way South Koreans began to rethink their military past. One of the by-products of these new historical re-evaluations was a drastic rethinking of South Korea's involvement in Vietnam. Indeed, the revival of memories of Vietnam has been an unexpected by product of post–Cold War South Korean society, and the struggle over these memories has occasionally taken a violent turn (Table 12.1).

South Korea began to re-remember its Vietnam War in the early 1990s. This is not to say that there had previously been no memory of the war at all; officially, the staunchly anticommunist ROK government maintained that its contribution to the American war effort in Vietnam had been a noble defense of the Free World against the communist onslaught in Asia, and that Korean soldiers had behaved admirably in that war. For the military-led regimes of Park Chung Hee and Chun Doo Hwan, the American ambivalence about the war was somewhat embarrassing, as well as a worrisome sign that the United States could not always be counted on as a trustworthy ally. Therefore, although the Vietnam War was not officially criticized, it was relegated to silence. At the popular level, the Vietnam War was part of the personal memories of thousands of war veterans and their friends, colleagues, and families. Perhaps the most enduring popular memory of the Korean soldiers in Vietnam was that of toughness: Korean soldiers were fierce, capable, manly fighters feared by the Vietnamese and respected by the Americans. On that the American veterans of Vietnam agreed. Koreans were tough (ROK soldiers were, appropriately, referred to as "ROKs" or "Rocks" by their American counterparts), but toughness could also mean brutality, as we shall see.

Both the official memory of the noble war and the popular memory of the manly fighters were called into question with the emergence of a more critical remembering of the Vietnam War, first in fiction, then in film, and finally in media investigations and official ROK government statements. If there was a single event in popular culture that marked a break with the uniformly positive memories of the war, it was the release of the film *Hayan chŏnjaeng* (White War) in 1992, the same year that South Korea normalized diplomatic relations with the Socialist Republic of Vietnam (SRV). The first South Korean film made on location in Vietnam (well before any American film was able to do so), *Hayan chŏnjaeng* painted a morally ambivalent picture of South Korean soldiers' behavior, including acts of gratuitous brutality against civilians, and portrayed traumatized veterans unable to readjust successfully to South Korean society—it was, in other words, not unlike American movies on the war such as *Platoon, Coming Home,* and *Full Metal Jacket.* But for South Korean audiences unaccustomed to such ambivalent portrayals of Korean soldiers in general, and Koreans in Vietnam in particular, the film—based on a novel of the same name by Ahn Jung-hyo, himself a veteran of the ROK White Horse division in Vietnam—came as a shock.[4] *Hayan chŏnjaeng* signaled the emergence of a counter-memory against the official memory of the war, but not until the turn of the millennium did the full extent of Korean atrocities in Vietnam became verified, publicized and widely debated within Korea.

The History of the ROKs in Vietnam

On August 31, 2001, *Apocalypse Now Redux* opened in Seoul. The original 1979 version of Francis Ford Coppola's epic hallucination about the American war in Vietnam had been banned under the military regime of General Chun Doo Hwan, himself a former front-line commander of ROK forces in Vietnam. Chun had been a regimental commander in the Ninth ("White Horse") Division in 1971–72; his right-hand man and successor, General Roh Tae Woo, served in the Capital ("Fierce Tiger") Division in Vietnam in 1968–69 as a battalion commander. One week before the *Apocalypse Now* opening, on August 23, Vietnamese State President Tran Duc Luong met President Kim Dae Jung in Seoul, the first Vietnamese head of state to visit the ROK since the two countries established diplomatic relations in 1992. By this time, the ROK had become Vietnam's fifth largest trading partner, with two-way trade totaling $2 billion, and the fifth largest investor in Vietnam, behind Taiwan, Hong Kong, Japan, and Singapore and ahead of the United States. South Korean pop music, TV dramas and films had become enormously successful in Vietnam, as they had in China. The two countries were no longer enemies, but Kim was not willing to let the past go unaccounted for. His predecessor, Kim Young Sam, had made been the first South Korean president to visit unified Vietnam, in 1996, but did not mention the war. Kim Dae Jung and SRV President Luong themselves had first met at the Association of Southeast Asian Nations regional summit in Hanoi in 1998. At that meeting, Kim Dae Jung alluded to the South Korean presence in the Vietnam war, saying "It is regrettable we had an unfortunate period in the past . . . I propose we overcome it and make joint efforts to build forward-looking relations for friendship and cooperation."[5] At the 2001 meeting Kim was more direct, giving an unambiguous apology to his Vietnamese counterpart: "I am sorry for the suffering caused to the Vietnamese people by our participation in that unfortunate war," Kim said, and promised financial assistance to build hospitals in the five provinces of central Vietnam where ROK troops had been most active.[6] This remarkable gesture of apology and offer of compensation sought to bring to close a particularly ugly chapter in the Cold War in East Asia, and brought together two countries that, while on opposite sides of that conflict, had developed ever-deepening economic and cultural ties since the Cold War ended.

Between 1965 and 1973 the ROK contributed a cumulative total of over 300,000 combat troops to the American war effort in Vietnam, second only to the United States itself and far exceeding all other foreign force contributions combined. Although Thailand and the Philippines sent support troops to Vietnam, South Korea was the only Asian nation that heeded U.S. President Lyndon Johnson's appeal for international combat troop contributions. Johnson's so-called "More Flags" campaign, begun in early 1964, attempted to make the American effort an allied endeavor similar to the Korean War, but this "coalition of the willing" conspicuously lacked most of America's major allies, including Britain and Canada. South Korea, however, was not lacking in enthusiasm for America's Vietnam War. As early as 1954, South Korea under Syngman Rhee—via the American embassy in Seoul—offered to send military forces to aid the French against communist insurgents in Vietnam and Laos. The Eisenhower administration turned down Rhee's unsolicited offer, in part out of fear of provoking China and North Korea at a time when the ROK itself was thought to be politically unstable and vulnerable to attack. However, after General Park Chung Hee's coup in 1961 and the establishment of a more stable military government in South Korea, coinciding with the escalation of the U.S. military presence in Vietnam, the perception of American planners changed. Despite some criticism by opposition politicians and the domestic media, Park again volunteered South Korean troops to fight for the Americans in Vietnam, in response to Johnson's "More Flags" request. This time the Americans agreed.

South Korean involvement in Vietnam began in September 1964 with a contingent of some one hundred and thirty members of a Mobile Army Surgical Hospital (MASH) and a group of ten Taekwondo instructors. In January 1965, the ROK National Assembly voted to send the first contingent of combat troops. The following month, a South Korean engineering team arrived at Bien Hoa; naval transport and construction teams soon followed. Finally, in September 1965, the first full division of ROK soldiers arrived, the Capital or "Tiger" Division that would produce future Roh Tae Woo. In October, the "Blue Dragon" Marine Brigade landed at Cam Ranh Bay. The Ninth Army

Divisions would soon follow. President Johnson requested a third division in December 1967, but it was never sent.

The motives of Park Chung Hee's government for assisting the American effort in Vietnam was partly political, to gain U.S. support for Park's dictatorship. Park's regime was also motivated by security concerns, hoping to ensure a high American force commitment to South Korea by showing ROK loyalty for Americans in Vietnam. But perhaps the most important motivation for South Korean participation was economic. Simply put, the Vietnam War was a gold mine for South Korea. The Brown Memorandum of March 4, 1966—named after the U.S. ambassador to Seoul at the time—stipulated increased U.S. assistance to the ROK in terms of military equipment, weapons, and training, as well as civilian aid, in exchange for the ROK commitment to the Vietnam venture.[7] Individual soldiers would be paid by the United States, with a salary many times what they could have made in Korea. The amount of money pumped into the still-struggling South Korean economy through direct aid, substitution of funds South Korea would otherwise have borne itself for its defense, military procurements, and soldiers' salaries was a major boost to South Korea's development. If the Korean War had been for Japan "a gift from the gods," as Japanese Prime Minster Yoshida Shigeru once put it, the Vietnam War played a similar role for the South Korean "economic miracle." War-related income is estimated to have amounted to $1 billion dollars between 1965 and 1973, when the last ROK troops left Vietnam. In 1967 alone, war-related income accounted for nearly 4 percent of South Korea's GNP and 20 percent of its foreign exchange earnings. In particular, South Korea's heavy industries, including construction, chemicals, and heavy equipment, were given an enormous and invaluable boost by the Vietnam War. Individual sectors, especially steel and transportation equipment were dependent on the Vietnamese market for a majority of their earnings (Table 12.2). Major South Korean companies that took off during the war later became household names, such as Hyundai, Daewoo, and Hanjin, the parent company of Korean Air. Park's first Five-Year Plan for Korean economic development was mapped out with Vietnam in mind. One can say that the Vietnam War paid for South Korea's first expressway, the Seoul-Pusan highway built between 1968 and 1970 (Table 12.2).[8]

Table 12.2. Republic of Korea Exports with Percentages to Vietnam, 1965–70

Commodity	Exports to Vietnam as Percentage of Total
Steel products	94.29
Transportation equipment	51.74
Beverages	44.20
Non-electric machinery	40.77
Glass, clay, stone	32.98
Printing and publishing	32.84
Glass, clay, stone	32.98
Nonferrous metals	16.53

Source: Jung-en Woo, *Race to the Swift: State and Finance in Korean Industrialization* (New York: Columbia University Press, 1991), 95–96.

If the economic windfall of Korea's Vietnam is one untold story of the war, another, much grimmer one is the brutality of South Korean soldiers in the war. This was hardly unknown to observers of and participants in the war at the time, including Americans. William Westmoreland's successor as commander of U.S. forces in Vietnam, General Creighton Abrams, once compared allied war efforts in Vietnam to an orchestra, remarking that the Koreans "play only one instrument—the bass drum."[9] The "ROKs" were viewed with a measure of respect and even fear by the Americans, who rarely mingled with Korean troops. The Koreans had their own separate command structure and operated with a degree of independence, with the largest force concentrated in the central coastal areas. ROK officers in Vietnam included future presidents Chun and Roh; it was soldiers hardened by combat in Vietnam who led the bloody suppression of the Kwangju uprising in South Korea in May 1980, as General Chun consolidated his grip on power.

For decades, until the South Korean journalistic investigations in 2000, evidence of Korean brutality in Vietnam was largely anecdotal. But even as anecdotes, many of the atrocity stories show considerable and revealing consistency. It was often reported, for example, that Korean soldiers regularly cut off the ears and/or noses of Viet Cong to keep a record of the enemy killed; ear-cutting scenes occur no less than four times in the film version of Ahn Jung-hyo's novel *White War.* Later eyewitness testimony confirmed this. Interviews conducted by the American Friends' Service Committee in 1972 uncovered hair-raising accounts of atrocities committed by members of the Korean Blue Dragon marine brigade, including beheadings of children and leaving severed heads at the side of the road as a warning against supporting insurgents.[10] Other reports claim that ROK soldiers removed the hearts of living victims, or flayed entire skins from their victims to hang on trees as warnings. While much research is needed to confirm the extent and nature of Korean atrocities in Vietnam, the ROK reputation for ferocity in the war is well established, and reported consistently by Korean, Vietnamese, and American witnesses. What explains this ferocity? First, the brutality of South Korean troops in Vietnam was indirectly a product of the brutality of the Korean War, which killed upwards of 2 million Koreans. Many of the Korean civilian deaths were the result of U.S. bombing, and not a few atrocities were committed by the North Koreans and the Chinese. But the newly formed ROK army seems to have been particularly indiscriminate, and civilian casualties racked up ROK troops during the three-month UN-U.S.-South Korean occupation of North Korea (September–December 1950 probably number in the hundreds of thousands.[11] Most of the ROKs in Vietnam had been young boys during the Korean War and had seen at close range the inhumanity and brutality of that conflict. Educated most of their lives to consider "Reds" as less than human, such men were well suited for an anticommunist campaign of violence. Also, the training of ROK frontline soldiers, partly because of the South Korean military's roots in the Japanese military, was—and to some extent remains—particularly harsh. It is not difficult to imagine these young soldiers, in the confusing conditions of war far from their homeland, unable to communicate with the local Vietnamese, losing their sense of discrimination and control in combat.

Second, the legacy of Japanese colonial rule was another factor behind Korean soldiers' brutality. As the South Korean historian Han Hong-koo has pointed out, the ROK army was founded by men with Japanese military background, albeit trained and equipped by the Americans; its officers included future president Park Chung Hee, a veteran of Japan's anticommunist counterinsurgency campaigns in Manchuria in the 1940s.[12] And, like Park and other Koreans who fought for the Japanese in their semicolony of Manchuria, Koreans in Vietnam were fighting a war that was not their own. They had no long-

term commitment to Vietnam and had less to lose than the main occupying power; the Korean soldiers were there to get the job done, by
whatever means necessary. Japanese counterinsurgency in Manchuria
was a harsh teacher of pacification and intimidation, successful in its
own way but at great cost to civilian life and property. Much more than
the Americans, the Korean military leaders who had come of age in
Vietnam were well aware of the brutal nature of "successful" counterinsurgency.[13]

Third, Korean behavior can partly be explained by the difficult racial
position of Koreans in a war with such glaring racial divides. Koreans
were well aware that, to the Americans, they "looked like" the enemy,
and therefore felt they had to doubly prove their worth. Just as, in the
1930s, Koreans in Japanese-occupied Manchuria could occupy a position superior to the local Chinese but below the Japanese-dominated
scheme of things, so Koreans could become more than "gook," if not
quite "white," in the eyes of the Americans in Vietnam. The South Korean novelist Hwang Suk-young, a veteran of the Blue Dragon marines
in Vietnam, illustrates this point in his semi-autobiographical novel
Shadow of Arms. As an American criminal investigation officer and his
Korean counterpart (and Hwang's alter-ego) drive through the streets
of Da Nang, they notice an attractive Vietnamese women riding by and
carry out the following dialogue:

> "You're a Korean, aren't you? Your girls are also nice. There were
> two Korean girls in the strip show at the club last night. Both of
> them looked exactly like American women."
> "You mean an American army club?"
> "Yes, but Koreans can go there if they're working for investiga-
> tion headquarters. No gooks though."
> "Who are gooks?"
> "Vietnamese. They're really filthy. But you're like us. We're the
> allies."[14]

One irony of this conversation is that the term "gook" itself was first
widely used as an American pejorative for Koreans during the Korean
War. But Koreans in Vietnam were lifted, at least slightly and temporarily, out of this discriminated status, and perhaps because of this

could treat the Vietnamese with even greater condescension and dehumanization than did the Americans.

Revelations, Confessions, Counter-Memory

Although the ROKs gained considerable notoriety among both Americans and Vietnamese for their brutality, accounts of Korean atrocities in Vietnam never appeared in South Korea itself during the long years of military dictatorship. Even in the newly democratizing ROK of the 1990s, images of Koreans abusing Vietnamese civilians were confined to fiction and film.[15] But at the beginning of the new millennium, South Korean academics, activists, and journalists began for the first time to investigate and report detailed, eyewitness accounts of Korean atrocities against Vietnamese civilians in the American War.[16] At the forefront of this investigation was the progressive daily newspaper *Han'gyŏre Sinmun* and its sister weekly, *Han'gyŏre21*.

In the spring of 2001, the two periodicals published a series of articles on South Korean atrocities in Vietnam War based on interviews with ROK veterans of the war and field work in Vietnam itself. As the wartime investigations by the American Friends' Service Committee and others had suggested, the "Blue Dragon" marine brigade operating in Quang Ngai Province in the central coast was particularly notorious, conducting a "scorched-earth" policy that left whole villages razed and civilians indiscriminately massacred in its wake.[17] The most extensively detailed testimony was that of retired colonel Kim Ki-t'ae, former commander of the 7th Company, 2nd Battalion of the Blue Dragons. By then in his early sixties, Kim told *Han'gyŏre* in April 2000 that as a 31-year-old lieutenant in November 1966 he had overseen the murder of twenty-nine unarmed Vietnamese youth in Quang Ngai.[18] Kim testified that from November 9 to 27, 1966, the 1st, 2nd, and 3rd battalions of the Blue Dragons carried out "Operation Dragon Eye," a campaign to mop up Viet Cong (VC) resistance in their area of operations in central Vietnam. On November 10, the 6th Company of the 2nd Battalion came under fire near the village of An Tuyet, although they suffered no casualties. Four days later, with memories of the attack fresh in their minds, the 7th Company came upon twenty-nine Vietnamese men in a rice field. The Koreans arrested the men as suspected

VC guerillas and tied them together by the wrists as the marines searched for weapons. Finding no weapons in the vicinity they were left with the choice of releasing the prisoners or handing them over the Army of the Republic of Vietnam (ARVN).

This was the last day of the first stage of Operation Dragon Eye. On November 15 the ROK forces involved in the operation were supposed to hand over control of the area to the South Vietnamese army, which the Koreans held in low regard. Releasing suspected VC to ARVN was tantamount to aiding the enemy, as far as many of the Korean soldiers were concerned. They felt that there was a high probability that the Vietnamese prisoners would escape, regroups, and possibly join the VC if they were not members already. The Koreans were exhausted from six days of jungle fighting, and in urgent need of results to show their superiors. As Kim recalled, a platoon commander asked him, "What do we do with these bastards?" His answer was to drag the men, bound together by rope, to a nearby bomb crater left by an American F4 fighter, and throw them in. The Koreans stepped back and threw grenades into the crater, splattering blood and flesh into the air. Even then, moans of the living could still be heard emerging from the crater. The marines fired their rifles into the hole and killed any survivors.

As company commander, the highest ranking field officer among the Korean troops in Vietnam, Kim was acutely aware his direct responsibility for the actions of his troops. He expressed great remorse for the "horrible acts" committed under his command in An Tuyet. Nevertheless, Kim explained, "Vietnam was a guerrilla war. We couldn't discriminate between VC and non-VC. Civilians were aiding the VC in villages, hitting us in the back of the head." Kim also revealed that a month earlier, on October 9, 1966, most of the population of Binh Tai village in the Phuoc Binh district—sixty-eight men, women, and children—were massacred by ROK troops, who set fire to the villagers' homes and shot them when they fled the burning buildings. After the war, the SRV erected a monument in Phuoc Binh to the civilians massacred by the South Koreans. The Blue Dragons themselves had also instigated a massacre at Ha My village in 1968, killing some 1968 civilians who are now memorialized by a marble stele.[19]

After Kim Ki-t'ae's testimony was published in April 2000, several more Vietnam vets told the *Han'gyŏre Sinmun* about atrocities they had witnessed or participated in. One officer described an ROK massacre in Phung Nhi, Quang Nam Province, in February 1968, as "a second My Lai" (although it had occurred one month before America's My Lai massacre) and said it also reminded him of Nogŭn-ri, the site of an alleged massacre of Korean civilians by American forces early in the Korean War that was under investigation at the time.[20] The comparison of Korean atrocities in Vietnam with American atrocities in Korea was rich with irony. The Nogŭn-ri story had broken with a 1999 Associated Press report, later published as a book, that offered strong evidence that American forces had killed large numbers of innocent civilians in the vicinity of Nogun Village (Nogŭn-ri) in July 1950.[21] The Pentagon launched its own investigation of the event, concluding in January 2001 that, although the U.S. military did not bear ultimate responsibility for the massacre, "significant numbers of Korean civilians" were killed or injured in the area by U.S. forces at that time.[22] The South Korean Ministry of National Defense carried out its own investigation of Nogŭn-ri, coming to the same conclusion as the Americans. Thus it was particularly embarrassing for the South Korean government, in the midst of discussions with the Americans over compensation for the Nogŭn-ri massacre, to have it revealed that Korean soldiers had committed very similar actions in Vietnam. As one spokesman for the Ministry of Foreign Affairs and Trade bluntly put it, "if accusations that our troops committed atrocities in the Vietnam War are made repeatedly, Seoul's bargaining power in the Nogŭn-ri talks with the U.S. will be weakened significantly."[23]

Han'gyŏre was the first media outlet to bring to light eyewitness accounts of Korean atrocities in Vietnam, and a few others followed suit over the next two years; the more conservative, mainstream newspapers and other media, however, were more reluctant to bring up the subject. The ROK Ministry of Defense (MND) denied that the massacres reported in *Han'gyŏre* ever happened, and in any case, as one MND General asked rhetorically, "Why bring this up after thirty years?" Besides, any such excesses could be explained by the fact that Korean soldiers "could not differentiate between innocent civilians from Viet Congs,"[24] an excuse exactly parallel to that of the Americans at Nogŭn-ri, not to mention the Americans in Vietnam itself. The Ministry of Foreign Affairs furthermore warned that such revelations could damage the warming political and economic relations between the ROK and Vietnam today, and "would not be good for the 5,500 Korean compatriots living in Vietnam."[25]

By far the most outspoken, not to say violent, response to the *Han'-gyŏre Sinmun* investigation came on June 27, 2000, two months after the initial articles were published. A group of several hundred members of the "ROK War Veterans Association," dressed in combat fatigues, demonstrated in front of the *Han'gyŏre* offices in Seoul beginning in the early afternoon. Over the course of the next few hours, shouts and slogans gave way to rocks thrown in the newspaper's windows; shortly before 5:00 PM, the group stormed the building, trashing offices, destroying computers and printing equipment, and injuring several workers. The demonstrators also destroyed a number of cars that were parked in the neighborhood.[26] Such intimidation did not cause *Han'gyŏre* to retract the articles; on the other hand, besides *Han'-gyŏre* itself, no other South Korean newspaper reported the attack.

The conflict over Korea's Vietnam War memories that erupted in 2000 had all but disappeared a few years later. Although Kim Dae Jung apologized for the actions of South Korean soldiers in Vietnam, the ROK government did not investigate any alleged atrocities. Nor has the Vietnamese government pursued the issue, no doubt in large part for economic reasons. South Korea has been quite generous with economic aid and investment to a Vietnam emerging from poverty and moving toward a market system. Reminders of the two countries' embattled past, both governments seem to believe, would needless complicated this mutually beneficial economic relationship. Nevertheless, the past remains a painful memory for many on both sides. Vietnamese survivors bear the scars, physical and psychological, of the horrendous acts committed upon their neighbors and countrymen by South Korean troops. Most ROK Vietnam veterans continue to reside on the margins of Korean society. The estimated seven thousand Korean victims of Agent Orange, the infamous defoliant used by the U.S. military in Vietnam and well-established cause of debilitating illnesses and birth defects, were not included in the 1984 class action suit that gave compensation to victims from the United States, Australia, Canada, and New Zealand.[27] Other victims include the estimated thousands of half-Vietnamese children abandoned by their Korean fathers. Yet, despite decades of enforced amnesia in Korea, the truth of Korea's Vietnam War began slowly to come to light.

In the absence of ROK government action on the issue, the Korean Truth Commission on the Vietnam War, a coalition of South Korean NGOs, conducted their own investigation of Vietnam atrocities and offered their own unofficial apology to the Vietnamese people. One of their members, the singer-songwriter Park Chi-ŭm, wrote and performed a song called "Forgive Us, Vietnam," which he performed in Seoul in the summer of 2000 and sent a recording of to Vietnam:

> Our meeting could have been beautiful,
> But the place where we faced each other was Asia's sorrowful battlefield.
>
> We as perpetrators, and you as injured victims,
> Tomorrow's dreams were thrown into the shadows of History.
> We know that your painful scars cannot be washed away.
> Not by any excuse, nor with words of consolation.
> But what I sincerely hope with my two hands joined together,
> Is for the river of peace to flow like the deep marrow of your scars.
> I want to live in a world without war.
> I want to sing of peace, hand in hand, with a friend.
> Understanding each other, helping each other,
> Let our dreams of tomorrow unfold under the radiant sun.
> Forgive us, Vietnam.
> Forgive us, Vietnam.
> For the tears that you shed in the darkness,
> For the shame that we left in the darkness.[28]

That same summer of 2000, the South Korean novelist Hwang Suk-young met the Vietnamese novelist Bao Ninh, former North Vietnamese soldier and author of the international best-seller *The Sorrow of War*, at an Asian writers' conference in Seoul. Hwang, himself a veteran of the ROK Marines who had served in Da Nang in 1968, upon meeting Bao immediately bowed to the ground before the younger Vietnamese writer, a supreme sign of respect in Korean culture. Hwang explained that his gesture, meant as an apology for the actions of his countrymen in Vietnam, had been inspired by a similar act by an elderly Japanese novelist, who had apologized to Hwang for the behavior of his fellow Japanese in Korea.[29] If the governments of the countries of Asia were reluctant to own up to the actions of the best, the Hwang-Bao Ninh encounter suggested, then perhaps the intellectuals and ordinary people of the region could address the grievances of their respective mutual conflicts, and bring East Asia's long bloody century to a belated end.

~ 13

Revolution, War, and Memory in Contemporary Viet Nam

An Assessment and Agenda

CHRISTOPH GIEBEL

AS A STUDENT I spent some time in Viet Nam in the late 1980s and early 1990s. After a hiatus of a few years, I have regularly returned to Viet Nam since the late 1990s. During these recent visits I have been struck by the frequency with which the Vietnamese wars against the French and the Americans and their Vietnamese allies are publicly invoked. To be sure, in 2000, on the 25th anniversary of the "liberation" (or "fall") of Sai Gon, such invocations were to be expected. But a year later, my subjective observation—confirmed by Vietnamese friends—was that public commemorations and celebrations of military-revolutionary exploits of the past half century had actually *increased*. Examples might be the frequent showing of war movies, media reports on educational meetings about the wars aimed in particular at the country's youth, or song-and-dance performances with military themes and by uniformed entertainers on state-run TV networks.

The ever-present orchestration of war references in contemporary Viet Nam seems odd in a sense, since the overwhelming majority of present-day Vietnamese were born either after 1975 or just prior to 1975 and thus have no memory of war. It is also hard to reconcile with Viet Nam's increasing move toward international integration, where it projects itself as "a country, not a war." Viet Nam has been at peace for more than a decade now, is not threatened militarily, is a respected member of ASEAN, and has all but normalized relations with the United States.

There is no comparison now to the utterly grim circumstances the country found itself in just prior to the onset of reforms in 1986. Then, perhaps, the Vietnamese psyche was in need of being reminded constantly of the glory days of past victories. But nowadays? The phenomenon has led Hue-Tam Ho Tai to describe current commemorations of war as "obsessive" and constituting "hyper-mnemosis."[1]

I would argue that the fixation on the wartime past goes far beyond a desire to keep alive the memories of those who gave their lives for their country. Such a gesture is indeed aptly undertaken by the thousands of "martyr" graveyards and memorials that dot the Vietnamese landscape. Rather, the constant public reminders of military heroism are meant to define a certain national identity, to communicate a perceived essential quality of "being Vietnamese." As discussed in the chapters on China in this volume, the collapse of the Soviet Union in 1991 and the loss of faith in communism that the Soviet Union's demise represented, have had important repercussion in contemporary Viet Nam. In this context, the revival of war memory is, in part, aimed at creating undivided, patriotic loyalty to the Party-led state. The constant public reminders of military heroism are attempts by an aging revolutionary generation to keep their hold on power. The invocations of war memory are also a response to the ever increasing lure of commercialism and materialism on Viet Nam's increasingly apolitical youth. One of Viet Nam's responses to the collapse of the communist world order is to offer public reminders of revolutionary sacrifice and struggle, in order to cement a certain way of being Vietnamese.

In this chapter I would like to situate such a modern Vietnamese attempt to formulate a coherent version of national identity not only within the political-ideological exigencies of post-independence developments, but also within French colonial rhetoric and precolonial models of describing the past. Many such narratives centered on themes of warfare in the service of the realm, the country, or the nation.

Already in precolonial, "imperial" times, writing about the past had been an intensely political endeavor. Rulers commissioned chronologies by historian-literati that marked important events and royal actions in the reigns of past kings and recorded the accomplishments of great scholar-officials. These were highly didactic, stylized writings, either extolling the virtue of a past ruler or exposing his flaws. The chroniclers were thereby invoking and reaffirming classical moral teachings and, in so doing, announcing the alignment with these precepts of the court they themselves were serving. During the long periods of warfare between rival power centers among the Vietnamese, contesting histories could emerge in which differing regional outlooks and ideological preferences were clearly exhibited, each one laying claim to legitimacy vis-à-vis royal "pretenders."

Another kind of historical writing can be found in the Viet Dien U Linh Tap ("Spiritual powers of the Viet realm"), a fourteenth century compilation of tales of tutelary deities. In these tales, powerful spirits—many of them historical heroes of bygone times—inhabiting the Vietnamese landscape are either called upon by, or announce themselves to, virtuous leaders passing through the locale. As Keith Taylor and Oliver Wolters have pointed out in separate studies, a subtext of these tales is the successful alliance between protective spirits and worthy leaders, who together are able to ward off danger to the polity from outside, or (re)establish harmony within.[2] Such stories also provided didactic models of correct behavior for kings, because legitimacy was seen to have been conferred on them if these protective spirits entered into the rulers' service. Subsequent eras built on the Viet Dien U Linh Tap and carefully recorded the changing make-up of the pantheon of tutelary spirits. Throughout the Vietnamese monarchy (i.e., until rather recently), royal courts added to or subtracted from the roster of guardian deities, and the question of who was "in" and who was "out" was an eminently political one depending on the ideological, religious, or regional allegiances or other current prerogatives of the ruler.

Prescription and teleology were thus established features of precolonial Vietnamese depictions of the past. Historical writing was a moral-political, more often than not officially controlled, act that sought to establish legitimacy of Vietnamese rulers or royal lineages, to whom history had moved because of their virtuous behavior. Likewise, history "worked" predictably in the ways in which flawed kings and corrupted officials were causing disorder and their own inevitable downfall. Their negative examples also could be used as ideological ammunition against contemporary political opponents.

French imperialism and the establishment by force of the colonial regime brought new dimensions to the ways in which Vietnamese educated elites thought about the past, especially after World War I. In particular, the two Western ideologies of nationalism and social Darwinism that fueled French actions in the latter half of the nineteenth century powerfully framed such conceptionalizations of history. For one, colonial rhetoric of a French "civilizing mission" necessitated a depiction of the recent Vietnamese past as in decline, "sick," and mired in barbaric, unenlightened backwardness. France's purported tutelage to bring the Vietnamese into modernity was therefore "in" history, and France in some ways the legitimate heir to a "lost" greatness of the past. Consequently, as Benedict Anderson has argued in *Imagined Communities*, the emerging colonial scholarship focused on rediscovering the "classical" period of, in this case, "French" Indochina and linking it to the colonial present. Nationalism (i.e., the idea that people are bound in time and space by a common destiny and a shared community) and social Darwinism (i.e., the crude notion that societies and civilizations were locked in a constant struggle for survival) were the paradigms on which this engagement with the past was predicated.

If nationalism and social Darwinism lent the French assurances of the righteousness of their historical "mission," they also created an enormous cultural anxiety and reorientation among Vietnamese intellectuals. After all, if the French had a claim to being "in" history, the Vietnamese, now increasingly imagining themselves as a distinct nation reaching back in time for millennia, were on the verge of being "out" of history, indeed in imminent danger of not being "fit for survival." The trope for this deep-seated angst among the Vietnamese intelligentsia was "a country lost" *(mat nuoc)*. *Mat nuoc* referred in the first place, of course, to the reality of France's usurpation of power and its division of the Vietnamese kingdom into three artificial, but supposedly discrete entities, the colony of Cochinchina and the "protectorates" of Annam and Tonkin. But "a country lost" also spoke to the sense that the Vietnamese were losing their cultural memory and historical voice as a nation.

Already in the late colonial period, therefore, especially after World War I, one can see the nationalization of Vietnamese intellectuals' engagement with the past. Faced with their French-imposed divisions and dominant colonial discourses of history, Vietnamese began to privilege themes of (national) unity and to deemphasize episodes of discord in the past. Vietnamese thus appeared unified in a common culture, in a shared history—in the sense both as a shared experience and as a shared destiny—and, indeed, in exhibiting a distinct "national soul" *(quoc hon)*. It is no coincidence that an anticolonial newspaper published by segments of the Vietnamese exile community in Paris in 1926 bore the title "The Soul of Viet Nam" *(Viet Nam Hon)*. It was during the decade of the 1920s in particular when Vietnamese nationalists were engaged—quite literally—in an essentialist soul-searching, to be (re)discovered, as it were, before it was "lost."

Not surprisingly, a product of this anxious search for unifying themes to define the Vietnamese nation was a Hobsbawmian invention of traditions. For example, in 1921 the historian Tran Trong Kim published the first comprehensive linear history of the Vietnamese *(Viet Nam Su Luoc)* in *quoc ngu*, the romanized script. (Space does not permit me to focus on the impact of the rapid dissemination of *quoc ngu* after the Great War, other than stating that *quoc ngu* itself played a paramount role in forging nationalist discourses into a powerful tool of political action). Around the same time that Tran Trong Kim was linking centuries into a common national story, the prominent writer Pham Quynh was tirelessly propagating the nineteenth century verse novel "The Tale of Kieu" by Nguyen Du as a national poem. To Pham Quynh, this literary work best exhibited essential characteristics of the Vietnamese nation, notwithstanding the fact that "The Tale of Kieu" was based on a Chinese story.

A few years ago, Shawn McHale and Keith Taylor pointed out that the misleading, but widespread notion of Vietnamese culture being deeply suffused with Confucianism was a result of similar efforts, again with Tran Trong Kim taking a prominent role, of defining unifying cultural traits during the late colonial period.[3] Teleology in narratives of Vietnamese history can also be found in the influential idea of the "March to the South" *(Nam Tien)*, that is, the Vietnamese equivalent to the American "manifest destiny," which depicted a practically inevitable southward expansion of the Vietnamese nation from the late fifteenth to the eighteenth century. Finally, Patricia Pelley has shown that the quintessential post-1945 trope of prescriptive nationalist historiography, the "Vietnamese tradition of heroic resistance against foreign aggression," already can be found, albeit less explicitly, in the decades before World War II.[4]

In sum, during the era of colonial subjugation, historical writing continued to be highly political. It could be used to legitimize imperialist aggression as well as to rally people to take part in organized anticolonial activities. History became even more of a political battlefield after 1945.

VIETNAMESE INDEPENDENCE WAS declared in 1945, but not secured until 1954 in the northern half of the country under Communist Party rule. And the exchange of French colonial control for American overlordship over a rival regime in the south meant that the nationalist vision of an independent, united Viet Nam came true only in 1975. The period between 1945 and 1975 saw organized violence and human tragedy of immense proportions in the region—thirty years of almost continuous warfare that became a symbol both for decolonization and for the Cold War and that was likely the defining conflict of the latter half of the twentieth century. It is no small wonder, then, that historical writing in Viet Nam did not develop into an academic discipline somewhat on the margins of society in terms of its actual intellectual influence or weight, as can perhaps be said of Western societies at peace. Instead, the interpretation of the past became an endeavor of high importance and centrality in the political arena.

In the initial years of the anti-French resistance, that is, the latter half of the 1940s, when the military situation for the Democratic Republic of Viet Nam (DRVN) under Ho Chi Minh was critical, there was little of an organized historiography. Nationalist appeals to "save the country" and act in unity against the foreign aggressors, however, successfully rallied popular support for the guerrilla war. In the early 1950s, when the security situation in the northern strongholds of the DRVN stabilized, historical writing became more systematic and institutionalized. Revolutionary historians confidently defined their project as "New History," emphasizing a radical break from what was seen as the obscurantist distortions and self-justifying ideologies of French-imposed colonial historiography. History in independent Viet Nam was also to be "new" in its commitment to the revolutionary cause, in general, and Marxism-Leninism, in particular. It was consciously to be used as a political weapon in the war for national liberation as well as in class struggle. Not coincidentally, the two most prominent figures in that first generation of historians, Tran Huy Lieu and Tran Van Giau, both had long been involved in revolutionary activities—eventually as members of the communist movement—and played important leadership roles in the upheavals of 1945.

From the beginning, the "New History" operated under the obvious contradiction of the dual orientation towards writing the history of the nation and of class struggle. Despite Western Cold War rhetoric of totalitarian and monolithic communist regimes, Vietnamese historiography never saw the imposition of ideological orthodoxy. In fact, as Patricia Pelley has convincingly argued, on central tenets of Marxist-Leninist historical materialism—for example, the question of "feudalism"—heated debates took place and consensus was never found.[5]

I would argue—leaving ideological details aside—that Vietnamese historiography attempted to solve the seeming contradiction of the "New History" by collapsing national and revolutionary struggles. The Communist Party was portrayed as being "in" history in a double sense: (1) Taking the nation as a fixed reference point of historical narrative, Ho Chi Minh and his communist government were rightful heirs to centuries of a common Vietnamese destiny. The trope of "Vietnamese unity" in its "tradition of heroic resistance against foreign aggression" gave voice to these concerns and was most emphatically promoted during the period of American intervention. (2) Adhering to a highly deterministic, Marxist model of history, the "party of the working class" was at the vanguard of inevitable historical developments and, consequently, the only one legitimated to rule the country.

But such an exclusive interpretation of history made the "New History" not new at all. In fact, post-1945 historiography clearly echoed earlier ways in which Vietnamese engaged the past. History was a given, and the writing of rulers "into" history (and their rivals "out" of it) legitimized existing power. It was a highly didactic and political project and was officially controlled, commissioned, and sanctioned.

History, however, does not work that way; with no fixed Truth existing in the past and waiting to be objectively recreated, with historical understanding wholly dependent on perspective, history can only be impermanent and indeterminate. Almost by definition, exclusive concepts of history necessitate teleology (or inevitability) and prescription (or models), which burden the self-appointed guardians of historical Truth with the endless task of making everything "fit." For example, by positing an age-old unity of the Vietnamese at a time, after 1955, when Viet Nam was divided geographically and politically, Vietnamese historians had to deemphasize the long periods in the past when Vietnamese were fighting one another. Instead, they externalized conflict with the notion of the "tradition of heroic resistance against foreign aggression." In the past, Vietnamese factions had quite regularly relied on non-Vietnamese allies in their struggle with rivals, just as was the case in the 1950s and 1960s with the DRVN's rivals of the Sai Gon governments. The "tradition of heroic resistance against foreign aggression" as a national essence wrote those people throughout the centuries out of (legitimate) history, and even today, soldiers of the U.S.-backed Sai Gon army are routinely referred to as "marionettes," that is, not part of what is defined as Vietnamese. The nationalist-revolutionary paradigm of the "tradition of heroic resistance against foreign aggression," which really had its roots in the anxiety of the lost nation during the colonial era, was so powerful and so effectively employed in post-1945 historiography and state propaganda that it gave the revolutionary side during subsequent wars a permanent political and moral advantage and significantly contributed to the victory in 1975.

If national liberation was a fundamental trait of nationalist history and the revolutionary ascendancy of the party of the working class that of historical materialism, and post-1945 historiography subscribed to both, then the year 1945 became the point to which the two historical currents had inevitably flowed and where they teleologically merged. As David Marr has meticulously demonstrated in his book *Vietnam 1945: The Quest for Power*, seizing power and declaring independence in the summer of 1945 was enabled by the advantageous circumstances after the sudden Japanese surrender and less coordinated throughout Viet Nam than commonly portrayed. Vietnamese historiography, however, describes the "August Revolution" of the communist-led Viet Minh as the inevitable and ultimate culmination of previous developments, most important of which is the founding of the communist party in 1930. The years 1930 and 1945, therefore, have become fixed and greatly overemphasized markers in the periodization of modern history. For example, between 1957 and 1961, Tran Huy Lieu published his influential, three-volume work "History of 80 Years against the French" (*Lich su tam muoi nam chong Phap*, by which he meant 1865, when Cochinchina was ceded to France, to 1945). Of the three volumes, the first covered the period to 1929, sixty-five plus years, and the fifteen years of 1930–45 were focused on in the two others. Vietnamese post-1945 historiography has until recently almost exclusively written political, social, and economic history around the dates of 1930 and 1945.

A GREAT DEAL OF historiographical energy has been expanded in Viet Nam in writing historical biographies and autobiographies. Most likely this is due to the unique ability of this genre to crystallize desired historical messages in individual lives. Party historians have openly advocated such biographical publications as providing prescriptive role models and inspiration for readers, in particular the youth. Historical figures like Nguyen Trai, the famous fifteenth-century scholar-official, who played a crucial role in defeating Ming occupational forces, found strong interest among party historians (and party leaders such as Pham Van Dong) in the 1950s and 1960s. During the height of the war against Americans and the Sai Gon regime, Nguyen Trai was celebrated as an upright official who rallied the people and as a counter-model to foreign occupants and their local collaborators. In 1966, a chapter in Tran Huy Lieu's book on Nguyen Trai was entitled "Nguyen Trai in our present endeavor to defeat America and save the country." Similarly, the late-eighteenth-century Tay Son-leader Nguyen Hue (emperor Quang Trung), who united the Vietnamese after almost 200 years of division and beat back a Qing-Chinese army intervening on behalf of one of his rivals, was a good guy. A bad guy was Nguyen Anh (emperor Gia Long), who, with the help of the Siamese court and French mercenaries, soon after defeated the Tay Son peasant forces and established the Nguyen dynasty (1802–1945)—the dynasty, of course, which was supposedly conservative and oppressive, buckled under imperialist pressure, and became a corrupt puppet monarchy for the French until replaced by Ho Chi Minh's Democratic Republic!

Biographies, autobiographies, and memoirs of twentieth-century revolutionaries are likewise populated by stock characters and pre-

dictable plots that enshrine communists as the only party aligned with
the correct historical forces. Peter Zinoman's recent analysis of prison
memoirs by prominent party leaders, published in significant numbers
after 1954, is instructive here. In these didactic texts, communist prisoners always unfailingly endure the most severe abuse and hardship
and use imprisonment as a party school to strengthen their determination and prepare for further revolutionary struggle. By contrast, fellow
political prisoners who are "out" of history, like Trotskyists, petty
bourgeois nationalists, and so on are remembered as weak in character
and in political resolve and easily crushed by prison life. Common
criminals, by far the great majority in colonial jails, appear only as pro-
letarians who can be converted to the revolutionary cause by communist inmates.[6] At the same time, Zinoman argues, the metaphor of the
party school in the hardship of prison served to erase the elite educational and class background of most of the party leadership.

Elsewhere I have compared these didactic and motivational revolutionary biographies to the project of the communist mausoleum.[7] Both
model biographies and the mausoleum indicate the historiographical
desire to prescribe and "fix" history. Just as the mausoleum fights physical impermanence and tries to present but one, carefully orchestrated
memory of the deceased, so is a historiography that is committed to an
exclusive historical model fighting the decomposition of the past. History is as it should be: the people are always good and fight the more
that they are oppressed, the (auto)biographical heroes and heroines are
well intentioned, learn from and help the people, but are initially often
unable to be fully effective in their political mission. Only when they
come into contact with cadres, who are of impeccable character and
teach them communist ideology, will the protagonists be able to fully
comprehend the situation and lead the people to revolutionary activities.[8]

More generally, Vietnamese historiography, because of the political
interests it must serve, has avoided topics that might be damaging to
the party's self-image as the fulfillment of history both in terms of national independence and unity and of social revolution. Many social or
political groups that would threaten the dominant narrative or the
image of unity remain historically silent or have their histories translated into the officially sanctioned interpretation. Examples might in-

clude the instances of crackdown against political dissent in the north, in the so-called Nhan Van-Giai Pham affair of 1956/58, and also in the mid-1960s. The most glaring examples of omission are the many shades of southern political and social visions expressed from, say, 1925 to 1975. For example, until now we know very little of authenticity about religious life in the south, about the so-called neutral or "third force" movements during the American era, or the noncommunist members of the National Liberation Front and its suborganizations. Thus far, we must rely mostly on accounts and memoirs of exiled Vietnamese. Southern cultural and intellectual diversity have found little reflection in official historiography.

Even within the party ranks, regional differences and tensions are usually not mentioned. For example, after 1975, General Tran Van Tra, one of the highest ranking southern commanders in the revolutionary forces, began writing a military history of the American War which he conceived to entail five volumes. After the first volume was published in the early 1980s, it was quickly banned, ostensibly for providing too much of a southern perspective. A similar expression of revolutionary southern discomfort with a perceived northern dominance in shaping historical narratives, the so-called Club of Old Resistance Fighters, which had among its members general Tran Van Tra, the prominent southern revolutionary and historian Tran Van Giau, and the underground Sai Gon party chief during the American era, Tran Bach Dang, was ordered to dissolve soon after.

There are other instances of historical engineering that go beyond the privileging of certain historical narratives or the writing out of history of social groups. In these instances, concrete manipulations were undertaken to fit facts to a preconceived message, mostly of revolutionary heroism.[9] To give just one example, a shipyard workers' strike in Sai Gon in 1925 was portrayed as the first political strike in Viet Nam. The workers were alleged to have been motivated by proletarian internationalism when they refused to repair a crippled French warship bound for China to help suppress anti-imperialist movements there. My research revealed that there had been concrete internal grievances at the shipyard, and that protesting workers had put the director on notice—weeks before the unannounced arrival of the warship—that they intended to strike if their demands were not met. However, Tran

Van Giau, in his history of the Vietnamese working class, published in several editions between 1957 and 1961, ignored the internal grievances and, despite the evidence, moved the protest meeting of the shipyard workers to the ship's arrival day. That way he could support his argument that the Vietnamese working class had shown a certain level of political consciousness and organization already in 1925, thereby enhancing the credentials of the Vietnamese revolutionary movements that would lead straight to 1945.

In 1986, when touring the Museum of the Revolution in Ha Noi, I saw a photo of a high-ranking Vietnamese state and party delegation laying a wreath during a visit to Moscow in the 1950s. On the photo's surface, white liquid paper covered up one person in that delegation. Given the time, place, and occasion depicted in the photo, this person could only have been Hoang Van Hoan, the Politbureau member who had defected to China at the height of the Sino-Vietnamese conflict of the late 1970s and early 1980s. The crude liquid paper treatment of Hoang Van Hoan in that photo revealed more than anger on a personal level. Hoang Van Hoan had committed an infraction so grave that it could not be explained or made to fit into the dominant narrative. In a historical museum and on a historical document, Hoang Van Hoan was kicked out of history. Not silently vanishing like Trotsky in that famous manipulated photo of Lenin as orator, but, paradoxically, erased for all to see. History was political, and power could be exercised to shape history how it was supposed to be.

⌒ IN CONCLUDING THIS OVERVIEW, I return to my initial observation of a contemporary Vietnamese state being ever more busily fixated on remembering recent wars and revolutionary sacrifices. While Vietnamese national identity with its externalization of conflict and supposedly essential antiforeign resistance impulse predates 1945, the communist movement has been most successful in using the imagery of nationalist struggle to gain and retain power. Yet, at the beginning of the twenty-first century, the Party's insistence on the centrality of this version of a Vietnamese identity reveals concerns over a society that is rapidly becoming very diverse and, in a way, less definable as a nation. The frequent invocations of war are attempts by an aging revolutionary generation to hold on to the power to prescribe what is properly Vietnamese, who is "in" and who is "out." As a new generation of more pragmatic party technocrats, whose lives have been much more defined by the 1990s than the 1960s, is poised to take leadership roles, invocations of war are meant to stay the course of the Party-led state. Evocations of war are a last attempt to drown out the wild and increasingly uncontrollable babble of commercialism, the Internet, and cable TV that have arisen from the new post–Cold War realities of an increasingly globally integrated Viet Nam. Evocations of war seek to turn a materialistic, often apolitical youth back toward revolutionary ideals. Evocations of war, tragically, seek to define narrowly a nation precisely at a moment when the country should and could make very good use of the richness and diversity of Vietnamese experiences, past and present.

I am convinced of two things: (1) a great deal of our present historical knowledge of "Viet Nam" will have to be revised significantly and (2) a younger generation of historians in Viet Nam is eager to do so. However, they will not be able to succeed fully if—despite some relaxation in the post-1986 reform process—historical inquiry in Viet Nam continues to be confined by political control, the paradigm of the nation,[10] and an exclusive conception of history that denies the pluralism of the human experience.

Thus far the signs are not promising. On November 12, 2002, CNN reported that Don Duong, a popular Vietnamese actor, had been put under house arrest, criticized for being a traitor, and in danger of being thrown into jail. His crime? Portraying, in two Hollywood productions (*We Were Soldiers* and *Green Dragon*), a People's Army officer in a crucial battle with Americans and a Vietnamese refugee in California. Regarding the former role, the government was assessing whether he should "be punished because *We Were Soldiers* did not accurately reflect history or paint that nation's soldiers in a good light." As to Duong's portrayal of a refugee, the character's anti-government views were held against the actor, who complained in a letter sent abroad: "Only idiots who know nothing about the movies would confuse Don Duong with the character Don Duong portrays."

⌐ So it is time to lay out an agenda for future research about Vietnamese history to be conducted where the circumstances are more favorable. The generation of U.S.-trained and U.S.-based Viet Nam scholars of which I am a part, mainly coming out of Cornell in the early to mid-1990s, have devoted considerable energies to analyses of the various historical aspects of the Vietnamese Revolution. Generally speaking, we have been motivated by a desire to disengage scholarly inquiry into Viet Nam from the emotionally charged environment of the Viet Nam War years and to connect Viet Nam studies to larger debates and newer theoretical directions in academic fields. Up to that point in the 1980s, Viet Nam studies had too often been characterized either by overtly anticommunist agendas within the Cold War context, or by similarly politicized antiwar sentiments that tended to read revolutionary self-representations as transparent texts. I have contributed to this refocusing of Viet Nam Studies with critical works on communist historical representations and the constructions of Vietnamese memories and have become interested in a new focus on the history of southern Viet Nam during the years 1955 to 1975. My own interest is the historiography produced in the south during these years, including self-legitimizing regime narratives, but also the various counternarratives produced among southerners with regard to "national character" and the ways in which the present was connected to, and prescribed by, an imagined past. How did the Diem and other subsequent regimes in the south, all of them sustained by U.S. support, view the past and the project of historical writing? Were southern intellectuals allowed a freer hand to write southern Vietnamese history, in particular, or Vietnamese history in general?

In general, I believe that the larger field of Viet Nam Studies needs to pay closer attention to the south before 1975. Whereas ten to fifteen years ago, there seemed greater urgency in critically reexamining the Revolution, shorthand often for the north, it is time now—a generation after 1975—to undertake sustained analyses of the south in a variety of fields. New and fresh scholarly representations of the south might look at a variety of southern historical experiences: political developments as well as social ones, religions, women, literature and popular culture, labor, and questions of human rights in a society under stresses of violence, to name a few. In addition, a focus on southern viewpoints—revolutionary, anti-revolutionary, and neutralist alike—which were often silenced both by postwar northern triumphalism and by Cold War American myth-making might well directly speak to renewed emphases in history to include the marginalized, silenced, and underrepresented and to decenter the historical representations purveyed by the state.

If an agenda would be to rediscover "Pluralistic Visions and For-gotten Voices in a Time of War and Violence," then one might also in-clude in academic inquiries those in the North who do not neatly fit into categories of the revolutionary or the anti-revolutionary. But that might lead to troubles similar to those in which actor Don Duong found himself.

Epilogue

New Global Conflict?
War, Memory, and Post-9/11 Asia

SHEILA MIYOSHI JAGER AND RANA MITTER

THE END OF THE Cold War marked the beginning of a new era in history that had optimistically promised the arrival of a better world order that would eliminate the threat of nuclear annihilation that had overshadowed human history since 1945. But the post–Cold War era that began with the collapse of one structure, the Berlin Wall on November 9, 1989, ended with the collapse of another, the World Trade Center's Twin Towers on September 11, 2001. For the United States, the events of 9/11 marked the closure of the first phase of the post–Cold War moment and the arrival of a second and deeply troubling one. Although the rest of the world felt the impact of 9/11 less immediately than the United States, the event's impact still had a global reach.

At a time when Western memory of the Soviet Union had just began to reassess its old enemy as kitsch, or as an opponent that had always been doomed to failure, it is worth recalling how menacing and alien the Soviet Union had once seemed: George Kennan's famous "Long Telegram" became an influential text in large part because of the new perception that Soviet behavior came from sources other than purely rational ones. Moscow's antipathy for the West, Kennan argued, grew out of both historical and cultural circumstances. Whether radical Islamism will prove to be such an elusive foe, or a sterile but ultimately containable threat, remains to be seen. Yet the global effects of 9/11, and the arrival of a new enemy that seems, once again, alien and other, have also altered the post–Cold War moment, although how significantly it is difficult to determine. Like the events surrounding the end of the Cold War, the events of 9/11 and the U.S. global war on terrorism have had a wide-ranging impact on world events. In this epilogue, we offer some preliminary reflections on how this second "turning point" of the post–Cold War period has impacted the realm of war memory in East Asia.

Chinese fears about U.S. hegemony have not been removed by the events of 9/11 and the subsequent decline in U.S. global prestige following the 2003 war in Iraq. On the one hand, the Chinese have been at pains to present themselves as a benevolent giant in the region. On the other, the memorialization of China's past as victim of imperialist aggression, whether from the West during the Opium Wars, or from the Japanese during the War of Resistance, shows no signs of stopping. China's entry into the World Trade Organization in 2001 coincided with a revival of memory of the "national humiliation" that the Opium Wars, another aspect of the world trade system of an earlier era, had brought to China. China's diplomacy with Japan in the early 2000s has been marked by frequent spats relating to the Sino-Japanese War of the 1930s. In 2005, China's relations with Japan took a turn for the worse when Chinese protesters took to the streets to protest Japan's bid to gain a permanent seat on the UN Security Council. Many Chinese also felt outraged that a recent Japanese revision of a school textbook failed to provide a fuller account of Japan's World War II atrocities. In what appeared to be government-orchestrated demonstrations, protesters overturned Japanese cars, tossed rocks at sushi bars and smashed the windows of Japanese diplomatic offices. Chinese activists have also pushed for a boycott of Japanese goods.[1] In part, the need to use war memory to stress China's victim status arises from a realization in Beijing that the rise of Chinese power in the region is not universally welcomed among its smaller neighbours.

Japan, meanwhile, faced with a rising China, an equally hostile South Korea (2005 also saw its share of anti-Japanese protests in Seoul as well), a nuclear-armed North Korea, and increasing tensions over Taiwan, is seeking to remilitarize, with the blessing of the United States, and despite concerns among some segments of the Japanese public and other Asian nations.

Two opposing trends thus appear to be taking place in Japan with regard to war memory. One the one hand, the increasing possibility of remilitarization and efforts to revise Article 9 of the constitution sets Japan on a path of confrontation with China. This seemingly inevitable confrontation has everything to with how the past is remembered in both countries and Japan's inability to offer an officially acceptable apology over its historical war crimes. In a painful act of symbolism, at least for the Chinese, one of the last official acts Junichiro Koizumi made as prime minister was to visit Yasukuni Shrine in Tokyo, a practice he repeated throughout his tenure in office. The new prime minister, Shinzo Abe, supported these visits, although he has declined to say whether he will continue them. The Chinese (and Koreans) regarded the Yasukuni visits by the Japanese prime minister as insulting and symbolic of Japan's continued unwillingness to atone for its historical misdeeds. For Harootunian, Japan's unwillingness to confront this past represent what he terms the "temporality of a permanent postwar." For many in Japan, the end of the Cold War has done little to change their country's attitude toward the past, and the events of 9/11, the current war in Iraq, and American pressure on Japan to become a "normal nation" and rearm, means that Sino-Japanese conflict over the past will continue to be a flashpoint for years to come.

On the other hand, post–Cold War Asia has actually brought with it evidence of a new reckoning of Japan's wartime past, if not by the Japanese officials in power, then by the emergence of what Carol Gluck has termed a civil society of "memory activists" in Japan, South Korea, and China who are intent on exposing Japan's war crimes. The post-9/11 era has done nothing new to change these attitudes except by giving them sharper contours. The decline of American power and influence in the region following the Iraq War means that a large sector of Japan's population recognize the allure of the geopolitical East over the geopolitical West. While China has now replaced the United States as South Korea's largest trading partner, South Korean popular culture has become all the rage in Japan, China, and Southeast Asia. These developments toward Asian regional integration have also led to the creation of a broad spectrum of activists who are committed to confronting Japan's "history problem." Not surprisingly, many of these same activists are also opposed to Japan's rearmament plan.

Meanwhile, in South Korea, the new reckoning of such "forgotten events" as the alleged massacre of civilians by American troops at No Gun-ri and the American role in the suppression of the events of the 1948–49 Cheju-do rebellion, among other incidents, are part of a widespread movement that is directly linked to South Korea's changing relationship to the United States. In particular, the policy conflict between the U.S. and South Korean administrations over how to best deal with the current North Korean nuclear crisis has fed into popular anti-Americanism in South Korea and revisions of the Cold War narratives of the Korean War. The disastrous U.S.–South Korea summit in March 2001 and George W. Bush's denunciation of North Korea as part of an "axis of evil" in his State of the Union Address on January 29, 2002 reveals the fundamental disjuncture between American hard-line policy and South Korean engagement policy approaches toward North Korea. Although these policy approaches may change in the future, it seems clear that the events of 9/11 and its aftermath have reinforced an ever-widening gulf between the two countries, exacerbated by the North Korean nuclear crisis, as South Korea begins to look toward North Korea, rather than the United States, for its national legitimization.

Yet the case of the "two Chinas" also suggests that the trend toward regional integration is neither simple nor inevitable. The simultaneous rapprochement and continuing hostility between China and Taiwan illustrates how common experience and culture do draw societies together, but that other issues, notably a significant disparity in values, means that the seams of unification are often messy. The post-9/11 moment proved an immediate boon to China, since its place at the top of the United States' hierarchy of geopolitical problems was instantly ceded to the Middle East. Yet although China made some gestures toward sharing in the international "war on terror," mainly as a means to crush dissent in the Islamic western border areas, it took advantage of its new freedom of maneuver to return to the question of reunification with Taiwan. China's tactics have been a mixture of threat and blandishments, as Edward Vickers' chapter emphasized. What has been notable is the complexity in Taiwanese responses even in the few years since 2001. The downplaying of U.S. interest in the region, and the repeated statements of both U.S. and Chinese officials that they will not tolerate a declaration of Taiwanese independence has meshed with a significantly changed domestic atmosphere in Taiwanese politics. Chen Shui-bian, elected president in 2000 on a wave of anticorruption and pro-Taiwan autonomy feeling, rapidly found himself losing control of events, as the economy stagnated and unemployment rose. In 2004, he was barely reelected following an assassination attempt that aroused mass scepticism from observers and that forced the Supreme Court to review and endorse Chen's election. The decline in Chen's prestige also served to dim enthusiasm for the shape of post–Cold War Taiwanese cultural politics, and allowed space for a revival in the politics of reunification, something that seemed highly unlikely in 2000. Thus Lien Chan, the leader of the opposition Kuomintang, and James Soong, leader of the pro-unification People First Party (Qinmindang), both made official visits to the People's Republic in 2005, and made very public statements stressing the necessity for "one China." International and domestic circumstances came together to bring Taiwan's relationship with China "back to the future"—a politics not, as many would have thought a year or two earlier, shaped by the simple desire of Taiwan no longer to be considered part of China, but once again forcing the issue of the unfinished business of the Cold War, as if it were 1955 and not 2005. Nonetheless, the wider issues that underpin Chinese-Taiwanese mistrust remain unresolved. The question of how a lively, pluralist democracy with a relatively egalitarian society can be reunified with an economically growing but potentially unstable authoritarian state has not yet been answered, and the early twenty-first century seems likely to see further changes as startling as those in the short period between 2001 and 2005.

Vietnam is the state that seems to have yielded least, so far, to the new historiographies. This is because Vietnam has not yet experienced the memory opening that has occurred in Japan, South Korea and China during the 1990s. Despite some relaxation on the post-1986 reforms, historical inquiry continues to be confined by the paradigm of the nation and the victorious North Vietnamese Communist Party. Precolonial Vietnamese depictions of the past, especially of colonial subjugation and resistance, continue to depict Ho Chi Minh and his communist government as rightful heirs of a common Vietnamese destiny. Yet, if we can use the cases of China and South Korea as examples, it seems at least highly likely that the Cold War historical divisions in that country too must eventually fade. In China and Korea, the revision of war memory has come largely through a desire to rejoin a territory physically separated because of the Cold War. Vietnam, of course, was physically unified in 1975, and the Chinese and Korean agenda is therefore a long-done deal for the Vietnamese. Yet South Vietnamese memories, culture, and identity are still there, and enough people who remember the now vanished southern republic may exist to revive its memory, at least in part, as Vietnam's society thaws.

WHAT ELSE LIES AHEAD? There seem likely to be at least two contradictory threads. On the one hand, there is scope in the region for a feeling that an integrated Asian identity, defined against the United States, may have a new significance. The emerging regional order is characterized by China's regional rise, the increasing technological and economic interdependence throughout the region, and the maturing of regional institutions that do not involve the United States. As David Shambaugh has observed, "in this new order, Asia's principal sub-regions (Northeast Asia, Southeast Asia, South Asia, Central Asia, as well as Oceania) are becoming increasingly interactive and enmeshed in a growing web of interdependence."[2] On the other hand, the growing political and economic dominance of China in the region has led to an unease among the region's other nations as to how the region's new giant might be restrained.[3] Linked to this realist fear of China's size, common to all other states in the region, is the concern among neighboring states which have political values, such as a commitment to pluralist democracy, that are at odds with those of the current regime. Yet among these very contemporary and specific issues, the continuing memory of war stands central. For China itself, the feeling that its current rise is merely a late flowering of well-deserved historical reward is fueled by a new concentration on imperialist invasion and oppression, whether during the Opium Wars or the War of Resistance against Japan.

While it is too soon to say how the post-9/11 era will play out in this region of the world, what does seem clear is this "second" phase of the post–Cold War period has not yet given rise to fundamentally new reassessments of the past. The post-9/11 period has merely given sharper contours to what was new in the decades following the end of the Cold War. But this, of course, may change. The reunification of the two Koreas, or an outbreak of war between China and Taiwan, may engender yet another jolt to history, in which case, the past would have to be remade once again. Meanwhile, the importance of East Asia's reflections on its often-repressed understandings of the great wars that shaped it—the Opium Wars, the Sino-Japanese Wars, the wars in Korea and Vietnam, and the Chinese civil war—must be noted by anyone who wishes to understand the region today.

Notes
Contributors
Index

Notes

Introduction

1. See, for example, Stephen Greenblatt, Istvan Rev, and Randolph Starn, eds., "Identifying Histories: Eastern Europe before and after 1989," Special issue, *Representations* 49 (Winter 1995); Sarah Farmer, *Martyred Village: Commemorating the 1944 Massacre at Oradour-sur-Glane* (Berkeley: University of California Press, 2000); Svetlana Boym, "From the Russian Soul to Post-Communist Nostalgia," *Representations* 49 (Winter 1995): 133–166; Richard S. Esbenshade, "Remembering to Forget: Memory, History, and National Identity in Postwar Central Europe," *Representations* 49 (Winter 1995): 72–96; Sarah Farmer, "Symbols that Face Two Ways: Commemorating the Victims of Nazism and Stalinism at Buchenwald and Sachsenhausen," *Representations* 49 (Winter 1995): 97–119.

2. Francis Fukuyama, "Re-Envisioning Asia," *Foreign Affairs* (January–February 2005): 76.

3. Ibid., 75–76.

4. Japan's inevitable decline is due to its population, which will begin to shrink drastically after 2010. Some demographers estimate that by the end of the century, the country's population could shrink by two thirds, that is, from 127.7 million to just 45 million. Whereas replacement fertility level is defined as 2.3 children per couple, Japan's birth rate in 2001 was 1.3, one of the lowest in the world. See Chalmers Johnson, "No Longer the 'Lone Superpower': Coming to Terms with China," *Policy Forum Online*, March 24, 2005, and Nicholas Eberstadt, "The Population Implosion," *Foreign Policy* (March–April 2001).

5. In a recent survey article on China's economy, *The Economist* provided the following scenario for Chinese economic growth based on its World Trade Organization commitments and moving to a market-based economy by 2005: 7 percent until 2005 then 9 percent during 2006–15, resulting in a $4 trillion economy by

2020 or equal to the U.S. economy in 2000. In "China's Economic Power: Whither the Dragon?" *The Economist* 358, no. 8212 (March 2001): 24.

6. A number of scholars have discussed the relative decline of the United States' influence in the region with the rise of China. Through its sheer size and population as well as the force of its culture, history, and nationalism, China will be emboldened to exercise its perceived rightful place in the world as a great power and continue to challenge and compete with the United States. See Jiyul Kim, "Continuity and Transformation in Northeast Asia and the End of American Exceptionalism: A Long-Range Outlook and U.S. Policy Implications," *The Korean Journal of Defense Analysis* 13, no. 1 (Autumn 2001): 229–261; Kenneth N. Waltz, "Structural Realism after the Cold War," *International Security* 25, no. 1 (Summer 2000); Michael Pillsbury, *China Debates the Future Security Environment* (Washington, DC: National Defense University Press, 2000).

7. The chain of islands known as Tokdo in Korea and Takeshima in Japanese was taken over by the Japanese in 1905, foreshadowing Japan's colonization of Korea in 1910.

8. John Dower, *Embracing Defeat: Japan in the Wake of World War II* (New York: W. W. Norton & Company, 1999).

9. Ibid., 2.

10. See Chapter 6 in this volume.

11. See Chapter 5 in this volume.

12. In distinct opposition to Japan, South Korea has not painted the rising China as a menace. As Samuel Kim has noted, "The ROK's Defense White Paper generally devotes four to five pages outlining briefly China's military modernization and ROK-PRC military exchanges, showing no trace of security concern. In striking contrast, the corresponding Japanese publication devotes about three dozen pages to China's various weapons programs and military policy in not so subtle terms." Samuel Kim, "The Changing Role of China on the Korean Peninsula," *International Journal of Korean Studies* 8, no. 1 (Fall–Winter 2004): 103.

13. See Chapter 3 in this volume.

14. Ibid.

15. Ibid.

16. Arthur Waldron, "China's New Remembering of World War II: The Case of Chang Zizhong," *Modern Asian Studies* 30, no. 4 (1996): 869–899; Rana Mitter, "Behind the Scenes at the Museum: Nationalism, History, and Memory in the Beijing War of Resistance Museum, 1987–1997," *The China Quarterly* 161 (March 2000): 279–293.

1. Relocating War Memory at Century's End

1. Laura Hein, "Citizens, Foreigners, and the State in the United States and Japan since 9/11," *ZNet Japan*, December 4, 2003, *http://www.zmag.org*.

2. This chapter is based on chapter 9 of my book, *War Memory and Social Politics in Japan, 1945–2005* (Cambridge, MA: Harvard University Asia Center, 2006). I am grateful to Steve West for reading an early draft.

3. Gerrit W. Gong, "A Clash of Histories: 'Remembering and Forgetting' Issues, Structures, and Strategic Implications," in *Memory and History in East and*

Southeast Asia: Issues of Identity in International Relations, ed. Gerrit W. Gong (Washington, DC: Center for Strategic & International Studies, 2001), 29–30.

4. Takabatake Michitoshi, "Citizens' Movements: Organizing the Spontaneous," in *Authority and the Individual in Japan: Citizen Protest in Historical Perspective*, ed. J. Victor Koschmann (Tokyo: University of Tokyo Press, 1978). Also see Ellis Krauss's thorough review essay in *Journal of Japanese Studies* 7, no. 1 (Winter 1981): 165–180.

5. Michel Foucault, *Language, Counter-Memory, Practice: Selected Essays and Interviews*, ed. Donald F. Bouchard (Ithaca, NY: Cornell University Press, 1977).

6. Oda Makoto, "The Ethics of Peace," in *Authority and the Individual in Japan: Citizen Protest in Historical Perspective*, ed. J. Victor Koschmann (Tokyo: University of Tokyo Press, 1978), 154–170.

7. Yamaguchi Keiji and Matsuo Sōichi, eds., *Sengoshi to handō ideorogii* (Tokyo: Shin Nihon shuppansha, 1981).

8. This movement is described in some detail in Kenneth J. Ruoff, *The People's Emperor: Democracy and the Japanese Monarchy, 1945–1995* (Cambridge, MA: Harvard University Asia Center, 2001), 183–201.

9. For a poignant analysis of the funeral as public spectacle, see Takashi Fujitani, "Electronic Pageantry and Japan's 'Symbolic Emperor'," *Journal of Asian Studies* 51 (November 1992).

10. See Carol Carol Gluck, "The Past in the Present," in *Postwar Japan as History*, ed. Andrew Gordon (Berkeley: University of California Press, 1993).

11. See "Seijō hōgyo," *Jinja shinpō*, Special Edition no. 8 (1989).

12. "Gekido no Shōwa ni mananda mono," *Nihon izoku tsushin*, February 15, 1989.

13. "Tennō no sensō sekinin o tou," *Nitchū yūkō shimbun*, January 15, 1989.

14. This English translation was published along with the Japanese as "Hearkening to the Voices of Millions of War Victims: In Protest of the State Funeral for the Late Shōwa Tennō," in *Ima koso tōu tennōsei: Kikusenman sensō giseisha no koe ni kikitsutsu*, ed. Nihon senbotsu gakusei kinenkai (Tokyo: Chikuma shobo, 1989), 242–245.

15. Suzuki Yūko, *Chōsenjin jūgun ianfu* (Tokyo: Iwanami shoten, 1991).

16. For an interesting analysis see Jiro Yamaguchi, "The Gulf War and the Transformation of Japanese Constitutional Politics," *Journal of Japanese Studies* 18 (1992).

17. Taguchi Hiroshi, " 'Nichi-doku heiwa foramu' ni sanka shite," *Wadatsumi no koe* (1988).

18. This movement is treated in some detail in Kimijima Kazuhiko, "The Continuing Legacy of Japanese Colonialism: The Japan-South Korea Joint Study Group on History Textbooks," in *Censoring History: Citizenship and Memory in Japan, Germany, and the United States*, ed. Laura Hein and Mark Selden (Armonk, NY: M. E. Sharpe, 2000).

19. For an English translation, see Richard von Weizsäcker, "Speech by Richard von Weizsäcker, President of the Federal Republic of Germany, in the Bundestag during the Ceremony Commemorating the 40th Anniversary of the End of the War in Europe and of National Socialist Tyranny, May 8, 1985." In *Bitburg in Moral and Political Perspective*, ed. Geoffrey Hartman (Bloomington: Indiana University Press, 1986), 262–273.

20. The speech itself was made available in translation and through commentary almost immediately. See Hidaka Rokuro, "Mitsu no 40-nenme: 'kioku o iki-iki to tamotsu koto' no imi," *Sekai* (September 1985); Nagai Kiyohiko, "Waitsusekka enzetsu ni gyakufu tsunoru," *Sekai* (July 1987); Nagai Kiyohiko, *Waitsusekka no seishin* (Tokyo: Iwanami shoten, 1991).

21. For example, Tokyo shimbun, ed., *Owari naki sengo: shōgen to kiroku* (Tokyo: Tokyo shimbun shuppankyoku, 1994).

22. Adapted from Volker Fuhrt, "Von der Bundesrepublik lernen? Der Vergleich mit Deutschland in der japanischen Diskussion über Kriegsschuld und Vergangenheitsbewältigung," *Japanstudien* 8 (1996).

23. Nishio Kanji, *Kotonaru higeki: Nihon to doitsu* (Tokyo, 1994). A more recent example of a similar argument is Kisa Yoshio, *"Sensō sekinin" to wa nani ka* (Tokyo: Chūō kōron shinsha, 2001).

24. For example, Mishima Ken'ichi, "Nichidoku sengo gojūnen no sawagi no ato de," *Sekai* (February 1996); Nakayama Tarō, *Futatsu no haisen kokka: Nihon to doitsu no gojūnen* (Tokyo: Yomiuri shimbunsha, 1995); Irokawa Daikichi, ed., *1945 nen haisen kara nani o mananda ka* (Tokyo: Shōgakukan, 1995); Awaya Kentarō et al., *Sensō sekinin, sengo sekinin: Nihon to Doitsu wa dō chigau ka* (Tokyo: Asahi shimbunsha, 1994); Yamaguchi Yasushi and Ronald Ruprecht, eds., *Rekishi to aidentiti: Nihon to doitsu ni totte no 1945 nen (Geschichte und Identität)* (Kyoto: Shibunkaku shuppan, 1993).

25. See for example, Kasahara Tokushi, *Nankin jiken to Nihonjin: Sensō no kioku o meguru nashonarizumu to gurobarizumu* (Tokyo: Kashiwa shobō, 2002); Kaneko Masaru, Takahashi Tetsuro, and Yamaguchi Jiro, *Gurobarizeshon to sensō sekinin* (Tokyo: Iwanami shoten, 2001); Abiko Kazuyoshi, Uozumi Yōichi, and Nakaoka Narifumi, eds., *Sensō sekinin to "wareware": "Rekishi shutai ronso" o megutte* (Kyoto: Nakanishiya shuppan, 1999); Komori Yōichi and Takahashi Tetsuya, eds., *Nashonaru hisutorii o koete* (Tokyo: Tōkyō daigaku shuppansha, 1998).

26. "Kokusai shimpojiumu no kiroku" henshū iinkai, ed., *"Kako no kokufuku" to shinsō kyūmei: Nichibeikan de susumu rekishi jijitsu chōsa* (Tokyo: Kinohanasha, 2002).

27. In English, the most complete monographic treatment of Unit 731 remains Sheldon H. Harris, *Factories of Death: Japanese Biological Warfare, 1932–45, and the American Cover-Up* (London: Routledge, 1994).

28. Perhaps the most moving, if brief, English-language reading on Unit 731 is Haruko and Ted Cook's interview with Tamura Yoshio about his work in Harbin in Haruko Taya Cook and Theodore F. Cook, *Japan at War: An Oral History* (New York: The New Press, 1992), 158–167.

29. Iris Chang, *The Rape of Nanking: The Forgotten Holocaust of World War II* (New York: Penguin Books, 1997). Many new publications on the history and memory of the Nanjing Massacre have followed in the wake of the debate about Chang's book. See, for example, Takashi Yoshida, *The Making of the "Rape of Nanking": History and Memory in Japan, China, and the United States* (New York: Oxford University Press, 2006); Fei Fei Li, Robert Sabella, and David Liu, eds., *Nanking 1937: Memory and Healing* (Armonk, NY: M. E. Sharpe, 2002); Joshua A. Fogel, ed., *The Nanjing Massacre in History and Historiography* (Berkeley: University of California Press 2000); Honda Katsuichi, *The Nanjing Massacre: A Japanese Journalist Confronts Japan's National Shame*, ed. Frank Gibney, trans. Karen Sandness (Armonk, NY: M. E. Sharpe, 2000); Timothy Brook, ed., *Documents on the Rape of*

Nanking (Ann Arbor: University of Michigan Press, 1999); Kasahara Tokushi, *Nankin jiken* (Tokyo: Iwanami shoten, 1997).

30. The first published collection of documents was Yoshimi Yoshiaki, ed., *Jūgun ianfu shiryoshu* (Tokyo: Ōtsuki shoten, 1992).

31. In English, see, for example, Yuki Tanaka, *Japan's Comfort Women: Sexual Slavery and Prostitution during World War II and the US Occupation* (London: Routledge, 2002); Yoshimi Yoshiaki, *Comfort Women*, trans. Suzanne O'Brien (New York: Columbia University Press, 2000); Laura Hein, "Savage Irony: The Imaginative Power of the 'Military Comfort Women' in the 1990s," *Gender and History* 11 (1999); "The Comfort Women: Colonialism, War, and Sex," Special Issue of *positions: east asia cultures critique* 5, no. 1 (Spring 1997); George Hicks, *The Comfort Women: Japan's Brutal Regime of Enforced Prostitution in the Second World War* (New York: W. W. Norton, 1994).

32. Ōnuma Yasuaki lists 2 million yen per person as private atonement money regardless of residency, and government medical welfare programs ranging from 1.2 million yen for Filipino victims to 3 million yen for Taiwanese and Korean victims. These statistics are based on Ōnuma Yasuaki, Shimomura Mitsuko, and Wada Haruki, eds., *"Ianfu" mondai to Ajia josei kikin* (Tokyo: Toshindo, 2000), 148.

33. Ōnuma Yasuaki, "Japanese War Guilt and the Postwar Responsibility of Japan," talk at Harvard University on March 3, 2002, published in Japanese as "Nihon no sensō sekinin to sengo sekinin," *Kokusai mondai* (December 2001).

34. Kerry Smith, "The Shōwa Hall: Memorializing Japan's War at Home," *The Public Historian* 24, no. 4 (2002): 35–64; Ellen H. Hammond, "Commemoration Controversies: The War, the Peace, and Democracy in Japan," in *Living with the Bomb: American and Japanese Cultural Conflicts in the Nuclear Age*, ed. Laura Hein and Mark Selden (Armonk, NY: M. E. Sharpe, 1997).

35. *Nihon izoku tsushin*, April 15, 1999.

36. Both *kinenkan* in Japanese, but written with different characters for commemoration hall and prayer hall.

37. *Nihon izoku tsushin*, February 15, 1999.

38. Ibid.

39. Utsumi Aiko et al., eds., *Handobukku sengo hoshō* (Tokyo: Nashi no kiseki, 1993).

40. Takagi Ken'ichi, *Jugun ianfu to sengo hoshō: Nihon no sengo sekinin* (Tokyo: San'ichi shinsho, 1994).

41. Inokuchi Hiromitsu and Nozaki Yoshiko maintain a Web site, "Court Cases, Citizen Groups, and the Unresolved Issues of War: Updates and Brief Commentary," at *http://www.jca.apc.org*. See also a list of compensation cases at *http://www.jca.apc.org*.

42. These percentages were decisively lower among those fifty years and older, with 41 percent approving compensation for former "comfort women," 68 percent in favor of compensating victims of Japan's colonial rule, and 64 percent affirming the need to compensate victims of Japanese war atrocities. Asahi shimbun sengo hoshō mondai shuzaihan, *Sengo hoshō to wa nani ka* (Tokyo: Asahi shimbunsha, 1994), 135–140 plus graphs.

43. Hein, "Savage Irony."

44. Tanaka Nobumasa, "Nihon izokukai no 50 nen," *Sekai* (September 1994).

45. In 1998, the Japanese Society for History Textbook Reform sent out booklets to all Japan scholars in the United States and perhaps elsewhere entitled "The

Restoration of a National History: Why Was the Japanese Society for History Textbook Reform established, and What Are Its Goals?" See also the group's Web site at *http://www.tsukurukai.com*.

46. Gavan McCormack, "The Japanese Movement to 'Correct' History," in *Censoring History: Citizenship and Memory in Japan, Germany, and the United States*, ed. Laura Hein and Mark Selden (Armonk, NY: M. E. Sharpe, 2000).

47. Nozaki Yoshiko and Inokuchi Hiromitsu, "Japanese Education, Nationalism, and Ienaga Saburo's Textbook Lawsuits," in *Censoring History: Citizenship and Memory in Japan, Germany, and the United States*, ed. Laura Hein and Mark Selden (Armonk, NY: M. E. Sharpe, 2000), 96–126.

48. For an introduction to the Tribunal with documents, see VAWW-NET Japan's Web site at *http://www1.jca.apc.org*.

49. Elazar Barkan, *The Guilt of Nations: Restitution and Negotiating Historical Injustices* (New York: W. W. Norton, 2000).

2. Operations of Memory

1. "Comfort women" (*ianfu* in Japanese) is a shortened form of "military comfort women" (*jūgun ianfu*) which, together with "comfort stations" (*ianjo*), were the terms used by the Japanese military during the war. To avoid their obviously offensive meaning, other names such as "sex slaves" are often used, or "comfort women" is placed in quotation marks. Because the term now appears in so many different national and international contexts, I use it here in plain form, but like Yoshimi Yoshiaki and others, I think of it as having invisible quotation marks around it. For background on the comfort women, see Yoshimi Yoshiaki, *Comfort Women: Sexual Slavery in the Japanese Military during World War II*, trans. Suzanne O'Brien (New York: Columbia University Press, 2000), 39–40; Yuki Tanaka, *Japan's Comfort Women: Sexual Slavery and Prostitution during World War II and the US Occupation* (London: Routledge, 2002).

2. The term is Herbert Butterfield's; for this and the analysis of the operations of memory that follows, see Carol Gluck, *Past Obsessions: World War II and Historical Memory* (New York: Columbia University Press, forthcoming).

3. Robert G. Moeller, *War Stories: The Search for a Usable Past in the Federal Republic of Germany* (Berkeley: University of California Press, 2001), 198.

4. *Asahi shimbun*, October 9, 2001.

5. See *http://www.showakan.go.jp*.

6. Franziska Seraphim, *War Memory and Social Politics in Japan, 1945–2005* (Cambridge, MA: Harvard University Asia Center, 2006).

7. *Ningen no jōken*, directed by Kobayashi Masaki (Shōchiku, 1959–61) in three parts with a total running time of 9½ hours, was based on the bestselling novel by Gomikawa Junpei, 6 vols. (Tokyo: San'ichi shobō, 1956–58), which sold 250,000 copies.

8. Andrei S. Markovits and Simon Reich, *The German Predicament: Memory and Power in the New Europe* (Ithaca, NY: Cornell University Press, 1997), 77.

9. *Asahi shimbun*, January 1, 1995; *Mainichi shimbun*, August 15, 2005; *Asahi shimbun*, June 28, 2005; *Kyōdō tsūshin*, October 19, 2005.

10. Daniel L. Schachter, *The Seven Sins of Memory: How the Mind Forgets and Remembers* (New York: Houghton Mifflin, 2001), 113.

11. Iris Chang, *The Rape of Nanking: The Forgotten Holocaust of World War II* (New York: Basic Books, 1997).

12. Robert O. Paxton, *Vichy France: Old Guard and New Order, 1940–1944* (New York: Knopf, 1972).

13. Daniel Goldhagen, *Hitler's Willing Executioners: Ordinary Germans and the Holocaust* (New York: Knopf, 1996).

14. See, among others, Laura Hein, "Savage Irony: The Imaginative Power of the 'Military Comfort Women' in the 1990s," *Gender and History* (July 1999): 336–372; Chungmoo Choi, "The Comfort Women: Colonialism, War, and Sex," *positions: east asia cultures critique* 5, no. 1 (Spring 1997), special issue; Takagi Ken'ichi, *Jūgun ianfu to sengo sekinin* (Tokyo: San'ichi shinsho, 1992); Suzuki Yūko, "*Jūgun ianfu*" *mondai to sei bōryoku* (Tokyo: Miraisha, 1993).

15. Senda Kakō, *Jūgun ianfu: "Koenaki onna" no hachimannin no kokuhaku* (Tokyo: Futabasha, 1973); *Jūgun ianfu* (Tokyo: San'ichi shobō, 1978); *Jūgun ianfu keiko: Chūgoku, Gatō, Biruma—shisen o samayotta onna no shōgen* (Tokyo: Kōbunsha, 1981). Earlier examples, including the 1947 novel by Tamura Taijirō, *Shunpunden* (A Prostitute's Story) and the film based on it, belonged to the era I have characterized as context blind to the comfort women. Senda published in the 1970s, a time when, after the normalization of relations with China in 1972, Japan's wartime actions were beginning to receive a different kind of media attention. For example, on Japanese atrocities in China and the Nanjing Massacre, See Honda Katsuichi, *Chūgoku no Nihongun* (Tokyo: Sōjusha, 1972); *Chūgoku no tabi* (Tokyo: Asahi shimbunsha, 1972).

16. Cynthia Enloe, *Maneuvers: The International Politics of Militarizing Women's Lives* (Berkeley: University of California Press, 2000), 49–107; Annette F. Timm, "Sex with a Purpose: Prostitution, Venereal Disease, and Militarized Masculinity in the Third Reich," *Journal of the History of Sexuality* 11, nos. 1–2 (2002): 223–255.

17. Margaret D. Stetz and Bonnie B. C. Oh, "Tomiyama Taeko's *A Memory of the Sea*," in *Legacies of the Comfort Women of World War II*, ed. Margaret D. Stetz and Bonnie B. C. Oh (Armonk, NY: M. E. Sharpe, 2001), 201–208.

18. See Yun Chung Ok, *Chōsenjin josei ga mita ianfu mondai: Asu o tomo ni tsukuru tame ni* (Tokyo: San'ichi shobō, 1992).

19. After Kim Hak Sun, one of the three Korean comfort women who filed suit against the Japanese government in late 1991, told her story on Japanese television, others began to come forth to tell theirs. For insight into the nature of these stories, see Dai Sil Kim-Gibson, *Silence Broken: Korean Comfort Women* (Parkersburg, IA: Mid-Prairie Books, 1999).

20. Ustinia Dolgopol, coauthor with Snehal Paranjape of the report, in a speech to International Symposium on Violence Against Women in War and Armed Conflict NGO Forum on Women, Beijing, September 4, 1995. Dolgopol, of Australia, was later a Chief Prosecutor at the mock Women's International War Crimes Tribunal 2000 in Tokyo.

21. Linda Chavez, "Contemporary Forms of Slavery" (United Nations Economic and Social Council, Commission on Human Rights, E/CN.4/Sub.2/1995/38, 1995), *http://www.unhchr.ch*; Radhika Coomaraswamy, "Report on the Mission to the Democratic People's Republic of Korea, the Republic of Korea and Japan on the Issue of Military Sexual Slavery in Wartime" (United Nations Economic and Social Council, Commission on Human Rights, E/CN.4/1996/53/Add.1, 1996),

http://www.unhchr.ch; Gay J. McDougall, "Contemporary Forms of Slavery: Systematic Rape, Sexual Slavery and Slavery-like Practices during Armed Conflict" (United Nations Economic and Social Council, Commission on Human Rights, E/CN.4/Sub.2/1998/13, 1998), *http://www.unhchr.ch*.

22. See Ōnuma Yasuaki et al., eds., *"Ianfu" mondai to Ajia josei kikin* (Tokyo: Tōshindō, 1998).

23. For example, Fujioka Nobukatsu, " 'Jūgun ianfu' o chūgakusei ni oshieru na," in Atarashii rekishi kyōkasho o tsukuru kai, ed., *Atarashii Nihon no rekishi ga hajimaru* (Tokyo: Gentōsha, 1997), 76–90. Fujioka was one of the leaders of the right-wing revisionist "liberal view of history" *(jiyūshugi shikan)* in the late 1990s. For a contrary view, see Tawara Yoshifumi, *"Ianfu" mondai to kyōkasho kōgeki* (Tokyo: Kōbunken, 1997).

24. For an intelligent summary, see Yasumaru Yoshio, " 'Jūgun ianfu' mondai to rekishika no shigoto," *Sekai* (May 1998): 137–47.

25. For example, Seungsook Moon, "Begetting the Nation: The Androcentric Discourse of National History and Tradition in South Korea," in *Dangerous Women: Gender and Korean Nationalism*, ed. Elaine H. Kim and Chungmoo Choi (New York: Routledge, 1998), 33–66.

26. Quoted in Paul Rodgers, "Court Gives Ex-Comfort Women Symbolic Victory," *Women's E-News*, July 9, 2002.

27. "Transcript of Oral Judgment," The Hague, The Netherlands, December 4, 2001, *http://www.iccwomen.org*. For a wealth of materials relating to the mock tribunal, see VAWW-NET Japan, ed., *Nihon gunsei doreisei o sabaku: 2000nen josei kokusai senpan hōtei no kiroku*, 5 vols. (Tokyo: Ryokufu shuppan, 2000–2002).

28. Chang-rae Lee, *A Gesture Life* (New York: Penguin Putnam, 1999).

29. Maria Rosa Henson, *Comfort Women: A Filipina's Story of Prostitution and Slavery under the Japanese Military* (Lanham, MD: Rowman and Littlefield, 1999), 91. On the Filipino comfort women, see Firipin "jūgun ianfu" hoshō seikyō saiban bengodan, ed., *Firipin no Nihongun "ianfu": Seiteki bōryoku no higaishatachi* (Tokyo: Akashi shoten, 1995).

30. Hayashi Hirofumi, "Survey of the Japanese Movement Against Wartime Sexual Violence," *http://wwsoc.nii.ac.jp*. The group first discussed the issue in fall 2000.

31. Ueno Chizuko, "Kioku no seijigaku: Kokumin, kojin, watashi," *Inpakushon* 103 (1997): 154.

32. For example, Julie Peters and Andrea Wolper, *Women's Rights, Human Rights: International Feminist Perspectives* (New York: Routledge, 1995).

33. John Lie, "The State as Pimp: Prostitution and the Patriarchal State in Japan in the 1940s," *The Sociological Quarterly* 38, no. 2 (Spring 1997): 251–264.

34. Rhonda Copelon, "Gender Crimes as War Crimes: Integrating Crimes Against Women into International Criminal Law," *McGill Law Journal* 46, no. 1 (2000): 217–40; quotation, 223.

35. See Nihon no sensō sekinin shiryō sentaa, ed., *Shinpojiumu: Nashonarizumu to "ianfu" mondai* (Tokyo: Aoki shoten, 1998).

36. Ueno, "Kioku noseijigaku," 170; see also Ueno Chizuko, " 'Minzoku' ka 'jendaa' ka: Shiirareta tairitsu—'Nashonarizumu to "ianfu" mondai' sono go," *Kikan sensō sekinin kenkyū* 26 (Winter 1999): 15–25, 84.

3. Living Soldiers, Re-lived Memories?

1. Matsuoka Tamaki, *Nankin-sen tozasareta kioku o tazunete: Moto heishi 102-nin no shogen* (Tokyo: Shakai Hyoronsha, 2002).

2. See, for example, Ara Ken'ichi, "'Nankin sen-moto heishi 102-nin no shogen' no detaramesa," *Seiron* (November 2002): 96–102; "'Nankin sen' moto heishi—giwaku no shogen," *Shokun* (November 2002): 162–174.

3. Indeed, the Chinese translation of Matsuoka's collected testimonies was published almost simultaneously as *Nanjing zhan: Xun zhao bei fengbi de jiyi: Qin Hua Rijun yuanshibing 102ren de zhengyan* (Shanghai: Shanghai cishu chubanshe, 2002).

4. John Dower, "Sensational Rumors, Seditious Graffiti, and the Nightmares of the Thought Police," in *Japan in War and Peace* (New York: The New Press, 1993), 121.

5. Azuma Shirō, "Fukuin gunjin no fuman," originally published on September 16, 1946, reprinted in *Azuma Shirō nikki* (Kumamoto-shi: Kumamoto Shuppan Bunka Kaikan, 2001).

6. See chapters by Itō Kimio and Takahashi Yoshinori in Takahashi Saburō, ed., *Kyōdo kenkyū Senyūkai* (Tokyo: Tabata shoten, 1983).

7. Takahashi Saburō, "Senyūkai wo tsukuru hitobito," in Takahashi, *Kyōdo kenkyū Senyūkai*, 137–138.

8. In Japanese, the best overall survey remains Yoshida Yutaka, *Nihonjin no sensōkan: Sengoshi naka no henyō* (Tokyo: Iwanami shoten, 1995), 86–97, 112–120. See also Fujiwara Kiichi, *Sensō o kioku rusu* (Tokyo: Kodansha shinsho, 2001). In English, see especially Yoshikuni Igarashi, *Bodies of Memory* (Princeton, NJ: Princeton University Press, 2000).

9. For a sensitive study of these Japanese veterans based on interviews and psychoanalytical case studies, see Noda Masaaki, *Sensō to zaiseki* (Tokyo: Iwanami shoten, 1998). A Chinese translation was published in 2000.

10. Chūgoku kikansha renrakukai, *Kaette kita senhan tachi no gohansei: Chūgoku kikansha renrakukai no 40-nen* (Osaka: Shinpu shobō, 1996). Interestingly, "sankō" was the subject of the first Sino-Japanese dispute over history that I personally experienced, when in the mid-1980s one of my Japanese classmates at Nanjing University raised doubts about the authenticity of such a practice on the grounds that the term is not Japanese and therefore could not have been a wartime Japanese official policy.

11. Soka Gakkai sennenbu Hansen chuppan iinkai, *Sensō o shiranai sedai e*, 56 vols. (Tokyo: Daisanbumeisha, 1974–79).

12. It was only years later that his daughter was able to overcome resistance from within the family to fulfill his wish. Noda Masaaki, *Sensō to zaiseki* (Tokyo: Iwanami shoten, 1998). Chinese translation, 247–257.

13. On Yokoi, see Igarashi Yoshikuni, "Yokoi Shōichi: When a Soldier Finally Returns Home," in *The Human Tradition in Modern Japan*, ed. Anne Walthall (Wilmington, DE: Scholarly Resources, 2002), 197–212. In addition to Yasuoka Shotarō, another well-known commentator with army experience—Yamamoto Shichihei—also credited the Yokoi episode for reawakening his war memories.

14. On the background of the Nanjing Massacre debate in Japan, see my "The

Malleable and the Contested: The Nanjing Massacre in Postwar Japan and China," in *Perilous Memories: The Asia-Pacific War(s)*, ed. T. Fujitani, Geoffrey M. White, and Lisa Yoneyama (Durham, NC: Duke University Press, 2001), 50–86; "Transmitted Experience: Individual Testimonies and Collective Memories of the Nanjing Atrocity," in *Historical Injustice and Democratic Transition In Eastern Asia and Northern Europe*, ed. Kenneth Christie and Robert Cribb (London: Curzon Press, 2002). See also the essay by Takashi Yoshida in *The Nanjing Massacre in History and Historiography*, ed. Joshua A Fogel (Berkeley: University of California Press, 2000).

15. Hata Ikuhiko, *Nankin jiken* (Tokyo: Chūkō shinsho, 1986), 28–32.

16. John Pritchard and Sonia Zaide, comps., *Tokyo War Crimes Trial* (New York: Garland, 1981), vol. 20, 49815.

17. Honda Katsuichi, *Chūgoku no tabi* (Tokyo: Asahi shimbunsha, 1972). This, together with some of his later writings on the Nanjing Massacre, has been translated into English and published as *The Nanjing Massacre: A Japanese Journalist Confronts Japan's National Shame* (Armonk, NY: M. E. Sharpe, 1999).

18. Suzuki Akira, *Nankin daigyakusatsu no maboroshi* (Tokyo: Bungei shunju, 1973).

19. Yamamoto Shichihei, *Watashi no naka no Nihongun: Aru ijo taikensha no henken* (Tokyo: Bungei shunju, 1974), 3. Yamamoto's book was hailed as a "classic that, on the basis of one's own army experience, smashes the "war-military legends" full of misunderstanding and prejudice. Bob Tadashi Wakabayashi analyzed one episode in "The Nanking 100-Man Killing Contest Debate: War Guilt amid Fabricated Illusions," *Journal of Japanese Studies* 26, no. 2 (Summer 2000): 307–340. Recently, the daughter of one of the executed officers filed a libel suit against Honda for defaming her innocent father.

20. Ara Ken'ichi, *Kikigaki Nankin Jiken* (Tokyo: Tosho Shuppansha, 1987); recently reissued in *bunko* form as *"Nankin Jiken" Nihonjin 48-nin no shogen* (Tokyo: Shogakkan, 2002).

21. "Iwayuru 'Nankin jiken' ni kansuru jōhō teikyō no onegai" (A request for information concerning the so-called "Nanjing Incident"), *Kaikō* 395 (November 1983): 35–37.

22. Katokawa Kōtarō, "Shōgen ni yoru Nankin senshi: Sono sōkatsu teki kōsatsu" (The history of the battle of Nanjing: An overall examination), *Kaikō* 411 (March 1985): 9–18. Although this statement was welcomed by many in Japan, including some of Kaikōsha's own members, it also met with strong opposition from many others. The organization even donated a set of its published *History of the Nanjing Battle* to China, with the hope of building some common understanding.

23. An infantry soldier who fought in China, Hino Ashihei was the author of several widely read Japanese war novels. See David M. Rosenfeld. *Unhappy Soldier: Hino Ashihei and Japanese World War II Literature* (Lanham, MD: Rowman & Littlefield, 2002).

24. Ian Buruma, *The Wages of Guilt: Memories of War in Germany and Japan* (New York: Farrar, Straus and Giroux, 1994), 129–135.

25. Ibid.

26. Ono Kenji, an ordinary factory worker in the Fukushima prefecture, began his own odyssey of visiting and collecting veterans' testimonies and wartime diaries in his hometown area in 1988. Nearly twenty diaries were published in 1994 as

Nankin daigyakusatsu wo kirokushita kōgun heishi tachi (Tokyo: Otsuki shoten, 1994). The collected testimonies, running over 200, have not yet been published.

27. Sone Kazuo, *Shiki Nankin gyakusatsu* (Tokyo: Sairyūsha, 1986), *Zoku shiki Nankin gyakusatsu* and *Nankin gyakusatsu to sensō*. Sone was alleged to have faked (or confused) his rank by some associated with various Revisionist groups. See Itakura Yoshiaki, *Shokun* (December 1988): 126–146. Interestingly, Itakura accused Hata Ikuhiko for continuing to believe in Sone's account, sparking a lively exchange between the two concerning the credibility of veterans' testimony. See " 'Zangeya Sone Kazuo' e no shinyō," *Ketsuyō hyōron* 1331 (October 5, 1997), 3.

28. Azuma Shirō, *Waga Nankin puraton* (Tokyo: Aoki shoten, 1987). The word "platoon" in the title may have more to do with the blockbuster American film in the previous year, which showed considerable brutality, than with the actual history: the term would not be familiar to imperial Japanese army veterans.

29. Shimozato Masaki, *Kakureta rentaishi-20i gekyu heishi no mita Nankin jiken no jisso* (Tokyo: Aoki shoten, 1987). Shimozato had previously collaborated with the well-known writer Morimura Seiichi, whose *The Devil's Gluttony*, about the infamous Unit 731, was a top bestseller in 1981.

30. Some of the letters were reproduced in the *"Dong Shiliang riji" an tuji* (Beijing: Xinhua chubanshe, 2000). This is a bilingual album in both Chinese and Japanese. Buruma wrote of Azuma keeping brass knuckles in his car for self-defense. The exact circumstance of his departure is not entirely clear. Peer pressure was definitely the key factor. The late Fujiwara Akira, a prominent historian on the Left who wrote extensively about Japan's war crimes, had himself been an officer in the Japanese army in China and was a member of the postwar senyūkai.

31. Takaike Katsuhiko, "Nankin soshō kara mita 'daigyaku jiken,'" *Kakushin* (June 1994): 30–31; Ara Ken'ichi, *"Nankin Jiken" Nihonjin 48-min no shogen* (Tokyo: Shogakkan, 2002); Ara Ken'ichi, "Kōsai mo shirozoketa 'Nankin gyakusatsu' no uso," *Seiron* (March 1999). In fact, a group formed after the first ruling in support of the platoon leader was located in the same office as a group openly challenging the existence of the Nanjing massacre.

32. Ara Ken'ichi, "Kōsai mo shirozoketa 'Nankin gyakusatsu' no uso."

33. After the court ruling, the platoon leader admitted to a TV crew from Hong Kong that war was about killing and that he did kill Chinese in Nanjing. I have not seen this interview, nor do I know the exact question and answer given.

34. See, for instance, comments by Mizutani in interview with Zhu Chengshan.

35. *Dong Shilang susongan yu Nanjing Datusha zhengxiang* (Beijing: Renmin chubanshe, 1998).

36. Li Zongyuan, " 'Dong Shilang susongan yu Nanjing datusha zhengxiang' chuban zuotanhui," *Kang-Ri zhanzheng yanju* 30 (1998); Zhang Lianhong and Xiao Yonghong, "Dong Shilang susongan yantaohui," *Kang-Ri zhanzheng yanju* 31 (1999).

37. Jing Shenghong, "Dong Shilang [Azuma Shirō] susongan de Zhongguo yiyi yu Riben yiyi," *Nanjing shehui kexue* (2001/4).

38. While most of them expressed admiration of Azuma for his courage, a few vented anger that given the suffering in their families, they could not bring themselves to forgive Japanese like Azuma. Some of the letters were later published in Japanese translations. Sympathetic to its goals, Sun Ge was critical of the Chinese intellectual circles that "failed to provide the needed nutrients to the program," so

that it simply adopted an emotional stance of seeking justice over the Nanjing Massacre instead of an in-depth analysis of the past and the present. Sun Ge, *Zhuti misan de kongjian* (Nanchang: Jiangxi jiaoyu chubanshe, 2002), 33.

39. One Chinese student in Japan wrote an essay highlighting the contribution of Yamauchi Koyako.

40. A publisher in Shanghai published a book entitled *Dong Shilang xiezui* (Azuma Shirō apologizes for his crimes) (Shanghai: Cishu chubanshe, 2002), the first in a planned series of cartoon books on the Nanjing massacre, intended "especially for teenagers and youth."

41. See, for example, *Dong Shiliang riji an tuji* (Beijing: Xinhua chubanshe, 2000); *Dong Shiliang he ta de susongan* (Haerbin: Beifang wenyi chubanshe, 2000); *Dong Shiliang zhandi riji* (Beijing: Shijie zhishi chubanshe, 2000).

42. Mizutani Naoko, "Watashi wa naze Azuma Shiro shi ni igi wo tonaeru ka," *Sekai* (August 1999): 219–225. See the rebuttal by Azuma's three attorneys Nakakita Ryūtarō et al., " 'Azuma saiban' no shinjjutsu wo uttaeru," *Sekai* (October 1999): 275–279.

43. Some of the letters were translated into Japanese and included in *Kagai to*. Sympathetic to its goals, Sun Ge also was critical that "in reality the Chinese intellectual world failed to provide the necessary nutrient to the program, thus simply returning to an emotional stance of seeking to evaluate the Nanjing Massacre." Sun, *Zhuti misan de kongjian*, 162.

44. Azuma attributed this to Honda's envy of his new fame in China.

45. Maurice Halbwachs, *On Collective Memory* (New York: Harper & Row, 1980), 50–51.

46. One can only speculate about the moment when the last veteran passes away from the scene. What does this imply for generational difference?

47. Joan W. Scott, "The Evidence of Experience," *Critical Inquiry* 17 (Summer 1991): 773–797.

48. Writing about stories of war atrocities during the Vietnam War, Geunter Lewy cautioned that "the fact that many of the allegations of atrocities in Vietnam do not stand up under critical examination does not warrant the conclusion that no atrocities took place. Such a conclusion would be as one-sided and wrong as the assertion that the conduct of American forces in Vietnam was but an unrelieved record of brutal war crimes. However, the ease with such allegations were produced and the transparent political motive manifesting itself in many of them does not indictate an attitude of caution. Assertion and allegation are not tantamount to fact and proof." Guenter Lewy, *America in Vietnam* (New York: Oxford University Press, 1978), 324. On the recent atrocities stories in the Korean War, see Marilyn Young, "An Incident at No Gun Ri," in Omer Bartov et al., eds., *Crimes of War: Guilt and Denial in the Twentieth Century* (New York: New Press, 2002), 242–258.

49. Mizutani, "Watashi wa," 223; Nakakita, "Azuma saiban," 281.

50. Yoshida Yutaka, "Senjo kiroku toshite no 'Azuma nikki' no igi," in *Kagai to yurushi: Nankin daigyakusatsu to Azuma Shirō saiban* (Tokyo: Gendai shokan, 2001), 79–108. This book published some of the letters written by the Chinese audeience of the aforementioned television debate.

51. Fang Jun, *Wo renshi de guizibing: Yi ge liu-Ri xueshen de zhaji* (Beijing: Zhongguo duiwai fanyi chuban gongsi, 1997).

52. A Chinese translation of selected chapters from three Chūkiren publications

is published as Zhongguo Guihuanzhe Lianluohui, comp., *Lishi de jianzhen: Rijun chanhui lu*, trans. Yuan Qiupai et al. (Beijing: Jianfangjun chubanshe, 1994). A collection of affidavits by Japanese "war criminals" in PRC custody has been published as Yuan Qiubai and Yang Quizhen, comp., *Zuie de jigongzhuang: Xin zhongguo dui Riben zhanfan de lishi shengpan* (Beijing: Jianfangjun chubanshe, 2001).

53. Sun, *Zhuti misan de Kongjian*.

54. Azuma, "Shisō toshite no 'Azum gensho'," *Sekai* (February 2001): 251, 252.

55. Ibid., 252.

56. An example is the recent work by Kitamura Minoru, *Nankin jiken no tankyū* (Tokyo: Bunshun shinsho, 2002). Although Kitamura wrote in the Afterword of the need to "understand the anger and sadness of the Chinese people," one Japanese reviewer pointed out that his book all but ignored his own admonitions and tended to focus on the "pitiful circumstances faced by the Japanese soldiers in Nanjing." Inoue Hisahi, "Jijitsu wo akirakani suru shisei wa doko ni?" *Shūkan Kinyōbi* 441 (August 2, 2002), 50.

4. Kamikaze Today

1. For example, *Kumo nagaruru hateni* (1953), *Aa tokubetsu kōgekitai* (1960), *Saigono tokkôtai* (1970), *MACRON-A kessen kōkŭtai* (1974).

2. Kobayashi Yoshinori, *Shin gōmanizum sengen, special, sensōron* (Tokyo: Tōgensha, 1998), 75–96. The Japanese print media, for example, kept producing writings on kamikaze in the 1990s and 2000s, which include: Fukahori Michiyoshi, *Tokkō no shinjitsu* (Tokyo: Harashobō, 2001); Kaneko Toshio, *Kamikaze tokkō no kiroku* (Tokyo: Kōjinsha, 2001); Kudō Yukie, *Tokkō eno rekuiem* (Tokyo: Chūōkōronsha, 2001); Mimura Fumio, *Kaminaki tokkō* (Tokyo: Tokyo keizai, 1996); Satō Sanae, *Tokkō no machi, Chiran* (Tokyo: Kōjinsha, 1997); Shiroyama Saburō, *Shikikantachi no tokkō* (Tokyo: Shinchōsha, 2001).

3. Given his early film career, the actor Takakura Ken (who plays Yamaoka Shūji) also personifies death. He appeared in the 1977 film, *Hakkōdasan*, which depicted the 1902 tragedy at Mt. Hakkōda. He also plays a young kamikaze pilot in the 1970 film, *Saigono tokkōtai*.

4. The 1993 film, *Gekkō no natsu*, breaks away from earlier cinematic convention that emphasized the masculine quality of the kamikaze's dedication by depicting two pilots' deep love of music—their "feminine quality." The totalitarian regime forces two nonaggressive youths into service for the nation. Facing their inevitable death, they only wish to play the piano at a local school. They cherish the final opportunity to play the piano even though they know they will be late reporting to headquarters. In the end, the more musically talented pilot of the two dies as a kamikaze, and the film makes sure to show in its final sequence that he kills no enemies: he is shot down on his way to Okinawa. The death of the young musician culminates a narrative that casts Japanese youth as victims of the war.

5. The screenwriter bases this scene on the anecdote included in Takagi Toshirō's *Tokkokichi Chiran* (Tokyo: Kadokawa shoten, 1973).

6. The story of Second Lieutenant Kim directly derives from the 1988 nonfiction book, *Tokkō ni chitta Chōsenjin* (Koreans Who Died in Tokkō) by Kirihara Hisashi (Tokyo: Kodansha, 1988), which carefully documents the maltreatment that Korean kamikaze received in their corps because of their ethnicity as well as

their desperate efforts to find a Korean nationalist cause within their service toward the Japanese empire. Many of them insisted that Japan must win in order for Koreans to achieve Korean independence.

The book even makes a surprising assertion that Second Lieutenant Kim actually attempted to seek asylum in China. In his final letter, Lieutenant Kim records that he received an order to lead five kamikaze planes to Okinawa as a commander. Once he confirmed the completion of their mission, he would land in Okinawa to report it to the local command and then return to sea to attack enemy ships as a solo kamikaze. Kim's conduct is actually against the conventions of kamikaze attack (the commander must lead other planes in an attack), and Kim's immediate superior officers deny ever making such an order. It is also strange to write the contents of his mission in a final letter: the vast majority of kamikazes' final letters articulate something more personal. Building the argument, the author speculates that the letter was part of the careful preparation for Second Lieutenant Kim's escape—he needed to convince the people around him that such an order was in place in order to camouflage his plan to escape to China after landing in Okinawa. This plot was his only way to fulfill conflicting obligations to different institutions: the Great Empire of Japan, Korea, and his family.

There is no way of proving that book's claim. Yet the argument carries weight because it tries to be attentive to the plight of Korean kamikaze pilots. Their Korean nationalism was mediated by their keen awareness that they were serving as cogs in the imperial Japanese military.

7. The screenwriter attempted to give the scene some feasibility when he expanded the screenplay into a book. In the book version, Yamaoka's and Tomiko's visit to Korea takes place in late summer. Takeyama Hiroshi, *Hotaru* (Tokyo: Kadokawa shoten, 2002), 215.

8. Fukahori Michiyoshi, *Tokkō no shinjitsu: Meirei to kenshin to izoku no kokoro* (Tokyo: Hara shobō, 2001), 293.

9. The local retired junior high school principal, Kakimoto Hitonari, provided this information in an interview at Banse, Kagoshima, on May 9, 2003.

10. "2001 nendo dokusha senshutsu Nihon eiga besto ten," *Kinema junpō* (February [second half] 2002): 50–52. In *Kinema junpō*'s critics' selection, *Hotaru* was ranked fourteenth.

11. Satō Tadao, "Kanshō dewa naku kui o komete," *Kinema junpō* (June [first half] 2001): 40–41.

12. The audience has been limited to those who saw the film at the special showings since it has not yet been released in Korea.

13. The town's Web site provides brief history of the museum and the Kannon temple *(http://www.town.chiran.kagoshima.jp)*. Takagi Toshirō also talks about the origin of the Kannon temple in Chiran in his *Tokkōkichi Chiran*, 325.

14. According to the town's Web page, the two Army generals, Sugawara Michiō and Kawabe Shōzō, brought the statue to Chiran *(http://www.town.chiran. kagoshima.jp)*. Sugawara was the Army's air force commander in charge of carrying out the Army kamikaze attacks; and, in the last phase of the war, Kawabe prepared the kamikaze attacks on the landing enemy forces as the highest commander of Japan's remaining air forces (Tokagi Toshio, *Tokkōkichi Chiran*, 325). Interestingly, Akabane Reiko attributes the building of the Kannon statue in Chiran entirely to her mother's effort. Akabane claims that Torihama Tome, the model for the Ya-

mamoto Tomiko character in the film, originally came up with the idea of building a Kannon statue for the deceased pilots and managed to convince the town's mayor to build one. Akabane Reiko and Ishii Hiroshi, *Hotaru Kaeru* (Tokyo: Shisōsha, 2001), 216–217. This story can best be described as a folktale originating in Torihama's personal remembrance. *Hotaru* incorporates this myth rather than the actual history into its cinematic narrative.

15. The following account is based on my visit to Chiran on May 8 and 9, 2003.

16. On February 9, 2001, two and a half months before becoming Prime Minister of Japan, Koizumi Junichirō visited the Peace Museum and was literally moved to tears by its displays.

17. One can find many of the same stories in *Hotaru kaeru* by Akaba Reiki and Ishii Hiroshi.

18. Yamane Sadao, "Sensō no kioku," *Kinema junpō* (July [second half] 2001): 144.

19. The director Arai Haruhiko offers an equally short and cryptic critique of *Hotaru* in *Eiga geijutsu*. He also lists the film as one of the worst in 2001. *Eiga geijutsu* (Winter 2002): 53–54.

20. Ishimaru Gen-show, *Kamikaze* (Tokyo: Asuka shinsha, 2001), 285–286.

5. Lost Men and War Criminals

1. Yuki Hideo, "Tuitō-kon no hōkokusho o kangaeru," in *Sensō to tsuitō: Yasukuni mondai e no teigen,* ed. Sugawara Nobuo (Tokyo: Hassakusha, 2003), 77.

2. In 2004, more than 200 teachers in Tokyo were fired by the Board of Education because they refused to stand for the flag and the singing of the national anthem. Court challenges to the Tokyo Board's policies continue.

3. Hirohashi Takashi, "Dokyumento: Yasukuni sanpai to Chidorigafuchi," in Sugawara, *Sensō to tsuitō,* 59–60.

4. See for example Komori Yōichi, "Kyōiku kihon-hō kaiaku to 'sensō o suru kuni,'" *Gendai shisō* 4, no. 32 (2004): 78–88; Koyasu Nobukuni, "Tatakau kokka to matsuru kokka: Kokka no renzokusei to matsuri," *Gendai shisō* 4, no. 32 (2004): 42–46; and Sugawara, *Sensō to tsuitō.*

5. Komori, "Kyōiku kihon-hō."

6. Carol Gluck discusses the role of public intellectuals as "agents of public memory" in constructions of national history and memory in "The Past in the Present," in *Postwar Japan as History,* ed. Andrew Gordon (Berkeley: University of California Press, 1993), 65–71.

7. Wesley Sasaki-Uemura, "Competing Publics: Citizens' Groups, Mass Media, and the State in the 1960s," *positions: east asia cultures critique* 10, no. 1 (Spring 2002): 82.

8. See Ian Buruma, *The Wages of Guilt: Memories of War in Germany and Japan* (New York: Farrar, Straus and Giroux, 1994).

9. See Laura Hein and Mark Selden, *Censoring History: Citizenship and Memory in Japan, Germany, and the United States* (New York: East Gate Books, 1999) for another comparison of Germany and Japan's approaches to their wartime pasts. An editorial in the January 19, 2004 *New York Times* praised Germany for the ways it had dealt with its past: "Few nations in history have so sincerely and deeply looked into the evils of their past and worked so hard to come to terms with them. Ger-

many is, and deserves to be, a full and equal partner in everything Europe does, without being made to feel that it bears a permanent taint." Inagaki Hisakazu urges Japan to learn from the European Union model of how to coexist with ones neighbors, "Kokyosei kara shin-tuitö setsubi o kangaeru," in Sugawara, *Sensö to tsuitö,* 189.

10. On the religious and social aspects of the Yasukuni controversy, see Helen Hardacre, *Shintö and the State, 1868–1988* (Princeton, NJ: Princeton University Press, 1987); Harry Harootunian, "Memory, Mourning, and National Morality: Yasukuni Shrine and the Reunion of State and Religion," in *Nation and Religion: Perspectives on Europe and Asia,* ed. Peter van der Veer and Hartmut Lehmann (Princeton, NJ: Princeton University Press, 1999), 144–160; Murakami Shigeyoshi, *Japanese Religion in the Modern Century,* trans. H. Byron Earhart (Tokyo: University of Tokyo Press, 1980); Murakami Shigeyoshi, *Kokka Shintö* (Tokyo: Iwanami Shoten, 1970); Murakami Shigeyoshi, *Kokka Shintö to minshū shūkyö* (Tokyo: Yoshikawa köbunkan, 1982); John Nelson, "Social Memory as Ritual Practice: Commemorating Spirits of the Military Dead at Yasukuni Shrine," *Journal of Asian Studies* 62, no. 2 (May 2003): 443–467.

11. The photographs of the war dead at Yūshūkan are displayed in a manner that is disconcertingly reminiscent of the display of photographs of the massacred Jewish inhabitants of a whole town in Europe in the U.S. Holocaust Museum in Washington, DC. Hardacre points out that the Japanese government provides information to Yasukuni about each of the war dead, in violation of its own policy. Thus each photograph in the museum also gives the name, place of death, and other personal information about the deceased.

12. Sugawara Nobuo presents a moving critique of the Yūshūkan, and the photographs on its walls. He insightfully comments that the museum and Yasukuni shrine emphasize regret *(kuyashisa)* rather than sadness, and speaks of the need of a memorial or graveyard that would evoke sadness instead, as a part of mourning for the dead. Sugawara, *Sensö to tsuitö,* 2–5.

13. On the bride dolls, see Ellen Schattschneider, "The Bloodstained Doll: Violence and the Gift in Wartime Japan," *Journal of Japanese Studies* 31, no. 2 (2002): 329–356.

14. Yasukuni Jinja, ed., *Yūshūkan zuroku* (Tokyo: Kindai shuppansha, 2003), 94.

15. Harootunian, "Memory," 148. On State Shintö before 1945, see Murakami, *Kokka Shintö* and *Kokka Shintö to minshū shūkyö.*

16. Hardacre, *Shintö and the State,* 5.

17. Ibid., 159.

18. Hardacre, "The Shintö Directive," in *Shintö and the State,* 167–170, 26–27; Murakami, *Japanese Religion,* 132, 158–160; Harootunian, "Memory," 145–158; Nelson, "Social Memory," 456–462. Franziska Seraphim refers to the Izokukai as "pressure groups."

19. Hardacre, *Shintö and the State,* 40.

20. Ann Sherif, "The Politics of Loss: On Etö Jun," *positions: east asia cultures critique* 10, no. 1 (Spring 2002): 11–139. On Etö's "search for family roots" and his "forefathers in the Meiji period" in his *Reuniting with the Forefathers (Ichizoku saikai),* see Reiko Abe Auestad, "The Looping Movement of Kaiki in Etö Jun," in *Return to Japan from "Pilgrimage" to the West,* ed. Yoichi Nagashima (Oakville, CT: Aarhus University Press, 2001), 291–294.

21. Among Etō's numerous publications on Occupation censorship are *Tozasareta gengo kūkan: Senryōgun no ken'etsu to sengo Nihon* (Tokyo: Bungei shunjū, 1989) and *Jiyū to kinki* (Tokyo: Kawade shobō, 1982).

22. Many scholars have disagreed with Etō's claim of the deleterious influence of Occupation Censorship, including Jay Rubin, Honda Shūgo, Reiko Auestad, Brett deBary, and Yoshiko Samuel.

23. Auestad, "The Looping Movement of Kaiki in Etō Jun," 296.

24. Karatani, "Dokusha toshite no tasha," *Kokubungaku*, 68–69.

25. Seraphim uses the term "healthy nationalism" in her review of *Memory and History in East and Southeast Asia* by Gerrit W. Gong, *Journal of Asian Studies* 62, no. 2 (2003): 561. In Katō Norihiro's *Amerika no kage* (Tokyo: Kawade shobō, 1985), the younger critic extensively critiques Etō's writings on contemporary literature, and on the constitution and the surrender. For a critique of the particularly alarming and incendiary nationalism of an even younger generation, in the form of best selling cartoon artist Kobayashi Yoshinori, see Uesugi Satoshi, *Datsu-Sensōron—Kobayashi Yoshinori to no saiban o koete* (Tokyo: Tōhō shuppan, 2000).

26. Tanaka Kazuo, *Etō Jun* (Tokyo: Keio gijuku daigaku shuppankai, 2001).

27. Takazawa Shūji, *Etō Jun* (Tokyo: Chikuma shobō, 2001), 43–44.

28. Takazawa Shūji calls this aspect of Etō's narrative a *"watashi-gatari"* (a personal tale) in his *Etō Jun*, 73–75.

29. Etō's many personal tales include *Ichizoku saikai* (1976), *Yōnen jidai* (1999), *Tsuma to watashi* (1999).

30. Etō, "Dorei no shisō o haisu."

31. See Michiko N. Wilson, *The Marginal World of Ōe Kenzaburo: A Study in Themes and Techniques* (Armonk, NY: M. E. Sharpe, 1986), 35–136 on the Ōe/Etō debate on postwar literature.

32. Oketani Hideaki views Ōe's moment of transformation as a moment of blindness, because Ōe, he claims, does not understand that the naïve belief of the child in his teacher's message—no matter what the message may be—is precisely the same impulse as blind acceptance of imperial propaganda used to mold citizens. Karatani Kojin also problematizes Ōe's narrative of liberation. *Gyōshi to hōkō* (Tokyo: Gentōsha, 1971), 158–159.

33. See J. Victor Koschmann, *Revolution and Subjectivity in Postwar Japan* (Chicago: University of Chicago Press, 1996); John Dower, *Embracing Defeat: Japan in the Wake of Word War II* (New York: Norton, 1999); Yoshikuni Igarashi, *Bodies of Memory: Narratives of War in Postwar Japanese Culture* (Princeton, NJ: Princeton University Press, 2000).

34. See Van Gessel, *The Sting of Life* (New York: Columbia University Press, 1989).

35. I am grateful to Michael Bourdagh for clarifying the importance of Sōseki's historical moment and innocence.

36. "Tanin no monogatari to jibun no monogatari," in Etō Jun, *Senkyūhyaku yonjū roku nen kenpō sono sokubaku, sono ta* (Tokyo: Bungei shunjū, 1995) [hereafter *1946 nen*], 185.

37. On the Japanese narrative of victimization and its connection to Hiroshima and Nagasaki, see James Orr, *The Victim as Hero: Ideologies of Peace and National Identity in Postwar Japan* (Honolulu: University of Hawaii Press, 2001) and Buruma, *The Wages of Guilt.*

38. The many considerations of Japanese nationalism include Mariko Tamanoi, *Under the Shadow of Nationalism* (Honolulu: University of Hawaii Press, 1998), 79–190.

39. Etō Jun and Kobori Keiichirō. *Yasukuni ronshū: Nihon no chinkon no dentō no tame ni* (Tokyo: Nihon kyōbunsha, 1986). The reactionary Kobori wrote critically about the Tokyo Trials, penned an introduction to Tanaka Masaaki's refutation of the Nanjing Massacre, and, from the 1980s, was active in a committee dedicated to shield Japan from political and moral "bashing." Kobori is an emeritus professor of literature at Tokyo University. See also his essay "Kaidai" in *Yūshūkan*, 108–111.

40. On neo-Nationalism in the 1980s and 1990s, see Aaron Gerow, "Consuming Asia, Consuming Japan: The New Neonationalist Revisionism in Japan," *Bulletin of Concerned Asian Scholars* 30, no. 2 (1998): 30–36; also Yoshikuni Igarashi, "The Unfinished Business of Mourning: Maruyama Masao and Postwar Japan's Struggles with the Wartime Past," *positions: east asia cultures critique* 10, no. 1 (Spring 2002): 195–218. On the links between modern Nihonjinron and Nativism, see Harootunian, "Memory," 437–438. I differ with Harootunian on his lack of emphasis on dissent, opposition, and political activism in postwar Japan.

41. See Etō Jun, "Senbotsusha tsuitō no kokoro," in *Yasukuni no Inori*, ed. Yasukuni no Inori Henshū Iinkai (Tokyo: Sankei Nyūsu Sābisu, 1999), 1. All quotes from *Kokoro* are from page 1. Etō gives "way of life" as his equivalent of "kunigara" in "Seisha no shisen, shisha no shisen," in Etō and Kobori, *Yasukuni ronshū*, 16–17.

42. On the *Man'y'ōshū*, see Robert Brower and Earl Miner, *Japanese Court Poetry* (Stanford: Stanford University Press, 1961); Haruo Shirane and Tomi Suzuki, eds., *Inventing the Classics: Modernity, National Identity, and Japanese Literature* (Stanford, CA: Stanford University Press, 2000); Robert H. Brower, "Masaoka Shiki and Tanka Reform," in *Tradition and Modernization in Japanese Culture*, ed. Donald H. Shiveley (Princeton, NJ: Princeton University Press, 1971), 379–418. On the validation of MYS "masculinity and martial values" from the Edo period Nativist thinkers, and as a repository of the "true words and deeds of the gods," see H. D. Harootunian, *Things Seen and Unseen: Discourse and Ideology in Tokugawa Nativism* (Chicago: University of Chicago Press, 1988), 361, 365, 370. Thomas LaMarre conceives of the differentiation between the MYS and the later imperial anthologies in different terms, not gendered or martial, but in relationship to the assumed degree of "native absorption of the foreign." Thomas LaMarre, *Uncovering Heian Japan: An Archeology of Sensation and Inscription* (Durham, NC: Duke University Press, 2000), 31–32.

43. The translation is mine. In *Man'yōshū Nihon Koten Bungaku Zenshū*, vol. 4 (Tokyo: Iwanami shoten, 1957), 27. Hiroaki Sato offers this translation: "Though the broad cove of Shiga in Sasanami may lie calm/will it ever meet again the people of the past?" In *From the Country of Eight Islands: An Anthology of Japanese Poetry*, ed. Hiroaki Sato and Burton Watson (New York: Anchor Books/Doubleday, 1981), 28.

44. Harootunian, *Things Seen and Unseen*, 423–424. Origuchi was a follower of leading ethnologist Yanagita Kunio (1875–1961). One of Origuchi's best-known texts is "Book of the Dead" (*Shisha no sho*, 1939), inspired by the *Egyptian Book of the Dead*. See James Fujii, *Complicit Fictions: The Subject in Modern Japanese Prose*

Narrative (Berkeley: University of California Press, 1993), 223–256. Origuchi's attempt to fuse nativism *(kokugaku)* with scientific folklore studies, furthermore, inevitably resulted in an unscientific approach, because of the focus in nativism on "the question of origins and ethical practicality." Origuchi's motives in fieldwork would thus be to "find in the present enduring examples of archaic Japanese practices" (Harootunian, *Things Seen and Unseen*, 242, 430). On Yanagita and the Yanagita Boom "in the age of multinational capitalism," see Tamanoi, *Under the Shadow of Nationalism*, 119–136, 197; Harootunian, *Things Seen and Unseen*, 415, 418–435. Harootunian also discusses the work of Origuchi Shinobu and Yanagita Kunio extensively in *Overcome by Modernity: History, Culture, and Community in Interwar Japan* (Princeton, NJ: Princeton University Press, 2000). See also J. Victor Koschmann, "Folklore Studies and the Conservative Anti-Establishment in Modern Japan," in *International Perspectives on Yanagita Kunio and Japanese Folklore Studies*, ed. J. V. Koschmann, Ōiwa Keibo, and Yamashita Shinji (Ithaca, NY: China-Japan Program, Cornell University, 1985), 131–164.

45. Harootunian, *Things Seen and Unseen*, 421–422.

46. Etō's use of landscape here resonates with Karatani Kōjin's theorization of the "discovery of landscape" in the Meiji period. See Karatani, "The Discovery of Landscape," in *Origins of Modern Japanese Literature*, trans. Brett de Bary (Durham, NC: Duke University Press, 1993), 11–44.

47. In an earlier essay on Yasukuni, Etō gave full treatment to this idea of visuality as a link between the living and the dead. See "Seisha no shisen to shisha no shisen," in *Yasukuni ronshū*, 11–49. This anthology of essays by scholars of Shintō, literature, and constitutional law specifically discuss the growing controversy over Yasukuni.

48. Harootunian, *Things Seen and Unseen*, 421–422.

49. Ibid.

50. On the advisory board, the LDP, and the controversy, see Hardacre, *State Shintō*, 150–153. Although the group did not succeed in producing a unified recommendation, one result was the suggestion that a secular memorial be built by the government. As of this writing, no such memorial has been built, although the plan has supporters in the Diet and among the public.

51. Etō and Kobori, *Yasukuni ronshū*, 28.

52. Ibid., 29.

53. See Lawrence Olson, "Intellectuals and the Search for National Identity in Postwar Japan: On Etō Jun" (Occasional Paper No. 15, Wilson Center, Washington, DC, 1983), 27–29; Etō Jun, "One Aspect of the Allied Occupation of Japan: The Censorship Operation and Postwar Literature" (unpublished paper no. 8, Wilson Center, Washington, DC, 1980). The uncensored version of Yoshida's poem "Senkan Yamato no saigo" appears in Etō, *1946 kenpō*, 397–433. The same volume contains several essays about Yoshida's poem and Occupation censorship, 343–394. The "Ujigami" essay is 233–257. See also Richard Minear's translation of the poem in Yoshida Mitsuru, *Requiem for Battleship Yamato* (Annapolis: Naval Institute Press, 1999).

54. *Yasukuni ronshū*, 15. In 2005 a historical museum called "Yamato Museum," which contains a ¹⁄₁₀ scale model of the battleship, opened in the city of Kure to much public acclaim.

55. Edmund Burke, *Reflections on the Revolution in France* (Oxford: Oxford World

Classics, 1999). See also Kevin Doak, "Building National Identity Through Ethnicity: Ethnology in Wartime Japan and After," *Journal of Japanese Studies* 27, no. 1 (Winter 2001): 1–39.

56. *1946 kenpō*, 184.

57. Hardacre, *Shintō and the State*, 35–38.

58. John Nelson, "Social Memory as Ritual Practice: Commemoration Spirits of the Military Dead at Yasukuni Shinto Shrine," *Journal of Asian Studies* 62, no. 2 (May 2003): 461. Harootunian also discusses what he terms a "coalition . . . active in trying to resuscitate State Shinto." "Memory," 145.

59. Harootunian, "Memory," 147.

60. In 2006, long after Etō's death, the Imperial Household Agency released internal documents to the media that suggested the Showa Emperor's disgust with the enshrining of Class A criminals at Yasukuni and his refusal to pay official visits to the shrine.

61. Ibid., 151, 147.

62. Hardacre, *State Shintō*, 22, 171n12.

6. The Execution of Tosaka Jun and Other Tales

1. Ernst Bloch, *The Principle of Hope*, vol. 1, trans. Neville Plaice, Stephen Plaice, and Paul Knight (Cambridge, MA: MIT Press, 1995), 295, 296.

2. Ibid., 297.

3. Gilles Deleuze, *Difference and Repetition*, trans. Paul Patton (New York: Columbia University Press, 1995), 104.

4. Walter Benjamin, *Illuminations*, trans. Harry Zohn (New York: Schocken Books, 1968), 257.

5. Étienne Balibar, "Elements for a Theory of Transition," in Louis Althusser and Étienne Balibar, *Reading Capital*, trans. Ben Brewster (London: Verso, 1998), 283.

6. Nakano Toshio, *Otsuka Hisao to Maruyama Masao* (Tokyo: Aonisha, 2001).

7. Ibid., 188.

8. Imai Nobuhide, *Maruyama Masao to Tosaka Jun* (Tokyo: Ronsosha, 2000), 60.

7. China's "Good War"

1. Studs Terkel, *"The Good War": An American Oral History of World War II* (New York: Pantheon, 1984).

2. Liu Binyan, *People or Monsters? and Other Stories and Reportage from China after Mao*, ed. Perry Link (Bloomington: Indiana University Press, 1983).

3. Arthur Waldron, "China's New Remembering of World War II: The Case of Zhang Zizhong," *Modern Asian Studies* 30, no. 4 (1996).

4. On Cold War frameworks in China's domestic political culture, see Rana Mitter, *A Bitter Revolution: China's Struggle with the Modern World* (Oxford: Oxford University Press, 2004), 190–194, 246–247.

5. A recent example is the comprehensive history of the war by Zhang Xianwen, ed., *Zhongguo Kang-Ri zhanzheng shi* (Nanjing: Nanjing daxue chubanshe, 2001).

6. This necessarily simplifies a complex issue. For a comprehensive discussion, see Waldron, "China's New Remembering." See also Rana Mitter, "Old Ghosts,

New Memories: Changing China's History in the Era of Post-Mao Politics," *Journal of Contemporary History* 38, no. 1 (2003), and "Behind the Scenes at the Museum: Nationalism, History and Memory in the Beijing War of Resistance Museum, 1987–1997," *China Quarterly* 161 (2000).

7. Robin Stummer, "Why Has the Great War Come Back to Haunt Us?" *The Guardian*, weekend supplement (November 7, 1998), 12–23.

8. On Soviet war memory, see Nina Tumarkin, *The Living & the Dead: The Rise and Fall of the Cult of World War II in Russia* (New York: Basic Books, 1994).

9. Song Shiqi and Yan Jingzheng, eds., *Jizhe bixia de kang-Ri zhanzheng* (Beijing: Renmin Ribao Chubanshe, 1995).

10. Chang-tai Hung, *War and Popular Culture: Resistance in Modern China, 1937–1945* (Berkeley: University of California Press, 1994).

11. Fang Jun, *Wo renshide "guizibing"* (Beijing: Zhongguo duiwai fanyi chuban gongsi, 1997).

12. Reflection on contemporary identity through investigation into one's community's experience of World War II has been a recurring phenomenon in the West for some years. One girl's experiences researching her own small town in Germany became the basis of Michael Verhoeven's film *Das Schreckliche Maedchen* (The Nasty Girl, 1990). A stunning recent example, on the Netherlands and its myth of tolerance and resistance, is Simon Kuper, *Ajax, the Dutch, the War: Football in Europe during the Second World War* (London: Orion, 2003).

13. Fan Jianchuan, *Yi ge ren de kangzhan: Cong ide ren de cangpin kan yi chang quan minzu de zhanzheng* (Beijing: Zhongguo duiwai fanyi chuban gongsi, 2000).

14. Fan, *Yi ge ren*, frontispiece.

15. Pei-yi Wu, *The Confucian's Progress: Autobiographical Writings in Traditional China* (Princeton, NJ: Princeton University Press, 1990).

16. One such author is the noted journalist Zou Taofen. See Wen-hsin Yeh, "Progressive Journalism and Shanghai's Petty Urbanites: Zou Taofen and the Shenghuo Weekly, 1926–1945," in *Shanghai Sojourners*, ed. Frederic Wakeman Jr. and Wen-hsin Yeh (Berkeley: Institute of East Asian Studies, 1992).

17. An outstanding analysis of the development of the genre in the first half of the twentieth century is Charles A. Laughlin, *Chinese Reportage: The Aesthetics of Historical Experience* (Durham, NC: Duke University Press, 2002).

18. Fang, *Wo renshide "guizibing,"* 286.

19. Ibid., 267.

20. Ibid., 12.

21. Ibid., 287.

22. Qianyan, Foreword, in Song and Yan, *Jizhe bixia*.

23. Fang, *Wo renshide "guizibing,"* 3.

24. Ibid.

25. See, for example, John Gittings, *Real China: From Cannibalism to Karaoke* (London: Simon and Schuster, 1996).

26. Fang, *Wo renshide "guizibing,"* 24.

27. Zheng Yi, *Scarlet Memorial: Tales of Cannibalism in Modern China*, trans. T. P. Sym (Boulder, CO: Westview Press, 1996).

28. Ibid., 149.

29. *Dikang* (Resistance, issue 12), September 26, 1937.

30. Song and Yan, *Jizhe bixia*, 368.

31. Ibid., 374.

32. Ibid., 375.

33. Fan, *Yi ge ren*, 73.

34. Ibid., 136.

35. Ibid., 75.

36. Ibid., 83.

37. In recent years, scholarship on Holocaust responsibility has moved further away from blaming leaders and showing the responsibility of ordinary citizens; for example, Robert Gellately, *Backing Hitler: Consent and Coercion in Nazi Germany* (Oxford: Oxford University Press, 2001).

38. Fang, *Wo renshide "guizibing,"* 284–285.

39. Ibid., 73ff.

40. Waldron, "China's New Remembering."

41. Fan, *Yi ge ren*, 104–105.

42. Ibid., 109, 123.

43. Ibid., 123.

44. Ibid., 159. Regional pride has also affected the way in which Northeastern China (formerly Manchuria) has reassessed its history of the war years, noting, for instance, that it endured Japanese occupation from 1931, six years longer than the rest of China.

45. Fan, *Yi ge ren*, 219–220.

46. Ibid., 105.

47. Ibid., 107.

48. Ibid., 4.

49. Ibid., 5.

8. Remembering the Century of Humiliation

1. The calculation of this era begins with the first Opium War of 1839 and runs to the end of World War II, the victory over Japanese imperial fascism.

2. For example, at the Museum of the Revolution on Tiananmen Square in Beijing, the grand narrative display of the Chinese revolution has been dismantled and put into storage. In its stead is a wax museum of great figures of twentieth century China.

3. Pierre Nora, "Between Memory and History: Les Lieux de Memoire," *Representations* 26 (Spring 1989): 7–24.

4. Ibid., 19.

5. For a fuller discussion, see James L. Hevia, *English Lessons: The Pedagogy of Imperialism in Nineteenth Century China* (Durham, NC: Duke University Press, 2003).

6. Paul Cohen, *History in Three Keys* (New York: Columbia University Press, 1997), 242–243.

7. Cohen provides a helpful catalogue of many of these publications in "Remembering and Forgetting National Humiliation in Twentieth Century China," *Twentieth Century China* 27, no. 2 (April 2002). One of the earliest of these was by Shen Wenjun, who published *A Short History of National Humiliations (Guochi xiaoshi)* in 1910.

8. Kang Youwei, *Yuanmingyuan* 2, 17, and 158–159.

9. Jonathan Spence, *The Gate of Heavenly Peace* (New York: Penguin, 1982), 47.

10. L.C. Arlington and W. Lewisohn, *In Search of Old Peking* (1935; reprint, Hong Kong: Oxford University Press, 1987).

11. Steve S. Smith, *Like Cattle and Horses* (Durham, NC: Duke University Press, 2002), 78, 197.

12. The list I work from can be found in National Archives and Records Administration, Record Group 127–138, Box 3.

13. *Selected Works of Mao Tsetung*, vol. 5 (Peking: Foreign Language Press, 1977), 17.

14. The work was first published in 1952 and in English three years later.

15. The latter assessment is well represented in Albert Feuerwerker, ed., *History in Communist China* (Cambridge, MA: MIT Press, 1968). More recently, Cohen has discussed the mythologization of the past; see *History in Three Keys*.

16. Franz Fanon, *The Wretched of the Earth* (New York: Grove Press, 1963).

17. There are now twenty-eight World Heritage sites in China; for a complete list see *http://whc.unesco.org*.

18. I have discussed this issue in greater detail in James Hevia, "World Heritage, National Culture and the Restoration of Chengde," *positions: east asia cultures critique* 9, no. 1 (Spring 2001): 219–244, where the focus is on the Bishu shanzhuang, the Qing summer palace at Chengde and its link to the UNESCO World Heritage Project.

19. See Geremie Barmé, "The Garden of Perfect Brightness: A Life in Ruins," *East Asian History* 11 (1996): 142–154.

20. The Beijing-based Zhuda Cumputer Company, which is making such an effort; see Barmé, *The Garden of Perfect Brightness*.

21. See, for example, Wang, ed., *Yuangming yuan*, 2 vols. (Beijing: Beijing Publishing House, 1999); and Barmé, "Garden," 153. There is also a project on the Internet where a virtual Yuanming yuan is being built; see *http://www.cs.ubc.ca*.

22. The original photographs are in Colombe Samoyault-Verlet, *Le Museé chinois de l'impétrice Eugénie* (Paris: Editions de la Réunion des músee nationaux 1994), 21, 24–25, 52, 59, and 67. I am grateful to Craig Clunas for being kind enough to send me a copy of this publication and to Regine Thiriez for arranging a special visit to the museum in 1997.

23. See Hevia, *English Lessons*, chapter 10 for a fuller discussion.

24. See the *New York Times*, April 29, May 1, and May 3, 2001.

9. Frontiers of Memory

1. As is evident in the new museum opened in 2003 in the Nanjing Zongtongfu (Chiang Kai-shek's former presidential palace).

2. Junior Middle School *(Guomin Zhongxue)* history textbook, Book 1 (Taipei: Guoli Bianyi Guan, 1987), 2–4.

3. See Edward Vickers, "Defining the Boundaries of 'Chineseness'—Tibet, Mongolia, Taiwan and Hong Kong in Mainland History Textbooks," in *What Shall We Tell the Children? International Perspectives on History Textbooks*, ed. Stuart Foster and Keith Crawford (Greenwich, CT: Information Age, 2005).

4. *Gaoji Zhongxue Lishi*, vol. 3 (Taipei: Guoli Bianyi Guan, 1985), 113.

5. Ibid., 114–119.

6. Ibid., 25–37.

7. Ibid., 26.

8. Ibid., 43–44.

9. Ibid., 33.

10. Ibid., 106.

11. For a fuller discussion of Taiwan's recent history, see Murray A. Rubinstein, "Political Taiwanisation and Pragmatic Diplomacy: The Eras of Chiang Ching-kuo and Lee Teng-hui," in *Taiwan: A New History*, ed. Murray A. Rubinstein (Armonk, NY: M. E. Sharpe, 1999), 436–480.

12. *Renshi Taiwan: Lishi*, 3rd ed. (Taipei: Guoli Bianyi Guan, 2001), 4.

13. On history textbooks and national identity in Taiwan, see Stephane Corcuff, "The Symbolic Dimension of Democratization and the Transition of National Identity under Lee Teng-hui," in *Memories of the Future: National Identity Issues and the Search for a New Taiwan*, ed. Stephane Corcuff (Armonk, NY: M. E. Sharpe, 2002), 72–101. See also Stephane Corcuff, "History Manuals, National Identity Politics and Ethnic Introspection in Taiwan," and Mei-hui Liu, Li-ching Hong, and Edward Vickers, "Identity Issues in Taiwan's History Curriculum," in *History Education and National Identity in East Asia*, ed. Edward Vickers and Alisa Jones (New York: Routledge, 2005).

14. *Yi Shan Kai Xiang Ya Zhou de Men: Guoli gugong bowuyuan nanbu fenyuan yuanjing* ("A Door that Opens onto Asia": Plan for the National Palace Museum) (Taipei: National Palace Museum, 2003), 4.

15. One prominent individual who falls into the latter category is Huang Kuang-nan, Director of the National Museum of History (interviewed by the author on January 20, 2004).

16. *Gaoji Zhongxue Lishi*, vol. 3 (Taipei: Guoli Bianyi Guan, 1997), 165–166.

17. *Renshi Taiwan: Shehui bian* (Knowing Taiwan: Society, 2nd ed.) (Taipei: Guoli Bianyi Guan, 2000), 60.

18. For example, a pamphlet entitled "Explaining 228" *(jiedu er er ba)* printed by the Chi Mei Cultural Foundation and distributed by DPP activists in Tainan during the 2004 presidential election campaign (author's own collection).

19. See Corcuff, "History Manuals, National Identity Politics and Ethnic Introspection."

20. Edward Vickers, *In Search of An Identity: The Politics of History Education in Hong Kong, 1960s–2004* (Hong Kong: Comparative Education Research Centre, 2005).

21. Robert Edmondson, "The February 28 Incident and National Identity," in Corcuff, *Memories of the Future*, 25–46; also Stephane Corcuff, "Taiwan's 'Mainlanders,' New Taiwanese?" in *Memories of the Future*, 163–195.

22. Interview with Director Hsieh, Taipei 228 Peace Memorial Museum, January 13, 2004.

23. See Ian Buruma, *Wages of Guilt: Memories of War in Germany and Japan* (New York: Farrar, Straus and Giroux, 1994).

24. Interview with Director Hsieh.

25. Ma Ying-jeou, "Mayor's Foreword," in *1998–1999 Yearbook, 228 Peace Memorial Museum* (Taipei: Taipei er er ba jinianguan, 1999), 4.

26. Edmondson, "The February 28 Incident and National Identity," 42.

27. Andrew Wilson, *The Ukrainians—Unexpected Nation* (New Haven, CT: Yale University Press, 2002), 21–39.

28. *Renshi Taiwan: Lishi,* 66–81.

29. Ibid., 65.

30. Kobayashi Yoshinori, *Taiwan Lun* (Theory of Taiwan) (Taipei: Qian Wei, 2001), 55.

31. Tu Cheng-sheng, *Ilha Formosa: Taiwan's Emergence on the World Scene in the 17th Century* (Taipei: Media Sphere Communications, 2003), 26.

32. Tu, *Ilha Formosa,* 63.

33. Michael Stainton, "The Politics of Taiwan Aboriginal Origins," in Rubenstein, *Taiwan: A New History,* 41.

34. Ernest Gellner, "Do Nations Have Navels?" *Nations and Nationalism* 10 (1996): 366–370.

35. See Liu, Hong, and Vickers, "Identity Issues in Taiwan's History Curriculum."

36. A point underlined by Rana Mitter in *A Bitter Revolution: China's Struggle with the Modern World* (Oxford: Oxford University Press, 2004), 305–308.

37. Wang Ming-ke, *Hua Xia Bian Yuan: Lishi jiyi yu zuqun rentong* (China's Frontiers: Historical Memory and Communal Identity) (Taipei: Yun Chen Ye Kan, 1997), 426.

10. The Korean War after the Cold War

1. The views expressed in this chapter are those of the authors and do not necessarily reflect the official policy or position of the Army, the Department of Defense, or the U.S. government.

2. Rana Mitter also notes that a similar shift has taken place in the contemporary treatment of the Second Sino-Japanese War (1937–45) in post–Cold War China. See Rana Mitter, "Old Ghosts, New Memories: China's Changing War History in the Era of Post-Mao Politics," *Journal of Contemporary History* 38, no. 1 (2003): 116–131. See also Arthur Waldron, "China's New Remembering of World War II: The Case of Chang Zizhong," *Modern Asian Studies* 30, no. 4 (1996): 869–899.

3. Choi Jang-jip, "Political Cleavages in South Korea," in *State and Society in Contemporary Korea,* ed. Hagen Koo (Ithaca, NY: Cornell University Press, 1993), 23.

4. Ibid., 23.

5. Other campaigns include the 1968 Charter of National Education *(kukmin kyoyuk hŏnjang),* the New Spirit Movement *(saemaŭm undong)* begun in conjunction with the New Village Movement *(saemaŭl undong)* in 1970, and the 1972 Yushin reforms.

6. Park Chung Hee, "On the Basis of the 'Second Economy,'" speech in commemoration of the 4th Export Day on November 30, 1967, in *Major Speeches by Korea's Park Chung Hee,* ed. Shin Bum Shik (Seoul: Hollym Corp., 1970), 150–151.

7. Park Chung Hee, "Let Us Have the Courage to Fight the Enemy, Risking Our Lives," speech at the activation ceremony of the Homeland Reserve Forces on

1 April 1968, in *Major Speeches by Korea's Park Chung Hee*, ed. Shin Bum Shik (Seoul: Hollym Corp., 1970), 230–231.

8. It should be pointed out that genealogy of the slogan "fight while working and work while fighting" goes back to Meiji Japan when *fukoku kyōhei* (rich nation, strong army) became a prominent and measurable vision for modern Japan. The concept also figured prominently in Kim Il Sung's nation building ideology as when he stated in a major party speech on October 5, 1966, "How to combine economic construction with the building of national defences [*sic*] is one of the fundamental questions on which the success of the building of socialism and communism depends." This notion actually had an even earlier incarnation as Kim Il Sung noted that "our Party set forth the line of carrying on economic construction in parallel with defence [*sic*] building already at the Fifth Plenary Meeting of its Fourth Central Committee in 1962." "The Present Situation and the Tasks of Our Party (Excerpt): Report to the Conference of the Worker's Party of Korea," October 5, 1966, in *On Juche in Our Revolution*, vol. 1 (Pyongyang: Foreign Languages Publishing House, 1975), 568–570. The South Korean slogan had many variations. The earliest example found is from a February 9, 1968 speech at a meeting of university presidents: *hanp'yŏn ŭro kŏnsŏl hamyŏnsŏ hanp'yŏn ŭro panggong t'ujaeng* (*Pak Chŏng-hŭi taet'ongryŏng yŏnsŏl munjip*), vol. 5 (Seoul: Daetongryŏng pisosŏl, 1969), 83. Other versions include *ilhamyŏnsŏ ssaugo ssaumyŏnsŏ ilhanŭn, ssaumyŏnsŏ ilhago ilhamyŏnsŏ ssauja, minjok charip ŭi chagak chawi chŏngsin* (realizing national economic autonomy, spirit of self-defense); *ilhamyŏ ssaugo ssaumyŏ ilhanŭngŏt, ilmyŏn chŏnjaeng ilmyŏn kŏnsŏl* (war on one hand, construction on the other). What is interesting is that there was no standard slogan, but a concept that could be expressed in a variety of ways.

9. DPRK industry grew by 25 percent per annum in the decade after the war and about 14 percent from 1965 to 1978. Official figures put annual growth rate in industry at 41.7 percept for the Three-Year Plan (1953–56) and 36.6 percent for the succeeding Five-Year Plan (1957–61). These plans stressed wartime reconstruction and development of major industries, which were given an added boost by massive Soviet aid that pushed the economy along at "world-beating growth rates." South Korea's economy during this same period, on the other hand, was largely dependent on American aid, which accounted for nearly 50 percent of the civil budget, 80 percent of the available foreign exchange, and 75 percent of the South's military budget. See Bruce Cumings, *Korea's Place in the Sun* (New York: W. W. Norton, 1997), 310. For nearly two decades after the Korean War, "the North's growth rate far outdistanced the South's, striking fear into the heart of American officials who wondered if Seoul would ever get off the mark" (Cumings, *Korea's Place in the Sun*, 424). It was only by the early 1970s that ROK's economy, under the leadership of Park Chung Hee, began to outpace the DPRK's. This feat alone makes Park the most revered South Korean leader, despite his dismal record of human rights abuses.

10. Emphasis ours. Park Chung Hee, "Peace Is a Pre-requisite to Unification," June 23, 1974, in *Toward Peaceful Unification: Selected Speeches by President Park Chung Hee*, ed. The Secretariat for the President (Seoul: Kwangmyong, 1976), 98–100.

11. Park Chung Hee, "New Foreign Policy for Peace and Unification," special statement made on June 23, 1973 in *Toward Peaceful Unification: Selected Speeches by President Park Chung Hee*, ed. The Secretariat for the President, 78–79.

12. Park Chung Hee, "New Year's Press Conference," 14 January 1975, in Taet'ongryŏng pisŏsil, *Pak Chŏng-hŭi taet'ongryŏng yŏnsŏl munjip* (Collection of President Park Chung Hee's Speeches), vol. 12 (Seoul: Daetongryŏng pisosŏl, 1976), 34.

13. Don Oberdorfer, *The Two Koreas: A Contemporary History* (Reading, MA: Addison-Wesley, 1997), 197.

14. The winter of 1991 inaugurated a period of great progress for North–South Korean relations. On December 13, 1991, North and South Korea concluded the first of the two historic accords entitled "an Agreement on Reconciliation, Non-aggression, and Exchanges in Cooperation." In the second of the two accords, entitled "Joint Declaration on the Denuclearization of the Korean Peninsula," North Korea agreed not to "test, produce, receive, posses, store, deploy or use nuclear weapons." The promises stipulated in the December Accords, however, were short-lived. In the wake of the 1990 Gulf Wars and the discovery of Iraq's nuclear program, the International Atomic Energy Agency (IAEA) decided to make North Korea the first test case of a more vigorous inspection procedure against nuclear proliferation (see note 24). North Korea balked at the new and more rigid requirements set by the IAEA inspections team, precipitating the 1994 crisis. For an excellent overview of the history of the North Korean proliferation crisis, see Oberdorfer, *The Two Koreas;* Leon S. Sigal, *Disarming Strangers: Nuclear Diplomacy with North Korea* (Princeton, NJ: Princeton University Press, 1998); and Selig Harrison, *Korea Endgame: A Strategy for Reunification and U.S Disengagement* (Princeton, NJ: Princeton University Press, 2002).

15. Sheila Miyoshi Jager, *Narratives of Nation-Building* (Armonk, NY: M. E. Sharpe, 2003), chapter 7.

16. Ibid., 132.

17. *Chŏnjaeng kinyŏmgwan chŏnsi yŏnch'u kyehoek* (Exhibition Display Plan for the War Memorial) (Seoul, 1990), 342 (hereafter *CKCYK*).

18. Recent scholarship on the Taejon massacres suggest that there were actually two massacres committed in the Taejon vicinity, one of which occurred in July 1950 and perpetrated by Syngman Rhee's forces, and the one described by the U.S. Army as having occurred in late September 1950 committed by the KPA.

19. For a detailed catalogue of these and similar NKPA atrocities see Paul D. Chinnery, *Korean Atrocity: Forgotten War Crimes 1950–53* (Annapolis: Naval Institute Press, 2000).

20. *CKCYK, 135.*

21. Paul Fussell, *The Great War and Modern Memory* (Oxford: Oxford University Press, 1975), 179.

22. Rana Mitter, "Behind the Scenes at the Museum: Nationalism, History and Memory in the Beijing War of Resistance Museum, 1987–1997," *The China Quarterly* 161 (March 2000): 278–293.

23. *New York Times,* July 1, 2003.

24. Until 1991, the International Atomic Energy Agency (IAEA) had limited itself to overseeing civilian nuclear facilities and materials that Nuclear Non-Proliferation Treaty (NPT) signatories reported in voluntary declarations to the agency. However, the aftermath of the Gulf War exposed that Iraq, which was a NPT signatory, had carried on "an intensive and sophisticated nuclear weapons program at secret sites to those being inspected by the agency" (Oberdorfer, *The*

Two Koreas, 267). Accused of ineffectiveness and timidity, the IAEA, under the directorship of Hans Blix, underwent revolutionary changes in both personnel and attitude. After 1991, the IAEA established the unprecedented right to accept intelligence information supplied by the Untied States and other member states in its investigations, including "the right to demand access to suspicious facilities through mandatory 'special inspections'" (Oberdorfer, *The Two Koreas*, 267).

IAEA inspection of North Korea's nuclear program was the first test case of its new hard-line approach. A signatory of the NPT since 1985, North Korea had agreed to new IAEA inspections of its nuclear facilities at Yŏngbyŏn as part of its historic December 13, 1991 accords with South Korea. But whereas inspectors had previously been allowed only in the area of Yŏngbyŏn's research reactor, the IAEA, determined not be embarrassed again, came to North Korea in May 1992 well briefed by U.S. intelligence reports and aerial photographs. They found large discrepancies in the reports made by North Korea about the amounts of processed of plutonium it had officially declared, and the estimated amounts that the IAEA had come up with in the tests performed at its laboratory in Vienna. As a result, the euphoria that had resulted from opening North Korea's nuclear program to international inspections in 1992 soon gave way to suspicion, antagonism, and eventually crisis.

When North Korea declared its withdrawal from the NPT on March 12, 1993, the Kim Young Sam administration was in its fifteenth day in office. Faced with the first post–Cold War nuclear proliferation crisis, the Kim government reacted to the events by instituting a hard-line approach, reversing the conciliatory trends of the Roh Tae Woo administration. As tensions began to mount to crisis level by the spring of 1994, Washington leaders began to draw up war plans for another bloody struggle on the Korean peninsula.

In a last—ditch effort to save the situation, former president Jimmy Carter flew to Pyongyang on June 15, 1994. There, he negotiated a deal to temporarily freeze North Korea's nuclear program until the completion of a third round of U.S.-DPRK nuclear negotiations. He also received concessions from Kim Il Sung to allow the two remaining IAEA inspectors, who were scheduled to be expelled from the country, to remain at the site. In a sudden and entirely unexpected reversal of fortune, the immense danger and tension in the Korean peninsula that had almost led the United States to the brink of war was suddenly lifted as North Korea agreed once again to come to the table to begin new U.S.-DPRK and North-South negotiations. As a result of the Carter mission, Pyongyang promised to freeze its nuclear program while negotiations proceeded.

These negotiations eventually led to the singing of the October 1994 Agreed Framework. Under the Agreed Framework, the DPRK pledged to remain a party to the NPT and to freeze its nuclear program. In exchange, the United States promised to move toward political and economic normalization, an exchange of liaison offices, and the lowering of barriers to trade and investment. It was also agreed that a U.S.-organized consortium would provide North Korea with two proliferation-resistant light water reactors and a supply of heavy fuel oil in the interim.

25. See Oberdorfer, *The Two Koreas*, 374. Following the death of North Korean leader Kim Il Sung in June 1994 and reports of mass starvation in North Korea the following year, policymakers in Washington and other world capitals began to focus on the imminent collapse of the failing state. It was during this period of renewed

engagement with North Korea, after predictions of Pyongyang's inevitable collapse had failed to materialize, that Kim Dae Jung was elected into office in December 1998, initiating a completely new diplomatic approach toward North Korea.

Meanwhile, as delays in the promised oil shipments began to fall behind schedule, North Korea, as early as 1997, began to cheat. Working in secret, North Korean scientists began to devise a second method to acquire fissile material. Rather than extracting plutonium from spent fuel, they tried to produce weapons-grade uranium from natural uranium under a new Highly Enriched Uranium program (HEU). This technology is distinct from the plutonium-based weapons program that precipitated the first North Korean nuclear crisis in 1991 that had led to the signing of the 1994 Agreed Framework. In June 2002, the CIA sent an intelligence report to the White House asserting that North Korea was engaged in building an HEU program with the help of Pakistani technology. Armed with CIA intelligence reports, Assistant Secretary of State for East Asian Affairs James Kelley confronted the North Koreans in October 2002. To everyone's surprise, Pyongyang admitted to the existence of the covert nuclear program. The United States and its partners responded to Pyongyang's outright admission in a November 14, 2002 announcement that all oil shipments would cease unless the DPRK agreed to halt its covert program. Refusing to bow, Pyongyang raised the ante and said it would reactivate the facilities frozen under the now defunct 1994 Agreed Framework. Pyongyang also announced its withdrawal from the NPT on January 10, 2003.

In the midst of this growing crisis, the United States launched its invasion of Iraq in March 2003. Pyongyang responded to the "shock and awe" of the United States' rapid military advance through Iraq by suddenly dropping its demand for face-to-face talks with Washington and agreeing to multilateral talks (the first six-nation talks aimed at ending the crisis took place in Beijing in August 27, 2003). Meanwhile, North Korea denied the existence of the clandestine program to produce a uranium bomb—a statement that contradicted U.S. intelligence and Pyongyang's own admission in October 2002. North Korea's denial, coming on the heels of U.S. intelligence failure to find weapons of mass destruction in Iraq, posed a major problem for the Bush administration as it sought the complete dismantling of North Korea's nuclear weapons program. In January 2004, China announced that it was not completely convinced of the existence of North Korea's uranium program. These efforts to downplay the revelation about North Korea's uranium enrichment program suggested that Beijing was preparing the diplomatic groundwork to merely freezing the nuclear facility at Yongbyŏn, which was shut down in 1994, leaving intact the issue of uranium enrichment, a position wholly unacceptable to the Bush administration. See Walter C. Clemens Jr., "Beyond the North Korean Nuclear Crisis: Peace in Korea? Lessons from Cold War Détente," *Confrontation and Innovation on the Korean Peninsula*, Korea Economic Institute (December 2003): 1–17. See also Seymour M. Hersh, "The Cold Test," *New Yorker*, January 27, 2003.

26. For a discussion of Kim Dae Jung's politics see Jager, *Narratives of Nation-Building*, chapter 8.

27. Wu Hung, "Tiananmen Square: A Political History of Monuments," *Representations* 35 (Summer 1991): 84–117.

28. Jager, *Narratives of Nation-Building*, chapter 7.

29. Ibid., 136.

30. In the 1999 blockbuster film *Swiri*, for example, which portrays a love relationship between a North Korean female spy (played by Kim Yun-chin) and a
South Korean intelligence agent (played by Han Sŏk-kyu), the North Korean
characters in the film are all imbued with strikingly humane characteristics. The
tragedy of the plot rests entirely with the tragedy of the division. The climax of the
film happens at the end of the film when the two lovers have to face each other as
enemies. The passion the lovers share for one another cannot transcend the political reality of the division, for which no one party is to blame, and in the end, they
are left no choice but to strike the other down.

Following on the enormous success of *Swiri*, the acclaimed film *Joint Security
Area* (2000), about the friendship of North and South Korean soldiers, also casts
the North Korean protagonist in a remarkably positive light. The film begins with
a scene of a South Korean soldier, on duty at the DMZ, who has strayed from his
group and has accidentally stepped on a land mine. Saved by a North Korean soldier, a deep friendship is soon struck up between the two men and their two
friends. However, like *Swiri*, this film also ends in tragedy as the soldiers' friendship cannot overcome the political division of the two Koreas, and they end up
killing each other and themselves. In each case, North Koreans are portrayed, like
their Southern counterparts, as victims of the division, which has turned friends
into enemies and lovers into assassins.

31. In this tale, the North Wind and the Sun have a test of strength to determine which one of them could strip the clothes of a traveling man first. After several tries, the wind gives up. It is the sun that eventually wins the bet as the traveler
could no longer stand the heat and takes off his coat.

32. Harrison, *Korean Endgame*, 83.

33. *Han'gyŏre Sinmun*, July 28, 2003.

34. 6/25 Chŏnjaeng chohyŏngmul chemaksik haengsa annaesŏ (Unveiling
Ceremony of the Korean War Monument Guidebook), 5.

35. Ibid., 5.

36. Hyung Il Pai, *Constructing "Korean" Origins: A Critical Review of Archeology,
Historiography, and the Racial Myth in Korean State Formation Theories* (Cambridge,
MA: Harvard University Press, 2000), 18.

37. Ibid., 18.

38. 6/25 Chŏnjaeng chohyŏngmul chemaksik haengsa annaesŏ (Unveiling
Ceremony of the Korean War Monument Guidebook), 5.

39. The Associated Press broke a story in September 1999 alleging that U.S.
soldiers had opened fire on hundred of civilians at the start of the Korean War in
July 1950. The report, which won the 2000 Pulitzer Prize, provided first-hand accounts of U.S. Army veterans who told the reporters of deliberate shootings of Korean refugees, many of them women and children and older men, under a bridge at
Nogŭn-ri, a hamlet about 100 miles southeast of Seoul. Not since My Lai has the
U.S. Army confronted such serious charges of war crimes. Immediately after the
story broke, then Secretary of Defense William Cohen ordered the Army Inspector General to investigate (the culmination of which resulted in a 300-page report entitled *Department of the Army Inspector General: No Gun Ri Review*, January
2001). Even before the report was published, however, doubts about the veracity of
the veterans' testimony began to be raised. Joseph Galloway was one of the first

journalists to investigate the Nogŭn-ri story and found that the principle source of the AP report, Edward Daily, had not been at Nogŭn-ri when the reported massacres took place. Similar inconsistencies were raised by the witness accounts of other veterans (*U.S. News & World Report*, May 22, 2000). The AP reporters, Charles J. Hanely, Sang-hun Choe, and Martha Mendoza, responded to these criticisms in their book, *The Bridge at No Gun Ri: A Hidden History from the Korean War* (New York: Henry Holt, 2001). See also Robert L. Bateman, *No Gun Ri: A Military History of the Korean War Incident* (Stackpole Books, 2002).

Another event that has also received a great deal of attention in South Korea after the Nogŭn-ri story broke in 1999 was the Yŏsu and Sunchŏn uprisings in 1948. While the anticommunist president Syngman Rhee (Yi Sŭng-man) and his American supporters attempted to create a separate Southern regime in 1948, a group of left-wing activists on Cheju Island and in Cholla province instigated mass protests. The government responded with force, leaving an estimated 30,000 civilians dead. Shortly after Roh Mu Hyun took office in February 2003, a group of twelve lawmakers began deliberating a set of special bills on the massacres said to have occurred at the hands of the South Korean government under U.S. occupation. The committee, led by Rep. Song Kwang-ho, aimed at getting the "true" picture of the uprisings. The Assembly move came after President Roh apologized on behalf of the national government for the April 3 Cheju Uprising. It was the first time an incumbent president made an official apology for the 1948 Cheju massacres.

40. See, for example, Pak Myŏng-nim's *Hanguk 1950: Chŏnjaeng kwa p'yŏnghwa* (Korea 1950: War and Peace) (Seoul: Nanam ch'ulp'an, 2002). A respected historian who teaches at Yŏnse University, Pak currently serves as an adviser for Roh Mu Hyun on North-South affairs. He is also a strong advocate of making July 27–August 15 a "peace celebration period" to change the focus of the Armistice Day celebration beyond the Korean War. The book, which is nearly 800 pages long, incorporates not only the new materials on Nogŭn-ri but other civilian massacres committed by North and South Korean military as well as those allegedly committed by U.S. forces in a section titled "War and Civilians: Unification, Eruption, and Massacre" (chapter 6, 330–339). In his conclusion he writes that as long as North and South Korea continue to confront each other, the two Koreas will not be able to "overcome Nogŭn-ri, indeed (the two Koreas) will remain sitting in place at the moment before Nogŭn-ri" (780–781). There is more than enough blood to implicate all parties. Pak contends that the memory of this blood-letting must be overcome through some sort of a truth and amnesty reconciliation process similar to what was implemented in South Africa. Otherwise, he warns, the Korean people will be unable to overcome their wartime animosity, which will hinder the reunification process. Also imbedded in Pak's account is ultimate U.S. responsibility and culpability in the atrocities committed by the South Korean military and police.

41. Ibid. See also Kim Chi-hyŏng, *Nambuk ŭl innun hyŏndaesa sanch'aek* (A Stroll Through Modern History Beyond the North and South Division) (Seoul: Tosŏ chu'ulpan sŏnin, 2003). The title refers to a unified history of modern Korea. One of the striking features of this collection of essays is the extremely positive and human portrayal of North Korean leaders Kim Il Sung and Kim Jong Il (Kim Jong-il). Newspapers and magazines in the immediate aftermath of the AP account

of Nogŭn-ri were divided along political lines, a process that actually started even
before the September 1999 AP Nogŭn-ri report. In June 1999 the conservative
monthly *Wŏlgan chosŏn* published as part of a series of articles marking the fiftieth
anniversary of the beginning of the war, a long article detailing North Korean massacre of South Korean soldiers in hiding and patients at the Seoul National University Hospital in Seoul on June 28, 1950 immediately after the city was captured
(June 1999, 118–130). When the AP report was published, the Left-liberal newspapers immediately linked it to a wider issue of U.S. responsibility and culpability
and strongly supported the call for apology and compensation. (See, for example,
Tong-a ilbo articles on September 30 and October 1. Also see the October 15 interview with Stanley Roth, who was then the Assistant Secretary of State for East
Asia, which portrays a recalcitrant, skeptical, and even defiant American attitude
toward U.S. involvement in the killing of civilians during the war; and the *Chungang ilbo* story and editorial on October 1 that unequivocally points to U.S. culpability in Nogŭn-ri and other alleged massacres and pointedly calls for U.S. apology
and compensation for the alleged killings. On the other hand, the conservative
press, while covering the AP story, did so in a matter of fact manner that did not
immediately point to U.S. culpability and instead highlighted the possible miti-
gating circumstances, such as untrained troops, fear of North Korean soldiers, and
confusion caused by North Koreans disguising as civilians, to try to conceptualize
the incident as something comprehensible while acknowledging its tragedy that required apology and compensation if proven true. (See, for example, *Chosŏn ilbo* stories on September 30 and October 11, 1999 and its editorial on October 1, 1999
that contrasts with the *Chungang ilbo* editorial mentioned above. Also *Han'guk ilbo*'s
side story on the U.S. unit involved in the Nogŭn-ri incident, the 7th Cavalry,
which is historically contextualized by recalling not only the destruction of the unit
at the Little Big Horn, but also its leading role throughout the Korean War at
Inch'ŏn and the advance north where it incurred many casualties. The thrust of the
article is to portray the unit as a positive contributor to the war.) The liberal press,
on the other hand, continued their attacks with further accounts of U.S. complicity
in atrocities committed against South Korean civilians, with additional stories of
deliberate destruction of bridges (at Waegwan and Koryŏng) in early August 1950
that blocked refugees from moving south, and another air attack incident at Kwegaegul in January 1951. (See *Chungang ilbo*, October 15, 1999 for the Waegwan
and Koryŏng story and *Tong-a ilbo*, December 3, 1999 for the Kwegaegul story.) In
January 2000 the liberal press broke a major story based on newly discovered documents and photographs from the U.S. National Archives that graphically show
the execution of 1800 political prisoners by the South Korean military and police,
an incident that was long believed to be true but unsupported by documentary evidence. The number believed to have been killed, according to these press reports,
was roughly 8,000 people, although this figure is not corroborated by documentary
evidence (*Han'gyŏrae 21*, January 20, 2000, 20–27). Another liberal journal, *Mal*,
stoked the flames of anti-Americanism further with a series of articles in its February 2000 issue that provide both documentary and photographic evidence of
killings of civilian political prisoners, allegedly Communists, by South Korean
forces in Seoul in April 1950 before the war began, at Taejŏn in early July 1950,
and at Taegu in August 1950 and April 1951. Both the January and the February
stories strongly implicated the United States with photos showing American offi-

cers calmly observing the executions. The April 1950 incident is made more significant by the fact that it allegedly occurred before the war while the country was under peaceful civilian control, and yet the executions were carried out by the South Korean military police. Also implicated in the killings is Syngman Rhee, who is portrayed as being in cahoots with the United States because purging the Left strengthened his dictatorial hold on power. While not the last in this Left-Right debate about wartime culpability, one additional example demonstrates the unending cycle of the accusatory debate, the kind of cycle that Pak Myŏng-nim calls for an end. In June 2000 *Wŏlgan Chosŏn* published a long article on the North Korean massacre of several thousand civilians and POWs, South Korean and American, at Taejŏn in late September 1950. It happened as the North Korean forces reeled back from the success of the Inch'ŏn landing (*Wŏlgan chosŏn*, June 2000, 264–287). This was a direct counter to the liberal media coverage of the South Korean killings at Taejŏn in July 1950. The article also made a semantic distinction between "massacre," which characterizes what the North Koreans committed, and "execution" of prisoners by South Koreans. The execution of political prisoners is indirectly justified, because their arrests, as menaces to national security, were legal under South Korean law at the time (and for long afterwards). The debate is far from over. Though Pak Myŏng-nim's discussion leans toward the liberal interpretation and U.S. culpability, his work does signify that perhaps South Koreans are thinking about moving beyond the memories of fratricidal killings. What has not changed is the critical stance taken toward the United States, which has actually become more pronounced in contemporary historical writings about the war. See the last section on anti-Americanism.

42. *Han'guk ilbo*, October 2, 1999.

43. On April 20, 1998, the South Korean government formally announced it would grant 38 million won ($27,400) to each South Korean woman forced into sexual slavery for the Japanese military during World War II. While the government spokesperson said the Korean government would not seek compensation from Japan, it demanded an apology from Tokyo for the sexual slavery. The government measure was approved in a cabinet meeting presided over by President Kim Dae Jung at the Blue House. Kim told the cabinet meeting that the government made "the right decision to pay money to help the victims." He reiterated, however, "this does not mean withdrawing a demand for the Japanese government to accept historical and moral responsibility for the comfort women issue." The South Korean government, in a statement released by the Ministry of Foreign Affairs and Trade, urged Japan to make a heartfelt apology. "Japan should express deep regret for the inhuman acts committed by imperial Japan during World War II, and apologize thereon" the statement said. *Asian Political News*, April 27, 1998.

44. *Korea Times*, February 27, 2003.

45. Yu Pyŏng-mun, "Chŏngjŏn hyŏpchŏng i anira chŏknarahan him ŭi taech'i ka chŏnjaeng makko itta" (War Is Prevented by Raw Power, Not the Armistice), *Minjok 21* (August 2003): 118.

46. Ch'oe Ch'ŏl-yŏng, "Pyŏnhwa hanŭn nambuk kwangye wa chŏngjŏn hyŏpchŏng ŭi taean (Changing North-South Korea Relations and Alternative Arrangements for the Armistice Agreement), *Yŏksa pip'yŏng* (Critical Review of History) (July 2003), 77.

47. *Han'gyŏre Sinmun*, July 28, 2003.

48. Ibid.

49. Ibid.

50. It is interesting to note that in light of the recent surge in the establishment of new civic organizations in South Korea devoted to achieving peace and pacifism on the Korean peninsula, particularly among the younger generation of South Koreans, President Roh has recently changed the name of Kim's "Sunshine Policy" to "the Peace and Prosperity Policy."

51. Kim Seung-Hwan, "Anti-Americanism in Korea," *The Washington Quarterly* 26, no. 1 (Winter 2002–3): 109–122.

52. According to a survey of 800 adults conducted on January 5, 2004 across the country, 39 percent of the respondents called the United States the bigger threat to their nation's security as opposed to 33 percent of the respondents who chose North Korea. Among those in their 20s, 58 percent said the United States was the bigger threat, while only 20 percent cited the North. See *Chosŏn Ilbo* (January 12, 2004).

53. Ibid., 109.

54. On January 15, 2004, Yun Yŏng-gwan, South Korea's foreign minister, resigned amid controversy that he was unable to quell a growing rift between so-called "pro-American" diplomatic officials at the Foreign Ministry and Roh Mu Hyun's young, progressive and "independent" advisors at the National Security Council (NSC). The dispute was triggered by an alleged comment by Cho Hyŏn-dong of the North American Affairs Division in which he likened the young NSC staff members to the ultraconservative Taliban of Afghanistan. Yun's sacking, according to one political commentator, "signals the closer movement of Roh's foreign policy toward that of the NSC, away from diplomats who put priority on consolidation of the alliance with the United States" (*Korea Herald*, January 15, 2004). According to Chŏng Ch'an-yŏn, the president's senior secretary for civil affairs, "a certain few individuals at the foreign ministry have been unable to grow beyond the dependent policy of the past. They have been unable to adequately carry out the independent foreign policies of the Participatory Government. These individuals repeatedly spoke in a manner that is outdated in public and private contexts, leaked sensitive information, and in doing so caused confusion in foreign policy." *Chosŏn ilbo*, January 15, 2004.

55. Aidan Foster-Carter, "A Bumpy Road Ahead," *Pacific Forum CSIS*, http://www.csis.org.

56. *Los Angeles Times*, August 20, 2003.

57. *Han'gyŏre Sinmun*, July 28, 2003.

58. *San Francisco Chronicle*, January 5, 2003.

59. *Korea Herald*, August 11, 2002.

60. *Asia Times*, February 24, 2003.

61. Emphasis ours. *Chungang ilbo*, May 23, 2003.

62. Kim Dae Jung delivered these comments during a lecture entitled "The Realities of the Korean Peninsula and the Four Powers" at Chonnam National University on October 11, 2006. The speech was reprinted in Koreans newspapers and Internet sites that same day. For excerpts of the speech, see *http://www.chosun.com*.

63. The poll was conducted by the *"Joins P'unghyang-gae"* (research.joins.com) polling company and published in the *Chungang Ilbo*, October 13, 2006. See *http://articlejw.joins.com*.

64. Norimitsu Onishi, "Tough Talk from Seoul, if Little Will for a Fight," *New York Times,* October 10, 2006.

11. The Korean War

1. "Korea: The Forgotten War" is the title of an article in *Illustrated US News,* May 21, 1951, 1. I am indebted to Arissa Oh for giving me this reference.

2. Martha Gellhorn, *The Face of War* (New York: Atlantic Monthly Press, 1988), 274–275.

3. Public Record Office, London, Foreign Office file 317, piece no. 83008, Stokes to Bevin, December 2, 1950.

4. Charles J. Hanley, Sang-Hun Choe, and Martha Mendoza, *The Bridge at No Gun Ri: A Hidden Nightmare from the Korean War* (New York: Henry Holt, 2001), 236–237.

5. *New York Times,* September 30, 1999, A1.

6. Thucydides, *History of the Peloponnesian War,* trans. Rex Warner (New York: Penguin Books, 1954), 147.

7. Michael Walzer, *Just and Unjust Wars: A Moral Argument with Historical Illustrations* (New York: Basic Books, 1977), 117–123.

8. See David E. James, "Documenting the Vietnam War," in *From Hanoi to Hollywood: The Vietnam War in American Film,* ed. Linda Dittmar and Gene Michaud (New Brunswick, NJ: Rutgers University Press, 1990), 245.

9. For extensive documentation on the violence and terror of the air war see Bruce Cumings, *The Origins of the Korean War,* vol. 2 (Princeton, NJ: Princeton University Press, 1991), chapter 21.

10. U.S. Archives, Diplomatic Branch, 995.00 file, box 6175, George Barrett dispatch of February 8, 1951; also Acheson to Pusan Embassy, February 17, 1951.

11. Thames Television, transcript from the fifth seminar for "Korea: The Unknown War" (November 1986); Thames interview with Tibor Meray (also 1986).

12. See, for example, James I. Matray, "Diplomatic History as a Political Weapon: An Assessment of Anti-Americanism in South Korea Today," in *SHAFR Newsletter* 20 (March 1989). Matray's essay, which amazed me in its naiveté, might also be called "diplomatic historian stumbles blindly into hornets' nest"—except that FOIA documents in my possession show that Matray's trip to Korea was planned with malice aforethought by USIA staffers.

13. Shim Chi-yŏn, *Inmin-dang Yŏn'gu* (On the People's Party) (Seoul: Kyungnam University Press, 1991); Shim, *Han'guk Minju-dang Yŏn'gu* (On the Korean Democratic Party), 2 vols. (Seoul: Ch'angjak kwa pip'yŏng-sa, 1982, 1984); *Mi-So Kongdong Wiwŏnhoe* (The U.S.-Soviet Joint Commission) (Seoul: Ch'onggye yŏn'guso, 1989).

14. Ch'oe Sang-yŏng, *Migunjŏng kwa Hanguk minjokjuŭi* (The American military government and Korean nationalism) (Seoul: Nanam sinsŏ, 1988).

15. A useful collection of his and others' work is *Yŏksa wa kidokkyo,* no. 9, *Nongch'on hyŏnsil kwa nongmin undŏng* (History and Christianity, no. 9, Realities of the villages and peasant movements) (Seoul: Minjung-sa, 1984).

16. See, for example, An Chong-ch'ŏl, *Kwangju-Chŏnnam Chibang Hyŏndaesa Yŏn'gu* (The modern regional history of Kwangju and South Cholla Province)

(Seoul: Hanol Academy, 1991); Ch'oe Myŏng-hŭi, *Honbul* (Fire spirit), 3 vols. (Seoul: Shin Dong-a, 1985–92). In the past few years the magazine *Mal* and the newspaper *Han'gyŏre Sinmun* have documented several massacres in which hundreds died after the Rhee regime reoccupied South Korea; this is only the tip of a rather appalling iceberg, and the record of South Korean political repression in occupied North Korea remains to be fully unearthed. All this is not to say that the North did not also commit atrocities; but to say so does not surprise anyone. My own work (in *Origins*, vol. 2) and that of the late Callum MacDonald suggests that the record will eventually show that the Rhee regime was the more atrocious during the Korean War, and that Americans who accompanied South Korean army and police units knew well what was going on.

17. Among many other new sources on Cheju, see Yŏksa munje yŏn'guso, eds., *Cheju 4.3 Yŏn'gu* (Study of the April 3rd Cheju [rebellion]) (Seoul: Yŏksa pip'yong-sa, 1999). On Yŏsu, see *Yo-Sun Sakon* (The Yŏsu-Sunch'ŏn Incident) (2 vols.) (Yosu: Yŏsu chiyok sahoe yŏn'guso [Yosu Community Research Institute], 1998); an international symposium on the Yŏsu Rebellion was held in October 2002 at Yŏsu University, attended by some 200 delegates from the ROK, Japan, Taiwan, and Okinawa (some of them refugees who fled after the rebellion). A "Truth Commission on Civilian Massacres during the Korean War" was founded in September 2000, including more than fifteen "victim's groups" throughout the country. A number of historians from Cheju have been conducting research in the U.S. National Archives in recent months, preparing a multivolume history of the rebellion.

18. The best English source on Nogŭn-ri, and one of the best books ever written on Americans in foreign wars, is *The Bridge at No Gun Ri*; there are, again, many Korean-language accounts and memoirs of this massacre.

19. David E. Mark's study of Korea since liberation, included in Muccio to State, 740.0019/Control (Korea); the study is undated, but the covering letter was stamped May 23, 1949.

20. Central Intelligence Agency, "Korea," SR-2, Summer 1947, and "The Current Situation in Korea," ORE 15–48, March 18, 1948.

21. The literature on Kwangju is now quite large, but it can be sampled in Donald Clark, ed., *The Kwangju Uprising: Shadows over the Regime in South Korea* (Boulder, CO: Westview Press, 1988).

22. *Han'guk ilbo*, March 15, 1994.

23. Doh C. Shin, *Mass Politics and Culture in Democratizing Korea* (Cambridge: Cambridge University Press, 1999), 203–208.

24. David R. McCann's translation, in *The Middle Hour: Selected Poems of Kim Chi Ha* (Stanfordville, NY: Human Rights Publishing Group, 1980), 51.

25. Friedrich Nietzsche, *On the Geneaology of Morals*, trans. Walter Kaufmann and R.J. Hollingdale (New York: Vintage Books, 1969), 57–58.

26. Ibid., 61.

27. Friedrich Nietzsche, *Beyond Good and Evil*, trans. Walter Kaufmann (New York: Vintage Books, 1966), 195.

28. Quoted in Richard Falk, "The Vietnam Syndrome," *The Nation* (July 9, 2001), 22.

12. Doubly Forgotten

1. Changyu Piao, "The History of Koreans in Northeast China and the Yanbian Korean Autonomous Prefecture," in *Koreans in China*, ed. Dae-Sook Suh and Edward Shultz (Honolulu: University of Hawaii Press, 1990), 66.

2. Qiang Zhai, *China and the Vietnam Wars, 1950–1975* (Chapel Hill: University of North Carolina Press, 2000).

3. ROK Ministry of National Defense, 1994. Cited in *Wŏlgan Chungan* (June 1994): 195. North Koreans also advised the North Vietnamese, but not in large numbers and not, as far as is currently known, in any combat capacity.

4. Ahn Jung-hyo translated his novel into English himself, giving it the English title "White Badge"—an inaccurate title that furthermore obscures the multiple meanings of the original "White War," with its racial overtones (a white man's war) and cultural implications (white being the color of death in Korean custom), not to mention the suggestion of a white-washed war in South Korea. Perhaps he did not want to offend his American audience. Ahn recounts his experiences in Vietnam in "A Double Exposure of the War," in *America's Wars in Asia: A Cultural Approach to History and Memory*, ed. Philip West, Steven I. Levine, and Jackie Hiltz (Armonk, NY: M. E. Sharpe, 1998).

5. "Putting the Past Behind," *Newsreview* (Seoul), December 19, 1998, 7.

6. *Han'gyŏre Sinmun*, August 24, 2001, 2.

7. Frank Baldwin, "America's Rented Troops: South Koreans in Vietnam," *Bulletin of Concerned Asian Scholars* 8, no. 1 (January 1976): 36–37.

8. John Lie, *Han Unbound: The Political Economy of South Korea* (Stanford: Stanford University Press, 1009), 64.

9. Quoted in Harry G. Summers Jr., *Historical Atlas of the Vietnam War* (Boston: Houghton Mifflin, 1995), 154.

10. Frank Baldwin and Diane and Michael Jones, *America's Rented Troops: South Koreans in Vietnam* (Philadelphia: American Friends' Service Committee, 1973), 24.

11. Callum MacDonald, "So Terrible a Liberation: The UN Occupation of North Korea," *Bulletin of Concerned Asian Scholars* 23, no. 2 (April–June 1991): 5–10; Bruce Cumings, *The Origins of the Korean War*: vol. 2, *The Roaring of the Cataract, 1947–1950* (Princeton, NJ: Princeton University Press, 1990), 673–680.

12. Han Hong-koo, "Massacre Breeds Massacre," *Han'gyŏre21*, May 4, 2000, 26.

13. For a study of Japanese counterinsurgency as a "qualified success," commissioned by the RAND corporation (and carried out by a Korean-American scholar) at the height of the Vietnam War, see Chong-Sik Lee, *Counterinsurgency in Manchuria: The Japanese Experience, 1931–1940* (Santa Monica, CA: RAND Corporation, 1967).

14. Hwang Suk-young, *Shadow of Arms*, trans. Chun Jyung-ja (Ithaca, NY: Cornell University East Asia Program, 1994), 25.

15. So Un-ju, "The Vietnam War through Korean Fiction," *Yoksa pip'yŏng* no. 30 (Fall 1995): 214–242; Ch'oe Won-sik, "The Vietnam War in Korean Novels," in *Saengsanjŏk daehwa rŭl wihayŏ: Ch'oe Wŏn-sik P'yongnonjip* (For a Productive Dialogue: Collected Essays of Ch'oe Wŏn-sik) (Seoul: Ch'angjak kwa pip'yŏngsa, 1997), 377–390.

16. See among others Hyun Sook Kim, "Korea's 'Vietnam Question': War Atrocities, National Identity, and Reconciliation in Asia," *positions: east asia cultures critique* 9, no. 3 (Winter 2001), 621–635.

17. Kim, "Korea's 'Vietnam Question,'" 628, based on interviews with surviving villagers.

18. *Han'gyŏre Sinmun*, April 19, 2000, 1; *Han'gyŏre21*, April 27, 2000, 34–37.

19. Kim, "Korea's 'Vietnam Question,'" 623–24.

20. *Han'gyŏre Sinmun*, May 4, 2000, 20.

21. Charles J. Hanley, Sang-Hun Choe, and Martha Mendoza, *The Bridge at No Gun Ri: A Hidden Nightmare from the Korean War* (New York: Henry Holt, 2001).

22. Available at: *http://www.army/mil/nogunri*.

23. *Korea Times*, April 20, 2000, A3.

24. *Han'gyŏre21*, May 4, 2000, 2.

25. *Han'gyŏre21*, April 19, 2000, 1.

26. *Han'gyŏre Sinmun*, June 28, 2000, 1.

27. *Newsreview* (Seoul), December 19, 1998, 7. Needless to say, the Vietnamese were the biggest victims by far, and have yet to be compensated for their suffering by the U.S. government or by the chemical companies that manufactured Agent Orange.

28. Translated and cited in Kim, "Korea and the 'Vietnam Question,'" 632–633.

29. Charles K. Armstrong, trans., "Parallel Lives: A Conversation between Hwang Suk-young and Bao Ninh, Two Veterans of the Vietnam War," *Critical Asian Studies* 33, no. 2 (September 2001), translated from South Korea's *Han'-gyŏre21* magazine.

13. Revolution, War, and Memory in Contemporary Viet Nam

1. *The Country of Memory: Remaking the Past in Late Socialist Vietnam*, ed. Hue-Tam Ho Tai (Berkeley: University of California Press, 2001), 8.

2. Keith W. Taylor, "Notes on the Viet Dien u linh tap," *The Vietnam Forum* 8 (Summer/Fall 1986): 26–59; Oliver W. Wolters, *Two Essays on Dai-Viet in the Fourteenth Century* (New Haven, CT: Yale University Southeast Asia Studies Program, 1988).

3. Shawn McHale, "Mapping a 'Confucian' Past: Vietnam and the Transition to Modernity, 1917–1940," and K. W. Taylor, "When Is Nho giao Confucianism?" papers for the workshop on "Modernity and Confucianism," University of California at Los Angeles, November 1997.

4. Patricia Pelley, "The History of Resistance and the Resistance to History in Post-Colonial Constructions of the Past," in *Essays into Vietnamese Pasts*, ed. K. W. Taylor and John K. Whitmore (Ithaca, NY: Cornell University Southeast Asia Program, 1995), 232–245.

5. Patricia M. Pelley, "Writing Revolution: The New History in Post-Colonial Vietnam," Ph.D. diss., Cornell University, 1993. See also her *Postcolonial Vietnam: New Histories of the National Past* (Durham, NC: Duke University Press, 2002).

6. Peter Zinoman, "Reading Revolutionary Prison Memoirs," in *The Country of Memory: Remaking the Past in Late Socialist Vietnam*, ed. Hue-Tam Ho Tai

(Berkeley: University of California Press, 2001), 21–45. See also his *The Colonial Bastille: A History of Imprisonment in Vietnam, 1862–1940* (Berkeley: University of California Press, 2001).

7. Christoph Giebel, "Telling Life: An Approach to the Official Biography of Ton Duc Thang," in *Essays into Vietnamese Pasts*, ed. K. W. Taylor and John K. Whitmore (Ithaca, NY: Cornell University Southeast Asia Program, 1995), 246–271.

8. See, for example, *A Heroic People: Memoirs from the Revolution* (Ha Noi: Foreign Languages Publishing House, 1960); *Nhung nguoi cong san* (Communists) (Ho Chi Minh City: NXB Thanh Nien, 1977); Tran Tu Binh (narr.), Ha An (rec.), *The Red Earth: A Vietnamese Memoir of Life on a Colonial Rubber Plantation*, trans. John Spragens, ed. David Marr (Athens: Ohio University Press, 1985); Nguyen Thi Dinh, *No Other Road to Take*, trans. Mai Elliott (Ithaca, NY: Cornell University Southeast Asia Program, 1976).

9. See Christoph Giebel, "Ba Son 1925—The Strike at the Arsenal in Sai Gon: A Closer Look at Events and Their Interpretations," M.A. thesis, Cornell University, 1989; Christoph Giebel, "Ton Duc Thang and the Imagined Ancestries of Vietnamese Communism," Ph.D. diss., Cornell University, 1996; and my *Imagined Ancestries of Vietnamese Communism: Ton Duc Thang and the Politics of History and Memory* (Seattle and Singapore: University of Washington Press and Singapore University Press, 2004).

10. Cf. K. W. Taylor, "Surface Orientations in Vietnam: Beyond Histories of Nation and Region," *Journal of Asian Studies* 57, no. 4 (November 1998): 949–978.

Epilogue

1. CBS News, "Anti-Japan Rampage in Shanghai," April 16, 2005, *http://cbsnews.com*.

2. David Shambaugh, "China Engages Asia: Reshaping the Regional Order," *International Security* 29, no. 3 (Winter 2004/5): 65. See also John Fitzgerald, "China and the Quest for Dignity," *The National Interest* (Spring 1999), and Peter Hays Gries, "Tears of Rage: Chinese Nationalist Reactions to the Belgrade Embassy Bombing," *The China Journal*, no. 46 (July 2001).

3. Hints of this growing unease is revealed by the emotional dispute between South Korea and China and over the latter's historical claim to the ancient Korean kingdom of Koguryŏ (AD 300–668). The Chinese appropriation of Koguřŏ, whose territory had encompassed all of North Korea and Manchuria, has raised deep concerns in South Korea that China is setting the stage to justify its eventual annexation of large parts of North Korean territory following the latter's collapse. See *Choson Ilbo*, August 8 and 9, 2004.

Contributors

CHARLES K. ARMSTRONG is Associate Professor of History and Director of the Center for Korean Research at Columbia University. His publications include *The Koreas* (2006), *The North Korean Revolution, 1945–1950* (2003), and two edited volumes, *Korea at the Center: Dynamics of Regionalism in Northeast Asia* (2005) and *Korean Society: Civil Society, Democracy, and the State* (2002).

BRUCE CUMINGS is the Gustavus F. and Anne M. Swift Distinguished Service Professor of History at the University of Chicago. His publications include *North Korea: Another Country* (2003), *Parallax Visions: Making Sense of American–East Asian Relations*(2002), *Korea's Place in the Sun* (1997), *Origins of the Korean War,* 2 vols. (1981, 1990), and *Dominion from Sea to Sea: Pacific Ascendancy and American Power* (forthcoming).

CHRISTOPH GIEBEL is Associate Professor of International Studies and Southeast Asian History at the University of Washington. He is the author of *Imagined Ancestries of Vietnamese Communism: Ton Duc Thang and the Politics of History and Memory* (2004).

CAROL GLUCK is the George Sansom Professor of History at Columbia University, specializing in modern Japan from the late nineteenth century to the present. Her publications include *Thinking with the Past: Modern Japan and History* (2007), *Asia in Western and World History* (1997), *Showa: The Japan of Hirohito* (1992), *Japan's Modern Myths* (1985), and *Past Obsessions: World War II in History and Memory* (forthcoming).

HARRY D. HAROOTUNIAN is Professor of History, East Asian Studies and the chair of the East Asian Studies program at New York University. His recent publications include *History's Disquiet: Modernity, Cultural Practice, and the Question of*

Everyday Life (2000) and *Overcome by Modernity: Historical Surplus and the Search for Cultural Authenticity in Interwar Japan* (2000).

JAMES L. HEVIA is Director of the International Studies Program at the University of Chicago. His publications include *English Lessons: The Pedagogy of Imperialism in Nineteenth Century China* (2003) and *Cherishing Men from Afar: Qing Guest Ritual and the McCartney Embassy of 1793* (1995), winner of the 1997 Joseph R. Levenson book prize of the Association for Asian Studies.

YOSHIKUNI IGARASHI is Associate Professor of History and Director of the East Asian Studies Program at Vanderbilt University. He is the author of *Bodies of Memory: Narratives of War in Postwar Japanese Culture 1945–1970* (2000). He is particularly interested in the legacies of the Asia-Pacific War in Japan's postwar society.

SHEILA MIYOSHI JAGER (co-editor) is Associate Professor of East Asian Studies at Oberlin College. She is the author of *Narratives of Nation-Building in Korea: A Genealogy of Patriotism* (2003) and is currently completing a book on the Korean War.

JIYUL KIM, a colonel in the U.S. Army, is Director of Asian Studies at the U.S. Army War College. He is completing doctoral work on modern Korean history at Harvard University.

RANA MITTER (co-editor) is University Lecturer in the History and Politics of Modern China at the University of Oxford. He is the author of *A Bitter Revolution: China's Struggle with the Modern World* (2004) and *The Manchurian Myth: Nationalism, Resistance, and Collaboration in Modern China* (2000).

FRANZISKA SERAPHIM is Assistant Professor of Japanese History at Boston College. She is the author of *War Memory and Social Politics in Japan, 1945–2005* (2006) and has published and translated numerous articles in German, Japanese, and English.

ANN SHERIF is Associate Professor of Japanese Language and Literature at Oberlin College. She is the author of *Mirror: The Fiction and Essays of Koda Aya* (2001) and is currently completing a book on Cold War culture in Japan.

EDWARD VICKERS is Senior Lecturer in Comparative Education at the Institute of Education, University of London. He is the author of *In Search of an Identity: The Politics of History as a School Subject in Hong Kong, 1960–2005* (2005), coauthor of *Education and Development in a Global Era: Strategies for "Successful" Globalization* (2006), and coeditor (with Alisa Jones) of *History and National Identity in East Asia* (2005).

DAQING YANG is Associate Professor of History and International Affairs at George Washington University. He is the author of *Technology of Empire: Telecommunications and Japanese Imperialism: 1930–1945* (forthcoming) and coeditor of *Contending Issues in Sino-Japanese Relations: Toward a History beyond Borders* (2005, in Japanese and Chinese).

Index

Kakehashi Akihide, 154
Kakinomoto Hitomaro, 139
Kako no kokufuku, 33, 34
Kamikaze (Ishimaru Gen-show), 118
Kamikaze missions, 99–101. See also *Hotaru*
Kang Youwei, 197, 202
Karatani Kōjin, 130
Katokawa Kōtarō, 86
Katō Norihiro, 131, 152, 153
Kawakami Hajime, 155
Kawashima Takayoshi, 161
Kennan, George, 322
Kettler Arch, 197
Kike wadatsumi no koe (book and film), 44
Kikuchi Kan, 165
Kim Chi-ha, 287
Kim Dae Jung (Kim Tae-jung), 73–74, 92, 234, 247, 250, 264, 281, 285, 286, 295, 304
Kim Il Sung (Kim Il-sŏng), 237, 277, 279, 287
Kim Ki-t'ae, 301–302
Kim Koo, 284
Kim Sŏng-su, 284
Kim Wŏn-ung, 263
Kim Young Sam (Kim Yŏng-sam), 246–247, 284, 293, 295
Kinema junpō, 113, 118
KMT. *See* Kuomintang
Kobayashi (Japanese army veteran), 187–188
Kobayashi Hideo, 164–165
Kobayashi Yoshinori, 100, 227
Kobori Keiichirō, 137
Kōdansha, 81
Koizumi Junichiro, 16, 52, 56, 123–124, 324
Kojima Nobuo, 133
"The *Kokoro* of Mourning for the War Dead" (Etō Jun), 136–141, 148
Konoe Fumimaro, 155
Kōno Yohei, 93
Korea: North-South Agreement, 2; comfort women from, 9, 67, 68; democratization in, 72; postcolonial hostility in, 73–74; transnational activism in, 76; kamikaze pilots from, 101, 102, 104, 110–111; reunification movement and anti-Americanism, 257–265; Japanese colonialism in, 263; in Chinese civil war, 292
"Korea: The Unknown War" (documentary), 277
Korean activist groups, 71
Korean-American women, 72
Korean-Canadian women, 72

Korean Council for the Women Drafted for Military Sexual Slavery by Japan, 44–45, 74
Korean schoolgirls incident (2002), 262–264
Korean Truth Commission on the Vietnam War, 305
Korean War, 6, 266–290; reremembering of, 10; memorialization of, 233; martyrs of, 245–246; as "forgotten war," 267–273; as civil war, 273–278; justification for, 279; U.S. strategy in, 279–281; U.S. responsibility for, 281; recent critiques of, 281–287; and forgetfulness, 287–290; and ROK brutality in Vietnam War, 299
Korean War Monument (KWM), 234, 250f, 251–257, 254f, 264
Koxinga Museum, 227
Kuga Katsunan, 165
Kume Hiroshi, 78
Kuomintang (KMT), 13, 210–214, 216–223, 225–227, 230, 231. *See also* Nationalist Party
Kwangju Uprising, 241, 247, 285, 286, 298
KWM. *See* Korean War Monument

Labor strikes, 317–318
Landor, Henry Savage, 205
Landscape, 140
LDP. *See* Liberal Democratic Party
Lee Teng-hui, 218, 221, 222
Lenin, Vladimir, 318
Liang Qichao, 197, 202
Liberal Democratic Party (LDP) (Japan), 20, 26, 27, 30, 31, 62, 73, 123, 129, 146, 166–169
Liberal View of History Study Group, 43
Lien Chan, 221, 326
Liu Binyan, 172
Lu Er Men obelisk, 228f
Lu Huinian, 185
Lu Xun, 181, 182
Lu Yi, 176

MacArthur, Douglas, 267–268, 280, 289
Macherey, Pierre, 270
Male psychology, 77
Manchuria, 52, 53, 55, 62, 154, 299–300
The Manchurian Candidate (film), 270
Mannheim, Karl, 163
Man'yōshū, 138–139
Mao Zedong, 185, 192, 198, 199, 248, 287
Mark, David, 283